for
edexcel

D

Travel & Tourism

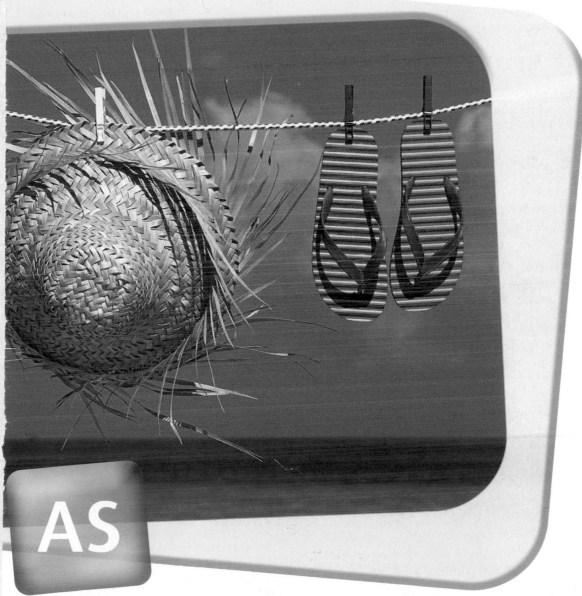

AS

Lindsey Taylor Stephenson

Collins

William Collins' dream of knowledge for all began with the publication of his first book in 1819. A self-educated mill worker, he not only enriched millions of lives, but also founded a flourishing publishing house. Today, staying true to this spirit, Collins books are packed with inspiration, innovation and practical expertise. They place you at the centre of a world of possibility and give you exactly what you need to explore it.

Collins. Do more.

Published by Collins
An imprint of HarperCollins*Publishers*
77–85 Fulham Palace Road
Hammersmith
London
W6 8JB

© HarperCollins*Publishers* Limited 2005

Browse the complete Collins catalogue at
www.collinseducation.com

10 9 8 7 6 5 4 3 2 1

ISBN 0 00 719809 4

Lindsey Taylor, Ray Barker and Nicki Stephenson assert their moral rights to be identified as the authors of this work

British Library Cataloguing in Publication Data
A Catalogue record for this publication is available from the British Library

Commissioned and project managed by Graham Bradbury

Cover Design by Blue Pig

Cover picture courtesy of Corbis

Page design by Patricia Briggs

Page layout by Ken Vail Graphic Design (www.kvgd.com)

Series managed by Kay Wright

Picture research by Thelma Gilbert

Production by Sarah Robinson

Printed and bound by Martins the Printer, Berwick upon Tweed

Acknowledgements

Many thanks as always to Kay and Brad for their hard work, support and encouragement. To Nick, Lucy and Alice for their patience and defrosted pizzas. To Mark Uttley, a past student who ended up teaching me a great deal. And finally to Sandra Gregory, whose wisdom and perspective on life provided some much needed motivation at times.
Lindsey Taylor

I would like to thank all those students who over the years have taught me how to teach; Lindsey, Brad and Kay who have taught me how to write; and my family Pete, Sue, Patrick, Sam and Rob who have taught me how to enjoy life.
Nicki Stephenson

The publishers would like to thank the following for permission to reproduce pictures on these pages (t = top, b = bottom, l = left, r = right):

Alamy 10, 14, 19, 28, 29, 32, 36, 37, 39(b), 42, 43(b), 44, 48, 59, 66(t), 67, 78, 81, 82, 88(b), 99, 106, 114, 120, 121(t), 127, 134, 149(r), 161, 166(r), 175, 189, 200, 209(l), 210(b), 212, 219, 224, 225, 226(b), 228, 241(r), 246, 247(t,b), 250, 251, 256(t,b), 257, 259, 265(tl), 270, 272, 273, 278, 279 280(l), 282, 285; Art Directors 258, 261(t); British Airways/Newscast 86, 138; Collections 60 Robert Hallmann, 69 Patrick Wise, 70 Geoff Howard, 80 Joy Whiting, 83 Neil Calladine, 155 Philip Craven, 157(t) Simon Bache, p158 Liz Stares, 159 Liz Stares, 168 Ashley Cooper, 172 Ashley Cooper, 174 Graeme Peacock, 178 Liz Stares, 180 Graeme Peacock, 180(b) Roger Scruton, 181(r) Paul Watts, 184 Ray Farrar, 188 Jill Swainson, 188(b) Brian Sheul, 191(b) Robert Pilgrim, 192 Paul Watts, 194 Nigel Hawkins, 195(b) Nigel Haggerty; Corbis 25, 49, 50, 79, 94, 97, 111, 125(b), 137, 139(r), 145,p166(b), 190, 195(t), 205, 214, 265(tr), 286(b), 280(r); The Deep 66(b); Easyjet 129; Empics 21, 40, 140, 157(b), 177, 193(t), 206, 218(r), 220, 226(t), 227(b), 230, 231, 233(l), 234, 235, 275; Eurocamp 121(b); Mary Evans Picture Library 22, 23, 24(l); Getty-Images 210(t); Sally & Richard Greenhill 62; Robert Harding Picture Library 26, 77, 109, 122, 123, 149(l), 165, 181(l), 186, 241(l), 256(t), 265(b), 266, 267; Kobal Collection 156; Langdale Quest 179(l); Photofusion 64; Rex Features 17, 18, 33(l), 34, 35, 39(t), 41, 43(tl,tr), 74, 84, 90, 108, 112, 117(t,b), 124(t,b), 125(t), 132, 133, 139(l), 143, 160(l), 179(r), 191(t), 193(b), 208, 222, 233(r), 261(b), 274(l,r); Science Photo Library 216, 217, 218(l); Roger Scruton 34(r), 33(t), 100, 142, 148, 160(r); Shutterpoint, Terry Maton p71, Andy Reed p152, 158; Superstock 209(r); Thomas Cook 58, 71, 73, 98, 227, 248, 268(t); Thomson Holidays 52, 240, 244, 264; Travel Ink 110, 128, 131, 146, 162; Topfoto 24(r), 204; Wallace Arnold 182; Russell Williams 11, 13 (all); York Archeological Trust 171.

Every effort has been made to contact copyright holders, but if any have been inadvertently overlooked, the publishers will be pleased to make the necessary arrangements at the first opportunity.

Contents

Unit 1

The Travel and Tourism Industry   8–55

1.1	**The nature and characteristics of travel and tourism and the travel and tourism industry**	
Topic 1	Different definitions of travel and tourism	10
Topic 2	Different types of tourism	14
Topic 3	Sectors and vulnerabilities	18
1.2	**The development of the travel and tourism industry**	
Topic 4	The development of the industry	22
Topic 5	What makes the industry grow?	28
Topic 6	Issues for the industry	32
1.3	**Structure of the UK travel and tourism industry**	
1.4	**Scale of the travel and tourism industry**	
Topic 7	Travel sectors of the industry	36
Topic 8	Resort and service sectors of the industry	42
Topic 9	Scale, inter-relationships and interdependence	46
Topic 10	Integration of the industry	50
	How Unit 1 is assessed	54

Unit 2

The Travel and Tourism Customer   56–103

2.1	**The organisation and its customers**	
Topic 1	Internal and external customers	58
Topic 2	The needs and wants of different customers	62
Topic 3	Providing free services	66
2.2	**Providing effective customer skills**	
Topic 4	Interpersonal skills	70
Topic 5	Communication skills	74
Topic 6	Product knowledge	80
Topic 7	Meeting different customer needs	85
Topic 8	Complaints procedures	90
2.3	**Measuring and monitoring the customer service of an organisation**	
Topic 9	Methods of measuring customer service	94
Topic 10	Quality criteria for customer service	98
	How Unit 2 is assessed	102

Unit 3

Destination Europe 104–151

3.1 Location and types of tourist destination

| Topic 1 | Coastal, city and business destinations | 106 |
| Topic 2 | Country, cultural and purpose-built destinations | 110 |

3.2 The features and appeal of destinations to different types of tourist

Topic 3	Features: climate, landscape and transport	114
Topic 4	Features: accommodation, facilities, attractions	120
Topic 5	Features: events, costs and local culture	124

3.3 Modes of transport and routes available to European travel destinations

Topic 6	Transport gateways	128
Topic 7	Rail links, roads and motorways	132
Topic 8	Transport: factors affecting choice	137

3.4 Factors affecting the popularity and appeal of European travel destinations

| Topic 9 | Accessibility, image and attractions | 142 |
| Topic 10 | Destination management, costs and political factors | 146 |

| How Unit 3 is assessed | 150 |

Unit 4

Destination Britain 152–197

4.1 Travel and tourism organisations that support tourism in the British Isles

| Topic 1 | Public-sector tourism departments | 154 |
| Topic 2 | The variety of tourist organisations | 158 |

4.2 Features of destinations in the British Isles

Topic 3	Coasts, cities and business conferences	162
Topic 4	Countryside, cultural and purpose-built destinations	168
Topic 5	Environment, transport and accommodation	172
Topic 6	Facilities, attractions, events and culture	178

4.3 Constructing itineraries for tourists

| Topic 7 | Constructing itineraries for tourists | 182 |

4.4 Scale of tourism to the British Isles

| Topic 8 | the scale of tourism to the British Isles | 186 |

4.5 The factors that affect the popularity and appeal of destinations

| Topic 9 | The factors that affect the popularity and appeal of destinations | 190 |

| How Unit 4 is assessed | 196 |

Unit 5

Travelling safely — 198–237

5.1 Legal and regulatory requirements

Topic 1	Aviation regulations and ABTA	200
Topic 2	EU and UK legislation	204
Topic 3	Consumer protection	208

5.2 Restrictions on travel

Topic 4	Passports and visas	212
Topic 5	Health restrictions	216

5.3 Emergency situations

Topic 6	Cancellation, curtailment and insurance	220
Topic 7	Losses and criminal activity	226
Topic 8	Large-scale emergency situations	230

How Unit 5 is assessed — 236

Unit 6

Resort Operations — 238–289

6.1 The activities of the resort office

Topic 1	Functional areas and departments of the resort office	240
Topic 2	Job roles of different overseas representatives	244
Topic 3	Activities carried out at the resort office	249
Topic 4	Links with the UK office	254

6.2 Duties of a resort representative

Topic 5	The welcome meeting	258
Topic 6	Selling products and services	264
Topic 7	Documentation	268
Topic 8	Dealing with problem situations	272

6.3 The significance of induction, training and product knowledge of staff in delivering high quality customer service

Topic 9	Induction and training	278
Topic 10	Product knowledge	282

How Unit 6 is assessed — 288

Index — 291

5

Travel & Tourism

About this book

Welcome to AS Travel and Tourism. This textbook is written specifically for students taking the Edexcel Travel and Tourism awards and provides you with the underpinning knowledge to be successful in both the coursework set by your school or college (internal assessment) and the one-and-a-half hour tests set by Edexcel (external assessment).

Collins *Travel & Tourism AS for Edexcel* is divided into six units. Each unit in this book relates to a unit of the Edexcel Travel and Tourism AS-level specification.

	Unit	Title	How is this unit assessed
AS single award	1	The Travel Industry	External assessment
	2	The Travel and Tourism Customer	Internal assessment
	3	Destination Europe	Internal assessment
AS double award (you will need to complete Units 1–3 and 4–6 to gain the double award)	4	Destination Britain	Internal assessment
	5	Travelling Safely	External assessment
	6	Resort Operations	Internal assessment

● **Explanatory introduction** to the topic shows what you will need to learn about each topic.

● **Activities** provide you with an opportunity to develop your understanding about specific aspects of a topic and practise your skills. Most activities are designed for you to work on your own, with a partner or in a small group.

● **Case studies** support your learning and set it in context.

The units in this book have been divided into topics and each topic provides a manageable chunk of learning covering the subject content. The contents list at the beginning of this book and at the start of each unit will show you how the topics correspond to the Edexcel Travel and Tourism AS-level specification.

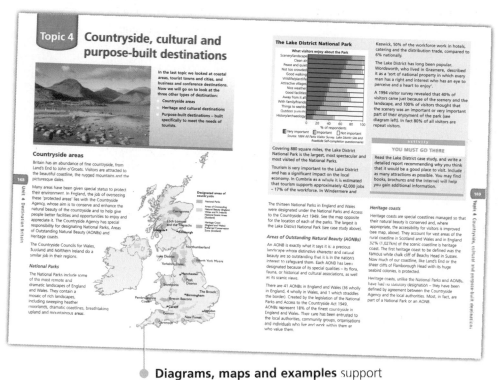

Diagrams, maps and examples support and clarify all the explanations in the text.

This book has been produced with considerable input from current practitioners in the travel and tourism industry. There are three **Industry Focus** interviews: Unit 1 The Travel and Tourism Industry features **Sam Wynzar, Sales and Marketing Executive, Leeds Bradford International Airport** Unit 2 The Travel and Tourism Customer features **Amanda Keers, Sales Office Manager, Superbreak** Unit 6 Resort Operations features **Nathan Millward, Resort Rep, JMC, Zante**.

Good luck with your GCE AS-level studies. This book provides you with interesting, supportive and motivating learning materials that we hope will help you to succeed in your travel and tourism course.

About this book

The combined travel and tourism industry represents probably the world's largest industry. Worldwide, it is worth over $6200 billion. The UK's share (2003), was £74 billion, and the industry employed 2.1 million people, according to star UK (the national tourism research and statistics website at www.staruk.org.uk).

It is also one of the most dynamic industries, offering new means of transport and new tourism destinations every year – such as dog sledding in Alaska or fly-cruise packages to Florida and the Caribbean, or budget flights to all night 'foam parties' in Ibiza. Many people now actually make up their own package from the internet and never visit a conventional travel agent at all.

However this diversity and global spread make it susceptible to world events such as terrorism, disease and disasters. The operators have to respond to new technological developments, and to changing social trends too, such as the collapse of Communism, demand for short breaks or the opening up of new frontiers such as China.

Travel and tourism, for business or pleasure, is a very competitive market, with organisations competing to outdo each other and supply us with ever more attractive tourism destinations and services.

In this unit you will gain a knowledge and understanding of what makes up the travel and tourism industry, which will underpin every other unit, so it is important you cover this one well, as it is a springboard to your other studies.

To fully understand why we love being travellers or tourists, means trying to understand our motivation (reasons) for going (such as escape, fun, or education), what activities we like to do when away (such as sunbathing, exploring or sports) and which mode of travel we prefer (such as planes, boats or trains).

Organisations offering travel and tourism products and services constantly strive to anticipate our needs in order to offer attractive deals, to satisfy our travel and tourism desires. These two sources – one of continuing customer demand, the other of the ongoing supply, create the travel and tourism industry and ensure its ever-changing characteristics.

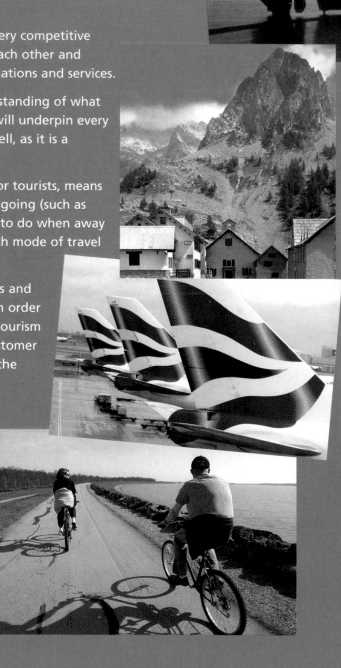

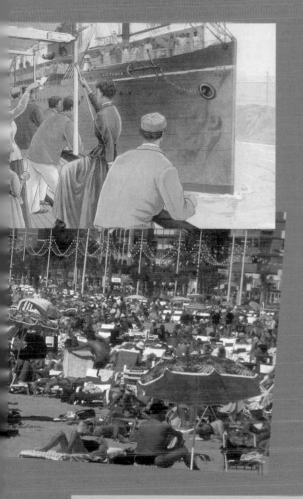

Unit 1

The Travel and Tourism Industry

1.1 The nature and characteristics of travel and tourism and the travel and tourism industry

Topic 1	Different definitions of travel and tourism	10
Topic 2	Different types of tourism	14
Topic 3	Sectors and vulnerabilities	18

1.2 The development of the travel and tourism industry

Topic 4	The development of the industry	22
Topic 5	What makes the industry grow?	28
Topic 6	Issues for the industry	32

1.3 Structure of the UK travel and tourism industry

1.4 Scale of the travel and tourism industry

Topic 7	Travel sectors of the industry	36
Topic 8	Resort and service sectors of the industry	42
Topic 9	Scale, inter-relationships and interdependencies	46
Topic 10	Integration in the industry	50

| How Unit 1 is assessed | 54 |

Different definitions of travel and tourism

Customers and operators hold different views of what travel and tourism means to them, which makes it difficult to create an ideal definition. Consequently you will need to draw from a range of areas, not only to give you the common themes, but also to identify why definitions might differ.

So in this topic we will present a range of suggestions as to how we can create a clear definition based on some commonly accepted travel and tourism ideas and interpretations:

- Organisational views
- Classification of tourism flows
- Purposes
- Defining by 'activity'
- Supply and demand views.

In the second part of this topic we will look at the factors that make travel and tourism products different from most other goods:

- Intangibility
- Perishability
- Inseparability
- Risk and quality.

Organisational views

Let's first look at a few published definitions. The definition from the World Tourism Organisation, given in 1998, is:

'The activities of persons travelling to and staying in places outside their usual environment for not more than one consecutive year for leisure, business and other purposes'

This gives a view of travel and tourism which could cover any tourist in any part of the globe. This contrasts with the UK Tourism Society, which gives a view reflecting the UK domestic travel and tourism scene:

'The temporary, short-term movement of people to destinations outside the places where they normally live and work, and their activities during their stay at these destinations.'

So already we can see some common threads emerging which help to define the true nature of the industry, e.g. 'movement' (travel away from home); for varying 'purposes' (visiting, leisure, business); 'stopovers' in different locations (destinations) and 'activities'.

Tourism flows

If we develop the first theme which comes from the definitions we can look at travel and tourism as a series of 'flows' (movements).

Monitoring tourism flows provides much statistical data to help inform tourism organisations about current volumes of flows, and about where tourists travel from and to. You can see examples of this opposite.

MAKE UP YOUR OWN DEFINITION

VisitBritain is the organisation formed when the British Tourism Authority merged with the English Tourism Council, creating a large travel and tourism organisation and website for use by professionals.

Use the website www.visitbritain.com to assess the key words, information and ideas they use on their site to reflect what travel and  tourism means to them, compared to the UK Tourism Society and the World Tourism Organisation, and then, based on the information from the three organisations, make up your own definition in a simple sentence. Present your definition back to the rest of your class.

Travel and tourism flows

Flow 1: 'outgoing' – tourists travelling away from their home on a trip abroad

Flow 2: 'domestic' – tourists travelling somewhere else in their own country

Flow 3: 'incoming' – other people coming to be tourists – in the UK for example, from abroad.

Purposes

Travel can also be classified according to its purpose. A common method of doing this is to use the following three categories:

Business travel	Visiting friends & relatives	Leisure travel
Trade fairs		Adventure activities
Meetings		Annual holidays
Conferences		Arts and entertainment
Incentive travel		Cultural visits
Corporate development		Sports-related visits
Training		Educational tours

Defining by 'activity'

A third theme which helps us define travel and tourism is the type of activities we like to indulge in while away. Most tourists nowadays want a lot more from their holidays or trips than the traditional sea, sand, sun and sangria. Let's use an activity to illustrate some examples, and you can add some more.

THE BUSINESS AND LEISURE CATEGORIES

Using the classification table and working with a partner, identify examples of the following for the business and leisure categories:

1 Two popular destinations for each category

2 One organisation working in each category.

Compare your findings with those of others in your class.

MATCHING CUSTOMERS AND ACTIVITIES

Match up the holiday activities to the customers, and add two of your own to each list.

Customer types

Couples over 60

Families with young children

Late teens/early 20s

Individuals

Single parents with children

Young couples

Disabled

TV or film stars

Holiday activities

Overland exploration

Sightseeing by coach and dinner dances

Activities on site with leaders

Going to clubs

Eating at local restaurants

Gyms and saunas

Supply and demand views

The leisure customer's view of holiday content will differ from that of the business traveller. The business traveller is more likely to require:

- a top-class venue for meetings/conferences
- a top-class hotel with high quality food
- first-class travel and business services.

The features mentioned above bring some new themes into our tourism definitions:

- level of accommodation for stopovers
- quality of support services
- mode of transport.

Here are some other considerations which customers can have in travel terms (which bring us back to our movement theme):

- Speed and comfort
- Affordability
- Frequency
- Location of terminals.

Every type of organisation in the travel and tourism industry (travel agents, airlines, hotels, tour operators) gathers data, through market research such as customer profiles, preferences and satisfaction levels, to help them define customer types, needs and wants in order to maintain their customer base and keep ahead of their competitors.

If we draw all of these views and concepts together we can find a few common strands that help us define travel and tourism for the purpose of your studies:

- It involves travelling away from your home area and usually staying somewhere else.
- It involves satisfying a need or purpose, e.g. leisure, business or social.
- Time spans vary from a short break, to a 2-week annual holiday, to a world cruise lasting months.
- We associate engaging in new activities with tourism – e.g. sampling new cultures and food, going on excursions, staying in a hotel.

Key ideas about the nature of travel and tourism

There are certain factors which make tourism products and services different to many goods you could also buy in the high street – and more difficult to provide.

Intangibility

A holiday or trip is largely intangible. You cannot touch it or test it before you pay for it, as you can with other leisure goods such as a tennis racket or a football. As a consequence, operators have to work hard to convince us that a real (tangible) product or service will be provided such as a coach trip or theme park visit. In fact all you really have, which is tangible sometimes, is a ticket, receipt or email. Although you may be able to visualise the benefits you hope to gain from your purchase, from a brochure or virtual tour, you have to wait to enjoy them.

Perishability

Your travel or tourism service cannot be stored up for sale later. It is only on sale for that trip or that holiday – your seat on the plane or bed in the hotel are only available once, because when the time passes, it's gone. It's a bit like eating a piece of fruit that is only ripe to eat for a single day of the year – after that it will perish.

Inseparability

The travel or tourism service provided and the consumption of it are done simultaneously (unlike the making of a tennis racket for resale later). This often requires a number of providers working in harmony, which makes quality control a lot more difficult. Your journey on holiday will start with a ticket purchase from a travel agency some time in advance, continue with a taxi to the airport, check-in by the airline, baggage handling by another company, flight by the airline, arrival by the foreign terminal services and on by coach to the hotel, and so on – plenty of opportunity for you to be disappointed or dissatisfied, as you have no doubt seen on TV documentaries.

Risk

Any investment involves risk, and a holiday sees us risking hundreds of pounds. We will all have our 'cut off' points at which something becomes too risky – it might be triggered by too high a cost, too dangerous a journey, or the risk of low quality accommodation or food.

Quality levels

Quality levels are always difficult to ensure, but are key factors for customers, especially at the upper end of the market. Staff delivering the service need to be competent, reliable, responsive and clear about what they need to do, for a business can sink or swim on its quality rating.

What do customers want?

It is clear then that travel and tourism services and products have important dimensions which affect customer choice:

- Attractions and activities at destinations are important in their decision to visit.
- Preferences about spending, where to go, and what to do there are called lifestyles factors, and have a role in our definition.
- Life-stages (young, family, old) give us our customer types, and help define the where, when, what and how decisions of travel and tourism.
- The image and quality of the destination can determine choice.
- The quality of information about a destination or travel mode is an important element in the decision-making process.

Prior to booking, individual customers are likely to consider other factors, which define what they want from their travels, such as a safe passage, a clean hotel and up-to-date services. These types of factors go to make up a detailed definition of travel and tourism.

Different types of tourism

In this topic we shall investigate types of tourism flows (travel) in more depth, and investigate specific types of tourism:

- Incoming
- Domestic
- Outgoing
- Business
- Leisure
- Visiting friends and relatives (VFR for short)
- Excursions
- Adventure trips
- Package holidays and independent travel.

Understanding these different types will add to your knowledge of the nature and characteristics of the travel and tourism industry.

Incoming tourism

Incoming tourism is also known as 'inbound tourism' and is defined as travellers arriving in a different country from their own. In other words, if you were arriving on your annual holiday on the Algarve, you would be an incoming tourist to Portugal.

Incoming tourism provides a valuable source of income for the country and for the local economy, because it is not just the hotels and attractions that benefit from the spending power of tourists. This is often known as the economic 'multiplier effect' as the tourists' money spreads out to benefit all sorts of local people. For example, some of the money that tourists spend in a hotel goes as wages to the waiters and cleaners, etc, who then spend it in the local shops. In addition, local businesses will supply food and services to the hotel, and some of the money they are paid will also be spent locally – most of it in shops that have nothing to do with tourism.

When tourism is successfully introduced to an area, the boost to the local economy can encourage more tourism to develop, and then more again. Let's imagine an old fishing port has just one new hotel built, between the harbour and the beach. This makes the destination more attractive, so other accommodation springs up, along with new attractions. More holidaymakers arrive and some buy second homes. The town decides to build a new road and update its station. New businesses are attracted, who in turn need a new road. The airport is built to fly tourists and goods into this bustling resort, while a marina is developed to accommodate yachts and pleasure boats. All this development – triggered by the arrival of just one new hotel – is not uncommon.

WHAT TRENDS CAN YOU IDENTIFY?

The UK incoming tourism sector was estimated to be worth £12 billion in 2002, with 24 million trips made into the UK. You can see some figures for 2003/4 in Table 1, comparing monthly totals with the previous year's figure. What trends can you identify?

Table 1	
	% change
2003	
May	+ 2.4
Jun	+ 0.2
Jul	– 0.5
Aug	– 3.5
Sep	+ 3.7
Oct	+ 2.1
Nov	+ 2.9
Dec	+ 5.4
2004	
Jan	+ 1.3
Feb	+ 2.2
Mar	+ 19.8
Apr	+ 19.2
May	+ 9.2

Source: BITOA

Domestic tourism

We are all familiar with domestic tourism – we create it as we travel around our own country – staying with family and friends, having short breaks or annual holidays. This is also known as 'internal tourism'. Just as with incoming tourism this sustains a large tourist industry in this country – for example heritage locations, rural destinations, coastal regions, and urban venues too.

Star UK estimates that in 2002, UK residents made 167 million trips within the UK, spending more than £27 billion. Table 2 shows the number of nights.

Table 2 UK domestic tourism: length of holidays, 2002		
Length of holiday	Trips (millions)	Spending (£ billions)
1–3 nights	65	8.7
4–7 nights	29	6.4
8+ nights	8	2.3
TOTAL HOLIDAYS	102	17.4

Domestic tourism in this country takes many forms – often determined by the seasons or the social habits that we follow. July and August are the traditional family summer holiday periods, coinciding with school holidays (and high peak-season prices). While the older part of the population (who prefer quieter locations with no kids and cheaper prices) usually take their breaks in May/June and September, when the weather is still quite good but prices are lower. Single people or couples with no children can take an annual holiday any time, dependent on their work commitments, so they can catch the best deals but maybe not always the best weather. Table 3 shows the spread.

Table 3 UK domestic tourism: months of all trips						
	Jan	Feb	Mar	Apr	May	Jun
% of trips	6	6	8	9	9	8
	Jul	Aug	Sep	Oct	Nov	Dec
% of trips	10	12	8	8	7	10

Short breaks are clearly popular. This is a social pattern we have evolved in this country, due, some would say, to work pressures encouraging us to 'get away from it all for a while'. These 'leisure breaks' boost and extend domestic tourism in the UK, but to compensate for the unreliable weather, we tend to want our short breaks to have high-value activities in them. Consequently accommodation providers, attractions and the entertainment sectors work hard to provide a broad range to tempt us, such as spa and health weekends, sports taster breaks, and rambling or gambling.

Outgoing tourism

Sometimes known as 'outbound tourism', outgoing tourism is travellers leaving their own country to go abroad.

In general, according to Keynote Publications, the USA is the most popular long-haul destination, with the Spanish 'Costas' and islands, along with France, the most popular short-haul destinations.

Outgoing tourism flows reflect seasonal factors, especially climate, in the home countries and in the destinations. In the winter, northern Europeans can escape to the warm sun of the Canaries, and Americans from the northern states can escape south to Florida. This flow is sometimes called 'snow zone to sun zone'. The skiing season also draws sports tourists to the Alps, Pyrenees and Rockies from December to April, for example.

UNDERSTANDING OUTGOING TOURISM

1 Factors which are important to outgoing tourists were covered in the previous topic. Can you recall some of these as they relate to travel or the stay in the destination?

2 Why is it important for operators to collect and analyse statistics on these types of flow?

3 What world events have slowed this rate in the new century?

4 Name two of the most popular international destinations worldwide.

Business travel

Business travellers go abroad for the purpose of work, but sometimes one of the perks of this type of travel is that after the business is over, they are able to enjoy other tourism attractions, such as local cultural entertainment or just sightseeing.

For some travel agents this is the most lucrative market, as business travellers often want first-class services and are often willing to pay more. Quality and speed, however, are key issues for this type of tourist.

Some travel agents have set themselves up to specialise in business travel, e.g. American Express, Hogg Robinson, Carlson Wagonlit. Large businesses have large business travel accounts, so competition to win one of these accounts is fierce.

According to Keynote Publications, contrary to public perception, not all business travellers travel in business class when flying. Low-cost, no-frills carriers are growing in importance in the UK business travel market, and internet use is particularly high among frequent business travellers abroad.

activity

WHO WANTS THE BUSINESS?

Carry out some research online, to identify what three of the larger airlines (see a selection of sites below) have been doing to try and attract business travellers to their company.

BA – www.ba.com

Qantas – www.qantas.com

Air France – www.airfrance.com

KLM – www.klm.com

Virgin – www.virgin-atlantic.com

Indonesian – www.garuda-indonesia.com

American – www.aa.com

Compare your findings with others in your class.

Leisure travel

Most of us are leisure travellers (or tourists if we stay over). Leisure travel can be as little as a day trip to a park or beach, or as much as a world tour lasting 6 months. Leisure tourism cuts across all types of tourism – holidays, short breaks, long-haul trips. It includes all types of people – young, old, families, and many different types of purpose – hobbies, exploration, relaxation. We will give more specific examples later in this topic.

Visiting friends and relatives (VFR)

Ever since travel modes were invented, people have travelled to visit their friends and relatives. There were 40 million VFR trips by UK residents in 2002. VFR trips do not benefit the accommodation sector much because we usually stay with our friends, but it does benefit the local economy because our friends buy in extra provisions for our stay, and we spend money in their locality on entertainment, visits and souvenirs. Next time you are caught in a busy bank holiday traffic jam you can bet that a good proportion of the cars are on their way back from visiting their friends and relatives.

Excursions

An excursion is simply 'a trip away to a tourist destination'. These are particularly popular with older people taking a coach trip for the day or overnight – for example from London to Brighton, or from Leeds to the Lakes. Children in school love excursions too, and I am sure you can remember yours. Your grandparents may even be able to tell you of 'mystery tours' they have taken, for this is another style of excursion, where the destination is unknown to the travellers, so they are really on a journey of exploration.

The essential nature of this type of tourism is that it is usually low cost, e.g. coach trips or tours, and it appeals to groups who are less able to get about, e.g. children and the elderly, and who also like going in groups. Excursions can also be run all year round, with the operators choosing destinations which suit the seasons – such as a visit to Whitby on the coast of North Yorkshire for the Dracula Festival, or Blackpool on the north-west coast for the 'illuminations', or the classic 'Edinburgh Tattoo' during the Festival there in August. A key concept for this market is the fact that many different types of provider are involved in what is called the 'supply chain', such as the one shown below (this will also be discussed later).

A simple supply-chain sequence

Travel agent → coach company → cafés en route → hotel → entertainment venue → visitor centre

What are the benefits of being able to run excursions all year round in the UK, for the supply-chain organisations shown above?

Adventure trips

These are usually for the purpose of challenge, exploration, skills development or thrills, and probably appeal more to the younger market at one end of the scale and the active over-50s who may have retired early. This sector is typified by what is called 'niche-market operations', that is, many small companies offering quite specialised products and services. Some examples are given below:

- Cycling for softies in France
- Ice climbing in the Alps
- Children's activity camps in the Norfolk Broads
- White-water rafting in Wales.

These are clearly not low-key trips or holidays, and may involve more than an element of risk, but that is why people go on them – for high activity, thrills and maybe spills – what we might call 'controlled danger'. Clearly the safety measures are very important here – no one wants any real spills at all, just the thrill of 'feeling' that they are at their limits. To operate in this market, companies have to ensure that risk assessments are done, staff are properly qualified, equipment is in excellent working order and clients are insured.

'Cycling for softies' is a specialised niche market.

Package holidays

These are the more conventional type of tourism experience. The original definition in the Tourism Dictionary described a package holiday as something 'that is arranged by a tour operator and bought by customers, that includes at least two of the following, travel, accommodation and food'. There are many more shades of that definition now, with self-catering accommodation, self-drive accommodation and activities, flight or ferry only, with or without food.

In the early days there were many problems with poor quality 'packages', which did not deliver what was shown in the brochure (the intangibility factor). There were stories of half-built hotels, poor health standards and food preparation resulting in sickness, and airlines or travel agents that went bust, stranding holidaymakers in their resorts. Some examples of this occurred in Spain and the Dominican Republic. Too rapid expansion and insufficient infrastructure, combined with poor hygiene, sanitation and water treatment, resulted in some major outbreaks of illnesses (such as food poisoning) amongst tourists.

All of this resulted in the key organisations having to make regulations to control the industry. The Association of British Travel Agents (ABTA) insisted that travel agencies had to lodge a 'bond' with them to cover contingencies such as flying passengers home if they went out of business. The European Parliament introduced 'The Package Travel Directive' setting out 'legal standards for tour operators that cover travel, accommodation and/or services for holiday trips booked in any EU country regardless of the destination'.

You can easily pick up a brochure from a travel agent to assess what is on offer these days. However, with the arrival of the internet and people able to put together their own 'packages', the lifespan of the package holiday bought at the travel agent is shortening every year.

An article in *Travel Weekly* (July 2004) reported that 'established travel agencies are scaling back their capacity, due to growth in market share by the online specialists'. It went on to say that 'the two largest online specialists, Lastminute and InterActive have added 700,000 passengers ... while TUI, MyTravel, Cook's, First Choice, Cosmos, Gold Medal, Trailfinders and Libra have had a general reduction of 8%'.

Independent travel

Independent travel is the 'opposite' to package travel. It is people making their *own* way – in many cases round Europe or the world. The features of this sector are that the travel modes are not often pre-booked, local accommodation is used and local food eaten, and stopovers are flexible. Independent travellers may have no fixed schedule or plans. Some will set out alone, but meet up with others to travel on or explore a destination together. There are many issues about independent travel, which are derived from the type of tourist it attracts. Some suggestions you might want to explore or discuss are given below.

Independent travellers are different

- They are 'doing their own thing' – not herding in crowds.
- Many are seeking authenticity – e.g., meeting Buddhist monks in Tibet
- They are more conscious about the native culture than package holidaymakers – they want to preserve, not change, whom they meet.
- They practise sustainable tourism or 'eco-tourism' and are more responsible – they 'leave no footprints'.
- They are keen to go to 'off the beaten track' destinations e.g. Vietnam and parts of Africa.

activity

COMPARING INDEPENDENT TRAVEL AND PACKAGE HOLIDAYS

Compare what you think is the 'appeal' of independent travel, with the 'appeal' of a package holiday. Write a short description of your key points.

Sectors and vulnerabilities

So far in the unit we have covered definitions, and the nature and types of travel and tourism. Now we will explore the composition of the industry, looking at the characteristics of the private and public sectors, and the industry's particular vulnerabilities:

- **The private sector**
- **Multiples (the largest organisations)**
- **SMEs (small and medium-sized enterprises)**
- **The public sector**
- **Factors causing change and vulnerability.**

Unit 1 The Travel and Tourism Industry

The private sector

The 'private sector' means companies which trade for a profit (as opposed to the public sector, which is not profit-oriented, but provides a service to the community, as we shall see later). The travel and tourism industry is predominantly made up of private companies, and much of its character comes from the global corporations and large-scale national enterprises, such as hotel chains, airports and travel agencies. However, the smaller and medium-sized enterprises still have a considerable presence, and a key role to play in delivering tourism and travel products and services.

Many of the private sector companies are 'household names'. Their brand image is very powerful – British Airways or Thomas Cook's, for example. These largest corporations tend to have a 'global network' – they trade in numerous countries around the world in their attempts to gain as much of the total market as they can (market share) and maximise their profits.

A handful of the largest private travel and tourism companies in the UK hold as much as 50% of the market. You might describe these as 'the big fish in the big pool'. Some examples include travel agents First Choice and Thomas Cook's, and tour operators Thomsons and MyTravel. The rest of the market is spread amongst small and medium-sized providers, including specialist providers.

Company sizes are usually determined by factors such as the number of employees, turnover and the network of locations. The largest operators have considerable power in controlling the markets, for they are able to obtain substantial discounts from other travel businesses, such as airlines or hotels. In some cases these large operators buy other parts of the chain of supply – hotels at one end and airlines at the other – to complement their original operations. This is known as 'integration' and allows the organisation to have control over quality throughout the chain, and save money through centralisation and the economies of scale. You can learn more about integration in Topic 10.

activity

IDENTIFYING THE BIG PLAYERS

Give examples of the following:

- An airline, rail and coach company
- Hotel groups, B&B
- Theme park, two private urban/rural visitor attractions
- Holiday/caravan park operator
- Travel agency.

Multiples

This is the name given to the largest companies which have multiple outlets, such as travel agents Tui or Going Places. The expansion of the large travel agents (which at the time was known as 'the march of the multiples') helped to bring mass tourism to the fore. Everybody had a local travel agency to drop into – and they all had a range of holidays to choose from and a range of carriers to take people. However, the term 'multiples' can now also be applied to large global hotel chains such as Marriot or national ones such as Premier Travel Inns and Travelodge. The scales of operation of current multiples can be discovered in the next activity.

A street full of 'small enterprises'

Although multiples and big nationals bring more affordable travel and tourism through lower prices, they are not all good news. Some negative impacts have emerged as well, such as:

- environmental damage and cultural change through mass tourism, such as the mess tourists leave behind after a busy season, or the changes to local culture through increases in property prices.
- low benefits for the local economy because senior positions are taken up by staff from outside the area and profit is returned to the company headquarters – and lost to the local economy in many cases.
- impact on small independents – many just can't compete and close down.

Small and medium-sized enterprises (SMEs)

'Medium-sized fish in biggish ponds' such as budget airlines, holiday camps, or ferry services, can still trade globally if they have an internet site, but tend to favour serving customers on a more regional basis. Examples are Jet2, flying out of Leeds Bradford airport, the Butlins holiday camps and Caledonian MacBrayne's ferries on the west coast of Scotland. Other examples might include the UK's theme parks such as Alton Towers and thousands of privately run visitor attractions round the UK such as The Deep in Hull or Beamish near Durham.

The 'small fish in smaller ponds' small enterprises (SEs) tend to serve local needs such as the B&Bs you can find in Blackpool, Bournemouth, Bangor and Bideford. Some other examples would be the single high-street travel agent in smaller towns, or small boat and bike hire companies in the Lake District, many of which tend to be family businesses or even sole traders, with few employees and low turnover.

Small and medium-sized organisations make up a large portion of the travel and tourism sector, but have very different characteristics and bring different features to the nature of the industry. Many of the smaller SMEs offer 'special interest' tourism packages, in what are called 'niche markets' such as adventure holidays, cultural tours or world heritage site visits.

The public sector

Organisations in the public sector have entirely different characteristics, motives and purposes from those in the private sector. Let's start with the government's role, which would be the same in all the EU countries. Tourism is a major industry, and the various governments work to:

- attract international tourists
- ease the movement of people across borders
- standardise and raise quality
- develop the tourism industry in a sustainable way.

Most government policies and financial support will be aimed at these principles, and use information from sources like the European Travel Commission to help create development strategies for the tourist organisations and institutions. So the public sector's motives are:

- co-operation
- information exchange
- joint research
- partnerships.

If we compare this to the private sector strategies they would be almost the opposite. What words would you suggest for them?

The UK government, for example, tries to 'fill gaps in the market' for the good of the people, businesses and regions in general, as shown below.

How the government can help tourism

- promoting the UK as a tourist destination
- building and maintaining infrastructure (transport routes)
- providing training and development opportunities
- ensuring equality and fairness of trading
- collecting and disseminating statistical data
- protecting the environment
- supporting tourism-oriented organisations, e.g. its own Department for Culture Media and Sport (DCMS) which includes tourism, plus the English Tourism Council, tourist boards, local authorities and development agencies around the country.

activity

YOUR LOCAL TOURISM ORGANISATIONS

Draw a chart or spider diagram showing how your local tourism organisations are connected. Start with two circles at the heart of it, one with the local authority tourism department in it and the other with the regional tourist board. Who else do think has an input – the highways department, hoteliers, holidaymakers?

In 2000 the government published 'Tomorrow's Tourism', its strategy for tourism in the new century. The prime minister said that 'the challenge facing us now is to create a competitive, world-class tourism industry in Britain'. Clearly there is a need for both private and public sectors to work together to achieve this aim.

Factors causing change and vulnerability

The travel and tourism industry is very vulnerable to change, which can be generated by a number of factors. Some of these factors have been predictable – such as the impact of cheaper air transport. Others have not been, such as the SARS epidemic of 2003. Let's look at some of the key factors.

New technology

New technology has possibly had the greatest impact. Technology in its broadest sense could cover a range of factors:

- the internet
- satellite and global transmissions
- high speed and high volume travel modes
- the mobile phone.

Do you think that new technology has been good or bad for the travel and tourism industry?

Currency fluctuations

Currency fluctuations happen when a country's currency changes in value in relation to other currencies, e.g. the pound valued against the euro or dollar. Changes in this 'exchange rate' can have dramatic effects on the buying power of tourists abroad – the costs of hiring accommodation, purchasing fuel or paying landing fees and tourist taxes. It affects the overall income that a destination or even a country can expect to make in a season.

Tourism businesses like stable exchange rates so that they can forecast costs and profits more accurately. When this does not occur companies often try to pass the extra costs on to customers through supplementary charges. When oil prices go up, for example, tour operators may charge a supplement on package holidays, as happened in the summer of 2004. Tour operators usually reserve the right to do this in the small print of their booking form. Of course, currency changes could also make holidays cheaper.

Government legislation

New legislation can affect the host tourism country or the departing tourist in their home country. For example, if a tourist destination's government decides to increase business taxes, tourists and operators would find themselves paying more. If the government imposed stricter health and safety laws on tourism businesses, then greater investment would have to be found to meet the new requirements – another cost.

Climatic change

Climate change usually results in a very gradual change in weather patterns, such as we have with global warming and the erosion of the ozone layer. These are long-terms effects, which organisations and tourists can plan for. They do have significant impacts on the industry, however. For example, today we are much more aware of sunbathing causing skin cancer, so people may spend less time lying baking in the sun, and look for other diversions in a holiday package, such as excursions and activities – so this changes the nature of products. Awareness of global warming has encouraged us to look after fragile environments more carefully – resulting in more sustainable and responsible approaches to tourism.

In the shorter term, tourism can be affected by weather patterns taking an extreme course. Freak storms and hurricanes can cause floods and mud slides (such as in Mexico in 2003 and Turkey in 2004). Quite often these dramatic events happen in poorer destinations where buildings are less substantial. The whole tourism infrastructure can be washed away, wiping out the local economy entirely. The Indian Ocean tsunami in December 2004 had just this effect (though the cause was tectonic rather than climatic).

activity

THE EFFECT OF CONFLICTS

List some examples of recent forms of conflict. Evaluate what impact they had on the travel and tourism industry.

Reports of terrorist attacks can put off potential visitors.

War, civil unrest and terrorism

Unfortunately, terrorist atrocities and bloody conflicts are all too common around the world. The Arab–Israeli conflict, the invasion of Iraq, al-Qaeda threats, and the uprisings in African countries – all have an effect on the vulnerable travel and tourism industry.

Economic climate

The basis of most economies is 'trade'. When trading conditions start becoming unstable or failing, businesses become worried, confidence in the system drops and share prices on the stock market fall – which brings a spiral of less trade and lower profits (recession) that can end with companies going out of business. As the world's largest industry, travel and tourism can be hit very badly by poor trading conditions. This is because, when times are tough, people first save money by cutting down their spending on non-essentials (like holidays) so that they can still buy the essentials (food, shelter and clothing). It is the same for local authorities with shrinking budgets. When cuts have to be made, leisure and tourism is often the easiest area to cut.

Impacts on host environments

The impacts of travel and tourism can be beneficial (positive) or detrimental (negative). The industry can bring income and development to a host area, but it can also disturb local communities and cause environmental damage. Examples of these negative impacts at countryside destinations might be:

- Car parking at popular spots can damage the verges and spoil the views.
- Congestion on the approach roads can annoy local people and bring atmospheric and noise pollution.
- The constant flow of visitors along popular routes can erode pathways.
- Visitors may bother animals in their natural habitat.

The tranquillity and attractiveness of the countryside – which is what the tourists have come to experience – can be completely lost as hundreds of people 'swarm like bees round a honey pot'.

A balance needs to be found between residents, tourists and environmental needs. In a sense the experience needs to be 'managed'. This is often achieved through a partnership between a number of organisations – the local park rangers, a residents committee or parish council, the local authority, tourist boards and environmental groups, or traders themselves.

The development of the industry

In the last topic we looked at the nature of the travel and tourism industry. At first impression it seems a fairly young industry, but, ask yourself 'have we not been travellers and traders since ancient times?'

In this topic we shall look at the key stages in the development and growth of the industry, and move on to discuss issues that currently affect it, and its likely future. This historical view will be organised under the following headings:

- Ancient times
- The Middle Ages
- The Industrial Revolution
- The inter-war years
- The post-Second World War period
- The postmodern era
- The new century
- The future.

Ancient times

Fixing our starting point for an 'ancient' view is difficult, because there are several nations which may lay claim to being the first 'tourists'. It's not too hard, for example, to imagine travel and tourism amongst the ancient Chinese civilisation thousands of years ago. Perhaps the ancient Egyptian empire of 2000 BC produced some of the first tourism. Or should we credit the ancient Greek civilisation with their 'sports tourism' as athletes and spectators flocked to the early Olympic Games? Perhaps you favour the Roman Empire, a clear example of 'international' tourism and the building of facilities all around Europe.

If we included VFR in our search for the earliest travel and tourism, we would have to go right back to cave-dwelling times, before any of the ancient civilisations existed – because people must have visited fellow tribesmen and women in neighbouring caves.

What is clear from these many examples is that tourism must have existed long before the development of the infrastructure we use today. Clearly, the motives of travel and tourism are part of human nature, and some simple facilities would have been created in the destination zone and en route. Many stories and myths would have been created to capture imaginations and build curiosity, just as in brochures today.

Would you agree that travel and tourism have been with us ever since we became *Homo sapiens*?

The Middle Ages

In the Middle Ages, ordinary people had to work hard to survive, and leisure and travel were only possible for the richer classes. The landed gentry would have carried out their own versions of countryside, cultural, and sports tourism. Can you give examples of what these activities might have been?

There were, however, some 'holy days' designated by the church, which gave local folk some time off from their labours for festivals, fairs and sport. This is the origin of the term 'holidays'.

In the sixteenth century some people began to rebel against the indulgent ways of the upper classes, which were in such a contrast to their own poor lives. This made travel a much less popular activity for the rich, who ran the risk of being robbed by bandits.

Although wayside inns grew in number, the state of the roads was still appalling, and every journey was uncomfortable. It was not until sprung coaches were invented, with teams of horses (and coachmen for protection) and roads were improved that travel became more comfortable, and what we know today as a tourism infrastructure began to be created. The gradual improvement in the design and technology which went into coaches, together with the building of turnpike (toll) roads, began to form the transport network.

This type of development went hand in hand with sea transport improvements too, as ship design (and fewer battles) made trips to the Continent possible – for the rich at least – as passengers on cargo vessels. Despite all this, a journey from Edinburgh to Paris via London in the eighteenth century would still take two weeks.

Following on from the Renaissance period it became fashionable for the young aristocracy of the late seventeenth century onwards to travel a little – to broaden their education and cultural awareness. Paris, Venice, Rome and Florence were always on the itinerary, as they were the great centres of culture and learning. This trip was known as the 'Grand Tour' and, although halted by the Napoleonic wars, it was the basis for many later cultural and educational trips throughout Europe. Perhaps it was the foundation for the Mediterranean holidays of today – to the Riviera, for example, or Ibiza – except that today we have pleasure and leisure more in mind than education.

activity
THE HAZARDS FOR THE EARLY TRAVELLERS
Design a display board to show five of the earliest ways of travelling, and list the hazards underneath.

'Taking the waters' at spas – originally a Roman pastime – became popular again in the eighteenth century.

There were periods of war and unrest, during which people probably indulged more in domestic tourism and VFR, but the Grand Tour was never forgotten.

Progressively, from the 1750s onwards, transport modes were becoming more sophisticated, roads were maintained and safer, accommodation was provided en route, and travel was back in fashion.

The Romans had originally given people the idea that 'taking the waters' elsewhere was good for their health, but it was not until the eighteenth century that 'spas' really became popular. Many of the smaller places on the Grand Tour had also been spa towns, e.g. Baden Baden, Biarritz, Cortina, and this led to the development of many British spas, such as Harrogate, Bath, and Buxton (you can still enjoy these today).

activity
MAPPING THE FIRST RESORTS
In the last few paragraphs and the next few, more than twenty towns and cities are given as examples. Using a map of Europe and a separate map of just the UK, plot them all to help you build up your knowledge of the first resorts and destinations.

By 1750, 'taking the waters' at spas had spread to taking the waters at the coast, giving Scarborough and Brighton their first popularity. These were followed by Blackpool and Southend. The 'resort cycle' had begun. But there was still little for the common folk – other than their fairs, festivals and market days.

The Industrial Revolution

This period (roughly 1750–1900), gave tourism a boost in an indirect way. There was a massive population shift, as people left the countryside to work in the factories, mills and mines of the growing industrial cities. The people worked long hours, in noisy, dirty premises, but made a better wage than in the old agricultural days, so it was no surprise that when they did have time off they tried to enjoy themselves in the bars, clubs and other types of entertainment houses of the cities. Many, however, would have liked to return to the coast and the country to breathe some fresh air and relax. These are the first ingredients of 'tourism demand'.

One factor made this possible eventually – the invention of the railways and steam-powered trains.

By 1830 it was possible to travel on a passenger-carrying train from Manchester to Liverpool, have a good time, and get back to Manchester the same day. The railway networks spread rapidly, and numerous seaside resorts were connected to the industrial cities. Mass tourism was born as the working classes travelled 'from smoke stack to blue sea and sky'.

The use of steam power spread to the sea too, and 'steamers' complemented the faster travel on land with faster sea travel. The tourist resorts were truly born – piers were built, entertainment blossomed, accommodation sprung up, and second homes were built. The 'resort cycle' had moved into the 'growth phase' and, at the same time, travel for business was much more common.

At this time, along came a man called Thomas Cook, who in 1841 proposed an 'excursion' by train, from Leicester to Loughborough, for the members of his 'temperance society'. Over 500 people took up his offer, paying a shilling (5p) each, and their outing was a great success. As a result, Thomas Cook set himself up doing excursions on a commercial basis, The rest, as they say, is history. Cook soon expanded to offer all-inclusive deals (packages) to the Continent. The railway companies began to offer their tours as well – short breaks to the coast, trips to exhibitions, sports events and grand occasions.

Developments at sea were also moving apace with the first 'long-haul' trips to India and the Orient possible with P&O, and Cunard liners going to America from the 1840s onwards.

The Victorian traveller was spoiled for choice. Henry Lunn came along to rival Thomas Cook with new tourism products and services.

There were major infrastructural developments too, as stations, feeder roads and hotels were needed for travellers. The great London railway terminuses, which we still use today, were created – Paddington, Kings Cross, Euston and Waterloo. Some other features also began to develop:

- Destination branding can be identified – spa towns, ski resorts, seaside, mountain resorts
- Classes of travel were designated – first, second and third
- Quality of accommodation was important – everything from large second homes to 5-star hotels, guesthouses and B&Bs
- Resorts took on a more sophisticated look – with entertainment complexes, casinos, piers, parks and attractions
- Souvenirs and photographs of the day out provided the memories that are the essence of travel and tourism experiences.

The inter-war period

The early years of the last century saw continued development and growth, with evidence that as many as 50,000 people travelled to spend the winter on the milder Riviera (rather like the British and the Costa Del Sol today, or the northern Americans and Florida).

Tourism and travel activities are vulnerable to conflict, and were badly affected by the First World War (1914–1918). But before the Second World War began in 1939, the 'inter-war' years of 1918 to 1939, saw a number of patterns develop:

- migration to the USA
- the introduction of passports after the First World War
- many soldiers (who had never been abroad before the war) came back with a taste for foreign parts
- mass communications were improving, with cinemas and radio able to broadcast a view of other countries

The first Butlins holiday camp opened in 1936.

- the recession of the 1930s halted much of the aspirations of poorer people
- travellers were safer from disease and attack
- domestic tourism strengthened, e.g. with the opening of the first Butlins holiday camp in 1936 and further expansion of seaside resorts.

The post-Second World War period

After the Second World War (1939–1945), travel and tourism was able to take a leap forward, for a number of reasons:

1 People were keen to have some pleasures back after the lean years during the war.

2 Travel modes changed as cars and coaches came into their own, and the railways eventually saw something of a decline.

3 As Britain was rebuilt, a new kind of affluence spread to more of the population, with middle-class consumers on the rise.

4 The annual 'two-week factory holiday' (with pay) was established.

5 Faster and bigger passenger aircraft were developed. This spelled the end both for the domination of the railways and the extensive use of steamships for transatlantic crossings.

6 The expansion of the Youth Hostels Association (YHA) gave the more adventurous travellers a cheap and cheerful location to head for in many towns and countryside locations throughout Europe.

The backdrop to all of these factors was the support for tourism by governments in Europe, for they recognised its foreign earnings potential, and its contribution towards reuniting Europe.

Airlines started using jet aircraft, such as the Comet and Boeing 707, for both scheduled and charter trips. Liners continued to operate across the Atlantic, but were soon to be overtaken (in the late 1950s) by the air routes in numbers of travellers. Jet airliners meant that travel times were sent tumbling, and aspirations to travel rose.

The Comet, the world's first jet airliner, which came into service on the London to Johannesburg route in May 1952.

The introduction of wide-body jets in the 1970s, and the establishment of a strong competitive market for holiday operators (Horizon, Cook's, Thomsons) assured the future of the industry. Mass tourism was here to stay. The 'superstructure' for the industry (the buildings above ground) blossomed, as hotel chains established themselves along with restaurants, entertainment venues and bars.

By this stage, the profile of the market (as shown below) resembled that of a barrel, with mass tourism bulging at the middle and a fairly stable luxury market at the top (e.g. long-haul and 5-star accommodation) and the economy market at the bottom (e.g. camping and caravanning).

Luxury market
(long haul and 5-star accomodation)

Mass tourism
(package holidays)

Very low cost base
(camping and caravaning)

The shape of the market in the 1970s.

The tourist flows were clearly established as the northern Europeans (usually from the more developed countries) in general flew south to the sun – to the cheaper (less developed) Mediterranean areas. The annual total was about 2.5 million in the 1970s, growing to 11 million by the 1980s.

By the 1980s, the industry was estimated by the World Travel and Tourism Council to be worth $3 trillion and employ 200 million people worldwide. The shape of the industry became more that of a wine glass, with a strong but upwardly mobile middle market, and fewer budget holiday makers at the base, with some niche-market providers in the middle beginning to emerge.

Luxury market (bespoke holidays)

Mass tourism (package holidays)

Many niche markets (independents)

Basic holidays (seaside and camping)

The shape of the market in the 1980s.

This was possibly the most dynamic period for the industry. It was not without its vulnerabilities, however, as tour companies went bust, sometimes at short notice, stranding customers. Food poisoning was not uncommon due to poor local hygiene, and allegations of hotels being misrepresented in brochures were common.

The postmodern era

This effectively means the late 1980s and the 1990s – the end of the industrialisation period, the arrival of electronic technology and a much more 'me-centred' society – more affluent, more mobile, more discerning, and more leisure-focused.

During this period the shipping industry reinvented itself to create the 'cruise market', aimed at the over-50s, many more niche-market operators came on the scene, offering individual products as 'special-interest tourism'. Can you name ten different types of 'special interests' that people go on holiday to pursue?

There were some economic shifts too, which boosted business travel as the Far East boomed, and many cities built 'convention or conference centres' to attract the world's business people. Social trends saw us become more discerning consumers wanting

quality as well as an attractive price. The popular, but much maligned 'timeshare' deals sprang up, tour operators offered 'fly–drive', 'drive–camp', 'drive–ski' and fly–cruise' packages and 'seat-only' fares and 'all-inclusive' holidays to tempt us. Exotic destinations, previously known only to the rich and famous – Phuket, Goa, the Seychelles – came within reach of the mass market. The opening up of the least visited locations, however, brought with it issues of environmental damage and cultural intrusion. More 'sustainable' approaches were therefore needed to ensure their survival.

Recent years have seen the mass market spread to more exotic destinations.

If we view the profile of the industry now it appears more like an egg-timer, with the luxury market intact at the top and the base broad due to the advent of the budget airlines, but the centre (the long narrow waist) is not dominated by anyone, but features many niche-market providers, stretching the market.

Luxury market

Mass tourism

Many niche markets

Short-break and basic holidays

The shape of the market in the 1990s.

The new century

If we take a snapshot of the industry, looking at the first few years of the new century, we can see further developments and new characteristics emerging under a number of headings:

1 The influence of the internet. This electronic tool has given us the capability to take a virtual tour before we go (helping with tangibility) and to book our travel and holiday online, from home, for anywhere in the world.

2 The rapid expansion of budget airlines such as easyJet, Ryanair, bmibaby, Jet2.

3 The boom in holiday-home buying. With property prices high in the UK, people with a surplus are now mass purchasers of second or even permanent homes in places such as Spain, France and Florida.

4 The trend for people to take more short breaks – to balance work pressures and because they now have higher disposable incomes.

5 New high-speed rail, ferry and plane links can whisk us to destinations in a matter of hours.

6 Travel and tourism, however, is now under great threat from the new wave of terrorism that the new century has brought.

Despite all of the threats, people seem determined to travel, explore, relax and enjoy activities, which is good news for the industry for the foreseeable future.

activity

IMPLICATIONS

a) What implications has the internet brought for the high-street travel agent?

b) What implications have budget airlines had for the larger more established airlines?

c) What implications does second-home buying bring – for the people making the move abroad and for those who are the host community?

d) What implications does the increase of short breaks have for other sectors of the industry such as accommodation providers and travel companies?

e) What precautions have had to be taken at departure terminals to help ensure passenger safety?

f) How have shorter journey times affected our horizons and expectations?

The future

There are a number of trends and developments which will help to determine the directions and characteristics of travel and tourism in the future:

- We continue to be socially and geographically very mobile, which will ensure that new destinations are always being sought.

- Improvements in transport infrastructure are always ongoing as new economies emerge, such as Latvia or South Korea.

- New technology has swung the promotional and selling channels to more personal modes (e.g. TVs, PCs, mobiles) giving us all what might be called a 'buffet service', with a wide breadth of choice.

- The opening up of many previously closed communist countries as tourist-generating regions (China, eastern Europe), and as destinations in themselves.

- Changes in work patterns are common now with shift systems and flexible working. Some commentators feel that this leaves us 'money rich and time poor'. So will we all become high-spending weekend leisure bingers?

- We shall also have to maintain sustainable approaches to preserve the authenticity of the people, locations, cultures and events, that attract our holiday interest.

activity

THE DEVELOPMENT OF TOURISM

Design a poster showing the development of tourism and likely future characteristics, to include key features, such as:

- New travel modes
- Old and new destination features
- The influence of new technology.

What makes the industry grow?

This topic will investigate in further detail the factors leading to the growth in the travel and tourism industry. Many have already been touched on briefly, as the historical stages were described. The factors will be covered under the following headings:

- **Motivators**
- **Enablers**
- **Socioeconomic factors**
- **Technology**
- **Product development and innovation**
- **Consumer needs (Products ranges, buying behaviour, consumer protection)**
- **Customer expectations**
- **Fashion trends.**

Motivators

We talked in Topic 1 of motivations as the needs and wants of tourists. These can be of two types. 'Intrinsic' (from within) motivation, such as having a burning desire to see the world, tends to 'push' us to travel away from home. 'Extrinsic' (from outside) motivation, such as being inspired by one of the Michael Palin trips, tends to 'pull' us towards a place or particular activities. We may also be pulled by the attraction of a destination because of its uniqueness, beauty, or nightlife. And we can be pulled by clever advertising on TV or the internet.

Motivators can be some one-off fancy that we have, such as trying para-gliding in the Alps, or it can be just getting away from it all for a while, to recharge our batteries. Some people may be pulled by a singular motivational feeling, such as 'discovery' of unique places for example, which we might call 'wanderlust'.

We might argue that tourism motivations are really just desires in us to pursue great memorable moments and experiences. We can take little home (other than films and souvenirs to remind us) – so are we just spending some time playing out our fantasies?

Some work has been done to categorise our motivators more concretely – McIntosh, Goeldner and Ritchie in 1995 suggested the following four categories:

Four types of motivators

- Physical and personal factors such as health, wellbeing and pleasure – tension reducers
- Cultural – the desire to know more about other nationalities, how they live and spend their leisure time
- Inter-personal – wanting to meet new people, perhaps escaping family, friends and the home place
- Status and prestige – these motivators hinge on our image and ego, and possibly our desire to better ourselves.

activity

WHAT ARE *YOUR* MOTIVATORS?

Study the suggestions in the box above. Which order would you put them into to reflect your motivations when selecting a holiday? Compare your list with those of others.

Marketing strategies in the travel and tourism industry make extensive use of this type of knowledge, in order to 'target' each motivational type with the right kind of offering, e.g. cultural tours for the more academic and curious, cruises for those who feel they have an image to upkeep, group tours for those keen to make new friends, and so on. These strategies are another factor stimulating growth, and creating more and more niche markets. In 1972 a researcher called Cohen suggested that there are four different tourist types:

Four types of tourist

The organised mass tourist	Low on adventure, likes to stay in a safe bubble during the trip, happy with ready-made holidays, and not bothered about meeting locals.
The individual mass tourist	Slightly more flexible than above, but still likes the set tour and safe bubble.
The explorer	Organises independently, wants to go of the beaten track but likes their comforts still.
The drifter	Little attempt to use the tourism industry, wants as little reminder of home as possible, mixes with locals and works their passage.

activity

WHAT TYPE ARE YOU?

Study the suggestions in the box above. Assess which type of tourist you feel you are, or would like to be. Compare your ideas with those of others. With a partner, interview each other to find out why they have chosen that type. Plot the range of types that occur in your class.

Enablers

Enablers are closely linked to motivations, but different. They are the 'tangible factual factors' (TFFs), which enable us to be travellers and tourists. The range of TFFs includes:

- Level of disposable income – what is left over for leisure spending after all essential goods have been bought and all bills have been paid.

- Level of urbanisation – this may reflects how 'civilised' or developed we are, and this often goes hand-in-hand with a greater ability and desire to travel and be tourists.

- Level of education – the more we know of the world, its geography, populations and culture, the more we seem to want to travel to see it all for ourselves.

- Level of mobility – usually linked to car ownership, but also airports, seaports and rail networks to help us get around.

Thailand is one of the many Far East destinations that are growing in popularity.

Countering these, and *reducing* the ability to travel and be tourists, are factors such as large families, poorer rural economies, and increasing age.

Socioeconomic factors

Some aspects of social change have greatly contributed to the development of the travel and tourism industry (see Topic 4 also). Population density is a major factor. As this increases in urban areas, it brings with it a desire to escape, and usually the better wages to do it. But of course as the urban population stream out on a busy bank holiday, it is often the more fragile rural or coastal environment that comes under pressure to absorb them, and clean up after.

The population profile can also be a factor in growth or decline of the industry. In this country, for example, we have an ageing population which may slew the market towards cheaper packages, certain types of food and accommodation, and familiar resorts.

A combination of high earnings, low interest rates and a stable economy makes us feel good, and encourages us to spend more on leisure goods and services such as tourism and travel.

Technological growth

We considered some examples of technological change, such as aircraft and ship development, in the last topic. In this section, the main focus is on the use of new business systems.

In order to gain the competitive advantage over rivals, travel and tourism companies have embraced the new technology as quickly as possible, for theirs is a global industry, which benefits most from rapid communications around the globe. The new technologies produce cost savings for operators and better value for money for customers.

Larger organisations in the industry have been able to adopt global distribution systems (GDS) and global booking systems (GBS). Most have sophisticated software programmes which can calculate the best prices for seats, cabins, etc. for different routes, at different times of the year.

By keeping information on customer preferences in a computer database and using it for targeted mailshots and after-sales service, companies are able to forge relationships with customers – almost for life!

Benefits of the new technology

- Databases provide valuable sources of customer information
- Quality control is easier, due to the detailed nature of data kept
- Systems are speedy, accessible, and have unlimited space
- All information is concentrated in one place (on a network).

Constraints of the new technology

- Expensive – smaller and medium-sized organisations might not be able to afford to install systems and train staff
- High levels of dependency – if a system crashes, major problems can result, e.g. air traffic control in the UK
- Global networks can sometimes require staffing 24/7 to accommodate customers in different time zones.

Product development and innovation

The development and innovation aspects of travel and tourism include:

- Diversity of product and location range – Club Med for example is not just a land-based organisation, but now has tours in over 80 countries, plus a fleet of boats and cruise ships.
- Service levels – in most hotels now you can expect a full range of services.
- Improved business class travel – some airlines now offer sleeping bays, with full IT and internet access (and, of course, 5-star service).
- Broader ranges from tour operators.

Consumer needs

There are three aspects to consumer (customer) needs – the growing product range to choose from,

---

activity

INVESTIGATING PRODUCT RANGE

1 Investigate a tour operator's website or brochure to assess their product range. Select some products, and place them somewhere along these three scales:

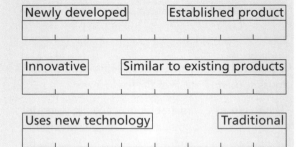

2 Comment on how these products are described. What words are used to attract/energise us?
3 Find a company that offers these innovative or newly developed products:
   - Fully serviced 'cabins' for business travellers
   - Activity holidays for the disabled
   - All-inclusive packages to China
   - Round the world fly-cruises
   - Spa health and wellbeing holidays in the new eastern European countries
   - Trips to the Arctic or Antarctic.

---

customers' buying behaviours, and protection for consumers after the purchase is made.

Product ranges

Tour operators work constantly to grow their product ranges to suit our needs. You can carry out a survey of all the latest developments, by reviewing Travel Trade Gazette or Travel Weekly magazines at www.travelweekly.co.uk and www.ttglive.co.uk.

Customers' buying behaviours

Research has shown that customers go through some fairly logical stages when choosing a holiday. Once their needs are aroused, they usually spend some time and effort in getting more information, and looking at several alternatives, before weighing them all up, and finally making a decision.

So after all of this effort and expenditure, consumers have a right to expect certain things with regard to their holiday purchase, and the industry and governments have worked hard to provide this.

Consumer protection

As the industry grew in the 1960s, 1970s and 1980s, travellers and tourists were really only covered by the normal Consumer Protection Acts:

In 1990, however – after years of customers finding that there was little they could do when companies 'went bust', when brochures misrepresented hotels, or when they felt annoyed by misleading small print on booking forms – the EU agreed to have a single 'Package Travel Directive'.

This gave the consumer greater coverage for packages which contained combinations of travel accommodation and other tourist services. Consumer protection is considered more fully in Unit 5, Topic 2.

Customer expectations

Customer expectations have gone up over the years, for a number of reasons:

- Rules and regulations tighten up poor practice – the industry is well regulated now.

- Codes of practice and ethical business practices have driven standards up.

- Staff are better trained – particularly in customer care.

- Companies striving for the competitive edge now try to 'exceed customer expectations'. Some use the phrase 'delight the customer'.

- Organisations know that if they do not reach customers' expected standards they won't get their business again.

- Customers are becoming better at complaining about, and to, organisations which have poor standards.

- Redress (getting compensation or something done about complaints) has been made easier by official institutions such as the Ombudsman, the Department of Trade and Industry (DTI), and Office of Fair Trading.

- Most good travel and tourist organisations belong to professional bodies and associations which monitor and control their activities.

Fashion trends

Just as with the fashion industry, travel and tourism has fashion trends too, for we are all influenced by our friends and family, advertising and persuasive operators. We have already seen that some people choose holidays for their 'status and prestige' – usually expensive holidays in exclusive places. Such places become very fashionable and, before long, the mass tourists are keen to go there too – to share the same exclusive experiences. The only problem is that to accommodate and satisfy mass tourism, often the whole original environment (e.g. south Tenerife) has to be reshaped. The authenticity that the tourists were seeking is destroyed as the big companies move in and create a tourism environment that looks just the same as others round the world – a sort of 'anywhere tourism'. Some writers have called this 'McDonaldisation'. Can you think of other examples that fit this description?

activity

TODAY'S FASHIONABLE RESORTS

Where are the current fashionable resorts for the following:

- 18–28 year olds
- the rich and famous
- independent/adventure travellers?

Issues for the industry

There are a range of current issues affecting the travel and tourism industry. Some, such as environmental damage, have been with us for a number of years. Others are more recent – such as the threats from al-Qaeda. And the industry itself has its own issues, about, for example, working practices, operations and use of technology.

This topic selects a few of the most important issues for the industry. Although most of them will be negative in focus, you should remember that tourism is generally a power for good in the world – helping with regeneration, sustainability, providing employment and much-needed income. These issues are more focused on how the industry can give the best benefit to all. Our selection will be broken into three types:

- Global issues – over-development, high investment costs, environmental concerns
- Recent development issues – falling investment, population shifts, expansion
- Operational issues – job losses, downsizing, disasters, low commission.

Global issues

Global issues tend to be those that are more long-term in nature, crop up all around the world, and need cooperative solutions.

Over-development and uncoordinated development

When tourism boomed in developing economies (e.g. Spain, Turkey) there was a frantic rush in some destinations to complete new hotels and other tourist facilities. The result now is that these resorts (e.g. on the Costa del Sol) are left with unsightly high-rise flats and hotels, partially completed apartment blocks and part-filled retail outlets, often with rubble and poor landscaping in between. When these resorts reach the end of their lifecycle there are some very poor buildings left. In the UK, you can see that happening now for some of our older seaside resorts built in the Victorian times – hence the range of 'renaissance' schemes underway at the moment.

Tourism development agencies and local governments need to have a planned approach, with accommodation that matches the local architectural style. They should plan what capacities the resorts can take without becoming eyesores. After years of mismanagement, Majorca, for example, has now adopted this policy.

activity

A RESORT REGENERATION SCHEME

Identify a resort renaissance or regeneration scheme somewhere (such as Hastings), and assess why it was needed and what the essential changes are. Compare your findings with those of others in your class to see if there are common themes and needs.

High investment costs

It is very expensive for local governments to create the tourism infrastructure (roads, water supply, sewage disposal, etc.) and this is a real problem for many poorer countries. Much of the considerable income eventually generated by the new tourism 'leaks' out of the local system back to the developer's home country, leaving the local authorities with little extra to pay off their massive debts. This has been the case with many Caribbean destinations.

Environmental concerns

The industry produces a wide range of environmental concerns – destruction of forests, soil erosion caused by trekkers' constant passage, loss of plants, animals and habitats as areas are cleared for development, air pollution from vehicle exhausts and jets, land pollution from rubbish and litter, water pollution from waste, poaching for game in Safari parks, congestion at peak holiday times. Agenda 21, produced at the 1992 Rio summit, and the 1997 Brundland Report both set out sustainable standards and an appropriate ethos to meet environmental concerns, but many countries do not really conform to this 'global agreement'. The USA and Australia, for example, have not signed the Kyoto Agreement.

activity

RESEARCH A PROBLEM AREA

Carry out some research on a particular problem area to find evidence of one of the issues given above. Assess what is being done to minimise or reverse the trend. Areas worth considering might be: the Himalayas, Brazilian forests, Kenyan safari parks, New York or Tokyo.

Cultural impacts

Cultural impacts include: disturbance of local communities, day and night, by tourists and revellers; corruption amongst businesses unashamedly 'chasing the tourist dollar' and giving the resort a 'rip-off' image; second homes forcing up house prices – which prices local people out of the housing market; exploitation of local people by developers paying minimum wages, etc.

Dilution and distortion of the local culture is a global issue. Local people may adopt tourist-friendly values and attitudes at the expense of their own long-established customs and cultural standards. Tourists travel to other countries to see different cultures and lifestyles, but operators can view these aspects simply as another valuable commodity to sell. They then stage 'traditional events' for tourists (dances and ceremonies) which are not really authentic at all.

'Traditional events', put on for tourists, are not always authentic.

activity

WRITE A 'CODE OF PRACTICE'

Working with a partner, create a code of practice which could be used by tour operators to ensure fair treatment of the local providers who will meet and entertain visitors.

Balancing the different needs

As mass tourism builds at a destination, great pressure can be put on the host community and the environment. The issue then becomes how to balance each one's needs, including the tourists' (see below). Any strategies to maintain the right balance must be 'sustainable' – although they must work now, they must not make things worse for the future.

The three sets of needs that a destination must meet.

Recent development issues

More recent issues probably only need medium-term solutions which are within the control/scope of the travel and tourism organisations themselves.

Declining public sector investment

Local authorities certainly don't have the capital to invest in major tourism works anymore. Today, this type of development can only be done in partnership with the private sector. These are sometimes called PPPs – private–public partnerships.

Population shifts

Demographics (the study of population statistics) clearly shows an ageing population in the UK. Over 50 per cent of the population was over 50 at the turn of the century. What are the implications of this type of population shift for travel and tourism?

Expansion

A large number of new airports, terminal expansions and runway extensions have recently been built around the world (e.g. Hong Kong, Manchester, Kuala Lumpur, Osaka) with many more planned – at Heathrow and Doncaster, for instance. These types of development throw up a range of issues (see below).

activity

NEW DEVELOPMENTS, NEW ISSUES

Identify and discuss the issues which each of the following bullet points might raise, under the following headings – social, environmental, political, economic.

- Bigger jets and cruise ships
- Changes in work patterns
- The internet.

Who benefits from expansion?

Even small developments at airports can cause disruption, as shown by the recent expansion at Leeds–Bradford Airport. There is a new international arrivals and domestic baggage hall, with extra administration offices and a large food hall, to cope with an estimated annual throughput of 2.5 million people. The original building is being doubled in size – a 4-year project. Bigger capacities, of course, mean more flights, more noise, more pollution, and more land swallowed up. The politicians and business people see these 'side-effects' as being balanced by more income, more jobs, and more capacity. How do you think local residents feel?

Operational issues

Operational issues, which sometimes apply only to specific sectors or even to single organisations, tend to cause short-term disruption.

Loss of jobs

Recent downturns in travel and tourism (e.g., after 9/11, the SARS epidemic or the invasion of Iraq) have seen many airlines either go out of business or reduce their routes, fleets and flights. The resulting job losses affect not only the companies themselves, e.g. BA, Swissair, but also the support companies which have to lay-off ground crew, catering staff and so on.

Downsizing, mergers and integration

One of the vulnerabilities of the industry which regularly causes problems for travellers and tourists is the amount of downsizing, merging and integration which goes on. Companies seem to be constantly reshuffling and re-organising themselves to survive, or to expand by swallowing up smaller companies, or to contract by trimming down. At the least it causes confusion for the customers, and maybe some lack of confidence. What other issues does this constant 'state of flux' cause for the industry?

Disasters

Disasters – whether natural, such as mudslides, or man-made, such as plane crashes – are not pleasant to consider. They sap confidence amongst travellers and staff alike, and can swing tourism flows away from disaster-prone areas. Under their association rules, companies, local authorities, terminals and ports must have 'disaster contingency plans' in place. A great deal of planning time, training and additional equipment costs have to be invested in such plans,

Hurricanes can wreck coastal buildings in seconds.

hopefully never to be used. Prevention of disasters needs a great deal of vigilance, and usually needs expert help, as you can see below.

Disaster management

For travel and tourism companies 'disasters' nearly always mean the loss of life and serious injury, plus a lot of media attention. Disasters mostly happen well away from companies' bases, with poor or confused communications, so organisations have to have effective systems in place to deal with contingencies 'at a distance'. Companies have to be ready for anything – we live in an increasingly litigious society (with charges of corporate manslaughter not unknown) and the media can be merciless in their coverage. Official investigations after a disaster are (understandably) very thorough.

So companies must be well prepared for possible disasters. Typically they will have a 'crisis-response team' who have regular training sessions and simulations to test the effectiveness of the planned procedures (which are all laid out in a special manual). Specialist back-up teams need to be on call, such as doctors, nurses, counsellors, communications staff and public relations (PR) experts. Some consultancy firms, such as 'Docleaf', are willing to come in and help prepare organisations for disasters. Good disaster preparation can also reduce insurance premiums, so it makes good business sense.

Low commission rates

With the advent of internet trading, meaning that many people with PCs never visit their high-street travel agent, their rate of commission has been driven down. In fact some travel agents now operate a fees system to ensure their income.

activity

THE VALUE OF GOING ONLINE

Identify ten benefits of putting a travel or tourism business 'on the net'.

The government's view

In 2000 the government issued a strategic plan citing tourism as a 'growth industry for tomorrow'. The plan, called *Tomorrow's Tourism*, had fifteen action points at its core, including several proposals aimed at trying to deal with issues in the UK industry:

- 'A blueprint for the sustainability of tourism', to preserve countryside, culture and heritage.
- 'A new internet booking and advertising system for the UK'.
- 'A more attractive hospitality sector as an employment area'. Traditionally this has been poorly paid and seasonal in nature.
- 'Innovative niche markets' such as sports and film tourism, as well as heritage tourism.
- 'New support for the regions and for seaside resorts' allowing self-direction and regeneration.
- 'A more joined-up approach to strategy'.

Proposals in 2005 give more responsibility to regional bodies for tourism development, such as 'Yorkshire Forward'. The government, of course, has an interest in supporting tourism because it generates wealth (and taxes), creates jobs, promotes entrepreneurship and enhances our culture.

Topic 7 Travel sectors of the industry

The travel and tourism industry, as it has evolved since the 1950s, is really an amalgam of many sectors, rather than a single cohesive industry. In this topic, after an introductory overview, we shall investigate the sectors concerned with travel:

- Travel agents
- Tour operators
- The four principal modes of transport.

Overview

Perhaps the easiest way to see how all the sectors come together is in a simple diagrammatic form (see below). The sequence represents the traditional process from booking to completing a holiday. This may not represent the process that you follow, but for many it is the normal sequence that is followed, because it answers some simple questions:

1 What is available?

Check at the travel agency

2 Who has the best deal?

Look at the brochures

3 How do I get there/back (easily)?

Train/Boat/Plane/Car/Coach/Bike

And, to be considered in the next topic:

4 Where will I stay?

Hotel/GH/BB/Caravan/Hostel/Tent

5 What will I do when I get there?

Attractions, entertainment, excursions

6 What extra services do I need?

Visa, guides, resort rep.

We shall review how well this diagram represents reality as the topic progresses.

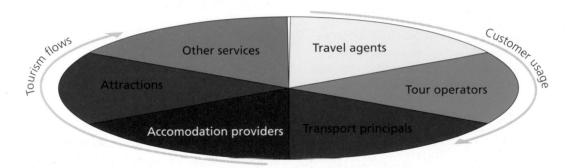

The different sectors of the travel and tourism industry

Travel agents

Traditionally, high-street travel agents have been the intermediaries (retailers) in the industry's supply chain. They sell the products and services produced by the tour operators, cruise companies, airlines and hotel chains to the travellers and tourists. Unlike most high-street retailers, however, travel agencies do not stock up beforehand – they sell 'on demand'. Agencies negotiate and then sign contracts with all types of leisure and tourism providers. The contracts license the agencies to sell tickets, seats, beds, and so on to the customers.

Travel agencies all belong to the private sector, whose prime purpose is to make a profit (and, if possible, to get the largest share of the market). In recent years that has proved to be much more difficult, as we will see later. Current market leaders include TUI, Thomas Cook's, MyTravel, and First Choice.

There are different types of travel agencies. Most provide for holidaymakers (the leisure travel sector), some provide for business travellers (the corporate sector) and others provide for both. The value of business clients is usually higher than that of holidaymakers (can you think why?). In the UK, there is a decline in the number of outlets (branches of the multi-national and national chains, regional networks, and independents) because of falling profit margins and because more people are now booking direct on the internet.

To trade, agencies normally have to be approved by their 'Association', who give them a charter to follow. The Association of British Travel Agents (ABTA), for example, has a set of articles, and the International Air Transport Association (IATA) scrutinises agencies for quality, standing, qualifications and competence. Today agencies have to deposit a 'bond' with their Association to cover their customers' needs, should they go out of business. This reassures travellers that they cannot be left stranded abroad, whatever happens to the company.

A travel agents in Japan

Until recently, travel agents were the most convenient way of selling to the public, because brochures, timetables, 'special deals' and specialist staff were all clustered together in one place.

However, with the arrival of the internet and direct sales, some argue that the days of the conventional high-street agent are numbered (do you agree?).

Travel agents have always made their income through commission payable after a sale has been made, but this commission has been squeezed to almost nothing recently, particularly by the tour operators. Different commission rates are paid by different sectors. Car hire commission, for example is usually higher than rail or cruise commission.

Some agencies are 'integrated' with tour operators and hotel chains (they are all part of the same company), so they have a tendency to 'sell' their own products, a fact that is not always made clear to customers. In the 1990s the best known set of integrated services were Thomson Travel, who also owned Britannia Airways and Lunn Poly (and a holiday cottages group), but Thomson themselves were taken over in 2000 by the German leisure group Preussag (now part of TUI). The following year, Thomas Cook's were taken over by another German group C & N Touristic AG.

Computer technology has both helped and hindered the travel agencies. It has helped, by giving them fast global communication and reservation systems (Galileo, Sabre or Viewdata), huge databases of customers, and efficient billing and ticketing systems. But now it has hindered them by giving customers direct contact with the operators and transporters (through internet access) thus helping to make the agencies – the intermediaries – redundant.

So already our traditional supply chain sequence is breaking up. Fewer and fewer of us are stopping at the travel agent as our first port of call to see what is on offer. More and more of us are doing this electronically from home, or at work, and booking online or contacting the call centres of the main travel and tourism operators.

Tour operators

Tour operators buy in and combine the various elements that make up a 'package deal' – the travel mode, the transfers, the accommodation, and the excursions or other activities. The products created (packages or tours), are then sold on down the line (supply chain) to the agencies, for distribution in the market place.

The majority of tour operators, like the travel agencies, are members of ABTA, which gives them credibility, and gives the customers security. Most operators offer a wide range of tour products, to suit the different seasons – from winter skiing to summer holidays, different timescales – from long-haul to short break, different social groups – from independents to large groups, different age ranges – from youth to ageing, and different levels of activity – from total relaxation to extreme sports. And the range usually includes almost every location on the globe! The section on TUI (page 51, Topic 10) shows the range offered by one major group.

Many independent operators have created their own little niche markets of special-interest packages, such as private villas, cottage holidays, or activity holidays (Exodus and Explore, for example).

Recently, tour operators have had to search for new, cheaper, destinations to keep down resort costs – hence Turkey's boom. They also adopt various tactics to ensure that their costs are at least covered – bulk buying, overbooking flights, selling off seats at a 'last-minute' discount ('late availability without guarantee'), and offering packages with unknown destinations (until the operator has filled the spare seats on the outgoing planes and the spare beds in the resort hotels).

Ferry companies, such as Brittany and P&O, organise their own package deals such as drive/gite/routier combinations in France. And, of course, there are tour operators organising package deals for incoming and domestic tourists as well, such as coach tours round Britain.

Because this is a very competitive market, quality and customer service have become paramount in gaining customers and keeping ahead of competitors. This (along with the internet) has allowed the smaller operators to survive, as they try to develop relationships with clients in what feels like a more personal way. Meanwhile the larger companies have tried more and more integration, but not all have survived. There have been some spectacular collapses over the years – Clarksons Holidays in the 1970s, for example, and Intasun and Best Travel in the 1990s.

Constant restructuring is a feature of this sector, making it one of the most volatile parts of the industry. Increasingly, the large companies with high levels of integration dominate. Currently a handful of the top organisations have around 50 per cent of the market. This situation does not concern the Department of Trade and Industry for it considers an

'oligopoly' (power resting in a few hands) to be healthy for the industry and the consumers – the Department would only intervene if just one company became too dominant.

Tour operators are now concentrating more on promoting short breaks, which are becoming more popular, especially to the attractive (and cheaper) eastern European destinations – in Poland, Bulgaria or Latvia, for example.

The nature of tour operating is clearly a complicated and risky business, for it encompasses integrated services, companies and add-ons – a recipe for potential disaster. Success is dependent on using bulk buying to put together packages at a cheaper price than the individual can do (or can be bothered to do). Tour operators must create a value-for-money package, by cutting costs – but not standards or safety – and loading hotels and planes to capacity. Consequently, customers may experience changes of departure times, even changes of airports, as airlines 'consolidate' capacities, as well as 'supplements' springing up, apparently from nowhere.

STEPS IN PLANNING A NEW PACKAGE

You work for a tour operator, and your boss asks you to search for a new destination idea. What steps would you take? Once you have decided on the best method, design a sequence that you could use every time when researching, planning, marketing and operating a new package tour. Use a flow chart with boxes for each step and some notes of what you need to do alongside each box. Prepare your flow chart on an acetate to present your ideas to the rest of the class.

The four principal modes of transport

There are four principal ways to travel – by air, on water, over land on rails, and over land on roads. This gives us four principal transport modes – aeroplanes, ships, trains, and motor vehicles. Once they all connect up, they make mass tourism possible.

Transport requires massive capital investment to create – just consider the cost of rail networks, airports, planes and ferries – so in most countries there are only a few main carriers.

Airlines

The new A380 Airbus could carry as many as 840 passengers, but will probably carry about 550 in three classes.

After the Second World War, faster and safer air travel revolutionised travel for ordinary people – and, in turn, revolutionised tourism. As technology has progressed, we have come to accept flying as a fast, safe and frequently cheap mode of transport. Wide-body jets now allow airlines to transport large numbers of tourists (300–400 at a time) worldwide, on a non-stop basis, every day.

The volume and frequency of air traffic, however, is now becoming a major problem, with congestion occurring at most of the world's largest airports.

The two main types of airline services are 'scheduled' and 'charter' flights (there are also air taxi services).

Scheduled flights fly to a published timetable on fixed routes, such as the frequent services between London and Paris, or the transatlantic flights from London to New York. The new 'no-frills' airlines operate scheduled flights too.

Charter flights fly to specific destinations for tourism purposes, e.g. taking holidaymakers on package trips in the summer to Turkey and Greece.

Scheduled services are provided by around 600 companies around the world.

The major airlines usually have a central base at one of the major airports, known as its 'hub', and the airline's smaller planes fly passengers into the hub from subsidiary airports. This is called a 'hub and spoke' operation – such as KLM has, based at Schiphol Amsterdam airport.

With the arrival of budget airlines, such as Ryanair and easyJet, offering no-frills scheduled flights to less busy airports, the major airlines have had real competition in recent years. The budget airlines' overheads are lower than the major airlines because they don't have so many additional costs, such as food on board and large amounts of administration. They also use airports with lower landing fees, and turn their aircraft round in quicker times – all helping to keep ground costs low.

Charter airlines often belong to the larger tourism companies, as we have seen, giving them full control of destinations, times and frequency. Examples are Monarch or Air 2000. Charters flights are mostly seasonal – to Malaga in the summer, for example, and to Geneva for skiing in the winter – but some destinations are year round, such as Florida and the Canaries. At airports, charters have to use the 'landing slots' that are left before, after (and sometimes between) the fixed scheduled flights. This means that they often fly at 'unsocial' hours (but it also keeps costs down). Charters also have an image of packing people in like sardines (load factors). Is that image fair?

Water transport

Conventional ferries may not be fast, but they have immense capacity and comprehensive facilities.

Water transport is one of the oldest modes of travel – just think of the ancient Greeks or the Vikings, for example. Today there are many types of vessel active in the tourism industry, but we shall look at the main two – ferries and cruise ships.

Ferry companies

Until a hundred years ago, the only way for people in the British Isles to go abroad (to become outbound tourists) was by water. Ferry services around the coast developed from sailing boats, to steamers, to diesel-powered vessels of ever-increasing size and capacity. Today's UK ferries vary in size from little 6-car open-decked boats plying their trade in the Scottish western isles, to large, almost cruise-ship-style channel ferries, carrying hundreds of cars and passengers. These 'ro-ro' (roll-on, roll-off) ships, sailing from massive terminal buildings on the British coast to similar terminals along the coast of France, Belgium and Holland, carry over 50 million passengers every year.

Key ferry companies for the UK are P&O and the French company Brittany Ferries. They link several of our English Channel ports to France's north-coast ports, carrying over 18 million people and 3 million vehicles each year.

The cross-channel ferries faced new competition when the Channel Tunnel was completed in 1994, and again five years later when budget airlines entered the market. The ferry companies responded by investing in better ferries, bringing the standards of comfort up to almost cruise-ship levels, and by introducing fast catamaran-type ferries, based on jetfoil designs, cutting travel times. Dover still remains the busiest UK port, with the shortest crossing route to Calais, now less than an hour away.

Even SeaCat ferries, which can cruise at 35 knots, have to slow down when they enter harbour.

activity

BRITISH FERRY SERVICES

Carry out some research on ferry services from Britain, and identify:

- the next four busiest routes from the UK (after Dover–Calais)
- the current volume of traffic for each route
- any new developments that have been brought in by the ports authority at one specific port
- three examples of new vessels
- the carrying capacities for two companies.

Cruise-ship companies

Cruise ships have taken over from the old ocean-going liners that used to take travellers vast distances around the world before long-haul flights were possible. Today, ships can't compete with planes on speed, but they can offer 5-star luxury, and style, and they can cruise from one exotic location to the next.

Most of the old liners were not suitable for adaptation to cruise purposes – they needed deep water to moor in, and tugs galore to push them alongside the quay. It was not until new marine technology was developed that purpose-built cruise ships could be built as we know them today – virtually floating entertainment cities, with every passenger comfort. Sizes increased during the 1980s and 1990s, as well as levels of sophistication – till we have today's cruise ship of advanced design. Long-term forecasts are good for this sector, with even larger ships, e.g. *The World* (see www.residensea.com).

The largest market is North America (followed by Europe), with the most popular departure port being Miami – just a short cruise away from the Caribbean. Just as with the busiest air routes, many shipping lanes and destinations are struggling to cope with the volume of arrivals. How can a small Pacific island cope with two or three cruise ships arriving within hours of each other and disgorging 4,000 passengers each – all looking for that deserted beach with white tropical sands, and no one else for miles?

These floating hotels can offer regular changes of scenery, great food, entertainment every night and leisure pursuits all day – the classic all-inclusive package. Fly-cruise packages are increasingly popular because tourists can get to their cruise's departure point quickly (and avoid the choppy Atlantic). New developments are themed cruises (Disney cruises, for example) and many companies are now targeting the younger age group to diversify their markets. The current top companies are Carnival, P&O and Royal Caribbean, and the newest ship is Cunard's 150,000-ton *Queen Mary 2*, described as the 'largest, longest, tallest, widest and grandest liner in the world'.

activity

RESEARCHING THE CRUISE BUSINESS

Visit the websites of Carnival, P&O, Royal Caribbean and Cunard to update yourself on their current capacities, routes and vessels. Identify who they collaborate with for cruise sales and linking travel.

Rail and Road

These two modes of transport were the original means of touring, but in many ways technology has overtaken them, and their roles for tourist purposes are now much smaller.

As a nationalised network (run by the government) the UK railways apparently soaked up investment and were slow to modernise, so in the early 1990s the government franchised off the various routes to private companies. Since then, however, the railways have had a chequered history of under-funding, accidents, lateness and strikes – hardly the record of an attractive tourist travel mode. Much investment has been made into both the track and the trains to bring them up to standards comparable with other European networks, but that is a very long process.

Business travel and commuter flows, plus VFR trips continue to keep most railways solvent, but it is very difficult to assess the future value of railways for tourism, other than the Channel Tunnel services (Eurostar/Shuttle) and perhaps the London underground.

There are one or two success stories for the railways among the many small private lines maintained by trusts and enthusiasts that serve the leisure market with classic steam-train journeys, such as the North York Moors Railway or the Welsh narrow-gauge railways, e.g. Towyn or Trawsfynnydd.

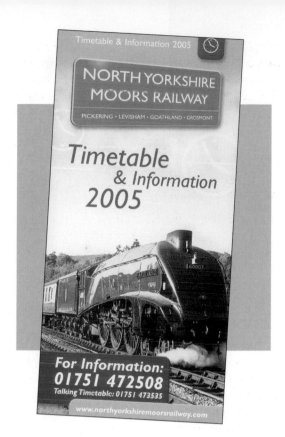

Where rail and road work together – the Channel Tunnel Shuttle service.

Road travel for tourist purposes can be represented by cars and coaches.

We tend to use our cars for VFR visits and the annual holiday trip to Europe (in conjunction with a ferry crossing and possibly towing a caravan or trailer tent). Some families will also hire a car while on holiday and this represents a large sector of the market with global companies such as Avis, Hertz, and Europcar. Many operate in conjunction with airports and railways, hotels and resorts. Who currently has the greatest market share of the worldwide car hire market?

Coach travel is widely used in the UK by people who don't drive, are not very personally mobile, or are on low incomes. What are the advantages for these types of traveller in using coaches? Coaches serve a range of markets:

- Day trips, e.g. to the seaside or to shopping centres
- Short breaks, e.g. to the Lakes or Scotland
- Continental journeys as scheduled services or charter trips.

---

activity

RESEARCHING THE RAILWAYS

Current franchises to train-operating companies (TOCs) include GNER, Virgin Trains and National Express. Investigate their websites to assess routes, development plans, and volumes of passengers.

---

activity

COMPARING MODES OF TRANSPORT

Make a comparison between the advantages of a rail journey, a car and ferry journey, and a flight, for a trip from Luton to a northern European destination.

Resort and service sectors of the industry

The operators, agencies, and modes of transport described in the previous topic are supported by the resort and services sectors, which will be considered in this topic. We will also investigate how most of the tourist organisations are regulated by certain outside organisations – organisations that you should know about because they are important to the whole industry. This topic therefore covers:

- **Accommodation providers**
- **Attractions**
- **Ancillary services**
- **Support services**
- **Other organisations involved with travel and tourism.**

Accommodation providers

This section will focus on the commercial providers, but you should be aware that there is also a vast range of non-commercial accommodation which exists to provide a service rather than make a profit:

Non-commercial types	Commercial types
Youth hostels	Hotels and motels
Local authority campsites	Guest houses
Home exchanges	Farmhouses and B&Bs
Staying with friends	Villa rentals
University halls of residence	Hired caravans/motor homes Caravan parks Holiday camps/centres

From the table above you can see how diverse the accommodation sector is. This is because it must meet the needs of the whole range of tourists and their budgets.

Hotels

Hotels dominate the accommodation sector. It is getting increasingly difficult, however, to define what you might expect in a hotel. The term covers everything from the 5-star accommodation and service that Gleneagles offers, including a host of supporting leisure pursuits, down to a tiny sleeping cabin. The 'rooms' in Japanese 'capsule hotels',

originally designed for businessmen, are little bigger than coffins. The hotels include all the conveniences one could ever need – sauna, bath, restaurant – and all for around $30 a night.

Gleneagles offers all the conveniences one could ever need too, but not for $30 a night! (You can visit websites to compare what's on offer – just key in 'capsule hotels in Japan' in a search engine, or find out about Gleneagles at www.gleneagles.com.)

Consumer demand has changed too, with business travellers needing very different services to the short-break holiday families, for example. This in turn has led to what are called 'branded multiples' creating niches for themselves in the market. This strategy of building exactly the same kind of hotel in every key geographical area (sometimes called McDonaldisation) is very cost-effective for the company, and reassuring for the customer, who can be sure of a familiar environment at a consistent standard.

Leading chains which offer more upmarket provision, with a bar, restaurant, leisure facilities and so on, include: American-owned Marriot and Holiday Inns; French-owned Novotel and Mercure, and the British Hilton and Jarvis chains.

Country house hotels are able to offer scenic locations and countryside pursuits, coupled with excellent food, making an attractive short-break package. Meanwhile the more traditional tourist-oriented family-run seaside hotels have suffered a decline.

RESEARCHING HOTEL CHAINS

Select two hotel chains and compare and contrast their:

- typical products
- additional services
- mission or vision statement
- values they feel are important for customers.

Farmhouses, guest houses, inns and B&Bs

Guest houses, and the other SMEs of the accommodation sector, appeal to many types of tourist and, together, still account for a significant share of the accommodation market. They offer a more personal service, especially as many of the locations are the owners' own home. In recent years, however, they have had increasing competition from the budget-hotel chains.

Camping and caravan parks, holiday centres, apartments and cottages

These accommodation types tend to cater for the lower-budget tourists. Camping and caravan parks can be quite diverse – everything from a simple farmer's field (registered with the Camping Club of Great Britain) to a massive Eurocamp complex in France, with entertainment, swimming pool, pizza cafe and children's activities.

Holiday centres, e.g. Club Med, Butlins or Center Parcs, offer 'the works', with a choice of entertainment, a range of activities, and 'fine and fast food'. Cottage and apartment rentals are self-catering, and give a 'home from home' feeling. They range from rural gites in France to the high-rise apartment blocks in Tenerife.

Attractions

Attractions represent what a destination has to offer. The two main types – man-made and natural – can be grouped under some further headings:

- historic/cultural/heritage-related – such as ancient sites and monuments, old buildings, and museums, e.g. Windsor, Warwick and Edinburgh castles
- modern and purpose-built – such as theme parks
- events-based – such as the Olympics
- entirely natural – such as the Grand Canyon.

The key issue for many of these attractions is how to manage them effectively and sustainably. They all have to cope with large flows of tourists and traffic at some stage, which brings with it issues of pollution and congestion. Host communities can often be disrupted by large influxes of visitors, though most now make the most of the 'secondary spend' – offering their visitors food, souvenirs, and facilities.

Many attractions around the world are based within the local native culture, which may be very different from that of the tourists. All sorts of impacts can be created by this clash of cultures – exploitation, the ever-present cola bottles, inflated pricing, and cultural

Being too popular with tourists can ruin the experience for everyone – as was long the case with the Mona Lisa in the Louvre, Paris. The display has now been improved to give more people a better view.

RESEARCHING TOP ATTRACTIONS

Select two top attractions in each category, and compare and contrast their:

- typical products
- additional services
- mission or vision statement
- values they feel are important for customers.

transgressions (such as under-dressing, not asking permission to take a photo, etc.).

Attractions, like many tourism sectors, suffer from seasonality, and also have their own problems – coping with queues, establishing authenticity, and getting funding to run and maintain the attractions.

Support services

Support services are the extra services that are provided by the tourist organisations, and the services supporting the whole industry that are provided by outside organisations. These include:

- Local tourist boards providing training for hoteliers, etc.
- Marketing consultancies offering business advice to local tourist organisations
- Employment agencies providing seasonal staff to a tourist attraction
- Laundry services for hotels
- Printing of leaflets, timetables, menus, etc.
- Entertainers for clubs, bars, hotels, etc.

When hotels display leaflets for local attractions, they are helping their own guests and supporting the local tourism industry.

- Technical support for computer systems
- Accommodation providers circulating brochures for local attractions.

Ancillary services

Usually, when people book a holiday or any sort of travel, they need to buy extra services, such as insurance or car hire, which are additional to the main product or service purchased. These 'ancillary' services cover a wide range of activities:

- Travel agents selling travel insurance as part of a package holiday
- Airport car parking, provided by private companies
- Local taxi and minibus companies
- Limousine and chauffeur services for business travellers
- Car hire, whether arranged through the travel agent or bought independently
- Bureaux de Change in travel agents, city centres or airports
- Agents offering express visa services
- The Post Office's 'Check & Send' service for passport applications.

activity

SUPPORT AND ANCILLARY SERVICES

Working with a partner, and using some of the suggestions given above as guidelines, make a list of other support and ancillary services that you can think of.

Other organisations involved with travel and tourism

Each of the sectors of the travel and tourism industry has its own national organisations, which regulate, control, advise and guide the sector.

Besides these sector organisations, there are also government departments and international agencies who oversee travel and tourism activities. A few examples will give you some understanding of these organisations and their roles, though you will also have to carry out some research and reading to answer the questions set below, and build up your knowledge by visiting the organisations' websites.

International agencies

- The World Travel and Tourism Council (WTTC) is a worldwide network of chief executives from all sectors of the industry. The WTTC works with governments to maximise the benefits that travel and tourism can bring to national economies.

- The World Tourism Organisation (WTO) is based in Madrid and provides a means for governments  and industry members to work together to discuss issues and set global standards.

Many of the industry's sectors have their own international associations. Examples are:

- The International Air Transport Association – who licence and monitor air transport

- The International Civil Aviation Organisation – a specialised agency of the United Nations.

a c t i v i t y

INTERNATIONAL AGENCY QUIZ

1 The WTO works in six main areas. What are they, and what is the WTO's motto?

2 What is the WTTC's 'Millennium vision'? What is the purpose of the WTTC's research centres around the world?

3 What role does the United Nations play in travel and tourism?

Government departments

Most countries have national tourism organisations (sometimes called NTOs). Their roles are usually to promote travel to that country and tourism within it, so they have policy-making powers and often funding power too. Government agencies may also have regulatory powers.

In the UK the Department for Culture, Media and Sport has a tourism division, which manages these aspects – it published the *Tomorrow's Tourism* strategy, as already mentioned. Building on *Tomorrow's Tourism*, the government published the 'Tourism Prospectus' in 2004, setting out the responsibilities of public- and private-sector organisations in the key areas of marketing, quality, skills and data.

English Regional Tourist Boards

Cumbria – www.golakes.co.uk

Northumbria – www.visitnorthumbria.com

North West – www.visitnorthwest.com

Yorkshire – www.yorkshirevisitor.com

Heart of England – www.visitheartofengland.com

East of England – www.visiteastofengland.com

London – www.visitlondon.com

South West – www.westcountrynow.com

Southern – www.southerntb.co.uk

South East England – www.southeastengland.uk.com

a c t i v i t y

WHAT HAPPENS IN YOUR AREA?

Identify your regional and local tourism boards, and find out what they do for travel and tourism organisations in your area.

The industry has recently formed a new body, the Tourism Alliance, to represent its views to government more effectively.

Each of the English Regional Tourist Boards provides detailed information on visiting their region (see box above). At the grass roots level, most tourism is controlled by the local authorities, who try to integrate it into local strategic plans.

National organisations

At national level, there is whole range of UK bodies setting out objectives, values and targets for travel and tourism providers, including:

- The Association of British Travel Agents (ABTA), controlling most large travel agencies

- Tourist Information Centres (TICs), providing information throughout the country.

Some sectors, such as accommodation, attractions, shipping and tour operators, do not have clear international 'key organisations', and are dominated by multinational corporations.

Scale, inter-relationships and interdependencies

This topic will draw together many of the threads that have been unpicked in the explanation of the travel and tourism industry so far – scale, importance, structure, and sectors. To do this we will look at some statistics, and at inter-relationships and interdependencies. The topic is arranged under the following headings:

- The scale of the travel and tourism industry
- Interpreting data
- An overview of functions
- An insight into the distribution chain.

The scale of the travel and tourism industry

Travel and tourism organisations constantly gather data – on visitor numbers, spending and employment – to help them assess whether the industry is growing or contracting. This is done at all levels – at a local level by individual attractions, regionally by a tourist board, nationally by a national operator or the industry lead body, and globally by one of the international associations.

The tables opposite present some recent figures on travel flows (how we travel), tourist movements (how many tourists and how often they travel) and economic value (spending).

Interpreting data

An important skill is the ability to interpret the data that has been collected, so that trends can be detected, recommendations made, and actions taken. Each new set of statistics will need new interpretation. The World Travel Organisation's annual market report for 2004, for instance, included several interesting statistics:

- Inbound tourism globally has grown remarkably by nearly 12% – double recent figures.
- Outbound trips from the USA have increased by 8% (to 59 million).

- Although passengers are concerned about security, just as important are affordability and quality of services.
- More people would travel (25% to 33%) if they were guaranteed upgrades or cheaper fares.
- The Middle East is considered an 'undesirable' destination by around 60% of the people polled.
- BA has reported pre-tax profits for the summer period of £220 million – double the previous year's figure.
- BAA reported that passengers passing through their regional airport network had risen by over 5%.

WHAT DOES IT ALL MEAN?

Imagine you are on the board of a large airline company based at five airports in the UK, and have just received the data above. What implications and interpretations might you make about the scale of tourism flows, and the operational implications for your company – in terms of numbers to be handled, for example, or spending and staffing forecasts?

Table 1 Purpose of tourism in the UK, 2002

	UK residents Trips (millions)	Overseas residents Visits (millions)
Holidays	102	8
Business	23	7
Visiting friends/relatives	40	6
Other	3	3
TOTAL	**167**	**24**

Table 2 Tourism expenditure by category, 2002

	UK residents %	UK residents £ billions	Overseas residents %	Overseas residents £ billions
Accommodation	30	8	33	4
Eating out	21	6	21	2.4
Shopping	17	4	26	3
Travel within UK	19	5	9	1
Entertainment	8	2.2	3	0.3
Services etc.	2	0.5	4	0.5
Other	3	0.8	4	0.5

Table 3 Distribution of overseas tourism, 2002

	Visits (millions)	Nights (millions)	Spending (£ millions)
Cumbria	0.2	1	41
Northumbria	0.5	4	169
North West	1.4	10	466
Yorkshire	0.9	8	303
Heart of England	2.6	21	881
East of England	1.7	14	616
London	11.6	75	5,788
South West	1.4	12	526
South East	3.9	31	1,504
TOTAL ENGLAND	**21**	**175**	**10,313**
SCOTLAND	1.6	15	806
WALES	0.9	7	252
N. IRELAND	0.3	2	126
TOTAL UK	**24**	**199**	**11,618**

Table 6 Social profile, trips by UK residents, 2002

	AB	C1	C2	DE
% of trips	33	31	19	18

Table 4 Top cities/towns visited by overseas residents, 2002

	Visits (thousands)		Visits (thousands)
London	11,600	Brighton/Hove	230
Edinburgh	850	York	230
Birmingham	670	Bath	200
Manchester	590	Nottingham	200
Glasgow	400	Liverpool	190
Oxford	390	Inverness	180
Bristol	310	Coventry	160
Cambridge	280	Reading	150
Cardiff	280	Canterbury	150
Newcastle	240	Leeds	140

Table 5 Overseas tourism by country of residence, 2002

	Visits (millions)	Nights (millions)	Spending (£ millions)
USA	3.6	30	2,443
France	3.1	18	733
Germany	2.6	15	743
Irish Republic	2.4	10	674
Netherlands	1.4	6	384
Spain	1.0	9	444
Italy	1.0	8	406
Belgium	1.0	3	180
Australia	0.7	12	531
Canada	0.7	8	338
Other countries	6.8	81	4,861
TOTAL	**24.2**	**199**	**11,737**

Topic 9 Scale, inter-relationships and interdependencies

  activity

HOW IS THIS DATA USED?

From the tables, try to identify the factors that a supplier of tourism products would want to find out, such as highest earning periods, most popular destinations, popular stopover periods, or country of origin of travellers, and discuss why these might be so. What plans do you think travel and tourism planners might make based on the data, e.g. investing in more hotel spaces or road improvements?

Sources of data

More detailed statistics on UK tourism are generated by Staruk (www.staruk.org.uk) – the official website of the UK Research Liaison Group which is made up of representatives from the UK's tourist boards and the Department for Culture Media and Sport. A sample extract is shown below.

Volume and spending of UK domestic tourism in 2003		
Trips	**Nights away**	**Tourism spend**
151 million	490 million	£26,482 million

[Average spend per night was £54. Average spend per trip was £175.]

This data was derived from a UK Tourism Survey. Further data on duration, distribution and type of holiday is also available, along with age groups and types of accommodation used. Further surveys have taken place on conference tourism, visitor attraction visits, and day trips.

Other sources of tourism statistics include:

- The Office of National Statistics
- The World Travel and Tourism Organisation
- Local tourism departments
- Regional tourist boards
- *Travel Trade Gazette* and *World Travel Guide*.

Overview of functions

The diagram in Topic 7 showed how all the sectors function together to create what we know as the travel and tourism industry. Each sector performs a role, and within each sector the organisations provide their separate inputs to complete the picture. What holds these parts together is the people who work in the industry. They provide the cohesion and the 'seamless transitions' that we all expect.

The distribution chain

This model focuses on the distribution of travel and tourism products and services. The distribution chain (sometimes called the 'value chain') is really a marketing term, coming under the 'place' part of the marketing mix.

Tourism is unusual because, as we have already seen, there is no tangible product to distribute – yet we have global selling systems and organisations, and identifiable points at which we purchase – all on trust.

For ease of explanation, the channels of distribution can be modelled as shown below.

- Route 1 – products and services are bought by the tour operators for direct sale to travellers and tourists.

- Route 2 – products and services are bought by the tour operators (wholesale) and sold on to the (retail) travel agents for direct sale to travellers and tourists.

- Route 3 – products and services are created by the travel agent for direct sale to travellers and tourists.

- Route 4 – intermediaries, e.g. 'bucket shops' and other types of agents buy 'job lots' of products and services for sale to travellers and tourists from various sources.

- Route 5 – products and services are sold directly to travellers and tourists.

The various routes depend on 'inter-relationships', where one set of organisations cannot really do without the other sets. There is also considerable 'interdependence' within the chain – if one section of the chain produces poor quality, the whole set of links will suffer. This is one of the industry's key vulnerabilities.

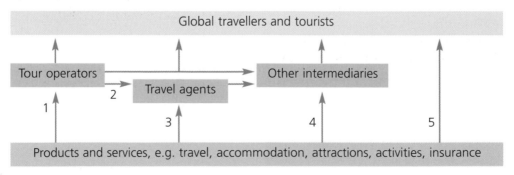

The channels of distribution model

The travel and tourism industry depends on all the various organisations working well together.

Products and services are supplied by both the private and the public sectors. Government strategies aim to produce some 'joined-up thinking' to help the two sectors work successfully together. At each stage of the chain some value should be added to the travel or tourism experience. For the customer, however, there should ideally be a 'seamless transition' from organisation to organisation and from experience to experience.

Let's use some simple scenarios to illustrate the points. Hopefully, they will help you gain an insight into how closely organisations have to relate to each other to sustain and develop themselves.

Scenario 1: An attraction

A medium-sized attraction (such as a small stately home) relates to the local authority in terms of its business relationships – it pays business taxes, has traffic-flow and parking needs approved, and consults on planning, environmental or health issues. It also works with the regional tourist board to market itself, gather tourist data and get advice on development plans. The owner of the attraction attends meetings of the local hoteliers' association to stay in touch with their promotions, and the chamber of commerce for business contacts. The company relies for marketing overseas on the work of visitbritain.com and has a presence on the region's website. The company offers day-trip specials to local and national travel agencies, and longer stays in conjunction with local hotels.

The company only uses ABTA-bonded travel agents, and occasionally hosts small conferences for the Tourism Society. From time to time they advertise in the larger travel or tourism magazines. Some domestic tour operators include them as an optional excursion.

Scenario 2: A regional airport

A medium-sized regional airport is owned by a consortium of two local authorities and a set of private investors, and is approved by the Civil Aviation Authority. Recently it has expanded to allow some other organisations to open outlets in the terminal: a travel agent (ABTA-bonded), three fast-food franchises, and a gift shop. Outside the terminal, a long-stay car park has been established, and a small helicopter training school is located on the corner of the site. Several airlines use the airport for business travellers midweek and leisure travellers at weekends and during the summer holidays. The local coach company has rerouted several buses to call at the airport. The board of directors is having talks with a group of local attractions, the regional tourist board and the local authority tourist department to assess if an 'attractions package' could be created, with budget flights into the area.

Integration in the industry

Most of the companies who dominate the market do so because of their size, spread and market share. These huge, multinational companies have been created partly through 'organic' growth, but mostly through 'integration' – formal mergers and take-overs, and informal alliances. This integration allows one company to offer the 'whole product' to customers – because it owns the travel agency, the tour operator, the carrier, and sometimes the accommodation provider as well. In this section we shall investigate the two main types of integration, and try to illustrate the extent of current integration in the industry with a look at TUI, the UK's largest holiday company. The unit concludes with an 'industry focus', illustrating how one airport integrates with carriers and ground services. The topic is organised, therefore, under the following headings:

- **Integration**
- **Vertical integration**
- **Horizontal integration**
- **TUI – an example of integration**
- **Industry focus**

Integration

Integration is the linking of organisations for economic benefit. It is a way of expanding a tourism business – by bringing in a wider range of products and services (vertical integration), or by gaining a wider share of the business's current market (horizontal integration). British Airways is a good example – its alliances with Qantas and American Airlines give them a global network of routes and destinations.

The Thomson Travel group seems to incorporate everything – from retail outlets to airlines. It is in fact part of the larger TUI Corporation, which we will investigate later. If we look first, however, at some of the mergers and sell-offs that Thomson were involved in at the turn of the century you can get an idea of the frequent 'movements' that go on in the turbulent world of the tourism industry:

Thomson Travel is to invest £100m in the development of its online sales, and a number of its Lunn Poly outlets will be closed.

3 March 2000

Thomson Travel has rejected a £1.3bn bid from C&N Touristic, the German travel company aiming to create the largest tourism group in Europe.

5 April 2000

Thomson Travel is to be acquired by Preussag of Germany for £1.8bn, which will create the world's largest package holiday operator.

16 May 2000

Thomson Travel has bought a £1.2m option to acquire a 10% stake in Travelchest, the online travel agency that is planning to open a flagship store in Surrey.

30 May 2000

Thomson Travel is seeking a further 200 staff for its new Glasgow call centre, which is due to open next month.

27 October 2000

Thomson Travel has sold Holiday Cottages Group, the cottage rental company, to Cendant for a sum thought to be about £60m.

18 January 2001

Thomson Travel is considering plans to cut jobs in its Britannia Airline business, in order to avoid overlap with parent company Preussag's own charter airline.

27 August 2001

Thomson Travel is to merge its three UK operations – Thomson Holidays, Thomson Travel and UK Distribution – with the loss of 400 head-office jobs.

30 October 2001

Source: UK business park

Let's put the idea of integration into a diagram to give you a picture of what we mean. We shall take tour operators as the heart of the process, and illustrate how integration can spread from them (though in practice this might not always be the organisation that starts the process).

Vertical integration

Vertical integration occurs when the connections are made along the distribution chain (the vertical axis in the diagram) – when an airline acquires or forms its own tour-operations company, for example. This is sometime also called 'forward integration' – into the chain. Tour operators acquiring their own airline would be 'backward integration'. Vertical integration can enable firms to gain competitive advantage over equally efficient rivals. It also quite often 'cuts out the middleman', saving on commission fees, for example – a problem now for travel agencies.

Horizontal integration

Horizontal integration occurs when two similar organisations (e.g., two travel agencies) merge or where one is taken over and absorbed by the other. This was common in the peak times of mass tourism in the UK, as larger travel agencies gobbled up smaller ones on their 'march' to become multiple chains, spreading across the country and gaining a large market share. Identity and brand image spread too – giving us the Thomas Cook's and TUI empires, for example.

Horizontal integration cuts operating costs, especially if the merged companies set up just one administration centre, when previously there had been two. Although large tour operators have done this type of merging as well, there has been a general retention of brands and products to ensure a familiar broad range is still available to the public.

Integration of this type is always subject to the UK monopoly and merger laws. The company formed must not be so big that it totally dominates the market and does not leave any room for competition. Nevertheless, this 'corporate concentration' creates huge buying power for the new large enterprises, which can often force profits down for the smaller providers – in the accommodation sector, for example.

TUI – an example of integration

TUI UK is the UK's largest holiday company, employing around 9,000 people, (7,000 of them abroad). There are a number of divisions within the UK group, many of which have been rebranded under the Thomson name. These include:

- Thomson Holidays – providing a wide range of holidays, and employing 3000 staff, most of them overseas. Their slogan is to 'provide customers with the best possible holiday for their money'.

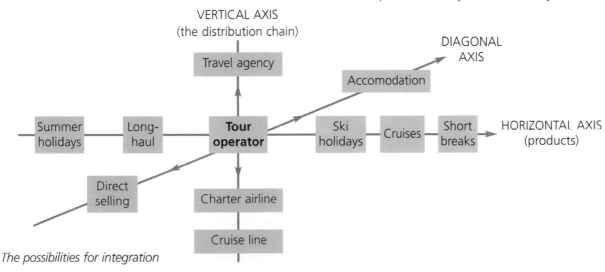

The possibilities for integration

Thomson Holidays has its own holiday airline, Thomsonfly (formerly Britannia).

- Thomson Retail Shops (formerly Lunn Poly) – with over 750 stores in the UK, a direct call centre, and an online booking service. Thomson Retail Shops sell around 2.7 million holidays per year – 20% of the market.

- OSL – the villa holiday specialists.

- Thomson Specialist Holiday Group (including the former Austravel, Simply Ski, Simply Travel, Jersey Travel, Jetsave, and Crystal Holidays).

- Team Lincoln – the UK's leading teletext and internet specialist sales division.

- Travel House Group – which covers the regions under many brands, e.g. Scotland (Sibbald), the North East (Callers Pegasus) and South Wales and the Midlands (Travel House). Together, they sell around 300, 000 holidays per year.

- Glasgow Call Centre – selling 1 million holidays for Thomson Direct, Portland Direct, Founders Club,.

TUI UK is just part of TUI Northern Europe, which employs 17,500 people in the UK, Ireland, Sweden, Norway, Denmark and Finland. TUI Northern Europe is, itself, just part of the global TUI Group, TUI AG, the largest tourism and services group in the world. The group employs 64,000 people in 500 companies. It has 3600 travel agencies in 16 countries, over a hundred aircraft, 285 hotels in 25 countries, and 37 incoming agencies looking after customers in 70 countries.

activity

ARE THERE OTHER GIANTS?

Can you identify any other tourist companies that are this large and as comprehensive? What impact do you think these massive companies have on the industry?

Problems with integration

Such large and complex mergers are not without their problems. In the past, these have included:

- Reductions in workforces

- Drawing up the legal agreements (especially across national boundaries)

- Falling confidence amongst shareholders causing fluctuations in share values

- Diversification which hasn't worked out, such as for Club Med in the 1980s and Hyatt Hotels in the 1990s, both of whom tried to take stakes in airlines.

- Falling profit margins, making future investment capital harder to find.

activity

ANY RECENT MERGERS?

Using current trade magazines, identify two other mergers, acquisitions, alliances or takeovers, which have happened recently in the travel and tourism industry. Assess what impacts might have occurred for employees, shareholders and customers. Compare your answers with those of others in your class.

Partnerships and collaborations

These milder forms of integration are based on limited deals between companies for specific purposes, rather than actual changes of ownership. Examples include:

- Hilton Family Breaks – 33 of the UK's Hilton hotels offer child-friendly facilities which include the Hamley's playroom, unlimited cartoon network/playstations in the room, access to a Livingwell pool and gym, and Mothercare products on sale.

- Chelsea football club have collaborated with Utell International to create the Chelsea Village Hotel complex next to Stamford Bridge football ground. Now corporate clients can combine a business meeting with watching a match and staying over afterwards.

activity

THE KEY FEATURES OF INTEGRATION

Find your own example of integration in the industry, and prepare a mini-presentation for the others in your class to show the key features of collaboration, alliances and partnerships.

Sam Wynzar, Sales and Marketing Executive, Leeds Bradford International Airport

What is your organisation's role in the travel and tourism industry?

Leeds Bradford International Airport is a regional airport serving a catchment area of 5 million people. We offer both domestic and international direct flights to a total of 43 UK and European destinations and worldwide connections through the 'hub' airports of London Heathrow, Amsterdam, Paris CDG and Brussels. We provide passengers with a choice of low-cost, scheduled and charter flights – and the facilities needed to start their journey efficiently and in comfort.

What is your role within the organisation?

My main responsibilities are to:

- Liaise with airlines and tour operators to maximise passenger numbers – in the form of promotions and incentives for travel agents
- Organise and participate in promotional activities (including holiday exhibitions and agent functions)
- Produce airport literature (airport magazine and timetables)
- Give presentations and training about the airport's services and facilities
- Analyse statistical information and produce marketing/sales plans
- Maintain regular contact, through visits and meetings, with travel agents
- Co-ordinate broadcasts and media visits
- Instigate the writing of copy for editorials and press releases – and creative ideas for advertising and promotional campaigns
- Deal with general enquiries by post and through the website
- Update the website.

And how did you get to where you are?

After leaving school with 5 O Levels (that shows my age!) I went to Park Lane College in Leeds to do a BTEC National Diploma in Travel and Tourism. After college I worked in retail travel – 6 years in two different multiples and then 4 years at an independent agency. Fortunately the main thing that the airport was looking for was knowledge of the retail travel industry – and I had 10 years knowledge

Do you have a personal philosophy of how to get things done?

Be honest, respectful and listen. If you do that for others, others will do that for you.

What types of customers do you serve?

Our main customers are:

- Tour operators
- Airlines
- Airport employees, including those that work for other companies within the airport – Servisair and Aviance (handling agents), Alpha (Duty Free), Select Service Partner (caterers), Co-op Travel, W H Smith, Group 4 (security).
- Press – including newspapers, TV companies, radio stations, magazines, etc
- The general public
- Local and national businesses
- Local authorities and outside bodies (e.g., Yorkshire Tourist Board)
- Travel agents – both business and retail agents.

Are there any regular problems you have to deal with?

Awareness is the biggest problem – people have preconceptions, and think that you can't fly to many places from here. I enjoy being able to explain that we are one of the fastest growing regional airports in the country – we hit the 2 million passengers per annum mark at the end of 2003 and that you can fly to practically anywhere in the world from LBA.

Does you organisation have any plans for expansion or new services?

The most recent phase of development was a new check-in hall with 16 extra check-in desks and an extended 'meeters and greeters' area. A Travelodge will be opening at the airport very shortly. Bmi are starting services to London City and Thomson are offering Zante as a new holiday destination.

What impact have new communication methods had?

Our website has created an invaluable information source. We have 4000 'visits' a day – previously these people would have to have written or phoned for information. Mobile phones mean that I can be contacted wherever I am – even in the middle of the Yorkshire Moors on my way to visit agents in Pickering.

Are there any ambitions or dreams you still have to achieve?

Having been in the travel industry for 15 years, I have been very lucky to have travelled to a lot of different places in the world, but the one thing I would like to see before I retire is the 'Terracotta Warriors' in China.

53

Topic 10 Integration in the industry

How Unit 1 is assessed

This unit is externally assessed. The format will be a $1\frac{1}{2}$-hour written exam, using a question-and-answer booklet. The booklet, provided by Edexcel, will consist of short-answer and longer-answer questions relating to scenarios and information. You should aim to be ready to sit the exam in January and/or June.

The Edexcel website – edexcel.org.uk – will have more guidance on external assessment, including specimen papers and example answers, or you can get more information from your school or college.

The grade you are awarded will depend on how well you meet the assessment objectives. The general areas that assessment objectives focus on are:

1. How you **demonstrate** your knowledge and understanding of specified content, related skills and vocationally related contexts.

2. How you **apply** your knowledge and understanding of the content and contexts.

3. How you use **research techniques** to obtain information and analyse issues and problems.

4. How effectively you **evaluate**, **judge, draw conclusions** and **make recommendation**s about issues and problems.

In general, to gain the higher grades your work will have to show that you:

- Have in-depth knowledge and understanding of the subject content of the unit

- Can apply your knowledge and understanding in vocationally related contexts

- Are able to use appropriate research techniques

- Can analyse vocationally related issues and problems

- Are able to evaluate information to make reasoned judgements, draw conclusions and make recommendations.

You written work will also have to convey appropriate meaning and use vocabulary well. You need to be able to interpret statistical data, from which you

extract key points, and to show that you understand trends and can support any conclusions which you might draw in your test answers.

To prepare for your assessment you will need to research a range of aspects about working practices and keep a record of your findings – in a 'revision portfolio' perhaps – in such a way that they will be easy to revise as the exam date approaches. The headings below should help you organise your revision portfolio.

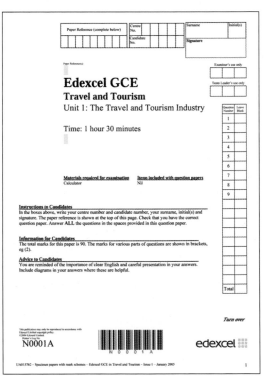

Specimen exam papers are available from the Edexcel website – edexcel.org.uk

1. The nature and characteristics of the travel and tourism industry

You will need to have a good working definition of tourism and appreciate its scope, plus understand the nature of the industry and its products. Types of tourism you need to be able to explain and give examples for: incoming, domestic, outgoing, business, leisure, excursions, adventure, package, independent, visiting friends and relatives (VFR).

You will also need to be able to explain the different characteristics of the industry, positive and negative impacts, and how some of the following operate:

the private sectors, small and medium-sized operators, new technology.

2. The development of the travel and tourism industry

You will need to show knowledge of the historical development of the industry from ancient times to present, but with more understanding of recent years. Questions are likely to cover the following growth factors (and ask for examples):

tourist motivation, 'enablers', socio-economic factors, technological change, product development and innovation, changing consumer needs, expectations and fashions.

3. The structure of the UK travel and tourism industry

You will need to be able to explain the different sectors of the industry and the key organisations in each sector, with their products, functions, objectives and values, including: transport principals, tour operators, travel agents, attractions, accommodation providers, ancillary service providers, support services.

Questions are likely to test your knowledge of roles and responsibilities, how each sector co-operates with the others and their relative dependencies and interdependencies.

Some key concepts are likely to be tested, such as chain of distribution and horizontal and vertical integration. You should prepare some examples and implications around these two topics to help you explain effects and impacts.

4. The scale of the travel and tourism industry

You need to be familiar with statistical sources and how to interpret and draw conclusions from the figures (as operators do) to identify trends, both nationally and globally, such as: visitor numbers, visitor spending, levels of employment.

Be prepared

You will need to plan your revision to be ready for the exam. Your tutors can also play a role by checking your revision portfolio and setting up a range of visits and speakers so that you have real examples to use. They should also check with the awarding body and brief you on structure, duration and any rules and regulations for taking the papers.

The marking criteria are likely to reward you for:

- Use and understanding of appropriate terminology
- Clear descriptions
- Real examples
- Depth or detail of answer
- Assessment or critical analysis
- Accuracy of interpretation.

Regardless of whether an organisation operates to make a profit or is non-profit making, its main focus will be on ensuring that customers want and, therefore, buy the organisation's products and services. One of the main ways in which travel and tourism organisations can ensure that customers buy the organisation's products and services rather than those of a competitor is by offering excellent customer service.

This unit explores the various ways in which travel and tourism organisations – and you, as a member of staff – can provide excellent customer service, and the benefits to both the individual and the organisation. We are going to look at the ways in which travel and tourism organisations provide excellent customer service and strive to continually improve the service that they offer.

All members of staff need to recognise the importance of good customer service and the role that they play in providing it. Customer service is very much a team effort, and it is vital that all team members recognise the important contribution that they are expected to make. This is why many travel and tourism organisations provide staff with training in customer service skills – if you have a part-time job in the industry you will probably have received training and already understand some of the aspects of customer service that are important.

Providing excellent customer service is an important part of everybody's job – but it is particularly important in the travel and tourism industry. This is because in the travel and tourism industry, there are many organisations which provide similar products or services to customers and it is often the quality of customer service which distinguishes one from another. Good customer service leads to customer loyalty, which in turn increases repeat business because customers will want to come back again – as well as encouraging their friends to visit.

Before you go on to the first topic consider the following ideas:

- What makes *you* want to go back to an organisation that you have used?

- To what extent are the staff a part of your desire to return?

- What would put you off using an organisation again?

Unit 2

The Travel and Tourism Customer

2.1 The organisation and its customers

Topic 1	Internal and external customers	58
Topic 2	The needs and wants of different customers	62
Topic 3	Providing free services	66

2.2 Providing effective customer service

Topic 4	Interpersonal skills	70
Topic 5	Communication skills	74
Topic 6	Product knowledge	80
Topic 7	Meeting different customer needs	85
Topic 8	Complaints procedures	90

2.3 Measuring and monitoring the customer service of an organisation

Topic 9	Methods of measuring customer service	94
Topic 10	Quality criteria for customer service	98
	How Unit 2 is assessed	102

Internal and external customers

The term 'customer service' is used to embrace all elements of the customer interface. In this context, it includes the concept of 'customer care' or 'caring for customers'. Customer service includes all direct and indirect contact with the customer as well as the products, services, systems and strategies that support the customer-service process.

The attitude and behaviour of staff is the foundation of all excellent customer service. It means that staff really have to care about their customers, and try to anticipate and satisfy their needs.

In this first topic we are going to explore what is meant by the term 'customer'. In particular we will look at:

- ■ **Internal customers**
- ■ **External customers.**

Internal customers

It may seem a strange place to start, but we are going to begin by looking at how staff should treat each other. This is because the way in which you treat your internal customers has a direct bearing on the quality of service that the 'paying' (external) customer receives. Internal customers are members of staff within an organisation or outside suppliers who contribute towards the service that is provided to external customers. They include:

- Colleagues – the people that you work with directly and who have a similar status to you.

- Management and supervisors. Most employees have a direct line manager in the organisation – a supervisor, head of department or manager.

- Staff teams – groups of staff who form a team to undertake specific functions or jobs. For example, a tourist attraction may have a health and safety team made up of staff from different departments. Many hotels have a fire evacuation team who work together to evacuate the building if the fire alarm sounds.

- Employees. If you are in a supervisory position you will have staff for whom you are responsible.

- Staff in other functional departments or organisations who do not work directly with you but contribute to the job that you do. For example, the personnel, finance, administration and maintenance departments in a local authority provide services to employees in the authority's tourism facilities, such as the tourist information centre, museums, art galleries, etc.

- Outside organisations. Many travel and tourism staff rely on other organisations to provide services that contribute to the overall product and service offered. For example, a hotel will have a number of outside suppliers who provide food, beverages, cleaning materials, linen, etc. Maintaining a good relationship with the supplier's staff is an important part of good internal customer service.

It is important that organisations are able to provide effective customer service to internal customers in order to establish good working relationships between all of the people involved in providing the products and services to external customers. The more successful

FIRST, KEEP THE STAFF HAPPY

The owners of a large stately home, open to the public, are aware that there have been frequent complaints recently amongst their staff, coupled with an unexpectedly high labour turnover during the last year. A meeting is called for staff to air their grievances to the management team. The main issues that arise are:

- Staff feel that they are paid a low wage in relation to workers in similar jobs, and are offered no employee benefits.
- The newer members of staff state that they did not receive adequate training and felt that they were not always able to carry out their role effectively.
- Some members of staff complained about the recent smoking ban in the staff canteen.
- Many staff felt that they were undervalued and that, whilst management were quick to criticise poor work, they rarely thanked staff for doing a good job.

- Workers complained that they were often not told about what was going on which resulted in mistakes and customer complaints.
- There was general complaint about the fact that staff no longer got free meals on duty or a taxi home if they worked late.
- Overall, staff felt that there was an 'us and them' relationship between staff and management and that their needs were not being listened to.

The owners are keen to address as many of these issues as possible, but are aware that business has been declining over the last few years and they cannot afford to spend a great deal of money improving terms and conditions of employment. In pairs, identify, explain and justify five courses of action that the owners could take to improve their internal customer care.

---

travel and tourism organisations are those that have a reputation for treating their staff well. Staff who are treated well will feel valued and be more motivated to do their job effectively – which means that the external customers will receive a far higher level of service. In addition, the staff are more likely to remain loyal to their organisation, which in turn reduces the expensive costs incurred by a high staff turnover.

Good working relationships help staff to do their jobs more effectively.

External customers

External customers are the people who actually buy or use an organisation's products and services. There are many ways of categorising external customers. To a large extent, the way this is done will depend on the type of organisation and the nature of the business it operates. Common categories of customers used will include:

- groups
- people of different ages
- business customers
- people from different cultures
- people with specific needs, e.g. customers with disabilities, adults with young children, medical conditions such as pregnancy, diabetes or age related
- language differences
- cultural differences.

We will look at the specific needs and expectations of each of these types of customers in the next two topics, but let's first explore what is meant by each type.

Groups and individuals

One of the most common ways of distinguishing between types of customers is based on whether they are on their own or form part of a group. Some travel and tourism products, such as 'singles holidays' are clearly going to attract more individuals rather than groups. However, it is important to recognise that although customers may use a product or service on an individual basis, they may also become part of a group. For example, customers on a singles holiday may go hoping to meet and socialise with others. Other customers may appreciate the fact that they are on their own and prefer to be treated individually rather than grouped together with others. The huge increase in spa facilities and resort hotels has been particularly popular with individual customers who appreciate the opportunity to spend time on their own being pampered. Likewise, businessmen and women are frequently individual customers.

Other travel and tourism products and services may predominantly attract groups rather than individuals. For example, few people go to a theme park on their own – preferring, instead, to go with friends, family or as part of an organised excursion.

Many organisations identify the specific types of individual and groups that use their products and

A coach party – a large group made up of smaller groups and individuals

services in order to provide the level of service that meets their needs and expectations.

People of different ages

Many travel and tourism organisations attract customers of specific ages. For example, cruise passengers tend to be in the 45+ age bracket, whereas the age of Club 18–30 holidaymakers is apparent from the name. The age of customers can be broken down into:

- children – babies, toddlers, older children, teenagers
- adults – young adults, middle-aged adults, senior citizens.

However, it should be remembered that customers will often be in the company of friends or relatives and that the group may therefore be a combination of ages. Some common combinations are:

- parents with young children and/or babies
- parents with teenage children
- adults with grandchildren
- adults with senior citizen parents.

Business customers

Whilst the travel and tourism industry is generally thought of in terms of satisfying the leisure needs of customers, it should be remembered that business customers are also a huge source of income for the industry. For example, businesswomen and men frequently stay in hotels, and use other travel and tourism products such as nightclubs, casinos, etc.

People with specific needs

Some customers have specific needs which may require special customer service in addition to that provided to meet the general needs of customers. This may be because of:

- Sensory disabilities, such as visual impairment, hearing impairment or speech impairment
- Mobility problems, such as the need for a wheelchair, zimmer frame or walking stick
- Literacy and/or numeracy learning difficulties
- Medical conditions, such as pregnancy or conditions such as diabetes
- Dietary requirements, such as vegetarian, nut allergy or religious restrictions
- Adults with babies or young children.

Due to the Disability Discrimination Act, it is now a legal requirement for all organisations to provide appropriate products and services for customers with a disability. However, most travel and tourism organisations have always welcomed customers with specific needs and tried to ensure that their needs are met.

Language differences

Foreign visitors are becoming an increasingly large part of the UK tourism market. Many such visitors may speak little or no English, but will expect staff to be able to deal with their needs despite the language barrier. Large organisations such as airports often employ multi-lingual staff to communicate with non-English speaking visitors.

Cultural differences

It is often important to recognise types of customer by their cultural background in order to provide effective customer service. Cultural background influences people's traditions, tastes, preferences and opinions, and it will therefore have an impact on the type and level of service they need and expect. For example, some cinemas show films in different languages to cater for the demands of large ethnic populations in their areas.

As with different age groups, the cultural background of customers is useful in identifying their needs, but it is equally important not to make assumptions based on culture. At best, this may result in customer dissatisfaction; at worst, this may offend and upset the customer.

WHICH TYPES OF CUSTOMER?

Look at the travel and tourism organisations listed in the table below. In pairs complete the table by listing the main types of customers that use each organisation. You will find that some of them attract a very wide range of different customers.

Organisations	Types of customers
Ryan Air	
Marriot Hotels	
Legoland	
P&O Cruises	
Madame Tussaud's	
Butlins Holiday Centres	

When you have completed the table, discuss the following:

1 Which of the organisations are likely to deal with the most non-English speaking visitors, and why?

2 Which of the organisations are unlikely to attract many individual customers, and why?

3 Which of the organisations are likely to list families with young children amongst their main types of customers, and why?

4 Which of the organisations are likely to attract individual businessmen and women, and why?

5 In what situations would each of the organisations need to be concerned about customers with food allergies?

The needs and wants of different customers

In the last topic we identified the different types of customers who buy travel and tourism products and services. In this topic we are going to look at the specific needs and wants of each of these types:

- groups
- people of different ages
- business customers
- those with specific needs
- language differences
- cultural differences.

Groups

One of the problems when dealing with groups of people is satisfying all of their individual needs. The customers may deliberately have chosen to experience a travel or tourism product or service as part of a group, but they often expect some personal recognition and attention as well. For example, a visitor on a guided tour of a stately home may well have particular interests and questions that the tour guide will need to deal with on a personal level. Likewise holidaymakers on a package holiday will expect the resort representative to speak to them personally and answer their specific questions. It is a fine juggling act for any member of staff to deal with the general needs of a group by providing advice and information, whilst also recognising the individual needs of the members of the group.

activity

A GROUP'S NEEDS

The Thackray Museum in Leeds is an interactive museum based on the history of health, disease, treatments and cures. It offers a number of educational days to schools and colleges, such as the one described below. In pairs, discuss what you think the needs and expectations of a group of twenty primary school children and three teachers would be. Then identify any individual needs and expectations that the staff at Thackray might need to deal with.

Victorians Alive!
A taught session available for Key Stages 1 & 2

Spend your day as a Victorian character at the Thackray Museum. Explore time packages of objects relating to six of the characters from the streets of 1840 Leeds. Build up a picture of their lives from the artefacts and documents. Discover where you live and work. What happens when you become ill, and decide whether to see a doctor, chemist or the quack – and can you afford your treatment? Return to the present day and see what your decision, treatment and fate would be now.

THACKRAY museum

England's Small Visitor Attraction of the Year 2004

WARNING! You don't know what you might pick up

THACKRAY museum

TELLING THE STORY OF MEDICINE

People of different ages

Generally speaking, the formality of the way in which customers of different ages are dealt with increases with age. Saying, 'Hi, young man that's a great smile', is appropriate for a 3-year-old little boy but hardly fitting for a 60-year-old man! However, we need to be careful not to make assumptions about customers' needs and expectations based purely on their age. The 13-year-old girl may be just as offended by being offered a children's menu as the active 70-year-old man who is offered an Austrian coach tour by a travel agent, when he was hoping to go skiing.

Dealing with groups of mixed ages is probably one of the hardest situations to handle in customer service – each will have different needs and expectations that need to be met. In addition, the enjoyment of each member of the group will be affected by how much their companions enjoy the experience.

Business customers

One of the main differences between the needs and wants of the business customer and those of the leisure customer is the importance of time. The business customer must purchase and use travel and tourism products that fit in around their work commitments. This means that such products need to be made available at such times. For example, international travellers arriving at UK airports require accommodation and food at all times of the day, and airport hotels are usually fully operational for 24 hours to cater for these needs. In addition, many business customers require facilities that allow them to continue working whilst they use products such as transport and hospitality (see box below).

Club Europe

Club Europe makes for an altogether smoother experience. By combining flexibility and personal control with the reliability and service you expect from British Airways, you have all the reassurance you need that your trip will go according to plan.

Lounges
Whether you wish to work, relax or snack, our Terraces Lounges offer all the facilities and comfort you need – ensuring you can make the most of your travel time.

Wireless LAN access from BT Openzone
Make even more of your time on the ground in British Airways' airport lounges with BT Openzone. You can send and receive emails, use the internet and access your corporate intranet wire-free in British Airways arrival and departure lounges where you see the BT Openzone sign.

Cabin environment
A separate cabin at the front of the aircraft with comfortable leather seats and a 34-inch seat pitch gives you the seclusion and space you need to relax, eat and work.

Service
Our dedicated Club Europe staff will take care of you throughout your journey providing a warm, responsive service.

In-flight dining
Club Europe menus have recently been refreshed to provide even greater choice and more appropriate food than before. Customers can enjoy a full English or Continental breakfast; hot or cold meals for lunch and dinner and High tea. All meals are served with freshly ground coffee, teas or a full bar plus a range of warmed breads.

Entertainment
In-flight entertainment is offered in the form of short programs on longer European flights including Moscow and Athens.

Beat the queues
There is an arrivals Fast Track channel through Passport Control at London Heathrow Terminal 4 and Terminal 1 for non-EU passport holders, enabling Club Europe customers to avoid unnecessary queuing.

source: www.British-airways.com

activity
JUST THE BUSINESS

Read the description of British Airways' Club Europe facilities and services, and explain how they have been designed to meet the needs of business customers.

Topic 2 The needs and wants of different customers

People with specific needs

It is important to remember that when dealing with customers with special needs they do not want to be made to feel different. However they may have different needs that require additional service.

The extract below is from the Disability Etiquette Policy from www.Tameside.gov.uk, and includes some useful advice.

Further specific needs can include a range of medical conditions. For example, pregnant women may require extra assistance, such as help with carrying luggage. There are also a number of conditions that create dietary restrictions for customers such as diabetes (limits the amount of carbohydrate that can be eaten), coeliacs disease (gluten intolerance) and allergies to specific foods such as nuts, shellfish or dairy products. In addition, an increasing number of customers are choosing to limit their diet through vegetarianism, healthy eating regimes or diets such as the Atkins diet.

LANGUAGE

It is important to gain a general understanding of words and phrases which may give offence to people with disabilities. There are no hard-and-fast rules – far better to try to keep in touch with disabled people and respect their preferences which may change over time.

DO NOT SAY 'victim of … crippled by … suffering from …'

DO SAY 'person who has/person who experienced …'

DO NOT SAY 'invalid'. This equates disability with illness and can be construed as 'not valid'.

DO NOT SAY 'wheelchair-bound' or describe someone as 'confined to a wheelchair'. Remember that a wheelchair represents freedom to its user.

DO SAY 'wheelchair user' or 'person who uses a wheelchair'.

DO NOT SAY words like 'spastic', 'cripple', 'retarded', 'defective' or phrases like 'blind as a bat', 'deaf and dumb', 'mentally deficient' as they are often used in general conversation as terms of derision or abuse or as jokes. This reinforces damaging and inaccurate images of disability. Such words and phrases should never be used, whether a disabled person is present or not.

MEETING PEOPLE WITH DISABILITIES

People who are deaf

Do not make assumptions about a person's ability to communicate or the ways in which they do it. Always ask the person to tell you. Remember that those deaf people who use sign language find this the easiest method of communication. If an interpreter is present, speak to the person you are meeting, rather than to the interpreter.

Do not assume that everyone who is deaf can lip-read. Always ask the person when you first meet them. If they do lip-read, remember that this skill is never wholly reliable. It requires intense concentration and is very tiring.

- Look directly at them and speak slowly and clearly.
- Speak with facial expressions, gestures and body movements which emphasise the words you use.
- Face the light, and keep hands, cigarettes and food away from your face while speaking.

Wheelchair users

- When talking for more than a few moments to someone in a wheelchair, try to put yourself at their eye level to avoid stiff necks.
- Speak to the person in the wheelchair and not their companion.

People with visual impairment

- First identify yourself clearly and introduce anyone else who is present. Try to indicate where they are placed in the room.
- When offering a handshake, say something like 'Shall we shake hands?'
- When help is needed on unfamiliar ground, say 'Let me offer you an arm'. This will enable you to guide rather than propel or lead the person.
- When talking in a group, remember to say the name of the person to whom you are speaking.

People with speech difficulties

- Give your whole attention to a person with a speech difficulty. Be encouraging and patient. Do not correct or speak for the person. Wait quietly while the person talks and resist the temptation to finish sentences.
- Where possible, ask questions that require short answers or a nod or shake of the hand.
- If you have difficulty understanding, don't pretend. Repeat what you do understand and the person's reactions will guide you.

Remember, at all times treat Registered Disabled People with Respect, Dignity and Patience.

Source: Disability Etiquette Policy from www.Tameside.gov.uk

Language differences

In an ideal world there would be staff who could communicate in the native language of all of their customers. However, even if you are not proficient in other languages there is still a great deal that you can do to help the communication process, such as:

- using gestures – when pointing out directions, for example
- using diagrams and pictures
- keeping various dictionaries to hand, so that you can translate key words
- making the effort to learn a few simply phrases in some common languages. Being able to say hello, goodbye, please, and thank you in two or three foreign languages will please your foreign guests and show that you care enough to make the effort.

You should not forget that even foreign visitors whose native language is English may still have difficulty in understanding some words. Americans, for example, have a range of different words and phrases from us – which can lead to confusion.

Cultural differences

Dealing with people from different cultures can give rise to a whole range of challenges. Variations in what and how they eat, dress, meet and greet each other, and communicate – all can create the potential for accidentally offending someone if you don't get it quite right. Certainly one of the main differences between many cultures is the way in which body language is used. The extract below is from the website www.executiveplanet.com which illustrates some of the differences between different cultures.

The Chinese

- Consider it rude to make expansive gestures and unusual facial expressions.
- Do not use their hands when speaking, and will only become annoyed with a speaker who does.
- Do not smile as noticeably, since there is a heavy emphasis on repressing emotion.
- Consider pushing and cutting ahead in queues acceptable.

The Indians

- Consider pointing with your finger is rude – they prefer to point with the chin.
- Think winking is either an insult or a sexual proposition.
- Consider grasping the ears signifies sincerity or repentance.
- Consider feet as unclean, so never point your feet at another person. You will be expected to apologise whenever your shoes or feet touch another person.

The Swedish

- Think that if women must cross their legs, it must never be ankle over knee.
- Consider that even in public, formal is always better than informal – no gum-chewing, slouching, or leaning against things.
- Believe a toss of the head means, 'come here.'
- Tend to stay slightly farther apart than North Americans.
- Never speak with their hands in your pockets, and always keep them firmly at their side when standing.

The Turkish

- Keep both feet flat on the ground when sitting. Displaying the soles of your shoes or feet to someone is insulting. It is impolite for women to cross their legs while facing another person.
- Consider it rude to cross your arms while facing someone.
- Keep their hands out of their pockets.
- Indicate 'yes' by nodding their heads up and down. The gestures for 'no' are different. Raising the eyebrows in a subtle way indicates 'no.' This arch look may be accompanied by the sound 'tsk'.
- The US gesture for 'no' (wagging the head from side to side) is a Turkish gesture for 'I don't understand.'

The Italians

- Stand much closer to you than you are used to or even feel comfortable with. Italian personal space is smaller than that of northern Europeans, and significantly smaller than that of Americans.
- Do not consider queue-jumping the 'crime' that it is in other countries. Italians are very tolerant of people who take advantage of the lack of strict queuing to get served first.
- Maintain direct eye contact – this is the way Italians show their interest. Be aware that looking away may be perceived as a sign of boredom or outright rudeness.
- Consider placing the hand on the stomach signifies dislike, usually for another person.

Source: www.executiveplanet.com

Providing free services

Whilst many of the needs and wants of customers are provided by products and services that are purchased, there are many that are provided free of charge by the organisation. Whilst no direct profit is made from such services they are of equal importance, since they have a considerable impact on the customers' overall enjoyment of the products offered. In this topic we are going to explore some free services, including:

- Late-night openings
- Telephone bookings
- Late check-in
- Translation service
- Car pick up and drop off
- Online services
- Interpretation
- Services for customers with specific needs.

Late-night openings

With increases in the number of international visitors to the UK and changes in working patterns, many travel and tourism providers are offering their products and services for longer periods of time. In recent years this has been shown through the increase in 24-hour availability of many products – from catering to transport. In an attempt to meet the needs of all of their customers, some tourist attractions are also joining the late-night-opening trend. For example, the Deep in Hull offers 'sleep-over' parties for groups of children where they can sleep beside the shark tank in sleeping bags.

The Deep *in Hull is one of the attractions operating late-night opening.*

Telephone bookings

Allowing customers to access and purchase products as easily as possible is a key concern for all travel and tourism providers. Taking bookings over the telephone is one of the main ways in which organisations make their products available. Organisations such as the tour operator Superbreak Holidays take all of their

bookings by either the telephone or internet. Many travel and tourism companies provide a telephone booking service free of charge or at a reduced rate. You can identify which these are by the fact that their telephone numbers begin with the numbers 08 (see box above right).

Phone services offered by travel and tourism organisations

Codes	Charges
080	no charge to the caller
0844	up to 5p per minute
0845	originating operator's local rate
0870	originating operator's national rate
0871	up to 10p per minute

activity

CHEAP TALK

Using national weekend papers, identify ten examples of travel or tourism organisations that offer a free or reduced-price telephone booking service.

Late check-in

As we have seen, many customers want to access travel and tourism products and services outside traditional trading hours. Providers such as those in the hospitality industry frequently find that customers

For guests at luxury hotels, having your car parked by a member of staff is a valuable free service.

wish to check in later than the traditional time. For example, whilst guests staying at one of the Center Parcs can check in from 3.00pm, many are unable to do this – perhaps due to a long journey or the fact that they have not finished work until late on their day of arrival. Therefore Center Parcs allows guests to check in as late as 10.00pm. In other situations, customers may require a late check-in simply because they are short of time. For example, most airlines provide a later check-in time for business class passengers.

Translation service

In Topic 2 we discussed the needs and wants of customers with language differences. For many such customers, enjoyment can only be achieved if information is translated for them. This is particularly true in visitor attractions where many provide a translation service. This may be in the form of foreign language leaflets/guides or audio guides. For example, at York Minster, foreign visitors can select from a range of languages when using the cathedral's audio guide.

Car pick-up and drop-off

A further example of a free service that may be provided is car pick-up and drop-off. This is often offered by hotels that are located in city centre locations. In such situations, guests may be able to drive to the entrance of the hotel, unload their luggage and check-in, whilst a member of staff parks their car.

Online services

With the increasing use of the internet, many travel and tourism providers offer services online. For example, customers can research and book holidays with tour operators as well as additional products such as car hire and insurance. Not only is this service free but can also result in the customer saving money because many tour operators offer a discount for holidays booked via the internet.

Interpretation

Interpretation refers to the ways in which a tourist attraction is explained to the visitors with the aim of increasing their enjoyment of the attraction. There have been huge advances in interpretation in recent years with imaginative use of actors, simulation,

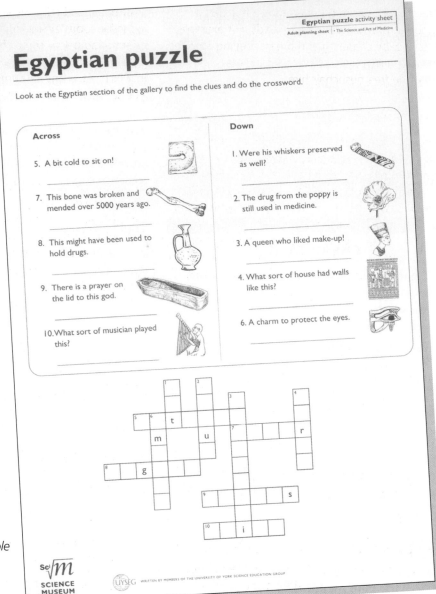

An activity sheet – an example
of interpretation material
available from the Science
Museum in London

virtual reality and interactive displays. Many visitor attractions provide interpretation as a free service. For example, visitors to any of the National Parks can pick up free leaflets as well as benefiting from clear and informative signage in the park. In addition, most have visitor centres that include displays and information. Private sector attractions also frequently provide free interpretation materials – for example, study packs and activity sheets for educational groups.

---

activity

FINDING FREEBIES

Use the internet to identify five visitor attractions that offer free interpretation materials.

Services for customers with specific needs

Possibly one of the largest areas where free services are offered is for customers with specific needs. Organisations do this for a number of reasons. The main reason is usually because the customer would not be able to enjoy the facility, service or product without the free service, although it is also good public relations to be seen to be looking after all customers. Let's look at some of the ways in which organisations provide free services for customers with specific needs.

Adults with young children

Adults with babies or young children have a range of needs in addition to those of the standard customer, and travel and tourism organisations are generally very good at providing for these needs. For example, most have baby-changing and breast-feeding facilities, offer bottle and baby food warming services, and may even provide free pushchair hire.

Customers with disabilities

The needs of customers with disabilities are met in a number of ways. For example, many travel and tourism organisations provide free wheelchairs for customers with mobility problems – at airports this is a standard service for passengers who have difficulty getting from the terminal to the plane. Most airlines also offer support to elderly or young travellers who may be nervous about the procedure for checking in and boarding aircraft. Customers with sensory impairments are often provided with free additional services such as information in Braille for sight impairment and induction loops or signing for hearing impairment. The information below comes from the Eden Project in Cornwall and is a good example of some of the ways in which travel and tourism organisations offer extra free services for customers with specific needs.

activity

WHAT FREE SERVICES?

In pairs, select one travel and tourism organisation that you are familiar with. This might be a tour operator, transport provider, travel agent, visitor attraction, hotel, etc. Identify who you think their main customers are, and then discuss what free services they should offer to each type of customers.

The wheelchair-friendly Eden Project

We have made every endeavour to make Eden as wheelchair friendly as possible, though please bear in mind that the site covers some 35 acres.

We have over 45 wheelchairs on site, available free of charge. These are available on a first-come, first-served basis only, and cannot be booked in advance. If you would like a wheelchair, ask a guide or steward when you arrive in the Visitor Centre. We do not have motorised chairs for hire on site, though users bringing their own motorised vehicles with them are most welcome.

The Visitor Centre has the following facilities for disabled visitors:

- There is a car park for disabled visitors which is very close to the Visitor Centre

- The footpath from the car park to the visitor centre is designed at the correct gradient for wheelchair users

- There are no stairs or lifts – the Visitor Centre is all on one level

- The land train has wheelchair spaces in the back, and the staff are trained in assisting wheelchair users

- Carers are admitted free of charge when assisting a disabled person.

The Eden Project welcomes people of all ages, backgrounds and disabilities. We are working to create equal opportunities for people to experience, learn and get involved in the Project. Interpretation programme

We are actively seeking ways of making our education and interpretation programmes as open as possible, for example through the use of new approaches and technologies. We are currently working on a project to incorporate into the mainstream signage pictorial icons developed for people with learning difficulties.

The way in which you present yourself to the customers and the interpersonal skills that you use will have a direct influence on the level of customer satisfaction as well as the image of the organisation you work for. In this topic we are going to explore the interpersonal skills that contribute to good customer service, in terms of:

■ **personal appearance**

■ **required resources available**

■ **use of initiative**

■ **problem solving**

■ **positive attitude**

■ **personality**

■ **industry standards.**

Personal appearance

Dress, physical appearance and personal hygiene are important parts of the overall impression that you give to customers, and help to create a favourable first impression. 'Dress and appearance' covers everything from clothes and footwear to your hairstyle, make-up and jewellery. Many organisations within travel and tourism provide their staff with a uniform. From a customer-service point of view, a uniform has many advantages:

• It helps create a positive first impression.

• Staff are instantly recognised as working for a specific organisation.

• It is easy to find a member of staff when a customer needs advice or assistance.

• It can indicate which department a member of staff works in.

• It helps to create a professional corporate image.

It is becoming more common for organisations to provide some sort of uniform – or specify what staff should wear. For example, many smaller hotel establishments may not provide uniforms but specify that staff should wear white shirts and black trousers/skirts. However they also rely on the good judgement of their staff in deciding what is and is not acceptable in terms of appearance. Aspects such as the type of make-up, hairstyles, jewellery and visible tattoos are issues that staff will need to consider.

Some organisations set ground rules. To a large extent, these will reflect the nature of the organisation and the type of customers it serves. For example, flight attendants have to conform to strict rules on how they can style their hair, and some airlines even specify the required shades of lipstick for female staff. Many luxury hotels and cruise ships will not employ staff with visible tattoos as they do not feel that a tattoo creates the right image. Other travel and tourism organisations may have less strict requirements. Some hotel bars, for example, allow staff to wear their own clothes, and have no rules regarding tattoos, hairstyles or makeup. This is because they feel that it is fitting that their staff are dressed in a similar way to their customers.

The most important consideration with dress and appearance is that it should suit the job, the organisation and the customers' expectations. The organisation, for its part, should ensure that uniforms are comfortable, easy to maintain and look equally appropriate on staff of all builds.

It goes without saying that anyone who is serving customers should ensure excellent standards of personal hygiene. No customer will be impressed by a travel consultant who breathes garlic fumes over them or a resort rep with dirty finger nails! Equally, dousing yourself with perfume or aftershave when you have not had time for a shower – or trying to conceal the fact that you have just had a curry or a cigarette by chewing gum – is just as off-putting for the customer.

In some situations it is appropriate for the staff to be dressed in the same way as their customers.

Some jobs in travel and tourism will have stricter requirements in terms of personal hygiene than others, due to the nature of the work. Someone employed in food preparation, for example, will be expected to wash their hands dozens of times a day between separate food preparation activities to avoid cross-contamination.

Required resources available

It is also important to understand the resources that staff will need to perform their job role effectively. This invariably requires commitment and support from their employers. From the perspective of personal appearance this may entail the provision of a clean and well maintained uniform. However, there are further resources that an employer needs to supply including:

- Adequate training to ensure that the member of staff is competent to undertake their responsibilities

activity

HANDBOOK EXPLANATION

The Phoenix Travel Agency employs eight full-time travel consultants. Each member of staff is provided with:

- 3 shirts
- 2 skirts (females) or 2 pairs of trousers (males).

The agency also specifies standards for shoes, hair, make-up and jewellery.

Write a page for their staff handbook outlining the requirements in terms of dress, appearance and personal hygiene.

- Sufficient information to allow the employee to give accurate and current advice to customers
- Support such as assistance when dealing with complaints or emergency situations.
- Physical resources such as equipment, computers and appropriate software, etc.

Use of initiative

Using your initiative means being able to 'think on your feet' and come up with a suitable course of action. Because travel and tourism is essentially a people-centred industry, any member of staff will face numerous situations where they will be called upon to use their own initiative. In such situations, you will need to be able to weigh up all of the possible alternatives and decide which one is most appropriate – *or call for help from a supervisor if you feel out of your depth!*

One of the problems often experienced is that a situation will involve a number of different issues, and the member of staff will have to decide not only what to do but also how to prioritise their actions – as the activity below shows.

activity

DON'T PANIC – PRIORITISE

You are working as a receptionist in a hotel and your fellow receptionist has just gone for their meal break. The Duty Manager is currently talking to a very important client about a large conference booking, and has asked not to be disturbed unless it is an emergency. You are checking in a coach party of elderly guests – some of whom are getting agitated about how long it is taking. The phone is ringing. A young child has just pushed to the front of the desk and said that he cannot find his parents and does not know which room he is in. The alarm on the lift is sounding to indicate that it is stuck between floors. And – you have just remembered that you have forgotten to book a taxi for two guests who are going to the theatre in 30 minutes. The only other member of staff that you can see is the Hall Porter – who only started today.

Take three minutes to write down what you would do, and then share your ideas with the rest of the group.

Problem solving

In the activity above you dealt with a stressful situation, but frequently travel and tourism staff need to deal with more substantial problems, such as a sudden illness, stolen belongings or missing luggage. These types of situations are very stressful for the customer, and require tactful and careful handling. Often the customer will be anxious, upset or even angry, and it is your responsibility to reassure them and show them that you are confident and in control of the situation.

Positive attitude

Your attitude towards the customer is crucial to your ability to deliver excellent customer service. All customers are sensitive to the way you feel about them and will know whether or not you are keen to serve them. For example, imagine that a customer goes into a travel agent with little idea about where they want to go on holiday – except that it needs to be hot, fun, with plenty of nightlife and cheap! They hope that they will be given some advice and suggestions on suitable options. If the travel consultant merely hands them a stack of brochures and tells them to come back when they've seen something they like, the customer will feel that:

• They are asking for too much by expecting personal advice.

• The travel consultant does not care about them enough to spend time advising them.

• The travel consultant does not really care whether they book a holiday with them or not.

In short, the travel consultant gives the impression by their attitude that they are not interested in the customer.

Your attitude towards customers may vary according to the situation. For example, it may be acceptable to be less formal with a child than you might be with an adult. You might address children by their first name but call adults 'sir' or 'madam'. However there are some general rules on attitude that should apply to all customers, whatever their age or circumstances. These might include:

Attentive
Thoughtful
Tolerant
Individual
Thorough
Unflappable
Dependable
Enthusiastic.

WHERE ARE YOU ON THE ATTITUDE SCALE?

Your attitude towards and understanding of particular customer-service situations says a lot about your attitude generally. Below is a quick quiz to see how you score on the 'attitude scale'! Consider the following statements and decide whether they apply 'always', 'sometimes' or 'never'. If you decide on 'sometimes', explain the situations in which this would apply.

1 It is all right to call a customer by their first name.

2 A member of staff should always stand up when dealing with a customer.

3 It is acceptable to chew gum when talking to a customer.

4 You should always wait for a customer to start a conversation.

5 You should maintain eye contact when dealing with a customer in a face-to-face situation.

6 It is old-fashioned to address a customer as sir or madam.

7 It is acceptable to get angry with a very difficult customer.

8 It is wrong to complain about one customer to another customer.

9 Customers will understand if you are tired or unwell, and make allowances.

10 All customers are equally important.

11 Your attitude and behaviour towards the customer will affect the extent to which he or she is satisfied.

12 The customer is always right.

Answers are given on page 290. Your total number of correct answers will show you where you are on the attitude scale:

• 8–12 correct answers: an excellent attitude.

• 4–7 correct answers: not bad, but you probably need a bit more practice. Try some of the role-play exercises.

• 0–3 correct answers: oh dear, perhaps you should read this unit again – slowly!

Personality

The overall impression that you give to customers will also depend on your personality and the way in which you project it. This is the way the customer sees *you* rather than the organisation as a whole. Of course, your personality will also influence the image that the customer has of the whole organisation. The difference is that only you can actually influence your personality and determine whether the customer is going to see it positively. It is important to realise that there is no *one* correct type of personality – different jobs in travel and tourism require different types of personality. The sort of personality required to work as a Club 18–30 resort representative is likely to be very different to that of a representative employed by SAGA holiday, aimed at retired people.

A children's rep must be prepared to join in the activities.

activity

RIGHT PERSONALITY FOR THE JOB

Using the list below, choose three adjectives that you think most closely describe the type of personality that would be needed for each of the following jobs (you can add your own adjectives if you like):

- Receptionist in a 5-star hotel
- Children's rep
- Customer service assistant at a railway station
- Coach tour manager.

Mature	Serious	Humorous
Calm	Friendly	Informal
Outgoing	Reassuring	
Fun-loving	Efficient	

Industry standards

One of the issues that we have highlighted in this topic is the ways in which personal presentation varies according to the job role and the organisation that someone works for. In many situations the personal requirements for staff will be influenced by the industry standards for the particular area in which they work. For example, standards for personal appearance are far more precise in job roles such as cabin crew, hotel staff or travel agency advisers than they may be for reservations staff. In the activity below you are asked to test your knowledge of some current industry standards

activity

WHAT ARE THE INDUSTRY STANDARDS?

Prepare a short presentation on what you think may be the minimum industry standards for the jobs listed below, in terms of interpersonal skills.

- Cabin crew
- Resort representative
- Tour guide.

Communication skills

A large part of effective customer service involves dealing with and communicating with customers. In this section we are going to look at the specific communication skills that are necessary, including:

- **Types of communication**
- **Listening and questioning**
- **Responding to customers**
- **Providing information**
- **Using appropriate documentation**
- **Using information communication technology.**

Types of communication

Let's start this section by looking at the various ways in which staff communicate with customers. In broad terms this could be broken down into:

- Face-to-face communication
- Non-verbal communication
- Telephone communication
- Written communication.

Face-to-face communication

Face-to-face situations have many advantages over other forms of communication, but only if you understand how to use them well. For example, your appearance can help to create a positive impression – particularly if you wear a uniform that immediately identifies you. You can also use facial expressions and gestures to help you to communicate more effectively such as smiling, nodding, shaking hands, etc. Of course, there are also some challenges when dealing with customers face-to-face – you are 'on show' and

the customer can see if you lack confidence or the right attitude. You also need to be able to think quickly and make the right response. Unlike written communication, you cannot spend time thinking about the best way of expressing something – the customer will expect you to respond to them immediately.

Oral communication is central to many face-to-face situations. Being able to speak well does not mean that you have to use a 'posh' accent. Of far greater importance is that you can speak in a way that is comprehensible and acceptable to your customers. 'Comprehensible' means that you need to speak in a way that is meaningful and easily followed by the customer. 'Acceptable' means that the way you express yourself should fit the personal image that you and your organisation are trying to create. As a quick guide, the following points are worth considering:

- Express your thoughts clearly. Do not mumble or ramble.

- Beware of using slang and jargon. In other words, use language that is likely to be familiar to the customer.

- Vary your tone of voice – it makes it more interesting and shows that you are interested.

- Listen to the customer. Good communication skills also involve the ability to listen carefully to customer requests and respond to their needs.

- React with interest by using suitable facial expressions as well as your voice.

Effective oral skills are often a matter of experience and practice. One situation that frequently makes staff nervous is making a speech or presentation. You may have experienced this already if you have been required to give a presentation to other students. You will know that it can be a nerve-racking experience, but have hopefully learned that good planning and preparation gives confidence and helps you to communicate effectively. The same advice can be applied to any situation where you have to speak to a number of customers at the same time.

Non-verbal communication

Non-verbal communication covers all aspects of communication that do not involve words – spoken or written down. There is a tendency to focus on what we say or write and to overlook the importance of what we communicate non-verbally. However, research has shown that as much as 80 per cent of communication is non-verbal, so it is clearly an important part of customer service.

Another term for non-verbal communication is 'body language'. This means the way we use our body to send out messages to someone else. It can include posture, mannerisms, gestures and facial expressions, all of which communicate messages about what we really think and feel. From a customer-service point of view it is useful to look at what is known as 'open' and 'closed' body language. Open body language persuades the customer that you are interested in them, that you are not hostile or aggressive and that you want to listen to them and please them. Closed body language suggests the opposite – that you are not interested, may be hostile or aggressive and are unwilling to listen to them or satisfy their needs. This table (below, left) gives examples of open and closed types of body language:

Smiling is the single most important aspect of non-verbal communication. It says that you like and take pride in your job, and that you like the customer and want to meet and satisfy his or her needs.

Open and closed body language

Open	Closed
Smiling	Frowning
Standing up straight	Slouching
Arms loosely at your side or behind your back	Arms crossed in front of you, or hands on your hips or in your pockets
Head held with chin level	Chin up or down to floor
Eye contact with customer	Avoiding eye contact with customer
Remaining in a comfortable position	Fidgeting, moving from foot to foot, crossing and uncrossing legs
No obvious mannerisms	Fiddling with your hair, hands, clothes
Using gestures that help you to explain what you are saying	Using gestures excessively or for no apparent reason
Showing interest	Showing no feeling at all
Showing concern	Showing lack of concern

Telephone communication

Most organisations use the telephone to provide part of their customer service. Indeed, some organisations that use call centres for reservations use the telephone as the main method of communication when dealing with customer enquiries.

With good telephone skills, we can usually meet or exceed the standard of service that customers expect. Many of the skills needed are the same that you would use in any customer-service situation. For example, you need to be polite, friendly, attentive and efficient. However, additional skills are needed when using a telephone because the customer cannot see you, and you cannot see the customer. This means that you cannot use expression or gesture to help the communication process but must rely totally on your voice and your ability to listen carefully.

Here are some basic rules for using the telephone effectively:

- Speak clearly. Do not eat, drink, chew gum or smoke while on the telephone, as this will distort or muffle the sound of your voice.
- Take notes. Always write down full details of what the customer wants, particularly if the message is for someone else.
- Identify the caller's needs. Remember that the caller is paying for the call and wants to be dealt with quickly and efficiently.
- Listen carefully. Do not interrupt when the caller is talking.
- Explain what is happening. If you transfer the caller to someone else, state what you are doing.
- Smile whilst you are talking – the customer will be able to 'hear' it in your voice!

It is worth noting at this stage that, with developments in technology, an increasing amount of telephone communication is automated – i.e. the caller receives a recorded response and has the option of pressing various numbers to obtain the information that they need. This has the advantage that calls are dealt with much more quickly since the caller does not have to wait for a member of staff to become available to take the call. However, on the negative side, callers can become frustrated at the length of time that it takes to work through the options – or simply want to actually speak to someone who can personally answer their specific queries! An effective automated telephone system will always give the caller the option of speaking to a member of staff at an early stage of the message.

Written communication

The definition of written communication extends to any information that is written and/or read and includes information that is provided electronically such as on the internet. For some organisations, written communication is the main way in which they keep in contact with customers. For example, internet-based reservations systems such as e-bookers and lastminute.com conduct the majority of their business through written communication.

However, for most travel and tourism organisations, written communication supports and enhances the other methods of communication that they use, such as face-to-face and telephone.

Typical examples of written communications used by travel and tourism organisations include:

- menus
- letters
- brochures and leaflets
- signs
- programmes
- faxes
- timetables.
- tariffs or price lists
- bills
- advertisements
- noticeboards
- tickets
- email

The same standard of care needs to be given to written forms of communication as to any other aspect of customer service. The quality of written communication will affect the customer's image both of you and of the organisation. For example, a holidaymaker may be very impressed by the friendly, enthusiastic attitude of the rep but that impression may change if he or she is handed a crumpled and badly photocopied excursions list. However, if the excursion details are presented in a professional and attractive manner the previous positive impression will be confirmed.

Formal business letters

The ability to write a correct business letter is a valuable skill that many staff in travel and tourism will need to master. Whilst the actual layout may vary between different organisations, the following rules always apply:

- The company name and address (fax and email) should be at the top of the page.
- The recipient's name, position and address should also be at the top of the page.
- The date should be written in full under the addresses.
- The letter should open with 'Dear Sir/ Madam (or the recipient's name if known – e.g. Mr Jones).
- The letter should finish 'Yours faithfully' if the name is not known or 'Yours sincerely' if the recipient's name is known.
- The sender's name and position should be typed at least three spaces below the 'Yours sincerely' with their written signature in between.
- If any additional information has been included with the letter this should be signified by writing 'Enc' (enclosure) at the bottom of the page.

Listening and questioning

So far we have explored the ways in which staff can communicate with customers. However there is an important aspect of communication that has not been mentioned – the ability to listen and ask appropriate questions. Communication is a two-way process and its effectiveness depends on the ability of both parties to be able to listen and respond appropriately. From the perspective of a member of staff this means listening carefully to what the customer is saying, identifying the key points that they are making and asking any questions that may be necessary to clarify understanding. In some situations, customers may be reluctant to talk at length – particularly if they feel that they are taking up too much staff time, or are simply nervous. There are a number of ways in which staff can encourage a customer to explain their needs more fully by employing good listening skills (see box below).

Questions are a good way of clarifying information that you are unsure of, and of confirming that you have all of the correct details. It is important that the nature and number of questions is right for the situation – too few and you will not have all of the relevant information; too many and the customer will think that you were not listening in the first place!

Good listening skills

- Maintaining good eye contact to show that you are interested. Constantly looking over the customer's shoulder suggests that you looking for something more interesting to do!

- Using appropriate body language – standing up, with relaxed but formal posture makes the customer think that you are interested in what they are saying.

- Using visual clues to encourage the customer to continue talking – such as nodding in agreement and smiling.

- Writing down key points to show that you are following the conversation and are aware of the customer's needs.

- Apologising immediately if you are distracted by anything – such as another customer asking for attention.

Responding to customers

As well as being able to listen to customers and ask appropriate questions, it is also important that a member of staff is able to respond to what a customer is saying and show that they have been listening. For example, in the role-play activity below, if the customer has said, 'I don't want to go to Spain, I've been there before and it's too overdeveloped', it would be inappropriate to suggest other similar destinations.

activity

WHERE DO I WANT TO GO?

In pairs, play the roles of a travel agency adviser and a customer. The customer starts the conversation with 'I would like to go for two weeks somewhere hot'. (You should have a very clear idea of where you want to go, but do not tell the travel agency adviser at this stage – that is for them to find out!)

The travel agency adviser should ask as many questions as is necessary to find out where their customer wants to go – but you cannot ask them 'where do you want to go?' or any questions of a similar nature.

Providing information

Providing customers with information is an important part of the communication process. For example, most resort representatives are expected to talk to a group of holidaymakers at the welcome speech and

Giving a 'welcome aboard' speech on a cruise liner.

provide information about the country, the resort and the accommodation, as well as health and safety, excursions, etc. Another situation where you may well be required to give a 'speech' is if you work for an organisation, such as a hotel or airport, which uses a public-address or tannoy system. The key to success in any situation where you are going to give a speech is to have a very clear idea about what you are going to say and how you will say it.

activity

ACCIDENT REPORT BOOKS

All travel and tourism organisations maintain an accident report book where they record details of any accident that staff or guests have on the premises. In pairs, identify five reasons why staff need to complete the appropriate documentation in the case of an accident.

Using appropriate documentation

In many situations, the communications process also involves recording information or completing relevant documentation. For example, travel agency advisers, hotel receptionists, resort reps and a wide range of other staff have to complete documentation for their customers. The need for documentation is to ensure that all relevant information is recorded and (where necessary) passed on to others within or outside the organisation who are involved in providing the travel and tourism product or service.

Using information communication technology (ICT)

The rapid rise in the use of information technology has had a huge impact on communications within travel and tourism, and most staff will need to be competent in its use. ICT is widely used as a communications channel for:

- Booking holidays
- Accessing information about tourist attractions and destinations
- Making transport reservations.

For many organisations, ICT is the main way in which they communicate with their customers, and the member of staff at the other end of the 'ICT link' needs to show the same level of care as with any other form of communication.

activity

USING A TANNOY

1 Imagine that you are going to make a public-address announcement in a hotel. Listed below are the seven main stages of using a tannoy, jumbled up. Rearrange them so that they are in the right order.

- Relay the message
- Switch tannoy off
- Plan (write down) what you are going to say
- Repeat the key points
- Switch tannoy on
- Thank customers for their attention
- Gain the customers' attention.

2 Now practise making the following tannoy announcements:

a) A telephone call at Reception for Mr Patel

b) Last orders for dinner in the restaurant is in 20 minutes

c) The coach has arrived to collect members of the Sharwood's party for their trip to Hever Castle

d) The cabaret is about to begin in the Ballroom.

IMPROVING COMMUNICATION METHODS

Read the following account of the experience of Mr and Mrs Ryan when taking a holiday at a holiday centre in Devon. In small groups, assess the communication methods and customer service used by the organisation, and suggest how they could be improved.

Booking the holiday

Mr Ryan had decided to surprise his wife and take her on a thirtieth wedding anniversary trip to Devon. His first approach to finding something suitable was to look on the internet, and he eventually found the ideal place – the Sandside Holiday Centre. Sandside offered 250 chalets in secluded woodland, each with their own patio and luxury features such as jacuzzi, satellite television and outside hot tub. Leisure facilities included a number of restaurants, spa facilities, water sports and leisure activities, swimming pool and a nightly programme of entertainment. Mr Ryan proceeded to make the booking on Sandside's website. However, when he tried to specify that they needed wheelchair access for his wife he was informed that for specific requests he needed to contact the centre directly by phone, and was given a phone number. The next day he phoned Sandside and was connected to an automated system that took 8 minutes before he was given the option of speaking to a

SANDSIDE HOLIDAY VILLAGE
Brixham, Devon

Dear Sir,

Thank you for booking your holiday with us. I have pleasure in confirming a week's stay in our 'Premium' one-bedroom chalet from August 1st – 8th 2005. We look forward to welcoming you to Sandside and hope that you have an enjoyable stay.

Yours sincerely

HR Roberts

HR Roberts
Reservations Manager

member of staff. He was then able to make his reservation and told that confirmation would be posted to him within 3 working days. After 8 days, the following letter arrived in a large envelope together with over twenty additional sheets of information about the holiday centre and surrounding area.

When they arrived

Mr and Mrs Ryan arrived at the packed check-in desk at Sandside on the morning of 1 August and were asked for their completed pre-registration forms by the receptionist. The receptionist, who was seated at her computer, was clearly very busy checking guests in and didn't look up as she requested the forms. Mr Ryan started to panic a bit at this point as he wasn't sure what forms the receptionist was talking about. The receptionist tutted at the delay and said, 'Form D34/101 – it will have been included in the information pack with your confirmation letter'. Eventually Mr Ryan retrieved the form, completed it and they checked in to their accommodation. On entering their chalet they found the television was displaying a message saying 'Welcome Mr and Mrs Rayn, we hope you enjoy your stay with us at Sandside'. Mrs Ryan decided to have a shower after the long journey, but found that the housekeeping staff had forgotten to leave any towels. So she rang through to reception. The line was engaged for over 20 minutes, but at last she spoke to the receptionist who assured her that the towels would be delivered promptly. When they still hadn't arrived after two hours she rang again. This time a member of staff arrived with the towels in ten minutes and said that she had only just got the message.

Topic 6   Product knowledge

In this topic we are going to look at three important issues within customer service delivery:

- **Knowledge of the range of products and services offered by an organisation**
- **Use of appropriate information sources**
- **How the needs of customers are met within different sectors of the industry.**

Knowledge of the range of products and services

We have already talked about the ways in which staff will often be required to provide information and advice to customers. In order to achieve this they need to have a sound knowledge of the range of products and services offered by their organisation. They should be able to provide product information that meets their customers' needs and expectations, and ensures total satisfaction. The sort of information that staff may need to be able to provide will vary according to their organisation and customers. However, typical product knowledge might include:

- Knowledge of the company and its operating divisions
- Main features of all the products and services offered
- Suitability of products and services for different types of customers
- Prices (including special offers and discounts)
- Location and directions
- Staffing
- Health, safety and security procedures

- Other local information (such as nearby attractions, medical facilities, transport, etc.)

In any customer-service situation, product information should be impersonal, accurate and objective. Let's look at what is meant by this in more detail:

- 'Impersonal' means that your own tastes and preferences should not limit or restrict the sort of information you give. For example, a customer at a travel agency needs information about holidays that are suitable for his or her needs, not about resorts that the member of staff would like to go to.

- 'Accurate' means making sure that everything you say is true. If you are not sure about something, say that you will check the information and let the customer know. For example, saying that a visitor attraction is suitable for customers in wheelchairs when you are not really sure could result in some very dissatisfied customers.

- 'Objective' means including all the information that customers need to know even if you think that it might put them off buying the product. Sometimes this may mean referring potential customers to a competitor – but the reputation that you gain for good customer service will mean that they will come back to you.

Impersonal, accurate and objective information is important in all situations, if you are to satisfy customers' needs and ensure that they return. Sometimes giving the wrong information can result in customers not being able to buy a product or service at all. For example, incorrect transport times could result in customers missing flights, trains or ferries.

Use of appropriate information sources

Staff cannot always be expected to automatically know the answers to all questions. Staff who work for organisations that deal with a very wide range of products and services are unlikely to have committed all information to memory – such as staff in travel agencies, train stations or tourist information centres. However, what is important is that they know where to find the information. Sometimes this may be a question of asking a colleague. Alternatively it may be necessary to use other sources of information such as printed materials, brochures, maps, etc. For example, customer service assistants at rail stations are constantly asked questions about train times, delays, departure platforms and connections. Clearly they cannot instantly recall all of this information – but they have computer screens and printed material that enables them to find the information quickly.

The type of information required will largely depend on what the customer asks you. They may want to know about the suitability of products or services in terms of meeting their needs and expectations. Alternatively they may require information on what prices include, or directions on how to get to

somewhere. There is a wide range of information sources available to travel and tourism staff including:

- manuals
- maps
- brochures and leaflets
- reference books
- guide books
- computerised information systems
- timetables recorded telephone information lines
- tourist information centres.

Many organisations include detailed information on how to get to them in their promotional materials, as this example from Beaulieu shows.

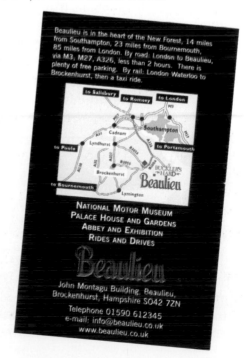

INFORMATION ROLE PLAY

Below is an extract from the P&O Cruises website, giving advice to customers who have not been on a cruise before. Take some time to read through the questions and answers. Then in pairs, role play a customer and an information clerk. The customer should ask a question based on any of the information provided. If the information clerk cannot remember the answer they can refer to the information – but they must use their own words.

How many formal nights are there on a cruise?
There are usually two per week.

Do I have to wear a suit on the formal nights? I don't want to buy a new suit just for the cruise.
You will need to wear a suit for formal nights.

What clothes should I pack?
Keep it simple. Casual shirts, shorts and beachwear by day with comfy shoes. A light jacket or coat for cool evenings.
   For the nights: men – a dark suit for formal evenings (if you have a tuxedo, by all means bring it). Jacket and tie for informal nights. Smart-casual for all other nights. Ladies – something elegant for formal nights, a cocktail dress for the informal, smart-casual for all other nights.

What else should I pack?
Dressing gowns are only provided in suite accommodation. For the swimming pool, towels are provided at the poolside. If you do forget anything, our onboard shops are very well stocked with 'ordinary everyday' goods.

How much luggage can I pack?
On cruises from Southampton, as much as you like. On fly cruises, restrictions vary according to airline, but you can bring at least 20 kg.

What is the Purser's Desk?
The Purser's Desk is something like the front desk at a first-class hotel. It is here that you can purchase stamps, settle shipboard accounts, etc. It is the place to go for information and action on almost everything.

What's the best way to carry spending money?
Sterling is the only currency used on board , so we recommend sterling travellers cheques, or your cheque book and card, to obtain cash – and currencies for the ports of call – at our Reception Desk. We operate a cash-free system on board; simply sign for all onboard purchases and settle your account by card at the end of your cruise. Foreign currency exchanges must be made at Reception with cash or travellers cheques.

What about tipping?
Please don't worry about it. You'll find a leaflet in your cabin with guidelines, but generally speaking about £3.50 per person per day should cover all your tips.

What if I'm not fully mobile?
We're delighted to welcome you aboard and we're sure you'll have a marvellous holiday. All four ships have wheelchair-accessible cabins.

What if I want to phone home?
Just pick up the phone in your cabin and dial. You can also fax home and send letters (we'll do the posting).

How do I get ashore?
Wherever possible, your ship will dock, and you come and go as you please via the gangway. In smaller ports, the ship will anchor and offer you a free and frequent shuttle service.

Source: www. pocruises.com

How the needs of customers are met within different sectors of the industry

It needs to be understood that whilst good customer service is a very high priority for travel and tourism organisations, this is not only because they want their customers to be satisfied. In reality, good customer service has a wide range of benefits for the organisation, including:

- more customers, increased sales
- a better public image
- an edge over the competition
- a happier and more efficient workforce
- satisfied customers
- customer loyalty and repeat business.

In effect, good customer service means that the organisation is more successful. In many situations (particularly the private, profit-making sector) this means reaching a balance between satisfying the customer and achieving the organisation's objectives. Specific situations where such a balance has to be found include:

- Staffing levels
- Access to products and services
- Health and safety
- Implementing procedures
- Ensuring the enjoyment of other customers.

Queues at attractions such as major theme parks could be reduced by providing more rides, but this would also reduce profitability.

Staffing levels

In theory, the best possible customer service would mean that all customers were dealt with instantly by a member of staff. However, in practice this is rarely achieved – simply because organisations cannot afford to employ large numbers of staff to ensure that there is always one available to serve a customer at once. For example a coach party arriving late at night at a motorway service station may often find minimum staffing levels and have to wait some time to be served. Likewise, customers going to a travel agency on a Saturday morning will often have to wait some time before seeing a consultant – despite all of the consultants' desks being staffed. Being able to guarantee instant service on a Saturday morning would be impractical – and unprofitable – since it would require much bigger premises to accommodate the large number of work stations that were only needed one morning a week.

Access to products and services

A further area where there often needs to be a compromise between the needs of the customer and the organisation's objectives is in terms of access to products and services. For example, visit any theme park during August and you will probably have to queue for some considerable time for the more popular rides. Clearly the problem could be solved by providing more rides or allowing fewer customers into the park. However, both of these options have huge cost implications and are likely to seriously reduce the profitability of the park – the operator's first objective.

Health, safety and security

There are many situations in which health and safety issues may result in the customer feeling that they are not getting the best service. For example, many catering establishments refuse to heat up babies' bottles of milk for customers. This is not because they are being difficult, but because they are concerned at the repercussions of a member of staff over-heating the milk and injuring the baby.

The rise in international terrorism in recent years has also impacted on the service offered by many travel and tourism organisations. Major attractions such as Disneyland Paris now conduct handbag searches of customers entering parts of the attraction. Whilst a necessary part of security this can dramatically increase queuing time and therefore reduce the customers' enjoyment.

Implementing procedures

Many procedures are based on health and safety concerns, whilst others may be purely organisational. They are generally implemented for sound reasons and aim to improve the overall level of service offered. However, customers may view them as unnecessary and as reducing their enjoyment. For example, if you have seen the 'fly-on-the-wall' documentaries about airlines, you will know that a recurring complaint is the refusal of ground staff to allow passengers to board a plane if they are late checking-in. Passengers frequently see this as petty-mindedness, and cannot understand why they should not board if the plane is still at the airport. In fact there are extremely good reasons for this. The amount of aviation fuel used for each flight is calculated very precisely, based on the number of checked-in passengers and the weight of down but too little fuel and the plane will not make it to the destination.

Ensuring the enjoyment of other customers

Whilst most organisations strive to meet the needs of all of their customers, there may often be some conflict which results in one group of customers being satisfied at the expense or dissatisfaction in others. A current and controversial issue is smoking. Many organisations have designated some or all of their areas as no smoking. Whilst this will clearly meet with satisfaction from non-smokers, there are many smokers who feel that their personal freedom and enjoyment is being eroded. Similarly, train companies such as Virgin have designated carriages on their trains where mobile phones are not permitted as some passengers find the noise intrusive.

VILLAGE RULES: OK?

Below are some of the aspects of customer service provided at Center Parcs. Not all customers believe that these practices enhance their enjoyment. In groups, discuss why you think Center Parcs implement these 'Village Rules' and how they may improve the overall enjoyment and satisfaction of their guests.

1 Most of the restaurants are non-smoking.

2 Booking most activities (such as tennis, bowling, squash, etc.) onsite can only be done one day in advance. There are often long queues at the booking desks as soon as they open, and some activities are quickly fully booked.

3 Center Parcs do not take group bookings for stag and hen parties.

4 No one under 16 years can have a beauty treatment in the Spa Centre.

5 Guests are only allowed to take their cars to their lodges on arrival and departure day for a limited number of hours.

6 At Center Parcs, Longleat there are no pubs.

7 When purchasing anything at Center Parcs (even a loaf of bread in the supermarket) you are required to give your lodge number.

8 Dogs must be kept on leads at all times.

Topic 7 Meeting different customer needs

In this section we will look at how travel and tourism organisations provide customer service to meet the needs of a range of different customers. In particular we will explore the ways in which organisations and their staff deliver good service through:

- **Giving advice**
- **Providing assistance**
- **Providing for specific needs**
- **Taking and relaying messages**
- **Maintaining health, safety and security.**

Giving advice

Giving customers advice is often an extension of giving them information. However, whilst information may be purely factual, advice requires you to make appropriate recommendations and suggestions. For example, a travel adviser may provide a customer with information on holidays by giving them appropriate brochures. However, the customer may ask for additional advice on what would best suit their particular needs. For example: 'Which destination would you suggest for some winter sunshine?' or 'Which Greek islands would be suitable for someone with mobility problems?' It is important that advice should always be impersonal, accurate and objective – in other words based on the customer's needs and not merely the opinion of the member of staff. So, for example, a young travel consultant may think a fortnight in Ibiza on a young adults' holiday is the ideal holiday, but it would probably be inappropriate to recommend the product to a retired couple.

Many travel and tourism products and services are complex, involving a wide range of different aspects. The first-time customer can often find this quite confusing, and it may spoil their enjoyment of the product if they have difficulty understanding how it is delivered. Therefore, one of the issues that many travel and tourism organisations have to deal with is giving their customers sufficient advice on the way in which services are delivered and used. For example, package holiday customers will be sent pre-holiday advice about when and where they check-in for their flight, baggage allowances, insurance, etc. Once they arrive at their accommodation they will usually be given advice on health and safety issues such as the use of lifts, swimming pools, hotel balconies, etc.

Providing assistance

We have already looked at how some customers may have specific needs and the ways in which customer service can meet these needs. In reality, any customer may have a specific need for extra assistance at any time. For example, the hotel guest who has locked himself out of his bedroom, the holidaymaker who cannot manage all of their luggage on their own, the wheelchair user who needs assistance getting through swing doors, or the train passenger who cannot find their reserved seat. In situations such as these, your responsibility is to try to anticipate when customers might need assistance and provide it. For example, if you see a wheelchair user struggling to get through doors you should not wait for her to ask for help – offer assistance quickly, to show that you really care and have anticipated her needs.

The extract above, from the British Airways website, is a good example of the assistance that they offer for unaccompanied children on their flights.

Providing for specific needs

Since the introduction of The Disability Discrimination Act (DDA) in 1995, all organisations have had a legal responsibility concerning the way in which they provide products and services to disabled people. The

DDA gives disabled people important rights of access to everyday services that others take for granted, and is particularly relevant to travel and tourism providers. Under the Act:

- Treating a disabled person less favourably because they are disabled has been unlawful since December 1996.
- Since October 1999, service providers have had to consider making reasonable adjustments to the way they deliver their services so that disabled people can use them.
- Since 2004, service providers have had to consider making permanent physical adjustments to their premises.

Many travel and tourism organisations far exceed the requirements of the DDA to ensure that specific needs are met.

Taking and relaying messages

Taking and relaying messages is an important part of customer service for both internal and external customers. There are many examples of when it may be necessary to take messages, such as:

- a customer telephoning to speak to a hotel guest who is not there
- a coach operator telephoning to say that they have been delayed

- a customer wanting to speak to the manager regarding a complaint
- a member of staff phoning to say that she is unwell and will not be in for work.

Standard message pads

Failing to take accurate messages or failing to ensure that they are passed on to the right person promptly can have disastrous effects on the customer's perception of the overall level of service offered. Most organisations have standard message pads to allow staff to record all of the necessary details – such as the one shown below.

TELEPHONE MESSAGE

Message for: *Mr Sinclair*   Date: *26/1/05*

Message from: *Miss J Collins*   Time: *3.40 pm*

Message:

> *Please call me at the office before 6 pm tonight.*

Telephone number: *01723 562189 Ext. 126*

Message taken by: *S Rawlins*

British Airways SkyFlyer Solo Service

British Airways offers a service for children travelling unaccompanied, called Skyflyer Solo.

Skyflyer Solo involves us taking special care of your child through the airport process – departure, arrival and, of course, in the air.

On British Airways your child can travel unaccompanied from as young as 5 if they are travelling on a single-sector flight. If the journey involves an onward transfer on the same or to another British Airways flight, they must be at least 6 years old.

At the airport

At most major airports we have a desk that is specifically designated for check-in of children travelling as unaccompanied minors. If you have difficulty finding the desk, please ask a member of our staff to help you.

We would like to remind you of the requirement

for an adult to accompany the child to the check-in desk and remain in the airport until the flight has departed. This is particularly important in the event that the flight is delayed for any reason.

At check-in our staff will ask you for the completed and signed Declaration Form, contained in a distinctive blue wallet with red and white stripes, that advises us who will be collecting your child at the end of the journey. We will also ask for your contact details just in case there is any disruption to flights.

Maintaining health, safety and security

Generally speaking, health and safety considerations take priority over all other customer needs and expectations – even if it means that the customer is not able to receive the products or services that they had hoped for. For example, the fire alarms sounding in the middle of a wedding reception would mean that the wedding party would need to evacuate the building – not the ideal event to include in a celebration, but clearly necessary. However, even if it is not possible to provide the expected service because of health and safety issues, it is vital that the customer is still treated politely and with consideration. The newspaper extract below outlines Air France's refusal to allow a passenger to fly with them due to health and safety concerns – however, the way in which it was handled is an appalling example of customer service.

Mail on Sunday, 15 August 2004

A Thalidomide victim with no limbs is suing Air France after being told she could not board a plane because 'a torso cannot possibly fly on its own'. Adele Price, 42, was travelling to New York and had already checked in her luggage when a gate worker allegedly told her, 'One head, one bottom and one torso cannot and will not be allowed to fly on Air France'.

She says the airline refused to let her on board without an able-bodied assistant and when she found a friend to fly with her she was allowed on a later plane – on condition she saw a doctor after the flight.

activity

WHAT WOULD YOU DO?

You are working as an overseas resort representative and have come into the office one morning to find the following message left by a colleague:

'Have just received a call from UK Head Office to say that the mother of one of your guests, Mr Nicholson, has been taken seriously ill and is in hospital. I've checked and we can get the Nicholson family on a return flight to the UK tomorrow evening. I could not contact the family as they are staying in a private villa on the outskirts of town. Please ensure that they get the message promptly.'

You go directly to the villa, but only the Nicholsons' 14-year-old daughter is there – the rest of the family have gone out for the day, and she does not know when they will be back.

Explain what you would do in this situation and why you think your method of dealing with the situation is appropriate.

A member of staff will then host your child throughout the journey until they are collected by the nominated adult at the arriving airport or by the transferring airline, if applicable. As you can appreciate, it is essential that we know who will be collecting your child.

On board

Our cabin crew will look after your child for the duration of the flight.

On some of our longhaul flights, where several unaccompanied minors are travelling together, we have dedicated escorts to assist the cabin crew.

At the destination airport

Our ground staff will host your child from the aircraft through all the arrival procedures until they have met up with the person nominated to collect him/her, or to the staff of the airline to which your child is transferring.

If the person collecting your child is delayed, it is essential that you advise us as we have limited hours of operation at some airports.

Source: www.britishairways.com

activity

UNACCOMPANIED CHILDREN

Having read the description of British Airways Skyflyer Solo service:

1 Write a list of the main ways in which BA provide assistance.

2 Explain what you think the main needs and expectations will be of:

a) The children travelling

b) Their parents.

3 In pairs, discuss what sort of questions you think parents might ask when booking the service for their children.

PRACTISE YOUR CUSTOMER-SERVICE SKILLS

For this activity you should select at least four of the situations below and role-play them in front of the group. Evaluate your performance with the help of the group and make recommendations as to how you could improve your customer-service skills in the future.

1 Role: Flight attendant

Passengers have already been advised that no smoking is allowed on the flight and one particular passenger has complained that he cannot last four hours without a cigarette. He has now lit a cigarette and is refusing to put it out, saying 'Just let me finish this one and I'll be OK for the rest of the journey'.

2 Role: Sales assistant in the souvenir shop of a stately home

A customer is unhappy that there is a £3.50 charge for the guide book to the stately home. She claims that she has already paid over £30 for her family's visit and that the book should be free.

3 Role: Resort representative

A family have booked and paid for an excursion to a nearby water park. On the day of the excursion they turn up 10 minutes late and the coach has left without them. They claim that the coach was early and demand a full refund.

4 Role: Airline check-in staff

A couple have arrived to check-in for their holiday flight to Malaga. On checking the passports, the member of staff finds that the wife's passport expired two weeks ago.

5 Role: Travel agency consultant

A young bride-to-be is planning to spend three nights away with friends for her Hen Party and would like advice on suitable destinations.

6 Role: Ride operator

A father and two children have been queuing for a ride for over an hour. As they get to the front of the queue, the ride operator realises that one of the children does not meet the height requirements for the ride.

7 Role: Airport representative

A family have just arrived on a night flight from Manchester. They produce documentation showing that they have reserved a hire car to be collected on their arrival at the airport. The rep has no record of the reservation and the car hire desk is now closed until the morning.

8 Role: Hotel receptionist

A Swedish guest indicates that he would like to know how to get from the hotel to the centre of town. He speaks very little English.

9 Role: Tour guide

Whilst showing a group around a tourist attraction the guide notices that one member of the group continually asks complicated questions and interrupts the guided tour. The other customers are clearly getting irritated.

**Amanda Keers
Sales Office Manager, Superbreak**

What is your role at Superbreak?

I run a department which provides sales support to a network of approx 7,500 UK travel agents who book with us. We control the distribution of over 11 million brochures a year, negotiate commercial deals with all our agency partners, and provide training on our products.

How did you get to be where you are now?

After studying Catering and Hotel Management at college, I worked for Ladbrokes Hotels, starting as a silver-service waitress and working my way up to 'Restaurant & Bar Supervisor'. Having had enough of split shifts, I returned to college to study Travel & Tourism, and then joined a tourism marketing consultancy, with clients as diverse as Falklands Island Tourism and the Wildfowl & Wetland Trust. From there I joined a visitor attraction production company as a project manager. My biggest project was a visitor attraction in Shrewsbury which celebrated the books of Ellis Peters (the Brother Cadfael author). From there I joined Superbreak, where over the last 10 years I have seen the company expand rapidly.

Who are your main customers?

Superbreak is the market leader in the provision of UK and European short breaks – we currently book breaks for over 1.25 million clients a year. Our customer base is broadly split 50/50 between clients who make their bookings directly with us and those who book through a travel agent. Our main Superbreak brochure is racked in over 90% of UK travel agencies and our website allows both travel agents and direct clients to book online.

How do you meet the needs of your customers?

We offer our customers unrivalled choice. We currently feature over 2000 UK hotels and 1,600 city and beach hotels in Europe. We hold allocations of rooms at all our hotels, so we can book up to the day of departure. If a client's first choice is not available we promise to offer a suitable alternative. Our 'price guarantee' promises that once a booking has been confirmed the price will not change, and should a client be offered a lower price for the same package by the hotel, we will refund the difference. Ticket and travel documents are dispatched within 24 hours of booking, and for bookings made on the web an instant (printable) confirmation is sent.

What training do staff receive to ensure that they can provide excellent service?

New reservations staff undertake two weeks of classroom training to learn our full product range, how to make bookings on our computerised system, and how to conduct a call (through role-play exercises). We do not script our staff, as we believe that a combination of product knowledge and personality are the best selling tools. We train them to efficiently identify the client's requirements and match them with the most suitable product. We teach our staff to go at the client's own pace, avoiding the use of jargon, and involving the client in the booking process.

After their 'starter training' our staff are continually monitored, and additional training on new products, particularly geographical knowledge, is given on a daily basis. Many of the hotels that we feature give presentations to our staff – who often get a chance to stay at the hotels themselves. Personal experience and recommendation is one of the most powerful selling tools there is! Staff also learn how to deal with difficult situations and which other areas of the business they may need to refer to, according to the client's enquiry.

How do you monitor the levels of service that your staff are providing?

We monitor individual staff performance based on the number of calls taken against the number of bookings confirmed – their 'conversion rate'. Less efficient performers will be 'silent call monitored' by one of our six trainers who will try to identify any product or selling weakness and give additional training on a one-to-one basis, if required. Each reservation adviser has a team leader who is there to act as a mentor and assist with any difficulties as they arise. Appraisals take place on a regular basis, and team meetings are held weekly.

As a company, we regularly benchmark our overall service levels against those in other sectors. In 2001, this resulted in the company winning the CBI's Yorkshire and Humberside Region 'Fit for the Future' challenge – a scheme to recognise best practice champions.

Complaints procedures

Strange as it may seem, dealing with customers' complaints is also a part of providing excellent customer service. This is because if a complaint is handled well a good relationship will be established – and the customer may well return in future. In this topic we are going to focus on:

- The importance of handling complaints effectively
- The reasons why customers complain
- Handling face-to-face complaints
- Handling complaints in writing or over the telephone
- Deciding what action to take following a complaint
- Complaints procedures.

The importance of handling complaints effectively

Research into customer complaints reveals some interesting facts:

- A happy customer will tell about four other people about the good service that they receive.
- A dissatisfied customer will tell at least fifteen people about the bad service they receive.
- 94% of dissatisfied customers do not complain – they simply walk away and don't come back.
- Most organisations lose between 45% and 50% of their customers every five years through complaints.
- Replacing lost customers costs a company five times more than keeping them.

Effective complaint handling is as much a part of customer service as providing information or dealing with specific needs. All travel and tourism organisations, however well they are operated, will receive complaints from customers about the products and services provided. Having complaints procedures and training staff how to deal with customer complaints is a vital part of the overall service provided by an organisation. In fact, if handled really well, the customer who complains may often feel more satisfied than if they had not had any original grounds for complaint. For example, read the following account of how a complaint can be turned to the advantage of the organisation.

'We'd never used Getaway Travel before but had heard good reports about them. Last summer they helped us to find a cruise holiday and made all of the arrangements. Two weeks before we were due to go, we received the final tickets.

But, three days before we were due to depart, my wife was reading through the details and saw that the departure airport was Newcastle, rather than our preference of Manchester. I rang Getaway in a panic, as we live a long way from Newcastle and don't have a car, plus the flight was at 6.00 a.m. – so there would not be any public transport to get us there. The travel adviser was really kind, although she did say (politely) that we should have checked the details at the time of booking as well as when the confirmation arrived. (To be honest, my wife and I are getting on a bit and cannot remember talking about which airport we wanted, as there seemed to be so much to think about when we were deciding where to go.)

Anyway, later that day the Getaway Travel manager rang back to say that she had booked us into a hotel at Newcastle airport the night before our flight – and reserved us train tickets. She said it was impossible to say how the error had occurred, so they would pay for the transport and hotel. I was really impressed by how much they cared, and will always use them in future. But next time I think I might read the details on the confirmation a bit more closely!'

The reasons why customers complain

There are as many reasons for complaints as there are customers. However, research continually shows that the main grounds for complaint are poor service, and standards not meeting customers' expectations. Complaints can vary from the seemingly trivial, such as no toilet paper in the Ladies, to the extremely serious, such as reported food poisoning. But what motivates a customer to complain in the first place?

- It may be through disappointment that the product or service has not met their expectations – such as an established customer who has always received good service in the past.

- It may be due to anger that they have not been treated as well as they expected – such as a customer who feels that staff have been rude.

- They may be embarrassed, such as a group leader who feels that they have let the rest of their party down because the service was not as good as they had promised.

- It may be because they simply want something put right, such as the customer who has not been left any towels in their bedroom.

- Or it may be because they want compensation to make amends, such as a holidaymaker who has had a disappointing holiday.

It is important to realise that a number of factors can influence a customer's overall satisfaction and their likelihood to complain. For example, tour operators know that unusually bad weather can often result in an increase in complaints about all aspects of a customer's holiday. This does not necessarily mean that the complaints are unjustified – however, the disappointment of being stuck inside a Spanish hotel room while it pours with rain outside, may make the customer more negative about other aspects of their holiday.

On a lighter note, there are sometimes 'complaint' situations that are clearly beyond the control of the organisation, as the following list of complaints received by tour operators shows:

> No one told us there would be fish in the sea – the children were startled.
>
> It is your duty as a tour operator to advise us of noisy or unruly guests before we travel.
>
> **I was bitten by a mosquito – no one said they could bite.**
>
> We booked an excursion to the water park – but no one told us we had to bring our swimming costumes and towels.
>
> I compared the size of our one-bedroom apartment to our friends' three-bedroom apartment – and ours was significantly smaller.
>
> It took us nine hours to fly to Jamaica from England – it only took the Americans three hours.
>
> **We had to queue outside – with no air conditioning.**
>
> There were too many Spanish people. The receptionist spoke Spanish. The food was Spanish. Too many foreigners.
>
> *Source: Daily Mail 26 July 2003*

Handling face-to-face complaints

No one likes dealing with customer complaints because it often suggests that you or a colleague have not done your jobs properly. Even when a complaint is about something totally out of your control you may still feel concerned that the customer is disappointed. Sometimes a customer may be angry or directly criticise you. They may even shout at you. Being able to deal with situations like this is all part of good customer service, although on the first few occasions that you receive complaints you may find them difficult to handle.

The following measures provide some useful tips when handling complaints.

- Listen carefully to the customer.
- Apologise in general terms for any inconvenience caused.
- Let the customer know that the matter will be fully investigated and put right.
- Try to see the problem from the customer's point of view.
- Keep calm and don't argue with the customer.
- Find a solution to the problem or refer the issue to a supervisor/manager.
- Agree the solution with the customer.
- Take action and make sure that what you promised to do gets done.
- Make sure that you record details of the complaint and the actions taken.

Handling complaints in writing or over the telephone

We have looked at the general guidelines for dealing with complaints in a face-to-face situation. Two further methods of dealing with a complaint are over the telephone and in writing. Both or either of these methods may be necessary when:

- following up a face-to-face complaint that could not be resolved at the time
- responding to a telephone complaint
- responding to a written letter of complaint.

Deciding which method is preferable will depend on the situation. The Strategic Planning Institute found that:

'95% of customers prefer a letter to a phone call when you are dealing with their complaints. This is because a letter is more personal, it demonstrates a greater commitment on behalf of the company and its tangibility suggests that the complaint has been taken seriously and is concrete evidence that something will be done.'

However, there will be some situations when a phone call is the most appropriate first method of contact. The great advantage of telephoning a complainer is that it is immediate and ensures that the customer knows that you are taking the complaint seriously. Many travel and tourism organisations have a policy of phoning a customer immediately they receive a complaint letter to confirm that something is being done about the complaint, and then following it up with a letter outlining the action that has been taken. The benefits of responding to a complaint in writing is that considerable thought can be given to the

planning and content of the letter to make sure that it is absolutely right.

Deciding what action to take following a complaint

One difficulty that many staff have when dealing with complaints is deciding what action is most appropriate – and, in fact, whether or not they have the authority to take it! If you are ever unsure about the appropriate action you should always ask a supervisor for help.

The best course of action will depend on the type of customer, the nature of their complaint and how serious the complaint is. It is very important to correctly identify what the customer would find acceptable or you may risk making them even more dissatisfied or even insult them. Many complaint situations will result in the customer being given some form of compensation such as a refund or complimentary product. The scale of the compensation should reflect the severity of the complaint. For example, passengers whose flight has been delayed for an hour on the runway may be given a complimentary drink but they would not expect to have their fare refunded in full. On the other hand, customers whose cruise has been ruined by mechanical problems on the ship may receive an invitation to return for a complimentary cruise at a

The complaints procedure at Superbreaks

Superbreaks is primarily a booking agency for hotels in the UK and abroad. A large percentage of their business is leisure, with short-break holidays and theatre breaks being particularly popular. Their customer-services department works to strict standards and procedures, which include:

- All customers are requested to put their complaint in writing. This is to ensure that the company has a full record of all of the details of the complaint.
- A response is guaranteed within 14 days, although in practice it is usually within 3–4 days.
- If Superbreaks needs to investigate the complaint further, due to it being about one of the hotels that they use, the customer is informed of this and guaranteed a further response within 21 days.
- Customer-service staff regularly visit the hotels used to enhance their product knowledge.

- There is no standard level of compensation because the company feels that all customers are different and will have different expectations.
- All customers who make a complaint receive a 10% discount voucher for their next booking with Superbreaks, regardless of the nature or severity of their complaint.

Superbreaks are also featured in the Industry Focus interview on page 89.

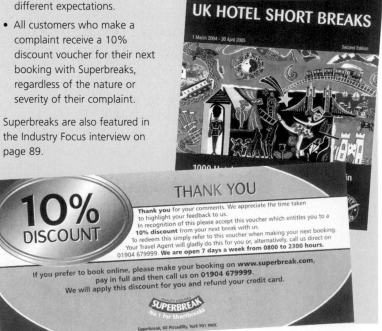

Unit 2 The Travel and Tourism Customer

later date. There are great advantages in providing compensation in the form of a free return visit, since it ensures that the customer will come back and it gives the organisation the opportunity to show that they can get it right.

Complaints procedures

Most organisations have a complaints 'procedure' which staff must follow when dealing with customer complaints. (see the Superbreaks example, on the previous page)

DEALING WITH COMPLAINTS

1 You work as a travel agency consultant and have received the following telephone message, which was taken during your lunch break by a colleague. You have identified the caller as a customer who you booked on a two-week holiday to Portugal.

> Message from: Mrs Rosemary O'Hara
>
> Date: 27 September 2005
>
> Time: 12.45 p.m.
>
> Message: Above customer rang to say that she was very disappointed with her trip to Portugal. Original hotel was overbooked and she was sent to alternative accommodation which was only three stars (not four stars as promised). Miles from beach and town centre which caused problems as her husband has mobility problems. Please call her on following number as she wants to know about claiming compensation and how to contact ABTA. Her number is: 01698 372 106.

In pairs, identify what information you would need to find out before you rang Mrs O'Hara – you might want to check the ABTA website for details of their arbitration scheme (www.abtanet.com) but bear in mind that ABTA intervention is a last resort. Write a list of questions that you need to ask Mrs O'Hara, and then role play the telephone conversation.

2 You are a receptionist in a hotel. The group leader of a party of guests has come to you to complain that several members of her party have developed severe diarrhoea and vomiting. They all had roast chicken for dinner in the hotel restaurant the previous evening and she believes the illness to be food poisoning. You are aware that several members of staff have been off work with a similar illness over the last week. Decide how you would deal with this complaint, and role play the situation with a colleague. You may find it useful to contact a local hotel and ask them what their policy would be when dealing with a complaint of this nature.

3 You work in the customer-service department at a local mainline station and have received the letter below. Identify what information you would need to find out before replying to the passenger. You will find it useful to access your local rail provider's website to see what compensation system they use. Then write an appropriate letter of response.

> Dear Sir,
>
> I am writing to express my absolute disgust at the service I received from your company on Monday, 15 January. I was due to attend a conference in London at 1.00 p.m. and had allowed ample time for travel – expecting to arrive at around 10.00a.m. Initially we were informed that our train had been delayed but no indication was given as to the anticipated departure time. Having eventually left 1 hour and 45 minutes late, we suffered further delays of over an hour and a half when the train ground to a halt just outside London. The guard on the train was most unhelpful – and in fact very rude – when I asked him for an idea of when we could expect to arrive. Needless to say, I was extremely late for my meeting and expect a refund for the full ticket price of £142.
>
> Yours faithfully,
>
> J.L Michaels

Methods of measuring customer service

In previous topics we have talked about how travel and tourism organisations and their staff provide customer service that meets the needs of their customers. In this topic we are going to explore how organisations ensure that customer service levels are maintained and continually improved through the ways in which they measure and monitor their customer service. In particular we will look at:

- Codes of conduct and customer service charters
- Mystery shoppers
- Observations
- Surveys
- Focus groups.

Codes of conduct and customer service charters

Many travel and tourism organisations outline their customer-service aims or strategy in what are known as a 'customer promise', 'customer service charter' or 'code of conduct' – in fact many organisations will have all three of these.

Customer promise

Generally speaking a customer promise sets out in broad terms what a customer can expect from the organisation and its staff. It is frequently a single sentence or a couple of sentences, such as the three tour operator examples that follow.

2 Thomson's Disneyland Paris Brochure

'At Thomson we want to ensure that you will get the most out of your holiday to Disneyland, Paris Resort. For this reason we endeavour to offer you the widest possible choice of hotels and travel options and we will try our very best to make your holiday run smoothly.'

1 TUI

'The world of TUI is as individual as you are and we go out of our way to cater for your individual needs. From the moment you pick up a brochure, to arriving at your chosen resort, you'll experience true quality, friendly service and a passion for holidays.'

3 Neilson

'We are completely committed to your safety, enjoyment and development. We will only make recommendations and suggest holiday options that suit your needs and not ours.'

a c t i v i t y

COMPARING CUSTOMER PROMISES

Each of the customer promises above has a different focus – this will be based on what the organisation sees as being important to the customer. In pairs, compare the three customer promises, and discuss why you think they vary.

Customer service charter

Whereas a customer promise provides a general idea, a customer service charter provides more detailed information on the aspects of service that are given a high priority. The example from Virgin Trains below is typical of the type of customer charter that many rail operators issue.

Virgin Trains Passenger's Charter

Any passenger purchasing a ticket for use on services operated by Virgin Trains should enjoy:

- a reliable and punctual journey
- clean and safe trains and stations
- a Customer Service team member onboard each train to be available to provide help if required
- a refreshment service on most trains
- a seat if reserved in advance

Some organisations include considerably more detail in their charters, and may specify measurable standards, such as this example from Allerdale Council:

Customer Service Charter

We want to give the best service we can to anyone who needs our help.

Our commitment to you!

- We will treat you with courtesy and respect.
- We will try not to keep you waiting.
- We will try to answer your query as best we can. If we cannot do this, we will pass you on to someone who can or get back to you.
- We will take responsibility when dealing with your request, making sure we do whatever is necessary.
- We will ensure services are as accessible as possible and consider individual circumstances/special needs, e.g. young and older people.
- We will give you choices about how and when to contact us.
- We will look for ways to improve services and will learn from comments and complaints.

When you contact us by telephone

- We will answer your call within 5 rings.
- We will ring you back if you ask us to.
- We will give you our name and if you need to contact us again, our direct telephone number and/or email address.

When you contact us in writing/by e-mail

- We will give you a meaningful response in 10 working days to letters.
- We will give you a meaningful response in 5 working days to emails.
- We will let you know when a full response can be provided if we cannot respond in this timescale.
- We will reply in plain English.

Source: www. allerdale.gov.uk

Codes of conduct

A code of conduct sets specific minimum standards of service that the organisation guarantees to achieve. Frequently, codes of conduct are set by regulatory bodies such as ABTA, and members are expected to abide by them. The extract overleaf shows the ABTA standards for information that must be given to customers making travel arrangements with an ABTA member.

Appendix 1, Clause 1.5

Details to be given to Clients before a contract is made if relevant to the particular Travel Arrangements.

1   The travel destination(s) and, where periods of stay are involved, the relevant periods, with dates.
2   The means, characteristics and categories of transport to be used and the dates, times and points of departure and return.
3   Where the Travel Arrangements include accommodation, its location, its tourist category or degree of comfort.
4   The meals which are included in the Travel Arrangements.
5   The itinerary.
6   Visits, excursions or other services which are included in the total price of the Travel Arrangements.
7   The name and address of the Principal, the Travel Agent and, where appropriate, the insurer.
8   The price of the Travel Arrangements, if the price may be revised in accordance with any contract term, an indication of the possibility of such price revisions and an indication of any dues taxes or fees chargeable for certain services where such costs are not included in the price of the Travel Arrangements.
9   The payment schedule and method of payment.
10 Special requirements which the consumer has communicated to the Principal or Travel Agent when making the booking and which both have accepted.
11 The possibility of the consumer cancelling or amending the booking and the method of so doing and the costs involved to the consumer.

Source: www. abtanet.com

Codes of conduct can be very detailed, as this example from ABTA shows.

activity

FINDING MORE EXAMPLES

In pairs see if you can find three examples of customer promises, charters or codes of conduct in travel and tourism organisations. Brochures, the internet and personal visits to organisations are all good sources of information.

Mystery shoppers

An increasingly common method of evaluating customer service is to use a 'mystery customer'. This is someone employed by the organisation, but not known by the staff, who visits the facility as a customer and analyses the extent to which service levels meet quality criteria. The mystery customer will usually have a checklist covering what needs to be looked at.

activity

PLAN A MYSTERY VISIT

Design your own 'mystery shopper' checklist for a travel or tourism facility in your area, and visit the organisation to carry out the mystery visit. Compare your findings with the rest of the group.

Observations

Many travel and tourism organisations realise the value of informal feedback from their staff observing customer behaviour or comments. All staff in travel and tourism organisations will receive informal feedback on a daily basis. They may overhear customers talking or customers may voice their opinions directly to staff.

Alternatively, feedback may be from other staff, management or even people who are not customers but voice an opinion about the products and services offered. For example, someone passing by a tourist attraction may comment on how untidy the outside is looking and how the plants need watering.

This type of informal feedback is very important to organisations in helping them to monitor and evaluate the service that they offer. Many customers feel more comfortable making informal comments and may not have the time or inclination to complete formal questionnaires. Of course, informal feedback can also be positive, and it is just as important to listen to this. Positive feedback tells an organisation what it is doing right and allows them to develop these areas to continue to satisfy customers' needs and expectations.

Surveys

Many travel and tourism organisations use formal feedback methods such as surveys and customer comment cards. If you have already studied the marketing unit you will have a good understanding of how questionnaires are designed and used. Questionnaires are very useful in terms of highlighting where any particular problems may be developing – or identifying a particular customer who is dissatisfied. Many organisations include questions on their customer service as part of a general customer questionnaire, such as the example above.

Center Parcs adds up the scores from their customer questionnaires every month, and the staff in the facility (i.e. restaurant, shops, sporting venues, etc) with the highest score receive an award. This system is a good incentive for staff to provide excellent service – although it has created a tendency for staff to constantly remind guests – 'Don't forget to give us two stars if you were happy with our service'!

Focus groups

A focus group is when a group of people is assembled by an organisation to discuss their opinions and feelings about one of their particular products or services or about a more general topic. It has the great advantage that the information collected is very detailed because customers can explain their feelings and opinions in depth. For example, a travel agency may hold a focus group discussion to identify how customers view the customer service that they get when choosing a package holiday.

Focus groups can produce detailed information about customers' views.

Measuring customer service: comparing methods

Method	Advantages	Disadvantages
Mystery customers	• Gives a realistic evaluation of customer service, as the staff are unaware that they are being assessed. • Is objective because the mystery customer has no personal interest in each outlet. • Allows the organisation to benchmark different outlets against specific quality criteria. • Can be motivating for outlets that perform well.	• Can be costly since the mystery customer will receive a salary as well as travel costs and the actual products and services experienced. • Can have a demotivating effect on staff who feel that they are being 'spied on'.
Observations	• Useful for assessing customer experience and behaviour. • Often effective for staff to visit other outlets in the organisation to observe the customer experience.	• Is largely subjective, and relies on good communication within the organisation. • Staff may only report back positive comments because they do not want to be criticised.
Surveys	• An effective way of acquiring quantitative data (i.e. facts and figures). • Is generally objective and can use quality criteria to benchmark and measure performance. • Is quick, easy and relatively cheap to implement.	• Many customers may not complete a survey. • Research shows that dissatisfied customers are more likely to complete a survey than satisfied customers.
Focus groups	• Provides in-depth information about customers' perceptions of the service provided. • Can be targeted to assess particular issues, such as complaint handling, promotional materials, etc.	• Can be very expensive as it is time-consuming and needs to be carried out by someone trained in research techniques (often a psychologist). • The information collected is only based on a small number of people, who may not be representative of all customers.

Topic 9 Methods of measuring customer service

Quality criteria for customer service

When measuring and monitoring customer service, most organisations have specific criteria that help them to judge the effectiveness of their service. In the last topic we looked at customer charters and codes of conduct – and this is often an effective way of evaluating whether or not standards are being met. In this topic we are going to explore:

■ Benchmarking

■ Quality criteria

■ The ways in which customer service is evaluated and improved.

Benchmarking

Many travel and tourism organisations use a system of monitoring and evaluation known as 'benchmarking'. This involves the setting of quality criteria (standards) and then measuring the organisation's performance against those standards. For example, a holiday booking service may set as a benchmark that all customers will receive a brochure the next day. Sometimes the benchmarks will be set according to standards offered by competitors. Rank Xerox define benchmarking as:

'The continuing process of measuring products, services and practices against the toughest competition of those recognised as leaders'.

Quality criteria

Different travel and tourism organisations will identify different quality criteria that are important for their particular products and services. For example, providing personal attention to individual needs would be one of the main criteria for an exclusive

5-star hotel, whereas providing value for money to groups may be one of the main criteria for a theme park.

Many travel and tourism organisations evaluate and monitor the quality of their customer service by using quality criteria identified by independent organisations. For example, smaller hotel companies may rely on organisations such as the AA, RAC, English Tourist Board, Egon Ronay, Relais Routiers, etc. to help them evaluate the service that they offer.

When using a benchmarking system, the first stage is to identify the most important aspects of service delivery. These will vary, depending on the type of organisation and the nature of the product and service being offered. Typical quality criteria that may be identified as important include:

• Health and safety

• Speed of service

• Availability of product

• Products and services offered

• Information and individual needs.

Health and safety

Health and safety issues are one of the key concerns for all travel and tourism organisations. In fact, failure to comply with health and safety requirements can result in an organisation not being allowed to operate. Most health and safety standards are set by legal requirements. Health and safety regulations have a varying impact on travel and tourism organisations, depending on the type of service and facility provided. For example, COSHH (Control of Substances Hazardous to Health) regulations have a greater significance for hotel swimming pools than for art galleries. However, all organisations must comply with the Health and Safety at Work Act 1974 which covers four main areas:

- the health, safety and welfare of people at work
- the protection of outsiders from risks to health and safety
- the controlled storage and use of dangerous substances
- the controlled emission of noxious or offensive substances.

Apart from complying with legal requirements, many travel and tourism organisations will also make it part of their customer service standards to provide customers with general health and safety advice. For example, tour operators know that the first few days of many customers' holidays are spoilt by spending too long in the sun – and ending up with sunburn or even sunstroke. Therefore, many resort representatives will give general advice about 'safety in the sun' at the welcome party.

Because travel and tourism is an international industry, many providers have to consider the implications of health and safety in foreign countries. For example in some countries child seats are not provided in rental cars whereas in the UK they are standard. Likewise, regulations regarding lifts and balconies in hotels are considerably less strict in some countries than in the UK. Whilst tour operators are not always directly responsible if accidents occur due to these differences (although under new EU law they have additional legal responsibilities), most try to ensure that their customers are aware of the potential risks.

activity

QUALITY CRITERIA BRAINSTORM

In small groups, brainstorm the key health and safety quality criteria that a tour operator might have for package holiday customers in a resort.

Speed of service

Speed of service is frequently one of the key quality criteria set by travel and tourism organisations. For example theme parks strive to minimise the length of time that customers have to queue for rides. Delays in service delivery are one of the most common complaints in the travel and tourism industry – particularly in areas such as transport and package holidays. However, it should be remembered that there is a difference between prompt delivery of a service and rushing the customer so that they do not enjoy the experience. For example, the travel agency customer hoping to find the perfect holiday does not want to feel that the consultant is rushing them in order to move on to the next customer.

Availability of product

Making it easy and straightforward for a customer to buy a product or service is also an important quality criterion. An art gallery will quickly lose customers if it is not open at the times specified, and it will be inaccessible to some customers if people in wheelchairs are unable to get through the turnstile. Similarly, accessibility can be affected by the provision of car parking.

The timing of a service also affects its accessibility. The success of Sunday trading, allowing shops to open on a Sunday, is an example of how a service has been made available to meet customer needs. Some travel and tourism organisations offer different prices to increase availability. For example a tourist attraction such as a theme park – which offers an experience that usually lasts several hours – may have a reduced admission charge in the late afternoon to encourage customers to experience part of the service.

Products and services offered

The reliability and consistency of products and services offered are perhaps two of the most important quality criteria, because they influence all of the others. They mean that customers can rely on the service being the same every time they use it. Therefore they can be confident that it will provide value for money, be enjoyable and ensure excellent staffing levels, health and safety, etc. For example, customers who use the same tour operator every year will probably do so because they know that they can rely on the organisation to maintain past standards of service. These might include:

- the accuracy of brochure descriptions
- the friendliness and efficiency of the staff
- the value for money
- the pre-holiday information
- the quality of in-flight service.

The actual 'qualities' that staff possess is also an important quality criteria in terms of service, and it is important to identify the specific aspects of dress, personal hygiene, personality and attitude as well as skills needed by staff in a particular job. Of course, this will vary enormously according to the type of organisation and the actual job.

activity

FIVE QUALITY CRITERIA

Write five quality criteria that you think might be used for travel agency staff.

Any quality standards will only be as good as the minimum that is offered. If a member of staff is usually friendly and welcoming but on a bad day is offhand and disinterested, then it is the bad day that sets the standard. This is because the member of staff cannot guarantee to be friendly and welcoming on each and every occasion. When setting quality criteria for staff, it is vital that they will always be able to live up to the standard.

Open-top-bus tours should be able to meet the needs of individuals as well as whole groups.

Information and individual needs

When setting standards for the provision of information it is important that all such information is accurate. 'Accuracy' means that the customer is given correct information about the products and services offered. So, for example, customers want accurate information on train timetables, with the trains departing at the published time.

One of the criticisms often directed at organisations that have well-defined quality standards is that it makes the service too inflexible and unable to meet the individual needs of customers. Fortunately, this is becoming less frequent, as organisations realise that quality standards are only effective if they truly satisfy the needs of all customers.

In assessing the quality of the customer service, therefore, the needs of individual customers must be considered. Generally this may be a matter of identifying the general needs of customers and then asking the question 'But what if one customer wants something different'. For example, a company running open-top-bus guided tours of an historic city may identify the general needs of customers as requiring friendly service, detailed and expert information, comfortable transport and value for money. But individual needs should also be identified, by asking such questions as 'But what if the customer:

- cannot speak English?
- is elderly?
- is in a wheelchair?
- is a child?
- wants extra information?

Ways in which customer service is evaluated and improved

An evaluation of customer service focuses on the extent to which the service provided meets the quality criteria and therefore the customers' expectations.

In essence, then, an evaluation of customer service seeks to ensure that the level of customer service is meeting the quality criteria, and that these quality criteria are, in turn, satisfying customer expectations. Some organisations use a mathematical process in their evaluation. The total scores are added up from each mystery customer checklist, with a minimum score being set as acceptable. Likewise many tour operators produce overall statistics and comparisons with other companies. The example below, taken from an Airtours brochure, shows how a company's evaluation of customer service satisfaction can be used for promotional purposes.

Other organisations use a comparison of the levels of complaints as one method of evaluation. For example, an increase in the number of complaints about a certain aspect of service – such as provision of information – would signify a problem.

Finally, having monitored and evaluated the level of customer service, an organisation will be in a position to make recommendations as to how the service could be improved. Remember that this is not always a negative process – i.e. putting right the mistakes. Sometimes it may be a question of identifying what the organisation does really well and doing it even better.

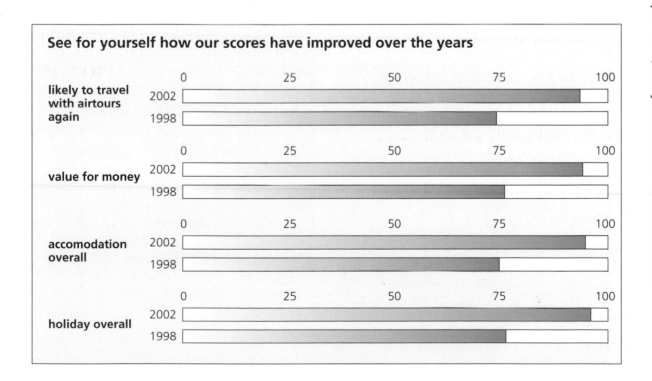

See for yourself how our scores have improved over the years

How Unit 2 is assessed

Unit 2 is assessed by coursework. The evidence should be in four parts, which we suggest you present as four sections within a portfolio. The following guidance outlines how you can achieve the assessment requirements for each of the four parts.

The evidence could be in many different forms to allow for your learning preferences, styles and strengths to be accommodated. Some of the evidence will be in the form of observation statements or witness testimonies with supporting documentation. There may also be written reports, completed documentation and data.

Task (a) How organisations meet customers' needs

(a.1) Customers' needs

Describe the needs of customers in one sector of the travel and tourism industry.

(a.2) Meeting those needs

Explain how organisations in that sector attempt to meet those needs. (Examples might include: late night openings, telephone bookings, late check-in, translation services, car pick up and drop off, online services.)

Task (b) Demonstrating your own customer service skills

Provide evidence of your involvement with customers in **four** real or simulated travel and tourism-related situations, demonstrating your own customer service skills by dealing with customers in different situations, including a complaint and completing relevant documentation.

(b.0) Introduction

Explain where your evidence has come from, e.g. role plays, work placement or part-time job.

(b.1) Different situations

For each situation (including the complaint), describe the type of customer that you dealt with and what their specific needs were.

(b.2) Customer service skills

Describe how you effectively used customer service skills in each situation. (These might include: initiative, problem solving, positive attitude, questioning, listening, responding to customers, providing information, etc.)

(b.3) Documentation

Explain how you completed the appropriate documentation, using Information Communication Technology, as appropriate.

(b.4) Evaluation

Evaluate the extent to which you were able to provide acceptable customer service and make recommendations as to how your performance could be improved in future.

NOTE: Your evidence for this section should be supported by signed witness statements that verify that you provided the customer service that you describe.

To achieve the higher mark bands the situations need to be more complex (a number of factors have to be considered at once and you will probably be working under pressure) and the complaint will be dealt with more fully.

Task (c) Research the standard of customer service within a travel and tourism organisation

(c.0) Introduction

Give a brief overview of the organisation to be researched.

(c.1) Method

Explain why the process of being a 'mystery customer' is an appropriate and effective way of evaluating customer service within a travel and tourism organisation. Explain how and where you undertook your mystery customer visit.

(c.2) Documentation

Describe the documentation that you used when carrying out the mystery visit. Examples should be presented in the appendices.

(c.3) Quality criteria

Explain what quality criteria you used to evaluate the organisation and why you thought these criteria were important. (Examples might include: health and safety, speed of service, availability of service, products and services provided, information and other needs met.)

NOTE: In this section, to achieve the higher mark bands you will need to use relevant and realistic quality criteria and justify why you have selected them.

Task (d) Evaluation and recommendations for improvements

(d.1) Evaluation

Using the results from your research of a travel and tourism organisation, evaluate the levels of customer service against the quality criteria that you identified.

(d.2) Recommendations

Based on your evaluation, make recommendations as to how your chosen organisation could improve the customer service that it offers.

NOTE: To achieve the higher mark bands your evaluation should be linked to benchmarked standards and cover a wide range of quality criteria appropriate to the selected organisation. Your recommendations should be realistic and justified.

Bibliography

List all of the sources of information that you have used to complete the assessment for this unit.

Appendices

Include any relevant supporting information in the appendices, such as examples of witness statements, organisational policies and procedures, mystery visit checklist, etc.

Improving your grades

Generally, you will get better grades by giving more comprehensive explanations, including better examples and showing a deeper understanding of each topic. Your school or college should be able to advise you in more detail, or you could visit the Edexcel website: edexcel.org.uk for more guidance.

General guidelines on presentation of assignments

See page 289 for advice on how to present your assignments.

How Unit 2 is assessed

Destination Europe investigates the most popular destinations in Europe (excluding the UK) for leisure and business travellers. Europe is growing in appeal as a tourist destination – nearly 400 million foreign tourists visited Europe in 2000. Of these, 190 million went to south-western Europe – an increase of 91% since 1985. The World Tourism Organisation expects this growth to continue, with an annual increase of more than 3% up to 2020. The three most visited countries in the world are France, Spain and Italy and this is unlikely to change over the next 10 years. However, the biggest growth areas are forecast to be central and eastern Europe, Poland, the Czech Republic, Hungary and Turkey.

This unit will develop your skills in identifying what gives destinations their appeal and you will learn how to categorise and locate them on a map. You will investigate the features making individual destinations attractive to specific groups of travellers. This unit also examines the major transport links between tourist generating and tourist receiving areas and their suitability for particular groups of travellers. In addition you will learn about the factors that have affected the popularity of destinations and how some are controllable and some uncontrollable.

Europe today is vastly different to the Europe of twenty years ago. Today, of the 45 countries in Europe, 25 are now in the European Union. Enlargement of the European Union is expected to unite the continent after generations of division and conflict. It should extend prosperity to a wider group of countries, and consolidate the political and social divides that have taken place in central and eastern Europe since 1989. The impact of enlargement is immense on the travel and tourism industry as so many more places become accessible as destinations. One example featured in this unit is Tallin, the capital of Estonia.

Unit 3

Destination Europe

3.1 Location and types of tourist destination

Topic 1 Coastal, city and business destinations	106
Topic 2 Country, cultural and purpose-built destinations	110

3.2 The features and appeal of destinations to different types of tourist

Topic 3 Features: climate, landscape and transport	114
Topic 4 Features: accommodation, facilities, attractions	120
Topic 5 Features: events, costs and local culture	124

3.3 Modes of transport and routes available to European travel destinations

Topic 6 Transport gateways	128
Topic 7 Rail links, roads and motorways	132
Topic 8 Transport: factors affecting choice	137

3.4 Factors affecting the popularity and appeal of European travel destinations

Topic 9 Accessibility, image and attractions	142
Topic 10 Destination management, costs and political factors	146
How Unit 3 is assessed	150

Coastal, city and business destinations

Before we start on the first topic, it is important that you have familiarised yourself with the location and geography of Europe. This is because you will only be able to fully understand the types of tourist destination if you can identify where they are situated. Tourist destinations can be broadly categorised under six types, though not all can be easily categorized and many overlap. In this first topic, we will explore:

■ **Coastal areas**

■ **Tourist towns and cities**

■ **Business and conference destinations.**

Location and geography

The best way to learn about the location of Europe is to study a map. Europe is located north of Africa and to the north west of Asia. It is surrounded on three sides by water, and borders the Asian continent on the east. Over 800 million people live here and the total land area is 4,809,200 square miles (12,456,000 square kilometres).

Europe is made up of a variety of different geographical regions. Most of us define a country by its borders. Sometimes these are physical features – mountains, lakes, rivers and seas, whilst sometimes they are decided by people, and may be signified by just a border crossing. Countries in Europe range from the landlocked states with no access to the sea, such as Switzerland, to those that are completely surrounded by sea, such as Britain. Some are dominated by high mountain ranges, such as Norway, others are split by long rivers that cross many countries in their path, such as the Rhine which starts its journey in Switzerland and meanders its way through France, Germany and then Belgium before joining the North Sea.

Coastal areas

The coast is mainly defined by the geography and climate of the location. The coastlines of Europe range from the deep mountainous fjords of Norway, to the large wide sandy beaches on the Atlantic Coast of France and Spain, to the small sandy coves found on many of the islands in the Mediterranean.

GETTING TO KNOW THE GEOGRAPHY

1 Check your understanding of Europe by looking at a map and locating in which country the following capital cities are situated:

   Helsinki, Vienna, Brussels, Sarajevo, Tallinn, Berlin, Luxembourg, Budapest, Reykjavik, Oslo, Madrid, Amsterdam, Bern, Lisbon, Stockholm, Warsaw.

2 If you were making the following journeys, by a direct route each time, which countries would you be going through?
   • London → Sofia
   • Oslo → Rome
   • Paris → Moscow
   • Athens → Copenhagen
   • Lisbon → Helsinki
   • Tallin → Bucharest

3 Use a map to find the location of the following coastal resort areas: Brittany, Costa Brava, Costa Del sol, Black Sea Riviera, Algarve, Adriatic Riviera, Norwegian Fjords.

4 Use a map to find the location of the following islands: Ibiza, Corfu, Rhodes, Malta.

Some coastal areas have been developed into beach resorts – the traditional 'sun, sea and sand' destinations so popular with European holidaymakers.

Spain is the most popular destination in Europe for British holidaymakers, most of whom head for its coastal areas and islands (see below).

Spanish coastal resorts – they're not all the same

Spain may be flanked to the north-east by the Pyrenees and to the west by Portugal, but most of the country is ringed with sand, rock, and sea water. That, coupled with almost year-round sunshine, has attracted many millions of beachgoers. But that doesn't mean that all the Spanish coastal areas are the same.

Costa del Sol

Stretching east from Gibraltar along the southernmost coast of Spain, the Costa del Sol (coast of the sun) is the most famous, 'party-hearty', and overdeveloped string of beaches in the Mediterranean. The beaches feature superb sand, and the sea is calm and warm throughout most of the year. But these charms have brought throngs of visitors, making these the most congested coastal resorts in Europe. The most important resorts here are Marbella, Torremolinos, Málaga, and Nerja, with their soaring skyscrapers, lots of sunshine, eye-popping bikinis, energetic nightlife – and interminable traffic jams.

Costa Verde

Radically different from the dry and sunbaked coastline of the Costa del Sol, the rocky Costa Verde (green coast) resembles a sunny version of Ireland's western shore. Being on Spain's northern coast, part of the Atlantic's Bay of Biscay, it's temperate in summer, when the rest of Spain can be unbearably hot. Much of the coast is within the ancient province of Asturias, a region rife with Romanesque architecture and medieval pilgrimage sites – and one that has not yet been overwhelmed with tourism. Premier resorts include some districts of Santander, Gijón, and, a short distance inland, Oviedo, the capital of Asturias.

The Balearic Islands

Just off the coast of Catalonia and a 45-minute flight from Barcelona, this rocky, sand-fringed Mediterranean archipelago attracts urban refugees seeking the sun, jet-set glitterati, and exhibitionists in scanty beachwear. The climate is even warmer here than on the mainland. The city of Palma de Majorca has the greatest number of high-rises and the most crowded shorelines. Much of Ibiza is party central for young people and gay visitors during the summer. Sleepy Minorca offers more isolation.

Source (adapted): www.in-spain.info

activity

WHICH COAST?

The following groups of people are looking to holiday in Spain this year. Which coastal areas would you recommend each to visit? Explain your reasons.

1 Daniel and his girlfriend are looking to have a really fun week, partying and sunning themselves.

2 The Strong family are keen walkers and want to enjoy a holiday in the great outdoors. They do not like very hot weather and want to enjoy the coast and its surrounding area to the full. Mrs Strong is particularly interested in culture.

3 Edward Simcox, his wife and two teenage children, look forward to a traditional hot summer holiday with lots of food and drink and plenty for the children to do on the beach.

Tourist towns and cities

Towns and cities have always been an attraction for the tourist, and Europe has hundreds to choose from. There are 36 cities with populations of more than one million, and the ten largest are shown below.

It is not the *size* of the city that attracts the tourists but the sights and attractions that are within it.

As well as cities there are many towns and villages throughout Europe that cater for the tourist. In some

Europe's Top Ten Largest Cities		
		Population
1 Moskva (Moscow)	Russia	8.3 million
2 London	UK	7.1 million
3 St Petersburg	Russia	4.7 million
4 Berlin	Germany	3.4 million
5 Madrid	Spain	2.8 million
6 Roma (Rome)	Italy	2.6 million
7 Kiev	Ukraine	2.6 million
8 Paris	France	2.2 million
9 Bucuresti (Bucharest)	Romania	2.0 million
10 Budapest	Hungary	1.8 million

Source: UN 2003 statistics

Topic 1 Coastal, city and business destinations

- France has the lowest number of large-city dwellers – just over 10%.

- Russia has one of the highest figures – almost 42%. Other former Soviet Union countries have similar high figures – Belarus, 40%, and Ukraine, 37%, for example.

- Statistics show that 51 per cent of Britons live in towns and cities with more than 150,000 inhabitants, but this figure is probably distorted because some smaller towns have been administratively amalgamated with their surrounding rural districts.

- Russia boasts 116 cities with more than 150,000 residents.

- Germany has 51 cities with more than 150,000 residents.

- France is a large country with relatively few large cities – only 16 above 150,000 people.

places the tourist may be a major source of income for a city or town, which is therefore reliant on the visitors. This is certainly true of the many small towns and villages in the Alps that host the skiers each winter, and the Mediterranean coastal resorts that rely on summer tourism.

The European Parliament building in Brussels. The EU administrative offices make both Brussels and Strasbourg significant travel centres.

activity

TOWNS AND CITIES

Select a country in Europe and research the following:

- The capital city
- Any other large towns or cities
- At least five smaller towns that have appeal to the tourist.

Research a little about each place and present your findings as a poster. Make recommendations as to why each destination would appeal to tourists. This may be done as a group with each member of the group investigating a different country. Your findings may then be used as a display.

Business and conference destinations

In some cities, a large proportion of the visitors are not holidaymakers but business travellers, who have come because the cities are major business or administrative centres.

European business traveller facts

- Business travellers account for over half of the client base of European hotels.

- The top four European economies – Germany, the UK, France and Italy – account for 63% of total business spending.

- Germany alone accounts for 20 per cent of the total, and is the world's number one in terms of attendance at trade fairs and exhibitions.

- Spain, meanwhile, has rocketed to the number two position for international meetings.

- Barcelona has become the number one city in the world for the business traveller.

Source: Mintel International Group, December 2003

Business travellers demand accommodation, food, places to entertain, functions rooms and various transport and communication facilities. The impact for the destination can be immense, and provide a large amount of lucrative income in addition to any regular tourist trade.

It is hardly surprising that a number of European cities are keen to attract business travellers as they guarantee business during the weekdays and at off-season times. For example, the main conference market is January to May, when holidaymakers tend to make least trips. The fact that business is conducted during the week is often reflected in the price of accommodation, which is generally higher on weekdays as compared to weekends.

According to Mintel, the outlook for the business market is looking healthy. Total spending on business travel and tourism in Europe is projected to increase by 73 per cent over the next ten years, with eastern European economies experiencing the highest growth rates.

WHY GO TO BARCELONA?

Read the information below on Barcelona, and identify the facilities it offers to a UK business traveller and why its location is important.

Barcelona's World Trade Centre

Barcelona for business

In business terms Barcelona is on the up and up. Over the last decade the city has fully utilised its potential as the gateway between Iberia and the rest of western Europe, a theme that Barcelona is pushing more than ever in the new millennium. The city has a strong background in manufacturing based on textiles and the large motor industry, and although it has a stock market it has failed to emerge as a major financial or banking centre to rival Madrid. It is, however, the country's major convention centre with impressive facilities like The Catalan Conference Centre and the state-of-the-art World Trade Centre at Port Vell (pictured).

The coming of the Olympic Games in 1992 was a pivotal event in business terms as it provided the impetus and investment necessary to improve the infrastructure of the city through $8 billion of investment. The Games' massive marketing project successfully promoted the city as an efficient, business-like centre and initiated a massive surge of investment in the hotel and tourism sector. The number of tourists visiting the city rose from 1.7 million in 1990 to over 3 million in 1999. About 50% of all foreign visitors are there on business.

The business community in Barcelona is used to hosting foreign visitors and many international business people speak English or French.

Country, cultural and purpose-built destinations

Having looked at coastal areas, tourist cities and business destinations, we continue our study of location and types of destinations by investigating, in this topic:

- **countryside areas**
- **historical and cultural destinations**
- **purpose-built resorts.**

Countryside areas

Countryside areas across Europe vary from the heavily forested areas of Scandinavia to the vast dry plains of inland Spain. Each area has its own appeal to the tourist. Some attract bountiful natural wildlife whilst others provide breath-taking scenery.

The Italian lakes, Swiss alps and the Pyrenees are some of the popular tourist areas visited for their appealing countryside.

'Europarc' is the umbrella organisation of Europe's protected areas. It unites national parks, regional parks, nature parks and biosphere reserves in 37 countries, with the common aim of protecting Europe's unique variety of wildlife, habitats and landscapes.

Europarc was founded in 1973, under the official title 'Federation of Nature and National Parks of Europe', and has since grown to become the recognised, professional organisation for European protected areas. An independent, non-governmental organisation, its membership brings together the organisations responsible for the management of over 400 protected areas, including national parks.

activity

APPEALING COUNTRYSIDE

Research a countryside area and explain the features that make it appealing to tourists.

Heritage and cultural destinations

One of the biggest appeals to the tourist is the vast number of heritage and cultural destinations located right across Europe.

'Heritage' means that a place has inherited (and still shows) the benefits of history or past events.

'Cultural' means that a place helps visitors appreciate and understand the customs and civilisation of a society, including their literature, art, music, etc.

It was Europe's overwhelming number of cultural centres that led to the 'European City of Culture' programme, as described below.

European City of Culture

The 'European City of Culture' programme was the result of an initiative by the Greek Minister of Culture, Melina Mercouri (the former world-famous actress). In 1983 she invited culture ministers to Athens and presented them with a project for promoting awareness of European cultures within the EC member states. She argued that the voices of artists should be heard as loudly as those of politicians, and as a result of her efforts the European City of Culture programme was launched just two years later, with Athens being the first title-holder.

At first, the member states worked together to select one city per year to be City of Culture, which then received a grant from the European Commission.

The start of the new millennium, however, represented a special case, and it was decided to award the title to nine cities in 2000, as a gesture of European unity.

As from 2005, the European City of Culture has been renamed the Cultural Capital of Europe, and now individual EU member states, in rotation, suggest one or more of their cities as Cultural Capitals, at least four years in advance of their allocated year.

Luxembourg, Cultural Capital of Europe, 2007.

CENTER PARCS – ALL OVER NORTHERN EUROPE

Center Parcs' villages are situated in France (including Brittany and Normandy), Belgium, Holland and Germany. Every holiday village features an 'aqua mundo' or 'sub-tropical swimming pool', with a host of waterslides, wavepools, whirlpools and a children's section, together with sauna and sunbed facilities – all set amidst the lush tropical surroundings which have become the trademark of Center Parcs.

Children of all ages are welcomed – the traffic-free environment is a safe haven for children to play in, and the 'Kids Klub', the children's farm, the playgrounds and the entertainment help to keep all amused.

The accommodation is in spacious cottages with an open-plan living/dining area, fireplace & TV, fully equipped kitchenette with microwave and four-ring hob, central heating, bathroom with bath and/or shower, terrace/patio, child cot, high chair and play pen. An upgrade to the deluxe cottage features a private sauna, turkish bath and/or shower, Hi-Fi/CD player and a daily continental breakfast delivery, with newspaper.

Each Center Parc village features a unique 'market dome' village with an indoor or outdoor square. Here you'll discover an array of shops including a bakery, foodstore, clothes shop, toy/souvenir shop, and a selection of cafes and bars with live entertainment.

Case study: Les Bois-Francs Center Parcs, France

3-night prices: from £75 per person
4-night prices: from £98 per person
7-night prices: from £142 per person

(Price based on 6 people sharing a Comfort Cottage on selected low-season dates, including mid-week off-peak P&O Dover to Calais crossing for one car plus passengers.)

Boasting its own elegant 19th-century chateau and 9-hole golf course, Les Bois-Francs lies at the heart of a country estate in a picturesque area of Normandy, surrounded by gently rolling hills and apple orchards. There is plenty for the children to do, with an Adventure Island, an animal farm, riding school and pony trekking. The golfing school gives lessons to adults and children of all abilities, whilst the action-packed Forest of Adventure offers aerial excitement with rope ladders, pulleys and footbridges. The Jardin des Sports provides a wide variety of sporting activities and you can pamper yourself at the Aqua Sana with its health and beauty treatments. In the Aqua Mundo you'll find an oasis of fun with waterslides, rapids, wavepool, jacuzzi and salt-water pool.

Facilities available at Les Bois-Francs: massage, tennis, aerobics, pitch & putt, wild water rafting, Adventure Island, animal farm, riding school, pony trekking, fishing and table tennis.

Local attractions: Monet's gardens at Giverny, Chartres Cathederal, Paris (75 miles), Parc Asterix, and Disneyland Resort, Paris.

Nearest ports: Dieppe (103 miles), Le Havre (108 miles), Cherbourg (158 miles), Calais (199 miles).

Source: www.clippersquaytravel.com

activity

JUST RIGHT FOR THE FAMILY?

Read the case study on the Les Bois-Francs Center Parcs in France and explain the features that would make it attractive to a family of two adults and four children from London. The children range in age from 4 to 14, and all are sporty, whilst the parents enjoy relaxing and sampling the local culture. Remember to consider the costs and choices of transport available to access the resort.

Purpose-built resorts

'Purpose-built', in this context, means built specifically to meet the needs of tourists. There has been a huge rise in the number of purpose-built resorts, with all their facilities on one site, designed to appeal to groups and families – where all the members want something different. Purpose-built resorts fall into three categories:

- Holiday complex, e.g. Center Parcs, Club Med
- Sport complex, e.g. golf and ski resorts
- Theme park resorts, e.g. Disneyland Paris, Alton Towers.

Holiday complex resorts are based on providing a wide variety of activities, restaurants, pubs and entertainment all on one site. Some, like Club Med, are located in the warmer Mediterranean climates, and base a lot of the activities and entertainment around their beach location. Others, such as Center Parcs, cope with the unpredictable weather by providing an enclosed central tropical swimming area for all-year-round use and a combination of outdoor and indoor activities. Center Parcs has 20 purpose-built sites across northern Europe (see previous page).

Sport complex facilities are mainly based around one sport. Purpose-built ski resorts, such as Avoriaz or Les Arcs in France, are built on mountain sites guaranteed to get snow for the majority of the ski season. There are many restaurants – and maybe some other entertainment facilities such as a swimming pool – but their primary function is to provide holidays for skiers. The same could be said for golf complexes. Vilamoura, in Spain, for example, is a purpose-built golf resort with access to five courses.

Some theme parks are purpose built and provide on-site accommodation, a host of attractions, shops and restaurants. The most famous theme park in Europe is Disneyland, Paris, 20 miles east of the French capital. Smaller theme parks, such as Alton Towers, provide a smaller version of Disneyland, with the main focus still being on the attractions – particularly the latest thrill rides.

activity

RESEARCHING PURPOSE-BUILT RESORTS

Gather information about one holiday complex, one sport complex, and one theme park. Then, for each, create a one-page fact sheet on their location, the main attractions available, the facilities, and the types of accommodation available.

activity

LOCATION AND TYPES OF DESTINATION

In the last two topics we have looked at the different location and types of tourist destination. Select a country in Europe and research the following features:

- Coastal areas
- Tourist towns and cities
- Business and conference destinations
- Countryside areas
- Heritage and cultural destinations
- Purpose-built resorts.

You should investigate countries right across Europe, including some newly emerging destinations. You may use information from a variety of sources – books, atlases, brochures, the internet – the more the better. Some areas may be difficult to categorise. You should explain what these areas are and what makes it difficult to categorise them.

Present your findings to the rest of the group. The presentation must be accompanied by a handout listing clearly the resources used.

Topic 2 Country, cultural and purpose-built destinations

Features: climate, landscape and transport

In the next three topics we will investigate the specific features that make certain destinations appeal to particular types of tourist. For example, hot beach holidays appeal to some people, whereas for others – such as a business traveller – it is the efficiency of the transport network and the communication networks offered by a location that are more important. This topic begins our look at the various features by considering:

- climate
- landscape
- transport and communication links.

Climate

Climate is the long-term average of weather conditions at a particular location. It is defined by three main factors:

- Latitude – the distance from the Equator
- The distribution of the land and sea areas
- Topography – the features of an area such as the mountains, plains, big cities, etc.

All of these factors affect the passage of airflows across Europe (see map opposite). Where the warm maritime air meets the cold continental air, depressions are created. It is the eastward movement of these depressions across Europe that has a significant effect on much of the climate.

In general there is a north–south variation in climate, with southerly areas being warmer than northern areas. In addition, there is an east–west variation, with places further east being drier, and experiencing greater temperature changes, compared with locations in the west.

Because the sea warms up and cools down much more slowly than the land, it tends to have a moderating influence on the climate of nearby land areas. In Europe, this influence is most marked in the north – beyond latitude 45°N – in Ireland, Britain and Scandinavia. During the summer the sea has a cooling effect on these places, but in the winter it keeps temperatures up. For example, Glasgow has a summer monthly average of 18°C and winter average of 3°C or 4°C, in contrast to a continental city such as Moscow which is hotter during the summer months – average 23°C – but much colder during the winter, when temperatures average –10°C.

Europe extends from latitude 71°N (northern Norway) right down to 35°N (Crete). This means that there are considerable variations in the amount and intensity of sunshine received in different parts of the continent. Annual sunshine varies from about 1000 hours in Iceland, to over 3400 hours in Portugal and South-east Spain. The amount of sunshine hours per day is often used in travel articles as an indication of the kind of weather to expect in different months of the year. But sometimes, it can get *too* hot (see case study opposite).

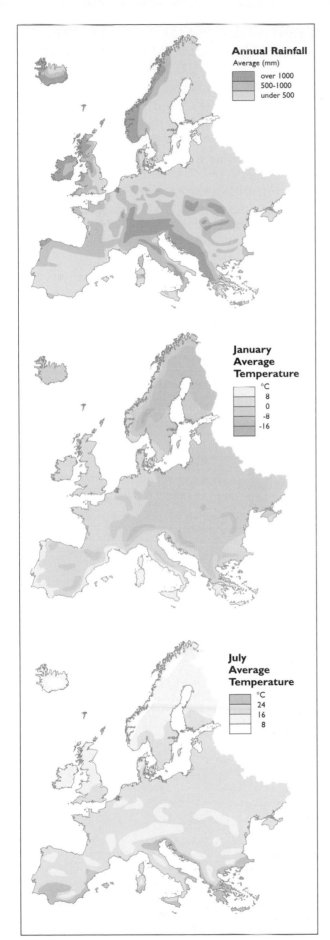

Annual Rainfall

Average (mm)

over 1000
500-1000
under 500

January
Average
Temperature

°C
8
0
-8
-16

July
Average
Temperature

°C
24
16
8

Dozens die in Balkan heatwave

A heatwave scorching the Balkan region this week has killed dozens of people. It has been blamed on hot air masses moving north from the Sahara Desert. In Croatian cities, some 40 people died of heart attacks caused by the heat, while hundreds more were hospitalised with serious health problems.

Greece is facing its hottest day of the year, with temperature expected to hit 44° C. Many Greeks have fled to the beaches for relief. The country also has to cope with power cuts and the threat of a strike by rubbish collectors. Two people have died from dehydration while dozens have been sent to hospitals.

The Bulgarian capital Sofia reported four deaths, and three people suffered heart attacks in northern Serbia, where one person who could not bear the high temperatures committed suicide. Croatia declared its north-eastern region – where the drought is expected to lower crop yields by 50 to 70% – a disaster zone.

Governments across the region have warned people to stay indoors. In Greece, the government has activated its Xenocrates emergency plan, which requires state buildings to provide air-conditioned spaces to the public.

Emergency services are on full alert and the authorities are watching out for forest fires. Meanwhile, public beaches are staying open late into the night.

Source: BBC News, July 2000

Rainfall levels are highest in western areas (because most of the rain-bearing winds come from the west) and over mountainous regions – because as the moist air rises over mountainous areas, it cools and tends to release its moisture, as rain (or snow). Annual rainfall varies from between 1000 and 2000 mm in the western coastal areas of the British Isles to less than 500mm in parts of Sweden, southern Spain, Greece and the Baltic States.

As we have seen, the European climate varies widely from place to place, and this provides the basis for a wide range of holiday choices. For example, for a summer holiday you can choose between mountain walking in the Scottish Highlands or cruising around the hot Mediterranean coastline. Winter activities range from skiing in the many highland areas of central Europe to catching the warmer weather on the coast of southern Spain.

Topic 3 Features: climate, landscape and transport

Landscape

The location and geographical features of the landscape such as mountains, lakes and coastlines affect the appeal of a tourist destination. Many mountainous areas of the world provide ideal tourist destinations as they provide scenic views and open countryside for many pursuits such as walking, climbing and skiing. For example, the lakes and mountains of Austria are popular tourist destinations. In the summer months many are attracted to the imposing mountains for walking holidays, whilst in winter these are transformed into a skier's paradise to provide some of Europe's leading ski resorts. The coastlines of Europe provide the most popular tourist locations in Europe – the beaches along the Mediterranean Sea.

activity

DIFFERENT CLIMATES, DIFFERENT HOLIDAYS

1 Examine the maps on the previous page, and explain the contrasts in temperature and rainfall between Helsinki, Dublin, Bucharest, Seville and Munich.

2 Identify which destination has the following features:
   - the wettest winter
   - the driest summer
   - the driest winter
   - the warmest winter
   - the coolest summer
   - the hottest summer.

3 Explain which location would have the most appeal to the following groups:
   - An elderly couple looking for a winter break
   - A family looking for a hot summer holiday
   - A group of tourists hoping to see the city sights.

4 Read the case study on the Balkan heatwave, and discuss who would be most affected by this type of weather.

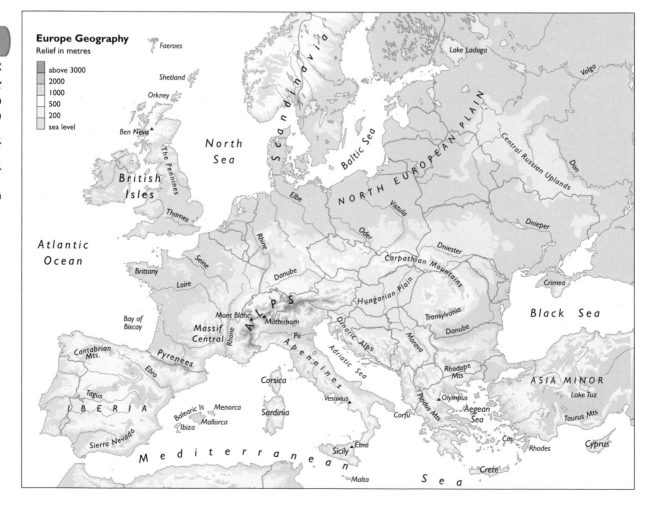

Europe Geography
Relief in metres

above 3000
2000
1000
500
200
sea level

FEATURES OF THE LANDSCAPE

1 Identify the location of the following features on the map opposite – mountains, rivers, and seas – and list six examples of each.

2 Obtain a map of one European country showing the landscape, and explain how this affects the appeal of the country as a travel and tourism destination.

The Millau Viaduct carries the French A75 motorway over the River Tarn, more than 1000 feet below.

Transport and communication links

The accessibility of a destination by various types of transport has a great effect on its appeal. For the business traveller, in particular, the efficiency of its communication services is also important. We will look at accessibility first – by road, sea, rail and air.

Roads

The European road network provides access for all types of vehicle right across Europe. In fact, many remote, rural places are *only* accessible by road, especially in high and rugged areas. For example, many popular European ski resorts are only accessible by road even if the traveller has chosen to fly to the nearest airport; which may be a two-hour bus or car journey away. The expansion of the motorways and autobahns has also made many areas accessible more quickly. Travelling by road in central Europe and through Germany, Belgium, France and Italy is now much easier than it used to be. Many cities in Europe now have major ring-roads circling them, reducing the traffic congestion, and allowing easier access for tourists.

Road building is to be an essential component in the development of eastern Europe. Currently the roads provide the main method of transport, as rail lines are limited and access by air restricted to the main towns and cities. But the roads are very basic, and in some places little more than tracks. One of the European Union's top priorities is to make the new eastern members more accessible by improving the transport network.

Seas and rivers

As most of Europe is surrounded by sea, many countries are still accessed by water. In fact, some are still dependent on water transport. For example, sea transport is very important in the Greek Islands, especially for those islands without an airport. Because of the high and rugged terrain along most of Norway's coastline, access to many of the inland Norwegian fjords is virtually impossible except by water. Similarly, it is access along the Rhine that has allowed for the development of the tourist trade in the Black Forest region of Germany.

High-speed trains, travelling at over 180 mph, make journey times across Europe much shorter.

Rail travel

The rail network across Europe effectively links the countries together. Special tickets, such as InterRail passes, provide access across the whole continent (see the activity opposite).

High-speed trains have really made an impact on the Mediterranean coastline as people living in northern Europe can access the coastline in half the time. For example the TGV from Paris to Marseille takes only 3 hours.

Air travel

In recent years the growth in low-cost airlines has meant many European cities have become accessible to more travellers. Places such as Palma, Naples, Venice, Madrid and Milan are now so much cheaper to fly to, as shown in the bmibaby advert. This has led to an increase in the number of people taking short breaks. It is now much easier to book a last-minute flight to a European city on Friday evening and be back at your desk for Monday morning.

Good transport links can make all the difference to whether a place attracts tourist development or not. For example, when Walt Disney was choosing where to site a Disney 'park' in Europe, the main contenders were southern Spain and Paris. In the end Paris won, and one of the main reasons was because it had access to 200 million Europeans within a four-hour travelling time. In terms of geographical location, southern Spain could not compete, even though it had a better climate.

Communication links

Once the traveller, especially the business traveller, arrives at a destination the methods of communication available (phone, email, etc.) become an important factor. The communication services, and prices, vary greatly from one country to another. If you are in a large city, such as Paris, London or Madrid then the communication services will be much better than if you are in a small town in an eastern European country. The services in eastern Europe, however, are improving dramatically, especially in the new EU members, which are looking to broaden their appeal to all types of traveller.

Business travellers, for whom good communications are essential, tend to go to the main cities for their meetings and conferences. Barcelona is the latest up-and-coming destination for business travellers, partly because of easier access with the introduction of low-cost flights but also because of the heavy investment in the city on the overall communications network.

500,000 seats at £25

Alicante	Madrid	Palma
Amsterdam	Milan	Edinburgh
Brussels	Nice	Naples
Venice	Dublin	and more

one way from Heathrow including taxes

winter fares
sale
book online by Tuesday

lowest fares at flybmi.com

bmi
A STAR ALLIANCE MEMBER

Unit 3 Destination Europe

GETTING THE RIGHT INTERRAIL PASS

InterRail, at www.interrail.net provides discounted rail travel, and is very popular with students travelling around Europe. However there are a number of rules; you must have been resident in a European country for at least six months to purchase one of these passes, and the pass cannot be used in that country. The passes are only for second-class travel, and you must pay a supplement on 'fast' trains such as the TGV and AVE (the Spanish bullet train). There are discounts ranging from 30 to 50 per cent on all ferry lines. You pay according to the number of zones you wish to travel through (see map).

Zones

Zone A
England
Scotland
Republic of Ireland
Northern Ireland
Wales

Zone B
Sweden
Norway
Finland

Zone C
Denmark
Germany
Switzerland
Austria
Liechtenstein

Zone D
Poland
Czech Republic
Slovakia
Hungary
Croatia
Bosnia-Herzégovina

Zone E
France
Belgium
Netherlands
Luxembourg
Andorra

Zone F
Spain
Portugal
Morocco

Zone G
Italy
Slovenia
Greece
Turkey

Zone H
Bulgaria
Yugoslavia
Macedonia
Romania

Fares

zones	Up to 25 years of age	26 and over
1 zone (16 days)	£159	£223
2 zones (22 days)	£215	£303
Global – all zones (1 month)	£295	£415

Source: www.interrail.net August 2004

Using the information given in the table above, discuss which ticket you would be best to purchase if you wanted to visit the following:

1 Six of the main cities in Europe. (Obviously, you first have to decide which these are.)
2 The main beaches in Europe. (Obviously, you first have to decide which these are.)
3 The Louvre, the Little Mermaid, the Sistine Chapel, the Ruhr.

119

Topic 3 Features: climate, landscape and transport

Features: accommodation, facilities, attractions

In the last topic we looked at the influence of climate, landscape and transport and communication links on the appeal of a destination. In this topic we will continue to look at the features affecting appeal, and focus on:

- Accommodation
- Facilities provided for activities, for business and in general
- Natural and built attractions.

Accommodation

Accommodation varies across Europe, depending on where you are. The cost also varies, depending on your location and choice of accommodation. In addition there are great differences to be found in the level of quality and service from country to country. As a result, each country has its own way of grading accommodation. Some tour operators have tried to overcome these differences by giving accommodation their own star rating. For example, Thomson's use a T rating system.

Depending on your budget, there is generally a wealth of accommodation on offer in all of the major European destinations. The main options for accommodation are:

- **Hotels** All major European destinations offer a variety of hotels that will cater for a range of budgets. Some offer 'full board accommodation' which includes all meals, others offer 'half board' which includes breakfast and evening meal. Some hotels now offer 'bed and breakfast' (B & B) or 'room only', as the trend for independent travel has expanded. 'All-inclusive' holiday accommodation extends full board to include unlimited bar snacks, meals and drinks.

- **Self-catering** is when no meals are provided but the accommodation has some cooking facilities.

The accommodation can vary from just one room to a whole house, with garden, pool, etc. Self-catering suits those travellers who may have individual dietary requirements or those just wishing to sample the local restaurants. Portugal has a high number of self-catering units, as do the Greek islands.

- **Hostels** For people on a tighter budget who prefer to spend their money on more exciting things than somewhere to sleep for the night, a youth hostel is probably the best option. Most European cities and towns will have a range of hostels that cater for travellers on lower budgets.

- **B & B and others** For the kind of person that prefers to sample the local culture, there are often more accommodation options open than just hotels and hostels. Many European towns and cities run schemes whereby locals open up rooms (or even parts of their homes) to tourists, for a fee.

- **Camping and caravan sites** There is wide variety of sites across Europe and those located in the warmer climates are particularly popular. Every summer, thousands of UK tourists flock to warmer Mediterranean sites for their annual holiday. Sites vary in standard, from the very basic to the 'village site' with shops, restaurants, bars and entertainment facilities all in one location (see below).

Self-catering accommodation for holidaymakers in Greece

RECOMMENDING A CAMPSITE

Research a European campsite of your choice. You may use the information from the Eurocamp study if you wish.

Imagine you are recommending the site to a friend. Write a letter informing your friend about how to get there, the accommodation, facilities available and the price. Include any maps that you think may be useful.

Facilities provided

The facilities of a resort range from the features available – such as pools, bars, restaurants, entertainment etc. – to conference facilities for a businessman. The facilities of a resort can be a major attraction and they are certainly one of the reasons many flock to the south of Spain each year. The resorts along the Mediterranean coastline offer a variety of accommodation together with water parks, beach activities such as water sports, restaurants, bars, nightclubs – the list is endless. For some the activities become a very important part of the holiday, which is why activity centre holidays have now become so popular.

Something for everybody

Eurocamp is the market-leader in self-catering holidays to Europe. The holidays cater for families and couples on 167 superbly equipped holiday parcs in 9 European countries.

For families
Families really love Eurocamp. The kids not only go free – they are free, with lots of room to play, new friends to make, and so many free activities.

For couples
Eurocamp offers an ideal holiday experience for couples, with the freedom and flexibility to plan your own itinerary, going when and where you want, at your preferred pace.

For families with toddlers
As the award-winning, most parent-friendly family holiday, Eurocamp take extra special care where babies and toddlers are concerned. Our selection of toddler-friendly parcs is quieter, with safe play areas, and many have a crèche area where little ones can play together.

Holiday homes
Our continental-style holiday homes, exclusively designed for Eurocamp, are modern and luxurious, with separate kitchen, dining area and bedrooms.

Under canvas
Accommodation under canvas is well equipped and includes everything from electric lighting to real sprung beds. So don't worry if you have no previous camping experience – your completely erected and fully furnished tent is ready for you to move in.

Source: www.eurocamp.co.uk

Activity centre holidays cater for those people who want an active outdoor holiday, often experiencing new activities under the guidance of fully trained staff in a relatively safe environment. They may include:

- Ski resorts
- Water sport centres
- Climbing and walking areas
- Cooking centres.

These activities are aimed at people who may think traditional holidays are mundane, and are looking for something more exciting and challenging. The holidays may be suitable for families, single-parent families, adults only, groups, couples, and singles.

Because of their mountainous location, many ski resorts double as activity centres in the summer months, providing the opportunity to white-water raft, canoe, climb and walk the once-snow-covered slopes. Many resorts rely on this dual economy from the tourist trade as they then cover two seasons, with winter and summer activities run from the same centre. For example many French resorts, such as La Rosiere, are dependent on catering for the two markets of skiing in the winter and walking and climbing in the mountains in the summer.

Less energetic, but just as stimulating, are the growing number of centres that provide a holiday relaxing in a different way, by cooking. France in particular has a number of cooking centres, often combining learning how to cook with sampling the local wines.

Walking in the Alps by Rachel How

There is something immensely invigorating about walking in the Alps, and it is not just down to the mountain air, so fresh and pure. If I had to give just one reason why I love walking in the Alps, it would have to be the grandeur of the scenery, breathtaking and humbling at the same time.

What could be better than walking along the Mont d'Or ridge, with Switzerland on one side and France on the other, with magnificent views of the Mont Blanc range and some of the peaks of the Bernese Oberland? In early summer, however, even spectacular views such as these must compete for your attention with the wild flowers that light up the meadows.

But there is much more to it than that. There is a real walking culture in Switzerland and Austria. It is not uncommon to see entire families out walking together, from 80-year-old granddad in his lederhosen to 8-year-old grandson. And everyone you pass is so friendly, greeting you with a warm *'Gruezi!'* (in Switzerland) or *'Gruss Gott!'* (in Austria). This love of walking has led to the development of an extensive network of superbly way-marked paths, which tends to astonish first-time visitors. Signposts at every

junction offer a multitude of options, all with estimated timings, and of course you can always 'cheat' by taking cable cars or chairlifts into the high mountains.

Walkers are never short of sustenance, either. Whereas in Britain it is rare to see cafés on mountainsides (the only ones I have ever encountered have been on peaks accessible by road or funicular), there are so-called 'huts' in the most inaccessible of spots in the Alps, the only neighbours being cows, whose bells clang in the distance. These 'huts' range from a few picnic tables outside a summer farm offering hunks of bread and mountain cheeses washed down with a cool beer, to 'proper' restaurants where you can enjoy tasty dishes such as local sausages, *Rösti*, or home-made goulash soup. There is a great sense of camaraderie, as everyone tucks into their food in the warm sunshine.

At the end of the walk you are able to relax at a high-quality hotel with views of the peaks, and excellent facilities, which often include sauna, jacuzzi or indoor pool. On top of all this, you can enjoy high-quality cuisine. I have enjoyed some memorable meals in the Lake Lucerne region, where menus have an accent on freshly caught fish from the lake.

Source (adapted): www.inntravel.co.uk

Unit 3 Destination Europe

activity
WHY DON'T YOU GO WALKING IN THE ALPS?

Read the article above and then write a short note to a keen rambling friend, recommending why you think they would enjoy walking in the Austrian and Swiss Alps.

Lake Garda, where natural and built attractions come together

Natural and built attractions

Natural attractions

The term 'topography' describes the natural shape of the planet's surface and includes features such as lakes, mountains and coastlines. Tourists are attracted to these natural features as they are visually appealing and provide the opportunity to get into the fresh air and exercise. These natural areas have always been popular as places for leisure and recreation. Today easy access across Europe has meant that many people travel further to visit the natural sights.

Many destinations depend on the appeal of their natural attractions. For example, the Alps rely heavily on large areas of countryside, which in the summer provides beautiful mountainous scenery for many walkers (see below) and in winter provides access to the many pistes popular with the skiers.

Coastlines are perhaps the most popular natural attraction in Europe for the tourist as millions flock to the Mediterranean beaches every summer. Whilst some beach resorts offer relaxation and the chance of walks along remote coastal paths others offer sun and excitement. Resorts such as San Antonio in Ibiza are popular with the 18–30 year old market because they offer a combination of hot weather, beaches, water sports and numerous bars, restaurants and nightclubs – a mixture of natural and 'built' attractions.

Built attractions

Many 'built attractions' were not originally built with the intention of becoming tourist attractions. Now, however, they are the historic sights that attract those millions of people who are interested in the past and its buildings. This is often called 'heritage tourism', and includes:

- Historic houses
- Castles, abbeys and palaces
- Ruined towns and cities
- Ancient monuments
- Museums.

The diversity of the history of Europe provides many opportunities to visit historic buildings right across the continent. For example, a lot of Paris's attraction is based around many historic buildings such as Notre Dame, the Louvre and the crowded streets of Monmartre. However, often the visitor is also attracted to the natural features of Paris's various parks, and of course the River Seine. The same is true of many destinations, where it is the *combination* of natural and man-made sights that creates the appeal. Many of us go for a hot beach holiday in the summer, but probably most of us will also explore the local town and visit a few of the historic sights and buildings too.

---

activity

SOMETHING FOR EVERYONE

Mr and Mrs Murton and their two grandsons are looking to take a three-night break in a European city. Mr Murton enjoys museums and historical sights, whilst his wife prefers to relax by visiting good shops and restaurants. The children like to be busy all of the time, and need the opportunity to 'let off steam'. In pairs, select Amsterdam, Rome, Madrid or Paris, and plan a three-day itinerary that includes some natural and built attractions that will appeal to the group.

Draw your itinerary on a poster, and present your ideas to the rest of the group.

Features: events, costs and local culture

In the last topic we continued to look at the main features that affect the choice of tourist destination. The remaining features of destinations will be covered in this topic:

- Events and entertainment
- Cost of visiting and living
- Local culture, including food and drink.

Events and entertainment

Today, events and entertainment are seen as an important part of the holiday experience. Most travel companies will go out of their way to tell you about the events and entertainment they have at each resort.

Events

Special events such as sporting competitions and festivals attract large numbers of tourists from within the country it is being hosted and from abroad.

Music festivals, which usually take place during the summer months, are held in a variety of settings such as parks, stadiums or on farmland. The Roskilde Festival, Denmark – Europe's biggest open-air rock event – is held in a small town near Copenhagen during the last weekend in June. Tens of thousands of tickets are sold in advance, and they claim to never turn anyone away.

Some of the largest events revolve around sport. The importance of the Olympics held every four years is hard to measure for the city that plays host. The Olympics in Greece in 2004 were a major event – not just for Athens but many of the towns and cities across the country. For example, the four Greek cities of Thessaloniki, Patras, Heraklio and Volos hosted the Olympic football tournament. The importance of these events is mirrored in many countries when they are chosen to host a World Cup or European football game. Fans will travel hundreds of miles to be at a match.

Many major cities host an event each year, as it is the key to attracting tourists. Each event has appeal for different reasons. For example, Oktoberfest in Munich (Germany) begins in mid-September. Huge tents are filled with massive crowds swilling beer and eating chickens and sausages. This event attracts tourists from all over the world. Semana Santa (Holy Week) is celebrated in Seville (Spain) from Palm Sunday to

Pamplona and the 'running of the bulls'

The Fiesta of San Fermin runs from the 7th to the14th of July in Pamplona, Spain. TV spectators all over the world are surprised, impressed or shocked each year when they watch the spectacle of bulls running through the streets of the town, and hundreds of young men, usually dressed in traditional white shirts and red belts, ahead of them. The bulls run every morning at 8 a.m., except on the first day of the festival. The men can't run if they are drunk or under 18.

The way through the town leads to the bullring, where in the evenings some of the most important bullfights of the season take place. All Pamplona is the scene of an enormous party, with dancing and singing and drinking – it is certainly the most exciting week of the year.

Source (adapted): James Martin, Europe for Visitors

Good Friday and is a mixture of extreme Catholicism and revelry – featuring hooded penitents and vast floats carried bodily by the crowds. Running bulls through the streets of Pamplona (Spain) is an event that has a different appeal, as shown below, left.

Entertainment

Entertainment can come in many forms, including theatre and concerts, nightlife, and animateuse.

Theatre and concerts

Theatres and concerts are very popular with some tourists. Many are led to discover a European city because they wish to attend a play or concert there. Such events are advertised in the UK, and quite often people buy a package with a tour company that includes the concert tickets, transport and accommodation.

Most major European cities have several theatres – London, Paris, Rome, Berlin. London has probably the world's greatest concentration of theatres, with over forty in the West End.

The opera houses of Europe are incredible monuments to the arts. London, St Petersburg, Budapest, Prague, Naples, Vienna and Milan are home to some of the world's finest opera houses. Prague, for example, hosts an incredible number of all sorts of musical performances, from voice recitals by soloists to chamber music to string quartets to full-blown symphony orchestras. There are often five or six concerts each night.

Nightlife

Nightlife is popular with tourists, particularly younger people – some state that it is the main reason for their trip. The nightlife can include bars, clubs, theatres and casinos.

Ibiza caters for those travellers seeking a lively nightlife, and has become established as the place for young people to party from dusk to dawn. All around the Mediterranean there are similar resorts that have set out to appeal to party-loving young people. That is not to say that other areas do not attract revellers. Stag parties in Moscow or Prague, and now the new destinations such as Riga (Latvia), have become increasingly popular. Dublin and Amsterdam are the traditional stag party favourites for the UK market, but they too are facing stiff competition. With the growth of the low-cost airlines, many other cities are now becoming popular for weekend parties. For example, easyJet has regular flights to Barcelona, Copenhagen, Geneva, Madrid, Naples, Nice, Prague, Rome, Toulouse, Venice, and many more.

Foam parties are just one of Ibiza's attractions.

Animateuse

'Animateuse' refers to 'actors' playing a role or a character to provide entertainment. This usually involves the person dressing appropriately and taking on the persona of the person or character they are pretending to be. For example, the Disney characters are a often a main feature of a visit to Disneyland Paris, particularly for the younger children, and people expect to see their favourite characters such as Mickey Mouse and his pals when they visit. The characters are the central theme to the main parade, which takes place each day with all the Disney characters taking part on floats or on foot and all are dressed magnificently for the part.

Animateuse can also be found at historical attractions where actors may re-enact a battle or other historic event such as how they used to 'amputate legs with no anaesthetic in the Olde Apothecary'.

Cost of visiting and living

The actual cost of a visit to Europe has decreased significantly over the last few decades. Destinations that provide low transport costs and accommodation are the most popular. Spain is still the number one choice of destination for UK tourists because it so competitively priced.

The graphs below, adapted from the 2004 Holiday Which report, show the cost of living when you arrive at a number of European destinations. The prices vary

activity

COSTS OF LIVING

1 From the graphs below, which country is the most expensive and which the cheapest for the following: car hire, petrol, a shopping basket, eating out.
2 In groups, discuss which destination would provide the best value for money for:
 • A family of four looking to enjoy a beach holiday
 • An elderly couple planning a driving holiday
 • A young couple looking to enjoy the nightlife.

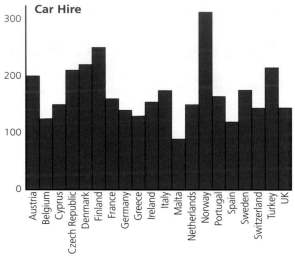

Average price of a week's hire of a small car, including insurance, CDW, unlimited mileage, and local taxes, pre-booked from the UK and collected from the airport.

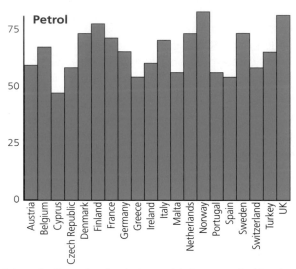

Price of a litre of unleaded petrol (prices supplied by the AA).

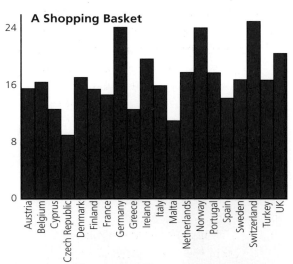

Prices are for a typical grocery basket, including bread, butter, mineral water, coffee, fresh milk, a small fresh chicken, a dozen eggs, cheese, a cheap bottle of wine, and a kilogram each of apples, oranges, and tomatoes.

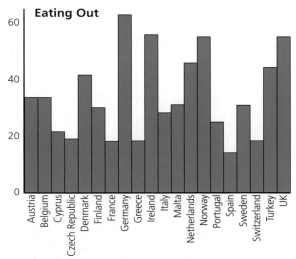

Guide prices indicate what you can expect to pay for a reasonable set three-course meal for two people, sharing a bottle of house wine and a bottle of water. Tax and service are included.

from country to country due to a number of factors. The opening up of eastern European countries is forecast to have a significant effect on tourism over the next few years. It is considerably cheaper in the east for the tourist to live, with a meal being only a couple of pounds and a drink a few pence. Now the low-cost airlines have started to provide cheap access to various locations so the eastern countries await a dramatic expansion as tourist destinations.

Local culture

For many people travelling to a different country may not be for the sun, sand and sea, but to experience a different way of life and the local culture.

activity

NATIONAL CUSTOMS

The French are renowned for their love of garlic and red wine. How many other customs can you think of relating to the following countries: Germany, Italy, Poland, Sweden, Netherlands, Greece, Austria, Switzerland? You could create a collage of pictures for each.

This may include many local customs – from how people dress and speak, to how they work, rest and play, to how they eat and drink. Restaurants are always popular with tourists and meal times often provide the focus of the day.

People who live in southern Europe usually take a siesta for a couple of hours at midday, which is traditionally to rest during the hottest part of the day.

Experiencing the local culture, including the food, is all part of the holiday.

Customs and culture vary from region to region. The customs and culture of the alpine resorts of France vary greatly from those who live in Paris.

The customs of the rural French resorts are traditionally established from people's farming background, with many still breeding animals for meat and growing their own vegetables. Entertainment is based around village activities such as boule competitions and rural shows. The Paris culture, on the other hand, is based on city life similar to that reflected in many other European cities. With limited space, people rely on shops and restaurants for food and drink, and their entertainment is often in a more commercialised form as they have access to theatres and cinemas.

Indeed many of the French rural population see the Parisians as a breed apart, as they are far more cosmopolitan and used to big city life and culture.

activity

RECOMMENDING A DESTINATION

Research and recommend a European destination for the following groups:
- A family of four looking for a hot beach holiday in the school summer holidays
- A young couple looking for an adventure holiday at Easter
- A retired couple looking for a quiet 2-day holiday
- A group of 12 young men looking for a holiday with lots of entertainment
- A businessman looking for a central European location so that he can visit Denmark, Italy, Lithuania and Portugal
- A Japanese couple wishing to visit all the major cultural sights in Europe in a week
- A newly married couple who are looking for a week-end city break in Europe. The man is blind and the woman is in a wheelchair.

For each group you need to consider the following features:
- Climate – for beach and activity centres
- Transport and communications
- Accommodation
- Facilities
- Natural and man-made sights
- Entertainment, e.g. theme parks.

Make your recommendations in the form of a presentation to the rest of the group.

Topic 6	Transport gateways

In the next two topics we will learn about the key transport gateways in Europe and the routes linking the main tourist receiving and generating areas. We will then go on to look at how each form of transport is suitable for different groups' travel requirements, in terms of length of journey time, cost of journey, quality, convenience, services available, safety and security.

Rail links, the Channel Tunnel, roads and motorways will be considered in the next topic. This topic looks at:

- Airports
- Ferry terminals
- Cruise ship ports.

Airports

Airports offer access to air travel between countries (international flights), and within countries (domestic flights). Flight times are relatively short within Europe, thanks to the compact geography of the continent. For example, you can fly from Frankfurt to Athens in less than three hours.

Heathrow, London's biggest airport, is the busiest airport in Europe and the third busiest in the world (see table). It handles over 60 million passengers a year. Frankfurt is the second busiest European airport handling 48 million passengers a year. Over the last few years, there has been a movement of passenger traffic away from the main airports to the smaller ones as the low-cost airlines find it cheaper to operate from them.

There are two main types of air travel, scheduled flights and charter flights. Scheduled flights operate to a published timetable, and depart whether or not the seats are filled. A scheduled timetable is essential to the many business travellers who fly around Europe. To offset the costs of empty seats, the flights tend to be more expensive, and airlines offer discounts to group bookings, known as 'special group inclusive

Top European airports, 2003				
European World Rank	Rank	Airport	Passengers (millions)	% change year on year
1	3	Heathrow	63.5	+ 0.2
2	7	Frankfurt	48.8	+ 0.2
3	8	Paris (CDG)	48.2	- 0.3
4	9	Amsterdam	40.0	-1.9
5	13	Madrid	35.9	+5.7
6	19	Gatwick	30.0	+1.3

Source: Airport Council International

tours' (SGITS). Package holidays which use seats on scheduled flights are referred to as 'inclusive tours by excursion' (ITX).

Charter flights do not follow a regular timetable, but are individual flights, 'chartered' for a specific destination and for a specific time. Charter flights obviously increase in the holiday months to the most popular destinations, such as Spain and Greece. Package holidays use charter flights, and this is called 'inclusive tours by charter' (ITC).

A message from Ray Webster, easyJet Chief Executive

Last month saw the start of an exciting year for easyJet, with many plans for growth and expansion throughout the network. You may have read that we will start operating three new routes in May, when we introduce daily services from Newcastle to Palma (Majorca), Paris Orly to Berlin Schonefeld, and Paris Orly to Naples. Seats for these routes are already on sale on easyJet.com. This will bring our total number of routes to main city destination airports to 127, flying between 39 key European airports.

But this is just the start of the easyJet expansion this year. In the spring we will be adding nine new Airbus A319 aircraft to our fleet, which will result in increasing frequencies on existing routes and the introduction of more new routes throughout Europe. We will be expanding by around 20% in 2004 with one of the world's youngest fleet of aircraft.

A very important element of the easyJet expansion is our new base in the German capital, Berlin. From May, we will be flying to 11 destinations across Europe from Berlin Schonefeld airport, bringing low-cost travel to millions more people, and creating hundreds of jobs in the local area of Berlin.

Source: easyJet onboard flight magazine, February 2004

Air travel has grown significantly in the last ten years as increased competition amongst the airlines has made air travel cheaper and more accessible. Fares within Europe are being pushed down further by European Union policies encouraging competition. For decades, most air travel in Europe was controlled by national airlines, which, because they were virtual monopolies could effectively charge what they liked,

activity

CHEAP FLIGHTS, CHEAP HOLIDAYS

In this activity you are going to investigate the cheap flights market. In pairs, you have one hour to find the cheapest deal for the following:

1 A trip, for a retired couple, to a European city, with 2 nights accommodation.

2 A week's holiday, for a family of four, to the Spanish Mediterranean.

3 A week's holiday for 2 adults, to Estonia or any other eastern European country.

4 A return flight next week to Athens for two people from an airport in the north of England.

You can use newspapers, magazines or holiday brochures, or you might like to visit some of the following online sites:

Online ticket agents

www.biztravel.com
www.expedia.com
www.travelcity.com
www.travelselect.co.uk

Discount specialists
www.air-fare.com
www.lowestfare.com
www.cheapflights.co.uk
www.travelzoo.com

Last-minute deals
www.bargainholidays.com
www.lastminute.com
www.lastminutetravel.com

and the customer could either take it or leave it. One of the best things to happen to European travel in recent years has been the rapid explosion of low-cost no-frills airlines operating across the whole continent. Airlines such as bmibaby and easyJet (see below) today provide affordable access to a vast number of countries and locations.

Along with competition from the low-cost carriers, the general decline in air travel after the September 11 attacks in 2001 was too much for the weakest national carriers. Sabena, Belgium's national airline, went bankrupt, and Swissair ceased flying entirely. Other carriers are fighting to survive. British Airways has dramatically slashed its European fares in a bid to recapture some of the market from its rivals

Ferry terminals

Europe: Major UK ferry destinations
- ferry ports
- ----- ferry routes

Ferry terminals are primarily ports for ferries, but hovercraft, jetfoils and other craft are also based at these terminals. The cross-Channel ferries transport cars, lorries and foot passengers, and provide modern onboard facilities including shops, restaurants, cabins, lounges, children's play areas and foreign-exchange services.

The English Channel is criss-crossed each day by hundreds of ferries, hovercraft, jetfoils and other craft. They are all in competition with each other, and with the Channel Tunnel, on price, journey time, convenience and levels of comfort.

The map above shows the main sea routes from the UK. The fastest crossing is between Dover and Calais, where the English Channel is at its narrowest. North Sea ports also link the UK to the continent. Hull, for example, is the terminal of the popular overnight route to Zeebrugge, in Belgium.

Ferries also link Bilbao and Santander in Spain with Portsmouth and Plymouth – a trip of about 29 hours. Regular boat services connect the major ports in the North and Baltic seas. Many linking Stockholm, Helsinki and Tallin resemble cruise ships, with elaborate entertainment and dining facilities.

Boats and ferries operate in many other parts of Europe. Many of these are primarily for tourists. Undoubtedly, if you are travelling around the Greek Islands you will travel by ferry at some point. The ferry crossing from Patras in Greece to Brindisi in Italy links the Greek mainland to the high-speed train network in Italy and is one way to get to the islands. Today, high-speed catamarans reduce travel times. For example, on the Brindisi–Corfu route they cross the Adriatic Sea in less than three and a half hours.

Turkey also operates coastal ferries, and runs boats to the Greek islands and to Italy. Steamers connect the Black Sea ports of Bulgaria and Romania.

Many of Europe's inland waterways are used to provide summertime voyages – paddle steamers on Switzerland's Lake Lucerne, for example, or river cruisers on the Rhine, Moselle, Elbe and Main rivers in Germany.

Cruise ship ports

Cruise ship ports are especially designed for loading and unloading cruise ships – with passengers and supplies.

Over the past 10 years, Europe has been the fastest growing destination for Americans who like to take cruises. Cruise ships serve as floating resorts, with restaurants, theatres, dancing and entertainment centres. There is a basic division into southern and northern itineraries. Southern itineraries focus on the Mediterranean, the Greek Islands, Cyprus and Turkey. Stops at Venice, Nice, Dubrovnik and Barcelona are popular too. To the north, Baltic cruises visit Scandinavia, Germany, Poland and Russia. A cruise along the Norwegian fjords is popular, and Copenhagen and Stockholm are regular calling ports.

activity

CRUISE SHIPS AND FERRIES

Read the two articles opposite, and then:

1 Write a short report highlighting the differences between the ferry and cruise markets in the UK.

2 Investigate the current prices of ferries to and from France for a family of four.

3 Investigate the price for a retired couple of a cruise around the Mediterranean.

4 Outline why you think it may be better for certain types of traveller to travel by ferry than to fly to the Continent.

Cruise ships can often get right into the heart of a city.

Cruise passengers sail past one million

More than a million Britons took to the waves last year and spent their holiday aboard a cruise ship.

According to figures from the Passenger Shipping Association (PSA), cruise sales rocketed by 12 per cent last year, resulting in the highest number of cruise passengers since records began.

Although a cruise is still popular among older and more affluent travellers – a third of the rise last year was due to the success of the Ocean village concept – the share of cruises sold for under £500 has nearly quadrupled during the last decade, indicating that the cruises are now popular across the generations.

At the other end of the price scale, ultra-luxury cruising experienced a 70 per cent increase in the past year, and PSA stated that the luxury sector had trebled in popularity over the last four years.

William Gibbons, a director of PSA, said: 'The sheer diversity of cruise holidays is helping to increase demand for cruises. The industry is responding by introducing many more new ship launches – 17 last year and 13 this year – and varied itineraries and styles of ships to suit different types of travellers.'

The PSA highlighted that an increase in variety – such as smaller ships, unusual destinations, luxury cruises and themed voyages – has had a particularly healthy effect on the industry.

Among the most popular destinations last year were Scandinavia and the Baltic Sea.

PSA also said that the recent introduction of Cunard Line's *Queen Mary 2* had stimulated a huge interest in cruising, and PSA predicts a 10 per cent increase in ocean cruising for 2004.

Source: Leisure Opportunities Magazine, 25 May 2004

Sea battle for passengers: ferries want their business back

Low-cost airlines already have British Airways and traditional carriers on the run. Now the ferries are having to respond.

In the wake of latest figures that show ferry usage is down 4 per cent year-on-year to May in the UK, a group of nine ferry firms has launched a website to highlight savings for those who choose to travel by sea across the Channel.

No-frills carriers have put a big dent in ferry travel on some routes over the past three years, with the Office for National Statistics finding the number of people travelling to France by sea down by about 400,000 to 4,567,000 last year.

Furthermore, ferry passengers to the Continent fell by 8 per cent in the first five months of 2003, according to FerryStat, a monthly report on ferry use compiled by IRN Research.

But www.sailanddrive.com hopes to break this trend by highlighting how families can save as much as 66 per cent by travelling by sea with their own cars.

On the offensive against the likes of Ryanair and easyJet, Bill Gibbons, a director of the Passenger Shipping Association, a group representing UK ferry operators, said, 'Airline pricing can be very misleading. Often the "from" price on a website is a single fare, excluding taxes, with very few seats available at that advertised amount.'

Sailanddrive show that a family of four (two adults, two children) travelling from Shrewsbury to Waterford in Ireland would save £458.66 by driving and taking a ferry.

This is based on an August "snapshot" of how much it would have cost the family to travel from Birmingham to Cork.

Meanwhile, a similar family would save £211.45 on journeys from Guildford to Chantilly in France, according to the new website.

The PSA estimates that, on all routes, more than six million British people travelled by ferry on holiday last year, up 300,000 from 2001.

Source: The Times, Travel News, 9 August 2003

Rail links, roads and motorways

The last topic looked at European transport gateways. In this topic we will investigate two further modes of transport:

- **Rail links and the Channel Tunnel**
- **Major roads and motorways.**

Rail links and the Channel Tunnel

Europe has a vast network of rail lines, ranging from the high-speed lines that link the major cities, down to the slower, local, scenic tracks. There is a long tradition of frequent trains (that run on time), reasonable fares, centrally located stations, and high levels of service. Trains are therefore widely used across the whole continent, with millions of people relying on their efficiency. In Germany, for example, every day 33,000 trains carry 4 million people.

The map opposite shows the major rail routes in Europe. On many middle-distance routes, high-speed trains compete with the air traffic. For example, Eurostar dominates the London–Paris market as it offers three-hour trips, city centre to city centre. The Eurostar service between London and Brussels (two hours, forty minutes) is equally successful. Over twenty Eurostar trains a day run between London and Paris, and ten per day between London and Brussels. Before the opening of the Channel Tunnel (in 1995) it used to take eight hours to travel between London and Paris by road and ferry, and seven hours between London and Brussels.

The last ten years has seen the spread of ultra-high-speed train routes throughout the continent. TGV (Trains à Grande Vitesse) in France, AVE (Trens de Alta Velocidad Espanol) in Spain and Pendolino in Italy are symbols of national pride as well as transportation. These trains travel at 120 to 150 mph and can cover long distances very quickly. The TGV train travels from Paris to Marseille in three hours. The Eurostar runs though the 31-mile-long Channel Tunnel and cruises at 185 miles an hour on the open straight track. The most extensive fast train networks operate in France, Germany and Italy.

The glamorous high-speed trains, however, make up only a small part of Europe's overall rail network. Standard trains are excellent as well, particularly the network of EuroCity express trains, with dining cars and sleepers that link major cities. Examples include: Frankfurt–Milan–Rome (14 hours) and Vienna–Venice (8 hours).

European trains are generally fast, convenient and reliable, and link a wide range of destinations. Tourists who want to travel widely across Europe usually buy a rail pass. The most popular kind, for visitors from outside Europe, is a 'Eurail' pass, which comes in a number of forms and covers from three to seventeen countries. These passes allow either unlimited travel over a period of time, or travel on a certain number of days within a given time period (e.g. five days within a month). Citizens of EU countries are ineligible for Eurail passes, but can buy the equivalent InterRail pass.

Trains are particularly useful as a method of transport in eastern Europe, where roads can be slow and flights limited. Special regional passes are available for these countries. For example the 'European East Pass' allows travel in Austria, Czech Republic, Hungary, Poland and Slovakia, and the 'Balkan Flexipass' covers Bulgaria, Greece, Macedonia, Romania, Turkey and Yugoslavia.

Europe: Rail links

—— high speed rail link

activity

FINDING THE BEST ROUTE

Study the map above and plot the best route for the following journeys:

1 London to Warsaw (Poland)

2 Budapest (Hungary) to Lisbon (Portugal)

3 Oslo (Norway) to Palermo (Sicily)

4 Brest (France) to Stockholm (Sweden)

5 Alicante (Spain) to Berlin (Germany).

Major roads and motorways

There is a large network of roads and motorways across Europe. Thanks to relatively short distances, motorists can find themselves driving in three different

countries in a single day, or from the seashore to the mountains in an afternoon.

Although motorways still constitute only a small part of the entire road network, their length has more than tripled over the last 30 years to 55,641km. Extraordinary growth can be noticed in Greece and Spain. Currently, the most extensive motorway network within Europe is in Germany, followed by France and Spain.

Driving in Europe in on the right-hand side of the road – except in the UK, Ireland, Malta and Cyprus. The network of highways is modern, well marked and expanding, most notably in eastern Europe and in Greece. Greece has rebuilt its main north–south motorway and is now working on the new east–west Via Egnita motorway and the Rio-Antirio bridge across the Gulf of Corinth. The border between France and Spain has also been the scene of much work, with the new Samport Highway tunnel through the western Pyrenees, and the spectacular Millau Viaduct over France's Tarn Gorge river, which completes the six-lane motorway between Paris and Barcelona.

Many of the motorways and major roads have been designated as 'European International' routes. These, therefore, have two numbers – a local (national)

motorway number and an E number, identified by distinctive green and white signs. This system follows the 1983 European agreement on the 'International Road Network', designed to simplify the use of road numbers across Europe. For example, the E-4 takes you from Helsinki to Stockholm to Copenhagen, and the E-55 goes from Salzburg to Brindisi. Unfortunately, not all countries in Europe have adopted the system. In the UK, for example, a number of motorways and major roads are designated as E routes, but are not actually signposted.

Some European motorways impose a toll (charge) to travel on them. Britain and Germany generally do not have toll roads. But tolls are charged on Italy's autostrade and France's autoroutes, and they can be expensive. Austria, the Czech Republic and Switzerland charge tolls through 'easy-pass' stickers,

activity

DISTANCES BY ROAD

Look at the map of road mileage between cities and calculate the length of the following car journeys: London to Rome; Athens to Lisbon; Moscow to Paris; Istanbul to Munich; Athens to Edinburgh.

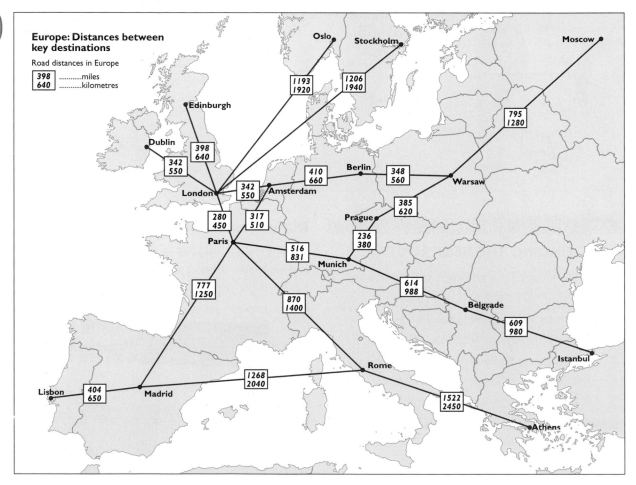

Europe: Distances between key destinations

Road distances in Europe

| 398 | ....miles |
| 640 | ....kilometres |

which are purchased in advance. The European Union is developing a common easy-pass system to work on all toll roads, bridges, tunnels, etc.

Away from the fast motorways there are many famous scenic drives. Examples include Germany's 'Romantic Road' from Wurzburg to Munich, France's 'Route Napoleon' from the Riviera to Grenoble, Croatia's dramatic Dalmatian coast drive south to Dubrovnik, and Italy's Amalfi coast highway.

The world's longest highway tunnel opened in Norway in 2000. The 25km Laerdal Tunnel takes the new Oslo–Bergen highway under a rugged range of mountains, eliminating a three-hour ferry ride and roads over high passes that are dangerous in winter.

Although it's for rail only, motorists can take advantage of the Channel Tunnel via special shuttle trains that carry vehicles. The shuttles operate between Folkestone and Calais terminals, running every 15 minutes during peak periods, and every hour at night.

Travelling by car gives the greatest flexibility to the traveller in terms of the choice of route, time of departure and of arrival. There has been a dramatic increase in the volume of car hire from airports, as the low-cost airlines make it cheaper to fly to your chosen destination and then hire a car.

Coach operators make the most of the fast motorway network across Europe. Coaches run from a variety of local departure points to a wide variety of destinations. Transporting people between destination and a resort is called a 'transfer'.

Not all tourists use the car as their main source of transport. For example they may get to their destination by air or sea. However, once there, they still have to consider how they are going to get around. In addition to hire cars, there are other methods to consider.

Public transport is available in all the major European cities. A combination of metros (underground), streetcars (trams) and buses provide the framework for city travel. The cheapest way to travel around a city is to buy a pass for a set period of time, from a day to a week.

Metros can be confusing. The separate lines are usually colour-coded, but may be known by their names (as in London), a letter or a number, or simply according to the final stop on the line. Most metro systems give out free pocket-sized maps with the tickets, which are usually purchased at the stations. Bus and tram tickets, on the other hand, are usually sold at news kiosks and tobacco shops – not by the bus drivers. Tourist offices sometimes sell daily and weekly passes.

Most European buses and trams and some metros operate on the 'honour' system. You cancel your own ticket in the punching machines in each bus or carriage. (Locals with monthly passes do not need to punch their tickets.) Inspectors make sure that the honour system is followed.

Euroline

The Euroline bus network, the largest in Europe, serves more than 1500 cities, in 28 countries. These include:

Northern Europe: UK, Ireland, France AQ, Belgium, Netherlands, Denmark, Norway, Sweden, Finland.

Central Europe: Germany, Austria, Croatia, Hungary, Czech Republic, Yugoslavia, Slovenia.

Southern Europe: Spain, Italy, Greece, Portugal (plus Turkey and Morocco).

Eastern Europe: Estonia, Latvia, Lithuania, Poland, Bulgaria.

In 2001, Euroline covered 19 million km, using more than 36,000 buses, transporting more than 1.5 million passengers.

In 1993, the Paris-Gallieni international coach station in France was opened. The biggest in Europe, it is designed to ease the movement of passengers. It is equipped with all the latest technology: central radio station, electronic ticket sales, electronic information, departure and arrival displays, bus positioning by satellite system, electronic luggage lockers, coffee shop, exchange office, direct access to taxis and the underground system, and even a little praying room for the Muslim customers.

Accessible Spain

All European countries are reliant on the modes of transport and routes to provide access to the tourist. Some have better access than others. One of the most accessible and popular destinations is Spain. More than 45 million tourists visit Spain each year, making it the third most visited country in the world.

Access is provided in a number of ways. Iberia, British Airways, easyJet and other no-frills airlines fly to the mainland and the Balearic Islands. There are decent rail and road connections with France and Portugal (although it is necessary to change trains at the French border). Ferries operate from Plymouth to Santander and from Portsmouth to Bilbao. AVE high-speed trains operate on the Madrid–Cordoba–Seville route and can whisk you from Madrid to Seville in just $2\frac{1}{2}$ hours.

activity

HOW CAN YOU GET THERE?

Select a destination in Europe and investigate the different transport routes available to get there. You need to consider the route by air, sea, road and rail. Atlases, travel guides and the internet provide good sources of information.

Transport: factors affecting choice

In the last two topics we concentrated on the different modes of transport available to people travelling between European destinations. In this topic we will examine the influencing factors that affect our choice of transport. In broad terms these factors include:

- Overall length of journey time
- Cost of entire journey
- Quality and convenience, e.g. departure times, transfer connections
- Services available, e.g. class of service, support for specific needs
- Safety and security.

It is important to understand that these factors will have varying levels of importance for different types of traveller.

Length of journey time

Speed, or length of journey time, is a major factor in the individual's choice of transport. Most people don't want to 'waste' time travelling – they want to maximise the time they have available at their destination. This is certainly true for most UK tourists taking their average 14-day holiday to the sunshine. It is also true for the business traveller, for whom time is money. Long journeys mean that they are missing valuable time in the office (or time at home with their families).

For some, however, speed may not be the major issue. This is because many travellers view the journey as part of the holiday. For example, a traveller may choose to take a 12-hour overnight ferry crossing rather than take the far quicker option of a fast catamaran because they want to relax and enjoy the on-board facilities of a longer journey. The overnight ferry from Hull to Zeebruge, for example, has the attraction of luxury accommodation, restaurants, cinema, bars and live entertainment.

Cost

Cost – the price one has to pay – is often a major factor in deciding which mode of transport to choose. For some people, price is no object, but for many it is the deciding factor. The cost of transport can contribute significantly to the total holiday price. It is true that the growth of low-cost airlines has made some destinations much more accessible than previously imaginable. The low-cost flights to parts of France and southern Spain have meant for many people in the UK that they can now, not only afford to holiday there but also consider buying a holiday home there. Low-cost flights have meant some other forms of transport have come under threat and are fighting hard to compete, as shown in the table (overleaf).

Cost can be a major factor is you are travelling in a family group. It may be cheap for one or two people to fly, but when you need to take a large family on holiday the flight costs soon mount up. Going by road and ferry, if it is feasible, will be cheaper because the

Changing modes of travel – shown by number of passengers leaving the UK, in 1998 and 2002, in millions			
Mode of travel	1998	2002	% change
Air	34.3	44.0	+28.3
Sea	10.5	10.0	−4.4
Channel Tunnel	6.1	5.3	−12.2
Total	50.9	59.4	+16.7

Source: Independent Passenger Survey 2002

Airlines are constantly trying to improve the luxury of the travel experience – for those prepared to pay.

cost of the car transport does not increase with more people – it costs virtually the same whether there is just the driver or a family of five. Many UK families certainly opt for this route when travelling to France for their annual summer holiday.

Quality and convenience

Quality and convenience are other important factors in our choice of mode of transport. 'Quality' often refers to the luxury of the travel experience and depends on the price of the transport and level of service you are buying. However, quality can also be down to customer service, and this is covered in Unit 2.

'Convenience' refers to meeting passengers' particular needs, and is another important factor in our choice of transport. For example, if the traveller does not own a car then the choice of road transport may not be feasible. Of course many people without cars, or those who do not wish to drive, sometimes choose to go by bus or coach, and this is often a good choice of transport as long as they have access to the pick-up point. For many who live in London, the underground

activity

COUNTING THE COST

In the table below are the costs for travelling from London to Paris via various forms of transport. Look at the information in the table and then answer the following questions:

1 Compare the cost of one person travelling from London to Paris by air, rail or road and sea.

2 Compare the cost for four adults travelling from London to Paris by air, rail or road and sea.

3 List the other factors you would need to consider before making your choice of transport.

For this activity you can assume that travellers already have a car.
Note: All flights have a £39.70 surcharge.

(Price research conducted on 3 August 2004 for journeys that week.)

Mode of transport		Adult	4 adults
Air	British Airways Heathrow to Charles de Gaulle	£13 outward journey £26 return journey Total £39	£13 out per person £26 return per person Total £39 per person
Rail	Eurostar (return) Waterloo International to Paris Nord	£66	£66 per person
Sea	Sea France – Ferry (return with car)	£145	£145
	Hoverspeed – seacat (return with car)	£158	£158

and the bus are the most convenient forms of transport around the city, and many choose not to use cars because of the heavy traffic or the congestion charge. Likewise, in many European cities the rail network, trams and buses provide the majority of the transport for the city traveller.

Convenience may also include departure times and transfer connections. For example, if you are travelling with a young family, a flight late at night or early in the morning may be impossible, and a long time spent in a transfer lounge may also be unbearable. On the other hand, the lone traveller may not see a night flight or changing flights as a big issue.

Convenience is also a consideration when you arrive at your destination. If it is important for you to get around during the time you are there, then going there by car may be the best option. This is why so many people still like to take their cars on holiday – it allows them to be more mobile when they are there.

Services available

The services available can have a significant impact on a traveller's choice of transport, particularly if the person requires support for specific needs. The special needs traveller is someone who has a special need over and above the average traveller. This may be physical or mental, and the category can cover a wide range of travellers – from someone who has difficulty walking and needs a wheelchair to someone who has a fear of flying. The individual need may determine

Some railway systems present no obstacle to wheelchair users.

the choice of transport selected. Some special needs travellers may not be hindered in their choice of transport at all, but for others it will be a major factor.

The business traveller often prefers first class travel, as it allows for more comfort and personal workspace. Getting from one destination to the next in the shortest time possible is a major consideration and it is for this reason that business travellers use scheduled flights, because they run to a fixed timetable and they can plan their working day around the flights.

The AVE rail service in Spain

AVE trains have been providing excellent service ever since 1992. Their success has been helped by their punctuality, together with the services offered on board and at stations, the levels of customer care, sales and after-sales service, and a ticket fare policy that is easy to understand.

First Class *Club*: Meal (choice of entree) at your seat, drinks, newspapers, audio/video, parking discounts, access to AVE lounges, access to conference room on train.

First Class *Preferente* : Meal at your seat, newspapers, audio/video, parking discounts, access to AVE lounges.

Second Class *Tourist* : Family area, children's board games, wheelchair facilities, audio/video.

Source: www.spanish-fiestas.com

activity

LEVELS OF AVE SERVICE

Discuss the advantages and disadvantages of each level of AVE service to a business traveller, family group, and an elderly man in a wheelchair. Consider the implications of each having to travel in all of the different classes.

Safety and security

It is an unfortunate fact that increasing crime is often a result of the development of an area as a tourist destination. This is particularly true in the less developed areas where the population have a relatively low standard of living and may be tempted into crime when confronted by the perceived wealth of foreign visitors. Prostitution, pick-pocketing, drugs and petty crime are often common problems in major tourist destinations. In fact, visitors to Barcelona are routinely warned to be vigilant with their belongings, as the city has the highest incidence of pick-pocketing in Europe.

Crime has always been a threat to the traveller, because people are vulnerable when they are away from home – they may be carrying a lot of money, they are unsure of their surroundings, may not speak the language, and they may be less vigilant of their possessions when travelling. Tourists have always made easy pickings for thieves, secure in the knowledge that most will reclaim the theft on their insurance when they return home. It is really up to the individual to be vigilant in looking after their own possessions, but many hotels now provide security boxes or a safe deposit for passports and valuables.

The threat of terrorism has now become a real deterrent to the traveller, particularly since 9/11 and the

activity

TERRORISM, TOURISM, AND TRANSPORT

Read the article, and answer the following questions:

1 What strategies are planned to combat terrorism in Europe?
2 Discuss which type of European destination might suffer from the threat of terrorism and which might benefit.
3 What are the implications for the choice of transport?

continuing actions of the Basque separatist movement in Spain (see article below). Terrorism affects everyone who is flying or travelling, especially those travelling to the major cities which are always the focus for terrorist groups. Since 9/11, airlines have increased security and when flying you will be asked a number of standard questions such as:

- Did you pack you own bag?
- Did anyone else help you pack?
- Are you carrying anything for anyone else?

Airport security has been increased since 9/11.

Leaders agree plan to combat terrorism

European leaders last night agreed far-reaching reforms to fight terrorism after the Madrid bombings.

In a hastily arranged summit in Brussels, Tony Blair and other heads of government agreed about fifty measures, including the beefing-up of security at airports, sharing information about stolen passports, making mobile phone companies store information about calls, and making development aid to poor countries conditional on them co-operating in the fight against terrorism.

Under one proposal, ferry passengers could be faced with airport-style security checks. There is concern that ferry passengers and freight face no security checks at all, making it easy for terrorists either to transport explosives and other weapons, or to make ferries the target of an attack.

There is also concern that people arriving by boat at small harbours face virtually no checks, making it easy for terrorists to smuggle themselves and equipment into and out of target countries.

Ministers have also proposed allowing 'cross-border hot pursuit' so that police from one country can carry on chasing terrorist suspects if they slip into another country. At present, police forces have to stop at the border.

Trade and aid deals with third countries will be conditional on them adopting appropriate anti-terrorism measures.

There will also be a European register of people convicted of terrorist-related offences and a database of forensic science evidence.

Source (adapted): Anthony Browne, The Times, 26 March 2004

MATCHING THE HOLIDAY TO THE TYPE OF CUSTOMER

Outlined below are eight types of travellers, and eight holidays available for the Easter period. Identify which holiday would be suitable for which type of traveller, and explain why. Consider these factors when deciding which trip best meets the needs of the customers: length of journey, cost, quality and convenience, services available, safety and security.

THE TRAVELLERS

1 An upmarket family with young children

2 A family with two teenage boys who are sports mad

3 Two ladies looking to pamper themselves

4 A young couple interested in history and culture

5 Two retired colonels interested in the history of the Second World War

6 Three families looking to holiday together

7 Four golf enthusiasts

8 A couple looking for activity and luxury

THE HOLIDAYS

It may help if you locate the resorts on a map so that you can examine the mode of transport and any other difficulties the travellers may experience. The websites may help you explore the different holidays available.

A. France: combine a healthy swig of Bordeaux with some top relaxation at Les Sources de Caudalie, a spa that specialises in vinotherapy. It has Merlot Wraps, Crushed Cabernet Scrubs and Pulp Friction Massages. Essential Escapes (www.essentialescapes.com) has three nights for £662, flying with BA on April 9. Spa packages from £200.

B. Norway: Inntravel (www.inntravel.co.uk) has an April 9 departure to the Lofoten Islands, inside the Arctic Circle. Stay in a former fisherman's *rorbu* (a wooden hut on stilts over the water), take cobweb-clearing coastal walks, enjoy lazy fishing expeditions or visit the Viking Museum. The three-night break costs £649, room-only, flying with SAS.

C. France: the Hôtel Royal Riviera, on the Cap-Ferrat peninsula between Monaco and Nice, will put its spectacular new Provençal garden to good use during the Easter festivities, with an egg hunt on April 12. Seasons in Style (www.seasonsinstyle.co.uk) has three nights from £450, room-only, flying with BA.

D. France: Ski Beat (www.skibeat.com) has good availability for April 10 departures, and suggests La Tania. Chalet Emeralde sleeps up to 18 in nine ensuite bedrooms; a one-week package costs £499, fully catered.

E. The Netherlands: this year marks the 60th anniversary of several key Second World War battles. Leger (www.leger.co.uk) has a four-day battlefield tour of war cemeteries and museums connected with Operation Market Garden in 1944. The package costs £209, B&B, departing by coach on April 9.

F. France: Esprit (www.esprit-holidays.co.uk) has a week's fully catered family skiing in the high-altitude resort of La Rosière, which is linked to the Italian resort of La Thuile, for £599 (discounts of up to 60% for children), departing on April 11.

G. Portugal: for those who believe golf is a good walk improved, Longshot (www.longshotgolf.co.uk) has a four-star week at the Vila Gale Ampalius, in the Vilamoura, within short-iron range of four courses, including the famous Old Course and the new Millennium layout. The price is £565, room-only, including car hire, flying with First Choice Airways on April 8.

H. France: in Le Touquet, the restored 18th-century Château du Broutel (www.chateaudubroutel.com) offers a peaceful lakeside setting, gourmet menus with an emphasis on local produce, and plenty of activities, including canoeing, archery, abseiling and raft-building. A week costs £549 (£379 per child), full-board, including ferry or Eurotunnel crossings with car, departing on April 11.

Source: 'Easter Escapes' by Susan d'Arcy, 2004 Sunday Times travel supplement, 14 March 2004

Topic 9 Accessibility, image and attractions

In the final two topics of the unit we will investigate the factors affecting the popularity and appeal of European destinations. You will gain some understanding of why some destinations with comparable features are more popular than others, and how some factors are controllable and others are not. Some destinations maximise their appeal and popularity by controlling certain factors. Destination management, cost of visiting, and political factors will be considered in the next topic. This topic concentrates on:

■ Accessibility

■ Image and promotion

■ Availability of attractions and other tourist facilities.

Accessibility

Accessibility is the measure of how easy it is to get to a destination. The various modes of transport were covered in the last three topics, and what is clear is that some destinations are more accessible than others. The vast European road network provides access to the popular and the remote destinations,
from the French Riviera to the Swiss Alps. Access by sea has been vital to the tourism development of many of the Greek islands and remote beaches. But more recently it is access by air and particularly cheap flights that is having the most dramatic effect on some destinations, such as Eastern Europe (see case study opposite).

activity

STAG PARTIES IN THE BALTIC COUNTRIES

Read the article on the growth of travel to the Baltic countries, then answer the following questions:

1 Why are the Baltic countries so attractive for stag parties?

2 How has their accessibility changed in recent years?

3 Why do you think that these countries appear to be keen to cater to this market?

4 What might the negative effects of this type of tourism be – to the host countries?

Image and promotion

The 'image' is the general impression of a destination and can be created by a number of factors. For example, Switzerland is the home of high mountains and clear air; Greece is a place of small islands, and Norway a country of deep rugged fjords. A country or destination may choose to promote these images or promote alternative ones. It has been proven that the increase in media coverage of particular tourist destinations across the world has had a dramatic effect on their popularity and growth. Media coverage includes:

• Advertisements

• Television and radio programmes

• Newspaper and magazine reports

Party time in Baltics for boozy Brits

Yes, the British stag weekend is on the move. Imminent EU expansion has the budget airlines and holiday operators falling over each other as they eye new destinations for Britain's thirsty hordes celebrating their last nights of freedom.

Already over the last five years, cities such as Tallinn in Estonia, Riga in Latvia, Vilnius in Lithuania, and Budapest in Hungary have seen a steady increase in the number of stag parties visiting from Britain.

Most are lured by the prospect of cheap beer and strip clubs in medieval cities that few know anything about.

'It's pretty much the edge of the world. No one's really heard of them. You can still smell the communists,' said Matthew Mavis, managing director of Lastnightoffreedom.com.

Nevertheless, they are sufficiently westernised for those who visit to feel comfortable. 'People experience good quality service wherever they go,' said Petra Stusek, a spokeswoman for the Slovenian tourist board. 'Most people speak English because this was the first foreign language they learnt in school.'

According to the company's website, easyJet will launch flights from Britain to Budapest in Hungary and Ljubljana in Slovenia,

with prices starting from as little as £6.99 one way. 'Within a couple of years, there will be a large number of airlines travelling to these new countries.' A spokesman for rival Ryanair confirmed that the Dublin-based company was also looking to expand into eastern Europe.

Already companies specialising in stag weekends are preparing tailor-made packages, starting at around £99 a person (excluding flights) for a weekend in Budapest during the low season – so many destinations are set to prove cheaper than traditional overseas venues, such as Dublin and Amsterdam.

Marco Walker, sales director with holiday firm Designadventure, said: 'Where the stag parties lead, the hens will follow. In five years' time, these eastern European countries will be the new Prague.'

The new party capitals are:

Budapest
Population 2,017,000
Flight time from UK 2 hours 30 minutes
Why go? Said to be the first city of eastern Europe – the 'Paris of the East'. More cosmopolitan than Prague. Wines are good, and it has 123 thermal spas.

Vilnius
Population 578,000
Flight time from UK 2 hours 30 minutes
Why go? Picturesque world heritage listed city with some of the friendliest people in eastern Europe.

Tallinn
Population 430,000
Flight time from UK 3 hours
Why go? The oldest and most beautiful capital city in northern Europe, a warren of spires and cobbled streets. Renowned medieval lesbian strip show.

Riga
Population 794,000
Flight time from UK 3 hours
Why go? Baltic boom town that has resisted westernisation. Dome Square is a haven for café society. Extensive gambling. Beer at less than £1 a bottle.

Source: Jamie Doward, Observer, 29 February 2004

- Travel guides and brochures
- Internet sites.

Advertisements have long been a traditional way of promoting a tourist destination – and many travel companies are still using this as their main form of selling. The advertisements provide a brief description of the holiday destination and then provide contact details to arrange booking.

Television and radio programmes providing advice to travellers have increased considerably over the last few years. Some people would argue that the television networks are saturated with travel programmes, indeed the Travel Shop channel is on all day, providing advice on destinations and the opportunity to book

immediately whilst watching the show. Any reports providing a negative report on a tourist destination can have a dramatic effect on people's holiday plans. The loss of tourists has been experienced in many European cities, especially London, due first to the 'foot and mouth' epidemic, and then to the threat of terrorism after the 9/11 attacks.

Newspaper and magazine reports provide regular updates on tourist destinations, sometimes accompanied by promotions from local travel companies providing the transport and accommodation to the featured resort (see example overleaf). These are most popular with the more mature traveller who often does not want to travel alone.

Three European cities to explore

THE treasures of Central Europe are revealed on this fascinating tour.

The holiday begins in Prague with sightseeing around the old town, which is renowned for its elegant architecture, historic landmarks and pretty medieval streets.

On the first evening, there will be an optional dinner, complete with traditional music and a folklore show.

Next its the Hungarian capital and spa city of Budapest which is a delight to explore.

The busy boulevards of Pest and the ancient castle district of Buda will be toured, and in the evening there is the option of a cruise down the Danube with dinner served on board.

The holiday concludes in the elegant city of Vienna where you can see the impressive St Stephen's cathedral and have the opportunity to visit the unspoilt countryside of the Vienna Woods.

There is also an opportunity to tour Vienna by night and go for a ride on a giant ferris wheel in Prater Park.

The price includes:
• 7 nights bed and breakfast.
• Sightseeing tours of Prague, Budapest and Vienna.
• Scheduled flights.
• The services of a Kaytravel tour manager.
• All transfers.
To make a booking contact the Kaytravel Office.

Travel guides and brochures provide detailed written information on many tourist destinations. The guides often provide the background to the geography, history and culture of the destination and lots of tips for travellers on the accommodation, food, language, etc. Travel information is promoted via the various tourist boards, located in the major cities and gateways across Europe. The advantage of written information is that the traveller can constantly refer to it. Many people still prefer to book their holiday from a brochure – because they can see pictures of the resort and the prices for the different types of accommodation available.

Internet sites have become the fastest growing method of purchasing in the western world, and the

---

activity

IMAGE AND PROMOTION

Compare the information below – from the Thomson's website – for four different types of beach holiday, and discuss the image each is trying to promote. Suggest which type of customer you would advise the resort to be suitable for and why.

Using the internet, brochures and advertisements, select three other European destinations and, with the use of examples, show how they each use image and promotion to present themselves to tourists. Present your findings in a portfolio.

Minorca

Peace and quiet are easy to find on picturesque Minorca. Great for family or friends, its beautiful beaches draw people back year after year. It is the second largest of the Balearic Islands; Minorca is perfect for a relaxing beach holiday, as there are over 120 beaches to choose from. It is also well worth exploring inland sights, from unusual hidden restaurants, to historic remains. The pace of life is relaxed and unhurried.

Ibiza

Ibiza, smallest of the Balearics, is an island steeped in history with a wealth of sights and sounds to discover. For years, Ibiza Town has been at the forefront of fashion and is still flamboyantly style-conscious. Head to San Antonio for streets full of bars, cafés and world-renowned nightlife. The landscape is equally colourful: sweeping bays, fantastic beaches, terraced hills covered in olive and almond trees and rugged pine-clad cliffs. The green rolling hills and open plains are fringed by a coastline dotted with secluded coves and sandy beaches.

Turkey

Turkey has some of the most unspoilt coastline around. Enjoy glorious beaches, dine on the delicious food and discover a fascinating heritage. Turkey presents a mixture of modern resorts and memorable beaches in the midst of an ancient, welcoming and very distinctive country. The coast is spectacular and dotted with small bays and glorious sand and pebble beaches. Rocky headlands reach into a sea so clear and blue it could have been distilled. The way of life belongs as much to the Middle East as to Europe.

Gozo

Gozo provides a tranquil haven for those who like to take their holidays in the slow lane. The charm of Gozo is apparent the moment you arrive there. Greener, more rural and smaller than Malta, life on Gozo moves at a leisurely pace. The rhythm is dictated by the seasons, fishing and agriculture. Gozo is steeped in myth. Thought to be the legendary Calypso's isle of Homer's Odyssey, it's a peaceful, mystical backwater with a rugged landscape and spectacular coastline.

Source: www.thomson-holidays.com

	Corfu Family Self Catering			Corfu Family Half board		
Prices based on	1 bed apartment for 4			SH WC		
Nights	7	14	All	7	14	All
Adult/Child	Adult	Adult	1st Ch	Adult	Adult	1st Ch
01 May–07May	195	225	65	225	319	155
08 May–18 May	215	245	85	239	355	185
19 May–25 May	289	325	95	289	435	215
26 May–31 May	385	419	195	335	455	255
01 Jun–9 Jun	299	329	145	315	445	255
10 Jun–16 Jun	299	329	145	325	475	255
17 Jun–23 Jun	315	349	145	339	485	255
24 Jun–30 Jun	325	365	145	345	495	295
1 Jul–07 Jul	325	375	165	345	495	295
8 Jul–14 Jul	375	425	235	369	525	325
15 Jul–21 Jul	409	489	245	375	549	335
22 Jul–03Aug	435	515	255	385	565	345
4 Aug–17 Aug	295	475	255	385	565	345
18 Aug–24 Aug	379	429	175	369	535	315
25 Aug–31 Aug	349	385	165	365	509	275

The detailed information in brochures allows people to compare resorts and prices.

travel market is no exception. Martha Lane Fox initiated the craze in the late 1990s with her website www.lastminute.com providing last-minute cheap travel bookings for many destinations. Most travel companies have now copied this trend, and easyJet's aim is to have all bookings done via its website, because it reduces booking costs and therefore reduces the price for the traveller. The internet also provides access to vast quantities of information that can easily be downloaded by the user. Webcams provide up-to-the-minute images of various resorts and destinations. For example, a keen skier can view the pistes of a number resorts before making a choice of their destination.

Availability of attractions

The provision of additional attractions to a travel destination usually adds to its appeal. This may be anything from the addition of an entertainment complex to an existing destination to the development of a completely new holiday complex.

Often a holiday is sold to the customer on the basis of the facilities that are being provided – and customers' expectations are increasing all the time. People now expect their hotel to have some additional facilities – such as a bar, pool area and games room. Some

destinations have invested heavily in the provision of new and additional facilities. Many hotel complexes are located on or close to the beach – some even with private beaches. Some of these provide all-inclusive holiday packages – all meals, drinks and activities for one pre-paid price. This type of holiday particularly appeals to families or groups of people who may have very different holiday requirements (see below).

Da Balaia Club Med

The Club Med at Da Balaia in the Algarve, (Portugal) is one of Club Med's 36 sites in Europe. It claims to be the village for everyone – close to one of the most splendid golf courses in Europe and with a magnificent panorama overlooking the ocean. Accommodation consists of 389 air-conditioned rooms equipped with bathroom/WC, telephone, TV, mini-fridge, hairdryer and personal safes. There are three restaurants to choose from, including one overlooking the ocean and another that specialises in Moroccan food. There is also a night bar. The sports available include golf, tennis, aqua-fitness, archery, fitness room and volleyball. Discovery events include day trips to Faro and Loule market, together with an off-road tour to see the local nature. The leisure facilities range from a multiform pool made from three pools, to Turkish bath, mini-golf, petanque, piano-bar, table tennis and Club Med evening entertainment.

Source: www.clubmed.co.uk

activity

ADDITIONAL FACILITIES

Read the Da Balaia Club Med case study, and identify the additional facilities available at the resort. Discuss which type of customer the destination would appeal to and why.

Topic 9 Accessibility, image and attractions

Topic 10 Destination management, costs and political factors

In this final topic of the unit we will look at the effects on the popularity and appeal of European travel destinations of:

- **Destination management**
- **Cost of visiting**
- **Political factors.**

Destination management

Destination management is a relatively new concept, which has become more significant as the number of visitors has increased to various locations over the last few decades. Management of a destination covers a variety of factors and may involve a number of different people in the public and private sector.

The type of destination that needs to be managed may vary from an isolated mountainous region which is home to near-extinct forms of wildlife, to an over-crowded Mediterranean beach resort. Both areas need management, but for different reasons.

The factors to consider when managing a destination are numerous, and range from physical and environmental to social, economic and political. The physical limitations of a destination are generally based on land space – the amount of people that can be physically accommodated on an area of land. The crowded beaches of some resorts are purely restricted by the amount of beach space available.

In a residential resort the number of beds may play a large part in the management of the size of the resort. This is certainly the case in many of the European ski resorts – they try to control the number of people on the slopes by the number of beds they

have in the resort. On the other hand, developing resorts – such as La Rosiere in France – actively promote the increasing number of beds in the resort each season.

One of the contradictions in the development of a destination is that as it rapidly grows in popularity it may then become unpopular because so many people go there and it becomes overcrowded. Benidorm in Spain, for example, became a victim of its own success (see below).

Managing Benidorm

By the late 1980s this purpose-built, mass tourist resort (pictured above) had become so overcrowded that it changed out of all recognition. It started going into decline, and needed careful destination management. Improvements were made in:

- the quality of the built environment
- the cityscape – with urban parks
- the infrastructure – sewage disposal and water treatment
- traffic management – reducing vehicle movements along the promenade.

Benidorm is now a tourist resort able to accommodate a large number of mass tourists, which if distributed over a much wider area, might be considerably more of a threat to the environment.

Other destinations have become victims of their own attractiveness. Islands such as Mykonos (Greece), Porquerolles and Re (France) and Capri (Italy) are experiencing increasing pressures and have already exceeded their carrying capacity for people in the resort. The coastal strip (500m from shore) of Majorca, one of the most popular European destinations, was already 27% urbanised in 1995. This is called over-commercialisation.

Over-commercialisation is when a destination loses its tradition and heritage to modern facilities such as bars and nightclubs. Mass-market tourist areas such as Torremolinos on the Costa del Sol in Spain have been criticised for being over-commercialised. Massive hotel complexes, bars, nightclubs and restaurants dominate the coastline leaving nothing of the traditional destination hidden under the sprawl of modern buildings. These complexes tend to cater for the standard holiday package market offering relatively cheap accommodation with access to entertainment and of course a warm climate.

Many of these destinations now rely on destination management to maintain their tourist appeal.

Cost of visiting

The actual cost of a visit to Europe has decreased significantly over the last few decades. Destinations that provide low transport costs and accommodation are the most popular. Spain is still competitively priced and is the number one choice of destination for the UK, as shown in the table below. It also attracts the highest spend of £5,055 million.

In the western economies there has been a rapid growth in the number of people taking second (or

The top 10 holiday destinations for UK travellers		
Country	Visits (thousands)	Spend (£millions)
Spain	12,525	5,055
France	12,112	3,591
Irish Republic	3,965	974
[USA	3,602	3,250]
Greece	2,958	1,311
Italy	2,650	1,327
Germany	2,275	706
Netherlands	2,149	542
Belgium	1,784	428
Portugal	1,779	739

Source: International Passenger Survey 2002, UK residents, visits and spending abroad

more) holidays. Over a third now fall into this category. This is a consequence of steadily rising incomes, plus:

- an increase in the number of days of paid leave
- the decreasing real cost of holidays
- the shift in exchange rates.

activity

BEACHENDERS

Rising incomes have meant that more and more people can now afford to take several holidays a year. This new affluence has even given rise to a new trend – 'beachenders' – people who go to European beach resorts for the weekend, taking a no-frills flight on Friday, finding their own accommodation when they get there, and sunbathing and clubbing until their return flight late on Sunday – just making it back in time for work on Monday.

1 Suggest three destinations that you would recommend to a 'beachender'.
2 Explain why you think that these destinations may be suitable.

The increase in the number of days of paid leave

During recent years, the length of paid holiday time has increased, giving people more time for tourism and leisure. Europeans now take multiple holidays in the year, rather than extending the length of their main holiday. The average length of holiday for the UK traveller is now 10 days, but they tend to have more than one holiday a year. Short holidays (less than 4 nights away from home) have increased significantly. This trend is the same across most of Europe. In France, the decrease in the working week, from 39 to 35 hours, has resulted in more holiday time, and there have been similar developments in several other European countries.

The decrease in the real cost of holidays

The actual cost of a holiday has decreased significantly over the last few decades. The increase in competition between tour operators and low-cost airlines has continued to provide cheaper and cheaper access to many European destinations, a trend which seems set to continue. The result of the low-cost holidays has been that the number of visits abroad made by residents of the UK almost tripled between 1982 and 2002, and the spending on these visits increased more than seven times.

Exchange rates, and the euro

Exchange rates – the value of sterling against foreign currencies – play an important part in the appeal of destinations to UK tourists. The amount of foreign currency that your pound will buy is displayed in windows of bureaux de change, in banks and in newspapers. Exchange rates go up and down all the time. In the long term, this can affect the overall cost of holidaying in foreign countries.

Many countries in Europe have adopted the euro (see above) which has the same exchange rate with sterling, regardless of the country. What the exchange rates *don't* show is what we can actually buy for the money. This depends on the 'cost of living', which varies from country to country – a hundred euros, for example, will buy a lot more in Greece than it will in France.

The different costs of living obviously affect the popularity of destinations, because the more you can buy with your money, the more attractive a resort will appear. Slovenia and Croatia are currently the cheapest countries, and Italy the most expensive. Certainly one reason so many people choose to take self-catering holidays in Greece is because the cost of living there is relatively low.

After decades of talking about it, most of western Europe has a common currency. The euro was designed to be a common medium of exchange that ultimately would be used by all members of the European Union. Not only would this eliminate the

problems of changing money, but also it would unite the countries of Europe against the rest of the world economically, allow cross-border banking and borrowing, and ultimately, tie the countries of Europe more tightly together. The euro was introduced in 1999. However, not all of the countries joined in, as the table below shows:

euro nations	Non-euro nations
Austria	Britain
Belgium	Denmark
Finland	Norway
France	Sweden
Germany	Switzerland
Greece	All eastern European countries
Ireland	
Italy	
Luxembourg	
Netherlands	
Portugal	
Spain	

Supporters of the euro see it eventually competing with the US dollar as an international medium of exchange. For the traveller, however, the euro is already a success, because money no longer has to be exchanged at every border crossing.

activity

EXCHANGE RATES

Get a copy of the latest exchange rates and work out the equivalent of £1 in the countries in the Euro zone and those that are non-Euro.

Political factors

Political instability has affected eastern Europe for many years, particularly a country like Estonia that has been one of Europe's top invasion spots – occupied in turn by the Danish, Swedes, Russians, Germans and the Russians again. The war in the Balkans disrupted the tourist industry in the former Yugoslavia and throughout eastern Europe. Neighbouring countries were also affected, with reduced bookings to the Czech Republic and Hungary. Political stability is the real reason many European countries are keen to be united under the European Union as they see it as reducing the threat of any future wars.

Croatia's tourist industry has revived after the war in the Balkans.

Budapest's tourist industry should be helped by Hungary joining the European Union.

A future rich in freedom and promise

For 74 million people across Europe, this weekend brings a formal end to decades of isolation and oppression and heralds the start of a future rich in freedom and promise. The journey of the European Union's 10 new member states has been an extraordinary one and it is something to be genuinely celebrated by the rest of Western Europe. Since the European Coal and Steel Community came into being in 1951, the EU's greatest achievement has been to bring together countries that had seemed irrevocably divided by war and ideology. That was true of France, Germany and Italy in the 1950s, and it is true now with the addition of former members of the Soviet bloc.

On raw figures, the new members have per capita incomes that average only a fifth of those they are joining. Even on the most favourable definition they are less than half as well off as their new western European partners. Starting from a low base, and having in many cases embraced western capitalism more enthusiastically than the countries they are joining, they know they have the chance to secure decades of strong economic growth and rising prosperity.

Source (edited): The Times 2 May 2004

activity

EASTERN EUROPEAN DESTINATIONS

1 In small groups discuss what effect joining the EU will have on the popularity and appeal of the new eastern European member countries.

2 Select one of the countries, and in a short report describe how it may be affected by the following factors:

• Accessibility

• Image and promotion

• Availability of attractions and other tourist facilities

• Destination management

• Cost of visiting

• Political factors.

Present your findings to the rest of the group. A useful internet site for this exercise is www.visiteurope.com

How Unit 3 is assessed

Unit 3 is assessed by coursework. The evidence should be in four parts, which we suggest you present as four sections within a portfolio. The following guidance outlines how you can achieve the assessment requirements for each of the four parts.

The evidence could be in many different forms to allow for your learning preferences, styles and strengths to be accommodated – maps, written reports, promotional material, witness testimonies of oral presentations, etc

You are required to investigate three destinations in total for the unit. You do not research all three destinations for all tasks. Each investigation will have a specific focus:

- one destination for task (b), focusing on features
- one destination for task (c), focusing on factors that have affected popularity and appeal
- one destination for task (d), focusing on accessibility.

Task (a) Location and types of tourist destinations

The six types of destination are:
- Coastal areas
- Tourist towns and cities
- Business and conference destinations
- Countryside areas
- Heritage and cultural destinations
- Purpose built – built specifically to meet the needs of the tourist.

(a.1) Six maps, one for each type of destination

Each map should locate the appropriate European travel destinations popular with UK tourists and highlight the relevant gateways and road and rail routes for these destinations from the UK.

(a.2) Six explanations

For each of the six types of destination, an explanation of the features that differentiate them and the difficulties in categorising some destinations, giving examples.

NOTE: To achieve the higher mark bands you need to show detailed and accurate location of all destinations, important gateways from the UK, major road and rail routes within Europe, clear and detailed explanation of features (relating to all types of destination) and specific examples illustrating the difficulty in categorising destinations.

Task (b) The key features that give destinations appeal to different types of tourist

(b.0) Introduction

Describe the key features that give destinations appeal to different types of tourist. Identify the different types of tourist.

(b.1) Recommendations

Recommendations for a European destination that meets the needs of a tourist whose needs and circumstances are given to you by your tutor in the form of a pen portrait. These might be complex.

(b.2) Description and explanation

A description of the main features that give the recommended destination appeal, and an explanation of how it meets the needs of the tourist specified.

NOTE: To achieve the higher mark bands you need to show a detailed and accurate description of how the features of the destination meet the needs of the specified tourist.

Task (c) Factors that have led to the growth in popularity and appeal of one European travel destination

(c.0) Introduction

Describe the main factors that can influence the popularity and appeal of European Travel Destinations. (These include: accessibility, image and promotion, availability of attractions, destination management, cost of visiting and political factors.)

(c.1) A European destination

Select a destination in Europe that has grown in popularity in the last fifteen years, and analyse the factors that have led to its growth in popularity and appeal. Analyse how the destination has controlled factors to maximise their appeal and popularity.

(c.2) Bibliography

Provide evidence of research undertaken to complete all tasks in the unit assessment – using a range of different sources of current information relevant to today's travel and tourism industry. (It is arguably better to make this your final task, as it will cover all of the other three tasks.)

NOTE: To achieve the higher mark bands you need to show that sources were obtained independently and referenced. The destination chosen would be one that has recently become popular, so the factors identified are mainly current. There would be analysis of a wide range of factors that have led to the destination's growing appeal with all the current and relevant factors identified and analysed. There would also be a clear and detailed analysis of how the destination has maximised the controllable factors to increase its popularity.

Task (d) Accessibility: modes of transport for a type of tourist

(d.0) Introduction

Describe the key transport gateways in Europe and the key rail and road routes linking the main European tourist receiving and generating areas.

(d.1) Assessment

Assess the suitability of different modes of transport to a European travel destination for a type of tourist. Details of the type of tourist and their needs and circumstances will be given to you in the form of a pen portrait. This will include details of their departure point and destination. The tourist might have complex needs and circumstances.

NOTE: To achieve the higher mark bands you need to show a clear assessment, referring to the tourists' complex needs, and that a range of factors and transport modes have been considered.

Bibliography

List all of the sources of information that you have used to complete the assessment for this unit.

Appendices

Include any relevant supporting information in the appendices, such as examples of maps, etc.

Improving your grades

Generally, you will get better grades by giving more comprehensive explanations, including better examples and showing a deeper understanding of each topic. Your school or college should be able to advise you in more detail, or you could visit the Edexcel website: edexcel.org.uk for more guidance.

General guidelines on presentation of assignments

See page 289 for advice on how to present your assignments.

We looked at the whole travel and tourism industry In Unit 1, and started to understand how it had developed, its characteristics and structure. It may be useful for you to look at Unit 1 again as a basis for understanding the industry before looking at this unit.

The term 'Britain' is shorthand for the British Isles. For the purposes of this unit we will focus on the United Kingdom, which occupies most of the isles. The UK is made up of Great Britain (England, Scotland and Wales) and Northern Ireland, and is one of the 25 member states of the European Union (EU).

According to Bob Cotton, Chief Executive of the British Hospitality Association, tourism is worth nearly £76 billion to the UK generally, and is the biggest industry in some regions of the country. Latest figures show that 2.1 million people are directly employed in tourism – 7% of all people in employment in Great Britain. The tourism industry consists of some 127,000 businesses, 80% of which have a turnover of less than £250,000 per annum.

Clearly tourism is important to Britain and we start by investigating the structure of the industry and the large number of government bodies and organisations that support it. We go on to investigate the different types of destination. London – the UK's top tourist destination – is examined in detail.

Visiting a destination as diverse as Britain requires careful planning, so this unit also includes a section on itinerary planning. Whether a tourist is on an organised trip or travelling independently, the impact on Britain is immense. Visitor numbers, spending and type of visitor are all discussed in relation to the scale of tourism to Britain.

The final topic considers how the popularity and appeal of destinations change in relation to a number of factors – accessibility, attractions, costs. For some resorts, destination management has become of vital importance. For others, their image and how they promote themselves has been a significant factor in their popularity and appeal.

Lastly the impact of political factors on tourism is discussed, in relation to events such as 9/11.

Unit 4

Destination Britain

4.1 Travel and tourism organisations that support tourism in the British Isles

| Topic 1 | Public-sector tourism departments | 154 |
| Topic 2 | The variety of tourist organisations | 158 |

4.2 Features of destinations in the British Isles

Topic 3	Coasts, cities and business conferences	162
Topic 4	Countryside, cultural and purpose-built destinations	168
Topic 5	Environment, transport and accommodation	172
Topic 6	Facilities, attractions, events and culture	178

4.3 Constructing itineraries for tourists

| Topic 7 | Constructing itineraries for tourists | 182 |

4.4 Scale of tourism to the British Isles

| Topic 8 | The scale of tourism to the British Isles | 186 |

4.5 The factors that affect the popularity and appeal of destinations

| Topic 9 | The factors that affect the popularity and appeal of destinations | 190 |

| How Unit 4 is assessed | 196 |

Public-sector tourism departments

A vast array of organisations support the travel and tourism industry in Britain, ranging from the small hill farmer offering B&B, to the many government agencies that provide a network of provision for the sector. In this topic we will look at the activities and responsibilities of the following organisations:

- Government departments and agencies
- Regional and national tourist offices
- Local authority tourism departments.

Government departments and agencies

Thousands of businesses depend in whole or part on tourism, not just hotels and accommodation providers but restaurants, transport businesses and a range of visitor attractions from art galleries to zoos.

The impact of all this activity is enormous – both on individual communities and on national self-image. It accounts for a significant part of Britain's economic activity. Yet it is still in some ways a hidden industry. Although they may be substantially dependent on income from tourists, a pub landlord, a coach operator, or a shop assistant may not see themselves as anything to do with the tourist industry at all. Part of the government's role is to help these diverse businesses recognise their common interest in working together.

The government places great importance on the significant contribution that tourism makes to the economy. The increasing productivity of tourism businesses makes a vital contribution to the government's wider objective of increasing UK productivity as a whole.

Since its establishment in 1992, The Department of Culture, Media and Sport (DCMS) has been the government department with the responsibility for supporting the inbound and domestic tourism industry. The Tourism Division of the DCMS works hard in partnership with the tourism sector to develop conditions that are right for the industry to flourish and increase its productivity. Since the tourism sector has a large proportion of small and medium-sized enterprises, an important part of the DCMS's work focuses on increasing productivity in such small businesses.

The DCMS acts as a 'champion' for tourism across all government departments and the regions, raising the industry's profile on a range of issues that affect the sector including regulation, financial and other policy issues. This includes co-operation with the devolved administrations of Scotland and Wales and the Northern Ireland Office to encourage a common approach to policy and delivery.

The DCMS aims are:

- to work with the Regional Development Agencies who have strategic responsibility for tourism in the regions;
- to support and encourage local authorities in their tourism promotional work.
- to work with the Greater London Authority to ensure that the unique role of the capital as a gateway is recognised.

The government plays a significant role in the development of many areas of the tourism industry – with its transport policies and its rural development initiatives, etc.

Regional tourist boards and national tourist offices

Regional Tourist Boards (RTBs) were established to promote tourism in their area. They are not government agencies. The RTBs are funded in part by the Department of Culture, Media and Sport (DCMS) and the Regional Development Agencies (RDA); the rest of their funding comes from business and local authority membership fees plus commercial income from training courses. All the regional tourist boards work in different ways to promote their local area. Some regions such as the south west of England or the Lake District are lucky to have the advantage of beautiful scenery and coastlines to attract the tourist. Other regions such as urban areas have to find different ways to attract people to their region. Some examples of the Regional Tourist Boards are: Tourism South East, Heart of England Tourist Board and the Yorkshire Tourist Board.

There are eight Regional Development Agencies that, along with the London Development Agency, have a role in the economic development of their region. Under the Regional Development Agencies Act 1998, each agency is responsible, among other things, for

regional regeneration and promoting tourism. The RDAs are developing regional tourism strategies and the Regional Tourist Boards will in some regions be principal delivery partners, while in other regions the RTBs' work will become part of the relevant RDA.

The aim of national tourist boards is to coordinate the diverse interests that make up the tourism industry and to provide it with a single voice. The four main national tourist boards in the UK are VisitBritain, Wales Tourist Board, VisitScotland and Northern Ireland Tourist Board. VisitBritain reports to the Department of Culture, Media and Sport. The Wales Tourist Board reports to the National Assembly for Wales, and VisitScotland reports to the Scottish assembly.

VisitBritain was formed in 2003 from the British Tourist Authority and the English Tourism Council to market Britain as a tourist destination to the rest of the world. It also markets England to the British. Working in partnership with the other national tourist boards, VisitBritain's role is to promote an attractive image of Britain, provide impartial tourism information and gather essential market intelligence for the UK tourism industry.

VisitBritain is funded by the DCMS. The grant to promote Britain overseas for 2003/04 was £35 million. Additionally, VisitBritain raises around £15 million in funding from non-Government partners.

The objective for VisitBritain is to generate interest in the UK and therefore encourage visitors and

Some regional tourist boards have picture-postcard locations to work with.

spending. It launched the 'UK City Experience' campaign, for example, which highlighted the exciting diversity of attractions to be found in 23 of Britain's cities – such as Oxford's dreaming spires, Cardiff's sleek, futuristic waterside and Manchester's buzzing nightclubs.

Research has shown that VisitBritain's activities work. It has been estimated that every £1 of public money it spends generates £31 of overseas visitors' expenditure in Britain.

One way of promoting the UK has been encouraging major film makers to choose British locations. The Harry Potter movies, for example, have massively boosted tourism in the areas used for filming. Alnwick Castle and the train stations at Goathland and Pickering in North Yorkshire are now crowded with tourists trying to retrace Harry's steps. Another example of VisitBritain successfully promoting tourism through links with a film is described on the right.

activity

VISITBRITAIN'S TWO WEBSITES

Visit the VisitBritain website, www.visitbritain.com and explain how it promotes Britain as a destination and the information it provides for the tourist.

VisitBritain also maintains an information site for businesses that work in the tourism industry: www.tourismtrade.org.uk. Visit this site and analyse the type of information available for a business in the tourism industry.

Local authority tourism departments

Local authorities (LAs) have a vital role in supporting the tourism industry because of their statutory duties and because of their wider responsibilities for local infrastructure, economic development and sense of place. Local authorities are the only bodies capable of joining up all aspects of tourism at local level, working in partnership with local businesses and other interests including the RDAs. A good example of this partnership is shown in the example on the next page, taken from the Isle of Wight's local authority website.

Visit Britain and *King Arthur and his Knights*

VisitBritain has joined forces with Touchstone Pictures and Buena Vista International to publish a 'King Arthur Movie Map. It is the seventh in VisitBritain's hugely successful movie-map series, which also includes 'Master and Commander', 'Johnny English – Mission to Britain' and 'Harry Potter – Discover the Magic of Britain' as well as those based on Bollywood films and Hollywood blockbusters and 'Brit-flicks'.

The unique guide features key destinations and attractions synonymous with Arthurian legend from the Dark to Medieval Ages, as well as Roman Britain's historical sites and locations. The 25 Arthurian and Roman locations on the map include Tintagel Castle, Merlin's Grave and Hadrian's Wall, along which much of the film's action and story is played out. King's Knot in Stirling and Caerleon in Gwent also feature, in addition to Roman locations such as Eboracum (York) and Londinium (London). On the reverse of the map, VisitBritain has identified locations that appear in more than 50 new movies, classic film favourites and TV shows from the 60s to the present day.

A VisitBritain spokeswoman explained: 'Around 1 in 5 overseas visitors are inspired to visit Britain because of something they've seen in a movie or on TV and, through our work with major motion picture studios, VisitBritain can reach huge numbers of consumers and persuade them to come here.'

activity

HOW MANY ARE INVOLVED?

Read the case study on Cowes Week and make a list of all the people that are involved in the event. Select an event in your local area and investigate how many people and organisations are involved.

There's nothing quite like Skandia Cowes Week – the sailing is great for spectators and competitors alike, and there's a fantastic line-up of live entertainment day and night. If you can only come for a day, make sure it's Friday 13 August – fireworks night. Staged from a pontoon moored in the Solent, hundreds of vessels from pleasure steamers to small powerboats lie at anchor, whilst the shore is packed with thousands of spectators watching the fireworks light up the sea and night sky.

Onshore there will be plenty to do and see, with street entertainment and bands in the Parade Village and throughout the High Street. Attractions will include live bands, stilt-walkers, comedians and magic shows suitable for all ages. Building on the success of the Parade Village last year, Wight Leisure and Mainsail are again working together to create an even better focal point for Cowes seafront. New this year will be a

model-boat sailing pool situated in the exhibition marquee and a chance for a close up look at one of the GBR Challenge America's Cup yachts. Next to the exhibition area, the Royal Yachting Association's 'Sail for Gold' bar, supporting British Olympic and Paralympic sailors, will be open to 11 pm each day. And don't miss the Red Arrows display on August 12.

Interdependence and interrelationships

Often it is the interdependence and interrelationship between organisations that leads to the success of many projects in the travel and tourism industry. One organisation may provide the funding but in most cases it comes from many sources, such as the Department of Culture, Media and Sport, the Lottery Fund and the local council. This working together is common practice across the UK, as the Stonehenge Project shows, below.

The Stonehenge Project

For thousands of years, Stonehenge stood in an isolated setting surrounded by chalk downland. Then two roads were established through the landscape and gradually upgraded, resulting in ever-increasing traffic and serious environmental problems, as more and more visitors came to visit this national monument. The visitor facilities were 'cramped' and denounced by Parliament as 'a national disgrace'. At last, national and local government, the Highways Agency, English Heritage, the National Trust and English Nature joined forces to deliver a plan – the Stonehenge Project, supported by the Heritage Lottery Fund.

The Stonehenge Project is designed to improve the setting and interpretation of Stonehenge. It will remove the sights and sounds of the roads and traffic from the area near the Stones, recreate chalk downland from arable farmland and transform the visitor experience with better access to the landscape and a new world-class visitor centre.

activity

WORKING TOGETHER?

Analyse the influence each partner may have on the Stonehenge Project. Identify the priorities of each organisation and how their input may influence this as a tourist attraction.

The variety of tourist organisations

In the last topic we looked at the government departments, national and regional tourist boards and local authority tourism departments. In this topic we will look at more organisations that work together towards the same end – promoting Britain as a tourist destination:

- Regional development agencies
- Tourist information centres
- Membership organisations
- Transport operators, accommodation providers and tour operators.

Regional Development Agencies

In England there are nine Regional Development Agencies (RDAs) and their main function is to oversee the economic development of their region. The RDAs aim to co-ordinate economic development and regeneration, to improve their relative competitiveness and address the imbalances that exist within and between regions. Together the RDAs have an annual budget of £2 billion.

The RDAs are now key players with government in leading tourism into the future. They work both

The Dorset World Heritage Site

The Dorset World Heritage Site is a stretch of coastline of significant historical importance with rock formations spanning the Mesozoic Era – some 185 million years of the earth's history. The area's important fossil sites and classic coastal geomorphologic features (see photo above) have contributed to the study of earth sciences for over 300 years.

individually and with one another, as well as with regional and local partners. Tourism is being repositioned as a driver of regional economies. In line with government policy, the RDAs are being encouraged to make tourism a key component of their economic development, linking it with other regional strategies, for example regeneration, skills development, transport and planning.

The South West Regional Development Agency is responsible for the largest region in England, and one of the most varied. Since 1999 it has helped enhance the image of the region as a tourist destination, as a region with a unique cultural heritage, as a location for new investment, and as a sustainable region with a high quality of life. It will also support projects that enhance the image of the region as a place where business excellence, manufacturing excellence and technology excellence contribute to it being widely regarded as a dynamic and innovative place to live and work. Activities and projects the RDA supports

activity

RESEARCHING AN RDA

Select one of the regional development agencies and compile a summary of the information that you find on the site. You could select you own region or research them all as a group project.

East Midlands – www.enjoyeastmidlands.com
West Midlands – www.visittheartofengland.com
East of England – www.visiteastofengland.com
London – www.visitlondon.com
North East – www.visitnorthumbria.com
North West – www.visitnorthwest.com
South West – www.visitsouthwest.co.uk
South East – www.visitsoutheastengland.com
Yorkshire/Humber – www.yorkshirevisitor.com

include the Dorset World Heritage Site (see above) and the Eden Project.

Over 2003–06, the RDAs will receive £3.6 million a year specifically for tourism. This money is ring-fenced to be passed on to the Regional Tourist Boards or to other designated tourism delivery bodies such as the Destination Management Organisations/Partnerships. Some of the money is ring-fenced for London.

London plays a vital role in the UK's tourism industry, with over half of visitors to the UK coming via the capital. Promoting London as a tourist destination and as a 'gateway' to the rest of the UK is a statutory duty of the Mayor of London, who works through the London Development Agency in implementing his Tourism Strategy for London. The budget for tourism is £1.9 million a year between 2003 and 2006.

London will host a number of events to encourage people into the city. For example, the Trafalgar Square Summer Programme was designed to encourage people into the centre of London on their way from work and after school, or simply passing through the area. Trafalgar Square is an internationally recognised public space and provides a unique platform for music, street theatre and other live performances from artists in the UK and overseas.

Since 1999, tourism has become the responsibility of the UK's devolved national administrations. For information on visiting Scotland, Wales and Northern Ireland see www.visitscotland.com ; www.visitwales.com , discovernorthernireland.com.

Tourist information centres

Tourist information centres are situated in many cities, towns and villages. Some are even sited at individual places of interest such as a castle. They provide up-to-date information on events, attractions, activities and public transport, sell tickets for local events and provide a free accommodation-booking service for the whole of the UK.

activity

PROVIDING INFORMATION

Imagine you are working behind the desk in your local tourist information centre. Role-play the following situations:

1 A family with young children are looking for the local play area to have a picnic.
2 A young French couple who do not speak much English would like to find somewhere to hire a car.
3 A business traveller needs somewhere to stay overnight.
4 An elderly couple would like to visit a local place of interest. The lady would need to use a wheelchair if much walking is involved.

Membership organisations

Many of the membership organisations are in the voluntary sector. Voluntary-sector organisations are usually non-profit making or charitable and managed and operated largely by volunteers. These include a wide range of conservation, countryside recreation and heritage pressure groups, such as the National Trust (see next page), the Ramblers Association and Tourism Concern. Membership organisations make a huge contribution to the industry, as their members are often associated strongly with tourism at the grass roots.

This is also true of 'destination associations', such as the Scottish Destination Management Association which promotes Scotland as a tourist destination. They have meetings with a variety of other organisations such as the Scottish Executive, VisitScotland, the various Scottish Tourist Boards, British Airways, Edinburgh Airport, Scottish Tourist Guides and the Edinburgh and Glasgow Hotel Associations.

activity

INVESTIGATE A MEMBERSHIP GROUP

Investigate a membership group that you are interested in and write a short report on its impact on the tourism industry. Refer to how it works alongside other organisations to reach its objectives.

The place to start when visiting a new town or city

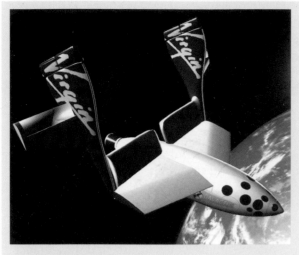

Virgin Galactic

Virgin Galactic is a company established by Richard Branson's Virgin Group to undertake the challenge of developing space tourism for everybody.

Virgin Galactic will own and operate privately built spaceships that will allow affordable sub-orbital space tourism for the first time in history.

Virgin's experience in aviation, adventure, luxury travel and cutting-edge design will be vital in contributing to the design of the spaceship, the smooth operation of the spaceline and creating an unforgettable experience unlike any other available to mankind.

Source: www.virgingalactic.com

Transport operators, accommodation providers and tour operators

There are many other organisations involved in Britain's travel and tourism industry, the majority of which are small and medium-sized private-sector enterprises.

However, the industry is dominated by the few larger organisations. These national and international organisations have a powerful impact on the whole industry.

Transport operators

The transport and communication links are covered extensively in Topic 5 of this unit. The transport operators vary from the small one-man bus company to large international organisations such as Richard Branson and his Virgin Group. Many of you will be familiar with the name Virgin Airways and Virgin Trains, but Virgin has now gone beyond the traditional forms of travel as shown in the case study above.

The National Trust

The National Trust is a registered charity and is independent of government. It was founded in 1895 to preserve places of historic interest or natural beauty permanently for the nation to enjoy. It relies on the generosity of its supporters, through membership subscriptions, gifts and legacies, and the practical contribution of many thousands of volunteers.

The Trust now protects and opens to the public over 200 historic houses and gardens and 49 industrial monuments and mills. It owns almost 600 miles of outstanding coastline and more than 248,000 hectares (612,000 acres) of the most beautiful countryside for people to enjoy. This includes forests, woods, fens, farmland, downs, moorland, islands, archaeological remains, nature reserves and villages.

It has the unique statutory power to declare land 'inalienable'. Such land cannot be sold, mortgaged or compulsorily purchased against the Trust's wishes – without special parliamentary procedure. This special power means that protection by the Trust is for ever.

Without its members, visitors and volunteers it would be unable to carry on its work. The Trust's enterprises include the popular National Trust tea rooms and shops, and National Trust holiday cottages.

The Trust invests over £160 m a year in the nation's environmental infrastructure and works with over 40,000 companies, including 2,000 specialist conservation businesses.

Source: www.nationaltrust.org.uk

Accommodation providers

Accommodation provision in Britain ranges from the small family-run establishment to the huge international hotel chains found all around the world. Choice of accommodation often depends on the tourists budget. Britain can accommodate the whole range – from the rich and famous in their suites at the Ritz or Savoy in London, to those on less expensive visits who are guests of the Youth Hostelling Association (YHA). The YHA provides valuable cheap accommodation for many tourists, as highlighted in the case study below. Accommodation is also investigated further in Topic 5 of this unit.

Tour operators

Tour operators assemble the components of tourism products and market them as packages to the customer. Unit 1 covers tour operators and the other major organisations involved with tourism in the UK. Ukinbound is the trade body which represents tour operators and tourism suppliers to Britain. (Before 2004 it had been called the British Incoming Tour Operators

Association – BITOA.) Members include national and regional tourist boards, tour operators, ground handlers, hoteliers, restaurants, visitor attractions and other suppliers to the inbound tourism industry.

activity

YOUR LOCAL ORGANISATIONS

From the information that you have gathered in the last two topics about travel and tourism organisations, investigate the names of the organisations in your local area that work within each sector. Are there any special projects that they are currently undertaking together to attract tourists to the area?

The Youth Hostels Association

The YHA operates a network of 225 youth hostels across England and Wales. Over 320,000 members receive a warm welcome, comfortable accommodation, good food and affordable prices.

The Youth Hostels Association of Great Britain was formed as a joint initiative between rambling, cycling and youth organisations, to meet the demand for simple accommodation for walkers and cyclists travelling throughout the UK. Shortly afterwards, it became the YHA (England and Wales) with separate associations for Scotland and Ireland.

The YHA is one Britain's' top 50 charities and its objective is:

To help all, especially young people of limited means, to a greater knowledge, love and care of the countryside, particularly by providing hostels or other simple accommodation for them in their travels and thus to promote their health, rest and education .

The YHA caters for individual travellers, families, and school and youth groups, recording more than 2 million overnight stays each year. It employs 1,200 staff including 600 seasonal staff, and has 2000 additional volunteer helpers. The annual turnover is £35 million.

The YHA is an active member of the International Youth Hostel Federation (IYHF), which embraces 60 countries, with 4,000 hostels and 3.2 million members worldwide. The IYHF is the largest budget-accommodation network in the world. The UK youth hostels cater for visitors from over 80 different nations.

The YHA plans to extend its network by offering new types of accomodation, such as guesthouses, bunkhouses, camping barns and backpackers hostels for young international travellers. It is inviting existing accomodation providers, such as owners of guesthouses and B&Bs, to join the YHA network.

Source: www.yha.org.uk

activity

THE PLACE OF THE YHA IN THE INDUSTRY

Discuss the effects that the YHA has had on the travel and tourism industry and how you think it will influence the industry in the future. For example consider the following questions:

- What is it doing to encourage overseas visitors?
- What impact will its plans for accommodation have on the industry?
- How does it work alongside other organisations?

Coasts, cities and business conferences

In the last two topics we looked at organisations that support the travel and tourism industry. The next two topics will look at the different types of destination in Britain. This topic looks at:

- Coastal areas
- Tourist towns and cities
- Business and conference destinations.

Coastal areas

The UK has over 9000 miles of coastline, with many stretches inaccessible. Some of the coastline is listed as heritage beaches, and the rest offers a variety of rural and resort beaches. Some stretches are steep craggy cliffs such as the White Cliffs of Dover, and some are deep little coves such as those common on the Cornish coastline with its quaint fishing villages.

However, probably the most common perception of the UK coast is the seaside resort.

Seaside 'resorts' are popular holiday places by the sea. Often these are heavily commercialised – full of amusement arcades and kiss-me-quick hats. Some have long sweeping bays of sandy beach like Blackpool, others have become established around small coves, such as Ilfracombe in Devon. The 'Seaside

---

activity

BEACHES AND TYPES

1 On the map, identify the location of the following beach resorts: Blackpool, Skegness, Bournemouth, Morecambe, Ilfracombe, St Ives, Southend, Aberystwyth, Great Yarmouth, Llandudno, St Andrews, Margate.

2 The groups of people listed below have decided to enjoy a day at the coast. Recommend the type of beach that you think that each group would enjoy and the type of activities you think they would be interested in doing. Try and think of some real beaches that you would recommend that they visit. For this exercise consider that distance and money is no object. You may find an atlas helpful.

a Mrs Brown is a retired schoolteacher living in Bedfordshire, who enjoys walking short distances and is particularly interested in bird watching.

b Jed and Tom are two sports-mad 18 year olds who live in London. Jed can drive and they are keen to try out any watersports that they can.

c The Curtis family live in Bradford and are keen ramblers, often walking 10 miles at a weekend.

d The McHugh family has two small children and they live in Taunton and enjoy having family picnics.

e John is a single man in his 40s who is into extreme sports.

Seaside resorts and beaches

St Ives ☀ Main seaside resort
▓ Main beach

Awards' define beaches as either resort or rural. Examples of each are listed below.

A lot of the beaches on the south cost are resort beaches, such as Brighton, which is one of the Londoners' favourite weekend retreats. Further to the west are Littlehampton and Bournemouth. Moving down to the south-west you will find the Cornish resort beaches of Tor Bay and St Ives, and to the north

of them lie the surfing beaches of Newquay and Ilfracombe. The Welsh resort beaches range from Pwllheli in the south to Aberystwth in the middle, up to Colwyn Bay in the north. The north-west beaches are dominated by Blackpool and smaller places like Lytham St Anne's. Down the east coast of England are the resort beaches of Scarborough in Yorkshire, and Skegness, Great Yarmouth and Southend-on-Sea – the favourite of the people living in east London.

Beach awards scheme

- The **Seaside Awards** recognise clean, well-managed resort and rural beaches. They are reviewed annually and a distinctive flag or plaque is on display at each beach.
- The **Blue Flag** scheme compares beaches throughout Europe and South Africa.
- The **Rural Blue Flag** pilot scheme recognises more remote, rural beaches that.
- The **Green Coast** is a scheme being piloted in Wales, which recognises the more remote rural beaches, which have sound environmental management.
- The **Resort Survey** is an independent report on the status of over 180 of the busiest beaches in the country. It is conducted every year and measures the performance of a variety of different management issues, including cleanliness, information, dog control and safety. Resorts are graded A–D, according to their overall scores.

Rural beaches tend be less easily accessible and less well known. Examples include Botany Bay (Broadstairs), Greatstone and Romney Sands in the south-east, and Bude and Kennack Sands in the south-west. Not surprisingly there are many rural beaches in Scotland, Wales, Northern Ireland and the north of England.

The needs of the visitor will influence their choice of coastal area to visit. A visitor with a pushchair or wheelchair, for example, will find certain parts of the coastline inaccessible, although recently more is being done to provide coastal paths that will provide access.

There are several different award schemes for beaches in the UK, designed to ensure that they are kept clean and safe. There are 374 Seaside Award beaches, although there are currently 552 official bathing sites in the UK, which are identified and monitored according to the EU Bathing Water Directive. The main UK beach awards scheme are shown above.

Tourist towns and cities

- A town is a substantial urban settlement, bigger than a village, which acts as the focal point of its area.
- A city is a large and important town, with special rights given by charter, and usually with a cathedral.

We will now look at each of these in turn – the types

Top towns visited by overseas visitors (2002)

City/Town	Visits (thousands)
London	11,600
Edinburgh	850
Birmingham	670
Manchester	590
Glasgow	400
Oxford	390
Bristol	310
Cambridge	280
Cardiff	280
Newcastle-upon-Tyne	240
Brighton/Hove	230
York	230
Bath	200
Nottingham	200
Liverpool	190
Inverness	180
Coventry	160
Reading	150
Canterbury	150
Leeds	140

Source: International Passenger Survey 2002

of visitors attracted to them and the factors that affect their popularity – and consider the impact that tourism can have on them.

The fortunate location of some towns has meant that they have been able to grow in importance as the travel and tourism industry has developed. This is particularly true of seaside towns, of course, such as Blackpool or St Ives, but it also applies to more rural inland towns, such as Penrith in Cumbria.

New towns, originally created to relieve the pressure on long-established and growing cities, have now become popular in their own right. Milton Keynes, for example, has grown substantially since its creation in the late 1960s. Dominated in the centre by a large commercial and covered retail-shopping complex, the town now boasts numerous other attractions such as an enormous cinema complex and more recently a snow dome.

Cities are large towns that have been awarded 'city' status under a special charter. There are currently 66 cities in the UK – 50 in England, 6 in Scotland, 5 in Wales, and 5 in Northern Ireland (see list).

English cities

Bath	Kingston-upon-Hull	Preston
Birmingham	Lancaster	Ripon
Bradford	Leeds	Salford
Brighton & Hove	Leicester	Salisbury
Bristol	Lichfield	Sheffield
Carlisle	Lincoln	Southampton
Cambridge	Liverpool	St Albans
Canterbury	London	Stoke-on-Trent
Chester	Manchester	Sunderland
Chichester	Newcastle-upon-Tyne	Truro
Coventry	Norwich	Wakefield
Derby	Nottingham	Wells
Durham	Oxford	Westminster
Ely	Peterborough	Winchester
Exeter	Plymouth	Wolverhampton
Gloucester	Portsmouth	Worcester
Hereford		York

Scottish cities	**Welsh cities**	**Northern Irish cities**
Aberdeen	Bangor	Armagh
Dundee	Cardiff	Belfast
Edinburgh	Newport	Lisburn
Glasgow	St David's	Londonderry
Inverness	Swansea	Newry
Stirling		

activity

WHERE ARE ALL THE CITIES?

Using an atlas, locate all the cities listed above, and mark them on an outline map of the UK.

activity

SOME FEATURES APPEAL, SOME DON'T

Identify a tourist town and write a short report on its features, distinguishing between those features that are key to its appeal to tourists and those which have less, or no, influence on its appeal. Consider the following factors:

- Location
- Transport links
- The local area
- Historical and cultural attractions
- Amenities and facilities provided in the town
- Competition from other towns and villages.

London is by far the most popular destination for overseas visitors (see table), and will be discussed in later topics. Edinburgh is the second most popular city in the UK with overseas visitors. Some of its diverse attractions are outlined below.

According to the 'UK Day Visits Survey' the majority of tourism trips (72 per cent) were to towns and cities. Some cities have more natural appeal as tourist destinations than others. For example, the old cities of Canterbury, Chester and York have more historical charm than those such as Peterborough or Kingston-upon Hull.

165

Topic 3 Coasts, cities and business conferences

Edinburgh Tops Travel Poll for Sixth Year

Readers of the Guardian and Observer newspapers have voted Scotland's capital their 'Favourite UK City' for an unprecedented sixth consecutive year.

'Edinburgh', said the writer Robert Louis Stevenson, 'is what Paris ought to be'. Its magnificent architecture shifts from the lofty buildings of its medieval Old Town, as they tumble down the spine of the Royal Mile, to the grace of the Georgian New Town. Above it all, in its towering splendour, stands the Castle.

Every step is a revelation – an alleyway that reveals an ancient courtyard, or a wynd,

which opens up a new panorama. And yet within this sweeping elegance is a compact city and a bustling city.

Edinburgh is famous for its many festivals from fringe theatre to international rugby fixtures to the Military Tattoo. Set against the stunning backdrop of the Castle, the Military Tattoo is the largest single gathering of military musicians in the UK. This spectacular event attracts visitors from across the globe and is usually a complete sell out.

Source: Edinburgh and Lothians Tourist Board

SELLING EDINBURGH TO DIFFERENT PEOPLE

Imagine you work for the Edinburgh Tourist Board. Role-play three scenes where prospective visitors, who have never been to Edinburgh, telephone for information on why you would recommend a visit. The callers, who will require different information according to their specific circumstances, are:

1 A Swedish businessman and his wife, who want to visit the major sights for the day.
2 A family with three children under 10, who want to visit the city for some fun.
3 An elderly couple who are limited in mobility, and want to visit two or three of the city's cultural attractions.

Business and conference destinations

Britain's position as one of the world's leading conference countries is confirmed by the statistics of both the ICCA (International Congress and Convention Association) and the UIA (Union of International Associations). The larger conferences tend to be held in the purpose-built business centres. Two-thirds of corporate events, however, involve no more than 50 delegates, and the majority are held in hotels.

According to the British Association of Conference Destinations (BACD), the UK conference business is worth an estimated £8 billion per year. The total value of the conference business is even higher when account is taken of delegate expenditure on such items as drinks in the bar, meals in local restaurants, entertainment and visits to attraction and transport

Conference venues provide large spaces that can be used in different ways.

Old, grand hotels can adapt their rooms for conference use.

costs. The BACD research was based on a survey of over 200 conference venues across the UK, the great majority of whom reported that business was increasing, and was expected to increase still further.

Companies using conference venues pay, on average, £170 a day for each residential delegate, and nearly £50 a day for non-residential delegates. The average conference has 35–40 delegates, and lasts between a $1\frac{1}{2}$ and 2 days. This 'average' conference would therefore cost over £10,000 – plus all the extras.

Conferencing is a year round activity, with peaks in September, October, June and November. The main international conference destinations in the UK are Aberdeen, Belfast, Birmingham, Bournemouth, Brighton, Cardiff, Edinburgh, Glasgow, Harrogate, London and Manchester. There are, of course, many more cities and towns ready to host a conference event. VisitBritain points out that Britain is ideal for business conferences because of the following factors:

- English is spoken here!
- Britain's leading tourist destinations ensure high delegate attendance
- Easily accessible
- Superb range of conference venues
- Excellent support services
- Knowledgeable convention bureaux
- Fast and efficient VAT reclaim
- And don't forget that Britain is a world leader in science and medicine, as well as in many other professional fields, making it the natural choice for many high-profile events.

It is clear that the conference industry is booming, and many destinations in the UK are realising the benefit of

WHICH CITY IS WHICH?

Identify the following cities from their descriptions below: Bath, York, Oxford, Newcastle, Manchester, Cardiff, Glasgow, Carlisle.

City 1 The symbol of the city's strategic importance is the castle. Founded by William Rufus in 1092 and once a prison for Mary Queen of Scots, it is still the home today of the King's Own Border Regiment. Historically, whoever held this city could influence the destinies of both England and Scotland.

City 2 For over 800 years, this city has been a home to royalty and scholars. Nowadays, it is a bustling cosmopolitan town, still with its ancient university, but home also to a growing hi-tech community – with businesses located all over the town and in the Science and Business Parks.

City 3 This city hosts major events such as the Network Q Rally, the FA Cup Final, the Worthington Cup, the Nationwide Playoffs and large-scale pop concerts at the Millennium Stadium, as well as smaller festivals such as the Mardi Gras and the Big Weekend.

City 4 This city has been reborn as a centre of style and vitality, set against a backdrop of outstanding Victorian architecture. It boasts world-famous art collections and the best shopping in the United Kingdom outside London. A 'must see' is the Art Nouveau splendour of the city's best known architect Charles Rennie Mackintosh.

City 5 This great city, once in the forefront of 19th-century industrial innovation, is now in the forefront of technical innovation, leisure and culture. Wander down to the transformed waterfront, the Quayside, now lined with stylish hotels, designer bars, restaurants and public art. The Millennium Bridge, a work of art in itself, arches across the Tyne to link the city to Gateshead Quays and the Baltic Centre for Contemporary Art.

City 6 Renowned for its rainy weather, there is inspiration (and shelter) to be found at the Lowry or the Imperial War Museum of the North.

City 7 Among this city's attractions are the Pump Room, the Assembly Rooms and the Roman Baths. See the Circus and the Royal Crescent, two of the best examples of 18th-century architecture, for which this city is famous.

City 8 With numerous award-winning attractions this walled city will surprise, inspire and stimulate you, with a stunning cathedral, the world's best railway museum, and the finest UK Viking attraction. Add to this the smaller gems like medieval guildhalls, Georgian town houses, and numerous National Trust and English Heritage properties, and this walled city does not disappoint any visitor.

encouraging the business traveller. Birmingham, for example, has been able to develop as a major conference centre by capitalising on its easy access. Birmingham International airport is already the second biggest airport outside London and one of the fastest growing with an estimated 10 million travellers in 2005. The airport is served by 28 scheduled airlines and 16 charter airlines. In addition Birmingham is at the centre of England's motorway system and has a half-hourly rail connection to London, just 80 minutes away.

Although the really large conferences need special purpose-built centres, it should not be forgotten that the majority of conferences are held in hotels. Many chains of hotels have large sales teams devoted to chasing business customers and in particular conferences. The Hilton International chain, for example, has 77 hotels throughout the UK and Ireland, and over 380 hotels worldwide. They can cater for any type of business meeting up to a 500-delegate conference.

WHERE SHALL WE MEET?

With the use of a variety of sources, such as the internet and brochures, research the best hotel location for the groups of business people listed below. Write up you recommendations and provide a choice of two venues for each, explaining the reasons for your choices.

- 100 UK business people travelling from the south of England to meet their northern equivalents, and needing a meeting room and overnight accommodation.

- 50 delegates from a variety of European countries needing a hotel with easy access to an airport, for a 2-day conference.

- 20 delegates who live and work between Doncaster and Newcastle, and need to meet on a monthly basis.

Topic 4 | Countryside, cultural and purpose-built destinations

In the last topic we looked at coastal areas, tourist towns and cities, and business and conference destinations. Now we will go on to look at the three other types of destination:

- **Countryside areas**
- **Heritage and cultural destinations**
- **Purpose-built destinations – built specifically to meet the needs of tourists.**

Countryside areas

Britain has an abundance of fine countryside, from Land's End to John O'Groats. Visitors are attracted to the beautiful coastline, the rugged mountains and the picturesque dales.

Many areas have been given special status to protect their environment. In England, the job of overseeing these 'protected areas' lies with the Countryside Agency, whose aim is to conserve and enhance the natural beauty of the countryside and to help give people better facilities and opportunities to enjoy and appreciate it. The Countryside Agency has special responsibility for designating National Parks, Areas of Outstanding Natural Beauty (AONBs) and Heritage coasts.

The Countryside Councils for Wales, Scotland and Northern Ireland do a similar job in their regions.

National Parks

The National Parks include some of the most remote and dramatic landscapes of England and Wales. They contain a mosaic of rich landscapes, including sweeping heather moorlands, dramatic coastlines, breathtaking upland and mountainous areas.

Designated areas of countryside

- National Parks
- Areas of Outstanding Natural Beauty (England, Wales and N. Ireland) National Scenic Areas (Scotland)
- Heritage Coast (England and Wales) Preferred Conservation Zone (Scotland)

Cairngorms

Loch Lomond and the Trossachs

Glasgow ● ● Edinburgh

Northumberland

Lake District

North York Moors

Yorkshire Dales

● Manchester

Peak District

Snowdonia

The Broads

● Birmingham

Brecon Beacons

Pembrokeshire Coast

● Cardiff

● London

Exmoor

New Forest

Dartmoor

The Lake District National Park

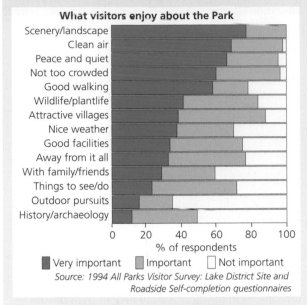

What visitors enjoy about the Park

Scenery/landscape
Clean air
Peace and quiet
Not too crowded
Good walking
Wildlife/plantlife
Attractive villages
Nice weather
Good facilities
Away from it all
With family/friends
Things to see/do
Outdoor pursuits
History/archaeology

0   20   40   60   80   100
% of respondents

■ Very important   ■ Important   □ Not important

Source: 1994 All Parks Visitor Survey: Lake District Site and Roadside Self-completion questionnaires

Covering 880 square miles, the Lake District National Park is the largest, most spectacular and most visited of the National Parks.

Tourism is very important to the Lake District and has a significant impact on the local economy. In Cumbria as a whole it is estimated that tourism supports approximately 42,000 jobs – 17% of the workforce. In Windermere and Keswick, 50% of the workforce work in hotels, catering and the distribution trade, compared to 6% nationally.

The Lake District has long been popular. Wordsworth, who lived in Grasmere, described it as a 'sort of national property in which every man has a right and interest who has an eye to perceive and a heart to enjoy'.

A 1994 visitor survey revealed that 40% of visitors came just because of the scenery and the landscape, and 100% of visitors thought that the scenery was an important or very important part of their enjoyment of the park (see diagram left). In fact 80% of all visitors are repeat visitors.

activity

YOU MUST GO THERE

Read the Lake District case study, and write a detailed report recommending why you think that it would be a good place to visit. Include as many attractions as possible. You may find books, brochures and the internet will help you gain additional information.

The thirteen National Parks in England and Wales were designated under the National Parks and Access to the Countryside Act 1949. See the map opposite for the location of each of the parks. The largest is the Lake District National Park (see case study above).

Areas of Outstanding Natural Beauty (AONBs)

An AONB is exactly what it says it is: a precious landscape whose distinctive character and natural beauty are so outstanding that it is in the nation's interest to safeguard them. Each AONB has been designated because of its special qualities – its flora, fauna, or historical and cultural associations, as well as its scenic views.

There are 41 AONBs in England and Wales (36 wholly in England, 4 wholly in Wales, and 1 which straddles the border). Created by the legislation of the National Parks and Access to the Countryside Act 1949, AONBs represent 18% of the finest countryside in England and Wales. Their care has been entrusted to the local authorities, community groups, organisations and individuals who live and work within them or who value them.

Heritage coasts

Heritage coasts are special coastlines managed so that their natural beauty is conserved and, where appropriate, the accessibility for visitors is improved (see map, above). They account for vast areas of the rural coastline in Scotland and Wales and in England 32% (1,027km) of the scenic coastline is heritage coast. The first heritage coast to be defined was the famous white chalk cliff of Beachy Head in Sussex. Now much of our coastline, like Land's End or the sheer cliffs of Flamborough Head with its huge seabird colonies, is protected.

Heritage coasts, unlike the National Parks and AONBs, have had no statutory designation – they have been defined by agreement between the Countryside Agency and the local authorities. Most, in fact, are part of a National Park or an AONB.

Heritage and cultural destinations

It is important that we first understand the terms 'heritage' and 'cultural' when they are applied to destinations.

'Heritage' means that somewhere has inherited (and still shows) the benefits of history or past events.

'Cultural' means that somewhere helps visitors appreciate and understand the customs and civilisation of a society, including their literature, art, music, etc.

The UK has plenty of heritage and cultural attractions, many of them built up through centuries of people's industrious work. Although many attractions may have both heritage and cultural appeal, in this topic we will consider them separately.

Heritage

The most popular heritage attractions in the UK are shown in the table top right, with the Tower of London being clearly the most popular. However this table also shows the spread of the attractions right across the country ranging from Windsor Castle to Edinburgh Castle.

Culture

Britain's 'culture' can be displayed in many different ways (and we go on to look at local cultures in Topic 6) but for the purpose of this section we focus mostly on museums and art galleries.

Most towns and cities have their own museums showing local historical and cultural artefacts, but the major museums – those likely to attract large numbers of tourists – are mainly based in London, as shown below.

Destination	Example of attraction	Visitors (2002)
London	Tower of London	1,940,856
Edinburgh	Edinburgh Castle	1,153,317
Windsor	Windsor Castle	931,042
Bath	Roman Baths	845,608
Amesbury	Stonehenge	759,697
Bakewell	Chatsworth	620,210
Knutsford	Tatton Park	564,300
Hampton Court	Hampton Court Palace	526,686
Woodstock	Blenheim Palace	465,562

Source: Survey of visits to visitor attractions 2002, sponsored by the UK statutory tourist boards

Popular London museums		
Museum	**Theme**	**Visitors (2002)**
British Museum	The history of culture from ancient times to the modern day	4,600,000
Natural History Museum	The history of life from dinosaurs to Darwin	3,000,000
Victoria & Albert Museum	The largest museum of the decorative arts in the world	2,700,000
Science Museum	Scientific, technological and medical change since the eighteenth century.	2,600,000

Source: Survey of visits to visitor attractions 2002, sponsored by the UK statutory tourist boards

Some cultural attractions have been developed recently to show tourists how people used to live. Although their theme is often historical they are cultural attractions because they are a re-creation of past times and cultures. The Jorvik Centre in York, the Ironbridge Museum in Shropshire, and Tales of Robin Hood in Nottingham are all examples of attractions that try to bring a certain period of history to life. The Jorvik Centre is described in more detail in the case study below.

Britain's art galleries, especially those in London, are known around the world and are an important attraction for tourists (see table below).

Popular London galleries		
Gallery	**Theme**	**Visitors (2002)**
Tate Modern	The national collection of international modern art	4,600,000
National Gallery	Western European paintings from about 1250 to 1900	4,100,000
National Portrait Gallery	Likenesses (portraits, busts and photos) of British people	1,500,000
Tate Britain	British art from 1500 to the present day, including the Turner Bequest	1,200,000

Source: Survey of visits to visitor attractions 2002,

Other cultural destinations focus on the theatre, music and entertainment. For example, Stratford-upon-Avon is home to the Royal Shakespeare Company, and Edinburgh hosts the annual Arts Festival. Glastonbury in Somerset has its annual music festival, which attracts over 100,000 people.

Between 1976 and 1981 some of the best preserved remains of the Viking world came to light, in the middle of York. York Archaeological Trust discovered wooden houses, fence lines, alleyways and backyards. Tens of thousands of objects from the Viking Age were uncovered, many of them in excellent condition thanks to the wet soils. The Trust had discovered Jorvik – the centre of Viking power in England.

Just three years later, in 1984, the Jorvik Centre opened its doors to the public, and has since welcomed over 13 million visitors. Situated on the site of the excavations, the centre used the newly uncovered evidence to re-create part of Viking-Age York, including the sights, sounds and even the smells of the time.

This groundbreaking experiment proved a tremendous success with tourists. The houses and shops are laid out in exactly the same pattern as they were in the year AD975, and even the faces of the people you see have been reconstructed from actual Viking skulls. The idea behind the centre has now been used all over the world.

activity

YOU SHOULD SEE IT!

Write a letter to your local primary school recommending why you think the Jorvik Centre would be of interest to the pupils.

Purpose-built destinations

Purpose-built destinations cater for all the tourist needs, including entertainment and accommodation. The most popular and well-recognised purpose-built resorts in Britain are Butlins (first resort opened in 1936 at Skegness) and Pontins (first resort opened at Brean Sands, Somerset, in 1947). Center Parcs is a relative newcomer to Britain. They have become popular largely because of their glass-domed activity centres, which house a large indoor leisure pool. With the unpredictable British weather this feature ensures the Parcs can offer an all year round attraction.

Some destinations are based around camping and caravanning holidays. The purpose-built Haven resorts offer sites with all the facilities a tourist requires, such as pools, entertainment centres, children's clubs and so forth. Its locations are in areas of natural beauty or near to a holiday resort.

activity

WHAT WOULD ATTRACT YOU?

Choose one purpose-built resort in Britain and locate it on a map. Identify and justify what specific types of customer the resort is likely to attract. Compare your findings with other people in your group.

171

Topic 4 Countryside, cultural and purpose-built destinations

Environment, transport and accomodation

In the last two topics we looked at the different types of destination in Britain, and in the next two we are going to focus on the features that give each of them appeal. We start by looking at:

- Climate
- Landscape
- Transport and communication links
- Accommodation.

Climate

The British Isles lie in the latitude of predominately westerly winds where depressions move eastwards across the North Atlantic, bringing with them unsettled and windy weather, particularly in winter. Between the depressions there are often small anticyclones that bring a welcome period of fair weather. It is the sequence of depressions and anticyclones that is responsible for our notoriously changeable weather.

Overall, the south of the British Isles is usually warmer than the north, and the west is wetter than the east. The more extreme weather tends to occur in mountainous regions where it is often cloudy, wet and windy.

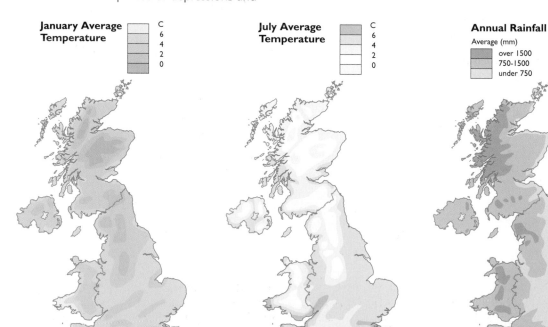

January Average Temperature
C
6
4
2
0

July Average Temperature
C
6
4
2
0

Annual Rainfall
Average (mm)
over 1500
750-1500
under 750

Landscape

Britain's landscape is full of contrasts, from the windswept moors of Scotland in the far north to the tranquil crystal clear waters of the Isles of Scilly; from England's 'green and pleasant land' of rolling hills and hedgerows to the dramatic beauty of the Welsh mountains and lakes. Whichever direction they travel, tourists will find a wide variety of landscapes and diverse cultures to explore.

The contrasts continue in other areas of the UK, from the densely populated Greater London area to the remote and practically deserted Scottish islands to the

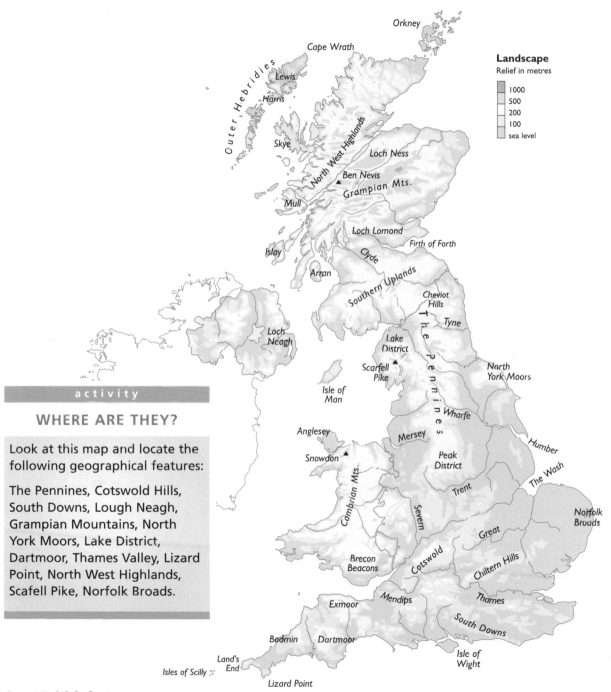

Landscape
Relief in metres

	1000
	500
	200
	100
	sea level

activity

WHERE ARE THEY?

Look at this map and locate the following geographical features:

The Pennines, Cotswold Hills, South Downs, Lough Neagh, Grampian Mountains, North York Moors, Lake District, Dartmoor, Thames Valley, Lizard Point, North West Highlands, Scafell Pike, Norfolk Broads.

Great British facts

Great Britain is about 600 miles (just less than 1,000 km) from the south coast to the extreme north of Scotland, and about 300 miles (just less than 500 km) across at its widest.

The coastline of Great Britain is 9,000 miles (14,500 km) long, with Scotland (including the islands) accounting for 65% of this distance.

The most northerly point on the mainland is Dunnet Head, Caithness. The most southerly point is Lizard Point, Cornwall.

far north. The urban areas vary from the idyllic thatched cottages villages in the Cotswolds to the highly commercial metropolitan cities of Birmingham, Manchester and Glasgow.

CONTRASTING LANDSCAPES

With the use of a map, select two contrasting landscape areas – for example the South Downs and the North York Moors. Research the main features of each landscape and identify the key attractions of the area, including climate. Describe two types of visitor who would enjoy each location and explain why it would appeal to them.

Newcastle International, one of Britain's many international airports

Transport and communication links

Transport links are of vital importance to the appeal of a destination. Those with a vast array of links, by air, train, road and sea are advantaged over those with only a few transport links. For example, good access links to Birmingham have led to its development as one of the major business centres in Europe. In contrast, difficult access to some of the remote Scottish islands – with perhaps just two ferries a week – has meant that many a tourist has been deterred from making the trip. We will go on to look at the different forms of transport under the following headings:

- Airports   • Port   • Road   • Rail.

Airports

Over recent years there has been a dramatic growth in air travel. According to the International Passenger Survey (2002), the proportion of overseas tourists arriving by air increased from 59 % in 1982 to 71% in 2002.

The BAA is the owner of seven main UK airports, including one of the world's busiest international airports, London Heathrow. Every year, nearly 200 million passengers travel through these 'gateways', and air traffic at UK airports is expected to keep on growing about 4% a year until 2020, according to the Department of Transport.

One of the main reasons that the numbers of people travelling by air has increased so dramatically has been the growth of the no-frills airlines. A MORI survey found that 30% of package holidaymakers had flown with a no-frills airline in the last two years. Just 14% had booked their no-frills flights through a travel agent – most people booked online.

activity

FIND THE FERRY PORTS

From looking at the map on p.31, identify where in Great Britain the ferries from the following destinations would dock: Bergen, Dublin, Calais, Hamburg, Rotterdam, Roscoff, Cherbourg, Stavanger, Bilbao, Rosslare.

Ports

Sea travel has slowly declined in recent years, as air travel has increased. According to the International Passenger Survey (2002) the number of overseas tourists arriving by sea peaked at 6.3 million in 1994, since when it has declined to 4.4 million. Visits by overseas tourists via the Channel Tunnel peaked at 3.2 million in 1998, falling to 2.7 million by 2002.

More than 45 million ferry journeys are now taken to and from Britain each year. Ferry services run to the UK from Ireland, Spain, Belgium, France, Holland, Germany and Scandinavia. There are also services connecting the Scottish Islands, the Channel Islands and the Isles of Scilly, Isle of Wight and Isle of Man with the mainland.

Although conventional ferries continue to be the main mode of water transport for most people when crossing to Britain, high-speed hovercraft and 'Seacats' are used on some popular passenger routes because they are so much faster. For example, the Seacat makes the Dover to Calais crossing in less than an hour, compared to the normal $2\frac{1}{2}$-hour ferry crossing.

Roads

Road transport has developed significantly over the last 50 years since the opening of the first motorway, the M6 Preston Bypass, in 1958. According to the United Kingdom Tourism Survey (2002), 73% of all trips are made by car (compared with 12% by train and 4% by plane).

The 4,800 miles of the motorway and trunk road network is managed by the Highways Agency. Although this network accounts for less than 4% of all roads by

'Spaghetti Junction', joining the M6, A38M and the A38, was opened in 1972.

Road Network

M20   Motorway and number

A30   Linking primary road and number

length, it carries 34% of the traffic, and provides the main routes for tourists. The Highways Agency is also responsible for the motorway service areas which are open 24 hours a day, 365 days a year. The 125,000 miles of other roads are the responsibility of the appropriate local highways authority.

activity

WHICH WAY TO GO?

From looking at the page 31, identify the easiest road route for each of these trips: Brighton to Inverness; Edinburgh to London; Glasgow to Birmingham; Penzance to Holyhead; Liverpool to Aberdeen; Folkestone to Carlisle; Fishguard to Thurso.

Rail

The rail system depends on two sets of 'providers'. Network Rail has the task of providing and maintaining the stations and the 21,000 miles of track. Safety is their primary concern, and £14 million a day is spent on maintaining, improving and upgrading every aspect of the railway infrastructure. The trains themselves are provided and run by many different private 'train operating companies'.

Although the safety of the track is of paramount importance for tourists, it is more often reliability, convenience and comfort that influence individuals choosing between trains and other forms of transport. Some train operators have been making a big effort to change the common perception of unreliable services and filthy carriages. Virgin Trains, for example, has invested heavily in updating some of its services, as shown in the case study below.

In addition to the national railway lines, there are a number of local transport rail systems in major cities. The largest of these is the London Underground – the world's first underground railway (1863) and, with 275 stations, one of the largest. It carries over 3 million passengers a day, using 500 trains at peak times. The system is based on 11 separate lines, most of which travel for twenty or so miles, right across Greater London, from one side to the other. In the central part of London, where all the routes criss-cross, the lines are all underground, but most of the 'underground' lines in the outer parts of London are actually above ground. The various lines are colour-coded on maps – the Bakerloo Line is dark brown, for example, and the District Line green. The simplicity of the system and the ease of use for newcomers make the underground very popular with tourists – who would actually see more of London by walking or taking a bus.

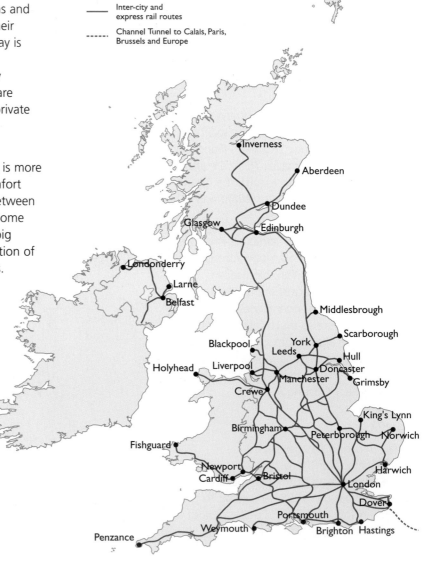

Rail Network

——— Inter-city and express rail routes

------ Channel Tunnel to Calais, Paris, Brussels and Europe

The West Coast train now tilting...

Virgin Trains has launched its Pendolino into regular tilting passenger service on the West Coast Main Line today [14 June 2004]. Virgin Trains is investing over £1billion in a fleet of 53 nine-coach Pendolino trains, which are now operating on over half of all services to and from London Euston. Fastest journey times, from September, will be:

• London–Birmingham: 1 hour 23 minutes
• London–Manchester: 2 hours 6 minutes
• London–Liverpool: 2 hours 30 minutes
• London–Glasgow: 4 hours 40 minutes

Accommodation

Most accommodation in the UK is in towns, cities and coastal resorts. Many of the hotels in cities are 3-star or above because they are aimed at the business market during the week. At week ends many hotels discount their prices to attract the leisure market.

There is also a vast array of accommodation in purpose-built resorts in the UK, ranging from the traditional holiday camp to the caravan park to the luxury hotels built alongside the main attraction, such as at Alton Towers.

Perhaps in most of our minds the typical purpose-built resort is the holiday camp, where the whole holiday experience is contained in one place. In the last 20 years the success and expansion of Center Parcs – providing unique all-year-round holiday resorts – has run alongside the decline in popularity of the traditional holiday camps, but other types of resort have developed. Caravan parks that offer facilities such as swimming pools, restaurant, bars and entertainment have become more and more popular as people enjoy the flexibility that this type of holiday provides. As many caravan parks, especially the smaller ones, allow camping too, this type of holiday provides a much cheaper option – because people can bring their own accommodation with them. The majority of these parks are located near traditional holiday destinations such as beach resorts and countryside areas.

activity

WHO LIKES CARAVAN RESORTS?

Discuss the advantages and disadvantages of caravan resorts for different types of holidaymakers.

Facilities, attractions, events and culture

In the last topic we looked at various features of destinations – climate, landscape, transport and communication links, and accommodation. This topic looks at the other features that give destinations appeal to tourists:

- **Facilities provided**
- **Natural and built attractions**
- **Events and entertainment**
- **Local culture, including food and drink.**

Britain's most popular holiday destination

Blackpool has taller, faster roller-coasters than anywhere else, bigger clubs and the biggest mirror ball in the world, plus world-class shows, cosmopolitan restaurants, vibrant nightlife, an active sports scene and breathtakingly beautiful scenery on the doorstep.

If you want to get away from it all, try leafy Stanley Park, Blackpool's award-winning horticultural treasure. Take in the showpiece Italian Gardens or float away lazy summer afternoons on the boating lake. Visit the multipurpose sports centre or admire the Model Village – complete with Blackpool trams!

The real-life versions trundle along twelve miles of Promenade. They're as much a tourist attraction as a vital public transport system, carrying more than 120,000 people on a busy summer's day. If you prefer to walk, then marvel at the musical high-tide organ, one of the growing range of giant sculptures on New South Promenade.

At the heart of Blackpool's famous Golden Mile is the Sea Life Centre, with more than 40 displays of marvelous marine life. Nearby is one of Blackpool's oldest attractions, Louis Tussaud's Waxworks, inviting you to meet the famous and the infamous in its many galleries. Then there's Coral Island, with its pirate town facade: the Terror Train awaits, along with the Parrot Flyer monorail, in this undercover family entertainment centre.

And down at the Sandcastle, white-knuckle water chutes, swirling slides and the giant Typhoon Lagoon wavepool combine to offer family fun amid a 'tropical' climate, complete with palm trees.

But of course you can't do everything in a day, which is why Blackpool offers a wealth of accommodation for everyone – from four-star luxury hotels to homely B&Bs – plus flats and caravans.

Source: www.blackpooltourism.com

Facilities provided

The 'facilities' are the additional attractions and services provided by a destination – things like leisure pools, restaurants and bars in a particular hotel, or, on a bigger scale, conference venues or the huge entertainment complexes found at purpose-built resorts like Butlins or Center Parcs.

For some people the facilities are the most important part of the holiday mix. The entertainment provided along Blackpool's Golden Mile, for example, makes it the most popular attraction in the UK, with over 6 million visitors a year (see case study below).

Of course, a destination's facilities will not appeal to everyone. Alton Towers, for example, has built its reputation on being one of the best places in Britain to experience thrilling rides. Some people will never visit Alton Towers for this very reason, and would prefer to visit a museum or art gallery.

Natural and built attractions

The UK has almost 6,500 visitor attractions, including country parks and farms, historic properties, theme parks, zoos, gardens, museums and galleries, and places of worship. They offer a wealth of unique experiences for international and domestic visitors alike. The UK's attractions are at the very heart of the tourism industry; with the top twenty major paid attractions accounting for 45 million visits alone in 2003.

Natural and built attractions are often located together, as buildings are often placed in beautiful

WHO CARES ABOUT FACILITIES?

Choose a resort (or use the Blackpool information), and analyse its appeal for the groups of people listed below, considering both the good and the bad points of the facilities and attractions on offer.

- 16-year-old Sam and five of his friends on a day trip.
- Richard, a single parent with three girls under the age of 10, taking a week's holiday.
- Doris and Bert, an active elderly couple looking for a weekend seaside break.

settings, such as the beautiful grounds of Windsor Castle or the attractions built along parts of Britain's beautiful coastline. However for the purpose of this section we will separate them into:

- Natural attractions
- Built attractions.

Langdale Quest

10,000 acres of North Yorkshire forest land makes Langdale Quest the UK's largest 4x4 driving site, with more than 80 miles of forest routes, including lots of mud, ruts, water pools and steep hills. The 5 standard routes are well maintained, so all types of 4x4 vehicles can be used – including the ones that normally just get polished on Sunday mornings.

Family-friendly 'treasure hunts' are provided along all the routes, and kids enjoy using the 2-way radios when 'checking in' with the instructors and helping with the navigating.

Langdale Quest provides an outstanding 'fun' recreational activity for the whole family, whilst achieving a safety record second to none.

Natural attractions

Many of Britain's natural attractions focus on the coastal and highland areas. We covered the coastal areas in Topic 3 of this unit, so we will focus here on the highland areas.

The hill and mountain areas of the UK range from the mountainous peaks of Helvelyn in Cumbria and Snowdonia in Wales to the lower more rolling hills of the South Downs in Sussex. People are attracted to these areas for different reasons. Some enjoy walking up the hills and mountains, and the more adventurous enjoy activities like abseiling, while others prefer sightseeing – driving around admiring the views and scenery.

The case studies below look at two activities in highland areas that appeal to different types of person.

Richardson Sporting

Richardson Sporting has access to some of the best dogging moors in northern Scotland.

The program is based on three or five days hunting and the accommodation (maximum of six hunters) is in a superb Victorian hunting lodge. Transport from Inverness Airport is provided. Each hunting day you will be taken by Land Rover to the hunting area. The hunt normally lasts for approximately 7 hours, so you must be physically fit. Each group of hunters can expect to shoot 8–20 brace of grouse per day.

The Royal Dornoch golf course is only 5 miles from the lodge, and there are six famous salmon rivers within an hour's drive. We can also provide transport for your wife and family, so that when you are hunting they may tour northern Scotland's spectacular scenery.

'APPRECIATING' UPLAND AREAS

The case studies above show two activities for people to enjoy in upland areas. List their similarities and differences, including the people they might appeal to.

Built attractions

'Built attractions' – walls, monuments, churches, museums – appeal to tourists today, but they were originally built, long ago, for some other purpose.

Hadrian's Wall, for example, was built nearly 2000 years ago by the Romans, to defend their empire. Today, it is a major tourist attraction (and a World Heritage Site since 1987) – the most important monument left by the Romans in Britain. Set against dramatic and wild landscapes, a visit to Hadrian's Wall is a must for tourists in the north of England.

Some historical monuments are amazing feats of engineering. We shall never know why hundreds of people struggled to build Stonehenge, for example, but visitors from all over the world come to marvel at it today. It was started in about 3,100 BC as a ring of wooden posts, and then rebuilt in about 2500 BC, using massive stones, and rebuilt again a couple of hundred years later.

Today only about half of the original monument remains. Some of the stones have fallen down, others have been carried away to be used for building or to repair farm tracks. Over recent centuries visitors have added their damage too – some even hired hammers from the Amesbury blacksmith and chipped bits off the stones as souvenirs. As you can imagine, this practice is no longer permitted!

Many of the historical buildings that have been well preserved right across the country are associated with religion – cathedrals, churches, abbeys and priories. Today, they are a big attraction for tourists, as the table below illustrates.

The two main organisations acting as guardians of our historical attractions are the National Trust (a charity) and English Heritage. English Heritage is funded by government and tries to make sure that the historic environment of England is properly maintained and cared for. It employs some of the country's very best archaeologists and historians, and aims to help people understand and appreciate why the historic buildings and landscapes around them matter.

Hadrian's Wall – built for defence, but now a major tourist attraction

Attraction	Visitors (2002, estimates)
York Minster	1,600,000
Canterbury Cathedral	1,100,000
Westminster Abbey (London)	1,060,000
Chester Cathedral	850,000
St Paul's Cathedral (London)	800,000
St Martin-in-the-Fields (London)	700,000
Truro Cathedral	500,000
Norwich Cathedral	500,000
St Giles Cathedral (Edinburgh)	400,000

Source: Survey of visits to visitor attractions 2002, sponsored by the UK statutory tourist boards

It's not known why Stonehenge was built – but tourists from all over the world now come to see it.

Events and entertainment

'Events' in Britain range from the annual village fete to the occasional lavish royal ceremonies, and each has their individual appeal to the tourist.

Large events attract huge numbers of visitors to a destination – having a positive effect on all aspects of the travel and tourism industry. For example, the Golden Jubilee celebrations in 2002 benefited many attractions in London, thanks to the huge publicity at home and overseas. Annual events such as the Glastonbury Festival and the Notting Hill Carnival are major European attractions for tourists (see case study below).

According to UK Sport, sporting events generate millions of pounds of additional spending within the host city or area. It is estimated that visitors to the Flora London marathon, for example, spend an extra £25m, and an Ashes cricket test can provide a £5m boost to the host city. Visitors to such special events spend, on average, just under £50 a day, and the ever-present media people register an average daily outlay of £100. Athletes and their entourages are also significant spenders.

activity

YOUR LOCAL CALENDAR

Create a calendar of local events and entertainment likely to attract visitors to your area. Explain the type of visitor each event would appeal to.

Local culture

Some destinations have an extra appeal for tourists because of their individual culture – their local dialect, customs, traditions, music and dance, or food and drink, for example. Many tourists to Scotland or Ireland (especially American tourists) are attracted by those countries' distinct cultures.

Sampling the food and drink of a region can often be an important part of the tourist experience. Britain is famous for its fish and chips and its beef and Yorkshire pudding. But in addition, each region has its specialities, from Cornish cream teas and pasties, to Irish Guinness and Scottish salmon.

activity

DIFFERENT LOCAL CULTURES

Select three different British places and compare their local cultures, including language, customs, food and drink.

Notting Hill Carnival

The Notting Hill Carnival is the largest arts festival in Europe, and the second largest Carnival in the world (after Rio). Centred on Ladbroke Grove – just north of Notting Hill – it has been held on the Sunday and Monday of every August Bank Holiday since 1966.

It started as a local affair, set up by the West Indian immigrants of the area, but has now become a full-blooded Caribbean Carnival, attracting millions of people from all around the world. There are scores of massive 'sound systems', spectacular floats and steel drum bands, and hundreds of food and drink stalls line the streets, selling Caribbean specialities.

In recent years the Carnival has grown and grown, reflecting the multicultural nature of our society. The organisers operate an all-inclusive policy, encouraging artists of all nationalities to celebrate their cultural traditions through art, dance and music. The traditional participants – from the Caribbean (all parts), Latin America, Africa and the UK – have now been joined, for example, by groups from Afghanistan, Kurdistan, Bangladesh, the Philippines, Bulgaria, and Russia.

Source (adapted): www.mynottinghill.co.uk

Constructing itineraries for tourists

An itinerary is a plan or schedule for tourists to follow. In this topic we will look at how to construct an itinerary of complementary destinations to meet a visitor's specific needs. You will learn to include the following in an itinerary:

- **Who the itinerary is prepared for**
- **Dates**
- **Timing**
- **What is included, such as accommodation**
- **Contact details**
- **Details of destinations, such as attractions featured.**

And finally we will look at:

- **Presentation of itineraries.**

Who is the itinerary prepared for?

The itinerary will vary immensely according to the visitor's specific needs. If a foreign tourist is visiting Britain for a short stay they may just be interested in visiting one or two English cities, starting with London. If they plan to stay a little longer, then many might enjoy a trip to Wales and Scotland too.

The itinerary may be planned for a group or an individual. Most of us probably think of an itinerary for a group – with a tour guide, bus and arranged accommodation and visits, but increasingly individuals are planning itineraries on their own and choosing their own methods of transport, accommodation and visits. Some specialist travel agents also offer tailor-made itinerary services for individual customers.

When planning an itinerary you first have to understand the visitor, taking into account the following factors:

- Age
- Individual/group
- Leisure/business
- Interests
- Special needs
- Language requirements.

Obviously, an elderly person will have different travel requirements to a younger traveller. Similarly a lone traveller may be much easier to accommodate than a group, particularly if none of the group speak the language. A business traveller will probably require good communication facilities to do his job, whilst people on holiday may just want to have fun, and time to pursue their own interests. Tourists with special needs may need additional support and help with their travel arrangements.

There are many organisations which provide itineraries for both group and individual trips, such as the England Travel Bureau, shown in the case study opposite.

Dates

The date of a trip can make a significant difference to the itinerary that is organised. Obviously there is little point offering trips to see the beautiful purple heather of the Scottish Highlands if it is not the months that it is flowering. Similarly an itinerary surrounding fixed events (such as exhibitions) would be useless if the dates did not correlate with when the events were happening.

England Travel Bureau

The England Travel Bureau is part of the Great Britain & Ireland Travel Bureau and is operated by Travel Match, online specialists in custom-built itineraries. They are staffed by local experts in the UK, rather than in the tourist's own country. The text below is adapted from their website and includes some of the features and attractions that may be included in an itinerary.

'A green and pleasant land' sums up England nicely. England offers something for every visitor: thousands of years of history – not just in the museums and galleries, but nearly everywhere you look; beautiful, green countryside; quaint little cobble-stoned villages; 15th-century smuggling inns; great walking and cycling; the world's best theatre; fantastic shopping and a vibrant nightlife.

England is like a Russian doll. At first glance, a very nice doll – a doll steeped in history and tradition. The same way you remove the outer doll to reveal another... and another... and another, England reveals more, the more you look.

Drive past a quaint little Tudor pub and you get a glimpse. Stop for a photo and you get a material memory. Venture inside, and you get to taste the beer. Buy a second, and you get conversation. Join a game of cards, darts or pool and you have laughter and new friends. By the time you're sitting with them by the open fire, patting a lazy old labrador, you'll realise you've discovered part of the real England. Just part, mind you.

Source: www.uktravelbureau.com

---

activity

WHERE SHOULD THEY GO?

Imagine you work for the Great Britain & Ireland Travel Bureau. Role play the conversations you would have with the following customers planning to visit the UK.

Jim is a 19-year-old Canadian travelling to the UK for the first time to visit the sights.

Derek and Madeline are an elderly couple. She is in a wheelchair, and they want to get a flavour of Britain's culture.

Ernest and Margot want to take their 8-year-old twins on a trip of a lifetime to Britain.

Timing

Timing is everything for an itinerary to be successful. For example, on an organised group tour it is vital that everyone meets at the right time (and place) throughout the trip so that the group can move on. The length of time allocated for eating meals, travelling between the attractions and the amount of free time – all need to be carefully calculated to ensure the itinerary runs smoothly.

The timing of a business trip will be vital if it is to tie-in with an organised event, such as an exhibition. The businessperson will want an itinerary based around the dates that give most access to the exhibition and is less likely to be worried about sightseeing.

Travellers who are not too worried about when they travel can get more competitive prices by travelling at off-peak times. For example, travelling into and out of London by train is considerably cheaper if you can avoid the commuter times, before 9.00am and after 4.00pm.

activity

PLANNING TRIP TIMINGS

Imagine that you are planning a day trip for yourself and a group of your friends to a local attraction. Create a plan of the timings for your trip. Fix the starting time, taking into account the length of time it would take for each individual to reach the meeting point. Then plan the time it would take for the group to get to the attraction and how long you would spend doing each activity, such as eating etc. Then plan the timings for your return trip. Make sure you take into consideration the individual needs of the group. Present your plan to a friend and ask for their comments on your timings.

Transport and accommodation

Itineraries for organised trips will include details of the various forms of transport to be used – flights, ferries, trains, coaches, minibuses, taxis, etc. Coaches, often including a tour guide, are particularly popular with tour organisers.

Cost often dictates the tourists' choice of transport, and this is also true in their choice of accommodation. The types of accommodation available in Britain are vast, ranging from the luxury 5-star hotels to youth hostels and camping grounds, with every other type of accommodation in the middle.

Contact details

The number of contacts needed on an itinerary varies. For an organised tour there will only be a few contact details, including the booking company and, on the trip, the tour guide – whose job it is to deal with all the other contacts. In case of an emergency, there might also be contact details for the coach company, the hotels, attractions, etc.

However, if you are planning your trip independently then you will have to make numerous contacts in relation to travel arrangements, accommodation and attractions. This can be a lengthy and laborious process – which is why many people prefer to travel with an organised party.

What to see in London

Madame Tussaud's, Planetarium, Regent's Park, Oxford Street, Regent Street, Piccadilly Circus and Eros Statue, Leicester Square, National Gallery, Trafalgar Square and Nelson's Column, Downing Street, Houses of Parliament and Big Ben, Imperial War Museum, London Aquarium, London Eye, South Bank Arts Centre, Covent

activity

CHOOSING WHAT TO SEE

Write an itinerary of attractions suitable for the following visitors who are staying in London for 24 hours. You may use books, maps, brochures and the internet to help draw up your recommendations.

- Jake, a young American, wants to see the sights and party as much as possible.
- Hans and Greta are German, retired and love history.
- Bernard and his family of four children aged from 2 to 12 want to see the sights.

Destination details: attractions

There are many varied attractions for the visitor to Britain. The choice of attractions will depend on the individual, or, for groups, on the selected tour itinerary. Entry to attractions may be part of the package, and is often the reason a customer chooses the trip. For example, an evening at the Military Tattoo may be the main selling point of an organised trip to Edinburgh, and also allows the organiser to negotiate cheaper group rates.

Because of its unique volume and mix of attractions, London is by far the most popular destination with foreign tourists (see box below).

Garden, St Paul's Cathedral, Monument, London Dungeon, Tower Bridge, Tower of London, Shakespeare's Globe, Tate Modern, Millennium Bridge, Westminster Abbey, Tate Britain, Buckingham Palace, Hyde Park, Speakers' Corner, British Museum, Science Museum, Victoria & Albert Museum – and there are more than forty theatres.

The Original London Sightseeing Tour 24-hour pass. Starting from £16 per person. See London's major sights on an open-top double-decker bus. Simply 'hop on and hop off' at your choice of famous landmarks.

Discovering London in 8–9 hours. Starting from £61 per person. London's bestselling tour! A day bringing history, pageantry and the sights of London to life including a pub lunch and a Thames cruise. Your experienced and qualified guide will take you through Westminster Abbey, Changing the Guard at Buckingham Palace, The Tower of London and much, much more.

Presentation of itineraries

Now that you have considered all the factors above, you have to present your itinerary to the customer. Good presentation is vital. The customer must be able to clearly see what they are going to be doing, and when, and also what they have paid for and what they have not (see example below).

Itinerary

Client's name: M. and Mde Dupont   **Date of tour:** Wed 8th–16th June 2005

Date	Location	Travel details	Accommodation	Extras
Wed 8th June	London	Arrive: Heathrow airport 12.15 • Depart: Heathrow aiport on HEATHROW EXPRESS at 13.32 • Arrive London Paddington at 13.48 • Taxi transfer to hotel	Two nights Dinner, Bed and Breakfast in a twin en-suite room at The Berners Hotel, Berners Street, London W1A 3BE	19.30: Two reserved tickets for The Producers at Theatre Royal Drury Lane, Catherine Street, London WC2
Thu 9th June	London		The Berners Hotel, London	Two tickets reserved for the day for the Big Red Bus tour. (Map and routes enclosed.)
Fri 10th June	Oxford	Depart: London Paddington on FIRST GREAT WESTERN at 16.00 • Arrive: Reading at 16.25 • Depart: Reading on VIRGIN TRAINS at 16.35 • Arrive: Oxford at 17.00 • Taxi transfer to hotel	Two nights Dinner, Bed and Breakfast in a mini-suite at The Randolph Hotel, Beaumont Street, Oxford OX1 2LN	
Sat 11th June	Oxford		The Randolph Hotel, Oxford	
Sun 12th June	York	Depart: Oxford on VIRGIN TRAINS at 10.00 • Arrive: Birmingham New Street at 11.14 • Depart: Birmingham New Street on VIRGIN TRAINS at 11.30 • Arrive: York at 13.44 • Taxi transfer to hotel	Two nights Dinner, Bed and Breakfast in a twin en-suite room at The Royal York Hotel, Station Road, York YO24 1AA	Two tickets reserved for Evening Dinner and Boat Cruise (Map of embarkation point enclosed)
Mon 13th June	York		The Royal York Hotel	11.00: Two tickets reserved for City Sight Seeing Tour (map of pick-up points and routes encl.)
Tue 14th June	Edinburgh	Depart: York on GNER at 11.00 • Arrive: Edinburgh at 13.37 • Taxi transfer to hotel	Two nights Dinner, Bed and Breakfast in a double en-suite room at The Roxburghe Hotel, 38 Charlotte Square, Edinburgh EH2 4HG	Two tickets reserved for HMS Britannia. Visit times optional
Wed 15th June	Edinburgh		The Roxburghe Hotel, Edinburgh	
Thu 16th June	London	Depart: Edinburgh on GNER at 10.30 • Arrive: London Kings Cross at 14.55 • Taxi transfer to London Paddington • Depart London Paddington on HEATHROW EXPRESS at 15.40 • Arrive: Heathrow at 15.55 • Transfer to terminal for return flight		

activity

CONSTRUCT AN APPROPRIATE ITINERARY

Using the outline plan presented above, write an itinerary for a week's trip around Britain, that would appeal to one of the groups listed below, remembering to consider their individual requirements. Use a variety of sources to try and make the itinerary as realistic as possible – research accommodation and attractions in as much detail as you can. Remember to include the following information: name of tour; dates; times; transport details; accommodation; day-by-day itinerary; contact details.

Groups to choose from: 30 Japanese tourists (from Tokyo); 20 French schoolchildren (from Paris); A middle-aged American couple (from Texas); A Danish family with teenage children (from Copenhagen); A family of four from the Republic of Ireland with three children under 5 years of age.

Topic 8 The scale of tourism to the British Isles

In this topic we research the scale of tourism to Britain, using a variety of sources. The importance of visitors to Britain will be looked at in relation to the following factors:

- Visitor numbers
- Visitor spending
- Type of visitor
- Bed-nights used (length of stay).

We will examine each of these in turn, using a variety of sources of reference. Several organisations produce statistics on the impact of tourism. Perhaps the best known are *Social Trends* and the *Annual Abstract of Statistics* published by Her Majesty's Stationery Office (HMSO). Other sources include VisitBritain (formerly the British Tourist Board), regional and local tourist boards, market research organisations such as Mintel, and industry bodies such as ABTA. The 2002 International Passenger Survey provides information on the number of visitors and their spend in the UK. Another useful site is www.staruk.org which provides a variety of information on the travel and tourism market.

Visitor numbers

According to the International Passenger Survey 2002, the number of visits by overseas residents to the UK more than doubled from 11.6 million in 1982 to a peak of 25.7 million in 1998, before falling each year to 22.8 million in 2001. The largest fall of 9.4% occurred in 2001 when there was Foot and Mouth Disease in Britain between February and September, and then terrorist attacks in the USA on 11 September. Between 2001 and 2002 the number of visits rose by 5.9% to 24.2 million. Although this indicated some recovery, the number of visits in 2002 was still lower than in 2000.

'Receiving areas' means the areas in the UK that foreign visitors go to visit. 'Generating areas' means the countries the foreign tourists come from.

The initial 'port of entry' for foreign tourists to the UK is usually a transport terminal – an airport or seaport. In 2002 there were 17 million visits to the UK made

Visits to the UK by overseas residents, 2002		
	Visits (millions)	Spending (£millions)
Holidays	7.7	3,702
Business	7.2	3,573
Visiting friends or relatives	6.4	2,514
Other	2.9	1,910
Total	**24.2**	**11,737**

Source: International Passenger Survey 2002

by air, accounting for 71% of all visits, with 18% made by sea, and 11% through the Channel Tunnel.

London is by far the most popular receiving area for overseas visitors – 48% of all overseas visits to the UK in 2002 included a stay of at least one night in the capital. (In fact, 85% of the UK's overseas visitors stay only in England.) Overnight visits to London totalled nearly 12 million. The second most popular destination, Edinburgh, received only 0.8 million. The most popular reason for a stay in London was for a holiday (42%), whereas stays in other parts of the country were more commonly to see friends or relatives. .

Visitor spending

The UK travel and tourism industry is immense – worth an estimated £76 billion – and very important to the UK economy. The proportion of the revenue generated by overseas visitors, however, is not easy to estimate.

The statistics show that overseas visitors spent nearly £12 billion in the UK in 2002, but we should add in the amount they paid to UK carriers (airlines, ferries, etc.) to get them here (see table below).

Spending by overseas residents, 2002, £billions				
	1999	2000	2001	2002
Visits to the UK	12.5	12.8	11.3	11.7
Fares to UK carriers	3.2	3.5	3.2	3.3
Total tourism expenditure In the UK, including domestic	73.3	75.1	74.0	75.9

Source 2002: United Kingdom Tourist Survey, International Passenger Survey

Currently the UK is ranked seventh in the international tourism earnings league behind the USA, Spain, France, Italy, China and Germany. A wide range of industries benefits from both direct and indirect income generated by overseas tourists, as shown in the table above, right. Direct income can be measured in terms of transport and accommodation but indirect income is more difficult to measure. Indirect income is generated through a process known as the 'economic multiplier effect' as the tourists' money spreads out to benefit all sorts of local people. For example, some of the money that tourists spend in a hotel goes as wages to the waiters and cleaners, etc, who then spend it in the local shops. In addition, local businesses will supply food and services to the hotel, and some of the money they are paid will also be spent locally – most of it in shops that have nothing to do with tourism.

How overseas visitors spend their money in the UK (2002)		
	% of total	£ millions
Accommodation	33	3,908
Eating out	21	2,418
Shopping*	26	3,052
Travel within the UK	9	1,080
Entertainment	3	340
Services etc.	4	469
Other	4	469
Total	100	11,737

* 50% spent on clothes
Source: International Passenger Survey 2002

It is difficult to actually measure the direct impact of the tourists, however. We know, for example, that in a tourist area the business in shops increases during the tourist season, but some of the increase may be caused by the local people buying more.

The travel and tourism industry also contributes to the national economy via taxation, including corporation tax and value added tax (VAT). Some of this money may be re-invested by the government in building the transport infrastructure, which will benefit the travel and tourism industry.

On a local scale, travel and tourism enterprises also contribute to local government through the payment of business rates. A hotel in central London, of course, has to pay significantly higher business rates than a hotel in a rural area, because the cost of public services in London is significantly higher, but throughout the country the business rates help to support the local economy.

activity

UNDERSTANDING OVERSEAS VISITORS

Look at the two tables on this page and answer the following questions:

1 Why have visits to the UK decreased?

2 What do overseas visitors spend most money on?

3 Why do you think overseas visitors spend so much money on shopping?

Topic 8 The scale of tourism to the British Isles

Where the most overseas visitors come from (2002)		
Country	Visits (000)	Spend (£m)
USA	3,611	2,443
France	3,077	733
Germany	2,556	743
Irish Republic	2,439	674
Netherlands	1,419	

Source: International Passenger Survey 2002

Just what the tourists want to see: pageantry at Windsor Castle

Type of visitor

The most popular reason for visiting the UK is for holidays (32%), followed by business trips (30%), and visits to friends or relatives (21%). The top five generating areas for the UK in 2002 are shown below.

There are many things in the UK that appeal to overseas visitors. Many put Britain's heritage as the number one reason for their visit. The cathedrals and the famous castles and palaces – especially those owned by the Royal Family – provide a unique appeal to the visitor. Buckingham Palace, Kensington Palace, Hampton Court and Windsor are all attractions. Museums, art galleries, theatres, the opera and ballet are all part of Britain's rich and varied culture which attract overseas visitors. Events such as Wimbledon, Henley Royal Regatta and the Open Golf Championships are all popular attractions. Some tourists are attracted by the excellent shopping facilities, not only in London, but also in historic cities such a Cambridge, Chester, Bath, Edinburgh and York.

activity

CITY FULL OF TOURISTS

Write a short report on the impact of tourism on London and where the visitors originate.

Tourists just love London

- 48% of all overseas visitors stay at least one night in London. Around three out of four overseas visitors pass through a London airport.

- In 2002, 11.6m overseas visits were made to London, with direct visitor expenditure equalling 5.8bn. On average, overseas visitors spend £500 per trip, and £77 per night.

- Holidays are the main reason for visits to London (42%), followed by business (24%), VFR (23%), and study (2%).

- The top five generating areas for London are USA (21% of visits), France (10%), Germany (8%), Ireland (5%), and Italy (5%). But even these countries make up less than half the total. The rest come from all the counties of the world.

- Overseas visitors are major investors in London's cultural landscape – they buy 30% of theatre tickets and account for half of all visits to London attractions.

Bed-nights used (length of stay)

The 'bed-nights used' depends on the number of tourists and how long they stay. The length of stay varies, depending on the purpose of the visit. People are more likely to stay longer if they are on holiday or visiting friends and family than if they are on business. The most common length of a business visit from overseas is 4 nights of a working week.

People who travel the furthest also tend to stay the longest, which means that those travelling from America and further a field tended to stay for at least 13 nights and people travelling from other parts of Europe only for two or three nights.

There is clearly a variety of accommodation for the visitor to chose from in the UK. Many establishments close during the winter months but these are mostly the smaller accommodation providers not used by overseas visitors in great numbers (see table below). Although there are tens of thousands of rooms and bed spaces available for tourists, not all are occupied every day of the year. In fact, the average annual occupancy rate for 'bed-spaces' in England is only about 45% , with slightly lower figures for Scotland (43%), Wales (40%) and Northern Ireland (31%). Some of this apparent 'shortfall' is explained by rooms being only partly occupied – one person staying in a twin room, for example, results in only 50% bed-space occupancy.

Accommodation used by overseas visitors to the UK	
	% of Visits
Hotels etc	45
Bed & Breakfast	5
Camping/Mobile Home	1
Hostel	4
Holiday Centre	0
Rented House	3
Paying Guest	3
Free Guest	39
Own Home	2

Source: International Passenger Survey 2002

activity

TOURISM TO BRITAIN – A SHORT TALK

Using the information provided in this topic, prepare a short talk about the scale of tourism to Britain. Your talk, which should be accompanied by a handout providing the relevant figures and sources you have used, should include answers to the following questions:

- How many incoming tourists are there to the UK and where do they come from?
- How much revenue is generated by the travel and tourism industry and by what methods?
- What type of visitor comes to the UK?
- How many bed-nights are used, and by whom?

The factors that affect the popularity and appeal of destinations

The final topic in this unit considers the factors that affect the popularity and appeal of destinations. We will cover:

- **Accessibility**
- **Availability of attractions and other tourist facilities**
- **Cost of visiting**
- **Change in customer needs and expectations**
- **Destination management**
- **Image and promotions**
- **Political factors.**

Accessibility

In the context of tourism to Britain, 'accessibility' means, first, the ease of getting here and, secondly, the ease of travelling around the country. Despite being an island, Great Britain is very easy for tourists to get to. Twenty-five of Britain's airports receive flights from abroad, and London is claimed to be the world's most accessible city. It is the focus of the global airline network with superb worldwide, European and domestic connections. There are regular ferry services from Ireland, Spain, France, Belgium, the Netherlands, Denmark, Sweden and Norway. And there is the Channel Tunnel. According to the 2002 UK Tourism Survey, 71% of visits to the UK were by air, 18% by sea and 11% through the Channel Tunnel.

The number of people travelling by air is rising, with 200 million passengers a year through the main UK airports. This trend is set to continue as no-frills airlines expand further by using smaller regional airports such as Leeds/Bradford, Liverpool and Southampton. In contrast, travelling by sea has slowly declined with only 4.4 million people accessing the UK via a seaport in 2002, and 2.2. million people via the Channel Tunnel.

Getting from the airport to the rest of the country is an important aspect of accessibility. The Heathrow and Gatwick Express provide fast, dedicated, rail links to the centre of London, but there are many rail links all over the country providing direct access from airports. One example of this is the train link that, from Manchester Airport, runs west to Liverpool and east – right across the country – to Scarborough, allowing easy access to a large part of northern England. There are also many coach companies that provide links from major airports to cities across the country. Virgin Atlantic has developed a completely new method (see box).

The various transport links *within* Britain, which make up the second half of the accessibility aspect for tourists, have been dealt with in Topic 5. The extensive road and rail networks mean that nearly all parts of the country are easily accessible to tourists – and even the remotest parts of the Scottish Highlands can be reached by determined walkers.

Virgin has developed a new mode of transport – the amphibious limo – to beat the traffic between Heathrow and the centre of London. The airline is planning to offer some of its Upper Class passengers arriving at Heathrow the chance to experience the Gibbs Aquada.

When it hits traffic, the driver simply heads for the nearest slipway and takes to the Thames before rejoining the roads for the final leg of the journey. Said a spokesman: 'This is a revolutionary vehicle providing a real practical solution to London's traffic – and there's no Congestion Charge!'

Source (adapted): www.aquada.co.uk

Availability of attractions and other tourist facilities

Up and down the country, there are many towns and cities that have benefited and grown because of the tourist attractions and facilities they provide. London is by far the most popular destination for tourists – because it has the greatest concentration of major attractions in Britain (see below).

Cost of visiting

The cost of visiting a destination can be a major factor affecting its appeal. London is notoriously expensive for the tourist, especially if the trip includes a stay overnight. The peak holiday seasons of July and August are the most costly, and many tourists choose to holiday in the UK out of season.

In addition to the cost of the holiday there are the additional costs of the activities and attractions. The Visitors to Attractions Survey 2002 showed the impact of the new policy of free entry to museums and art galleries, particularly those in London. Visits to the Science Museum, for example, increased 94% (to 2.6 million). Visits to the Victoria and Albert Museum increased 84% (to 2.7 million), and to the Natural History Museum 74% (to 2.9 million).

Why tourists choose London

- Six of the top ten 'free attractions' and three of the top ten 'paid attractions' (2002) are in London.

- The West End is the UK's leading retail centre, with Oxford Street the busiest shopping street in Europe, with 200m visitors a year.

- There are four World Heritage Sites (Palace of Westminster, Tower of London, Maritime Greenwich and Kew Gardens) in London.

- There are over 100 theatres in London, including 50 in the West End. London theatre accounts for 45% of all UK theatre admissions and over 70% of box-office revenues.

- London has 3,800 pubs, (9% of Britain's total) and 233 nightclubs (15% of Britain's total).

- With over 30% of its area green open space, London boasts more parks, many of which are *Royal Parks*, than any other city of its size in the world.

Source: London Visitor Statistics 2003/04

Speakers' Corner in Hyde Park

Change in customer needs and expectations

The customers' needs and expectations are constantly changing, which makes some locations more popular at some times than others. British beach resorts have seen many of their traditional customers changing to foreign holidays, and some resorts have invested heavily in trying to halt their decline by appealing to foreign tourists, as shown in the example of Fowey, Cornwall below.

Destination management

Destination management deals with the complex roles of public, private and partnership organisations in the tourism industry. These roles range from managing the effects of tourism on our communities, environment and economy to providing the key services for sustainable tourism development.

Planning and implementation involves a range of activities such as marketing, human resource management and operations, and also coordinating

A new destination for foreign tourists

Fowey is not your common-or-garden seaside resort. This historic seafaring town has more sea walls than sandy stretches, and not many buckets and spades in evidence. But the quaint town has long attracted 'discerning'– affluent and elderly – holidaymakers, and now it is also chasing the lucrative cruise liner market.

This year, the deep-water port will play host to 14 cruise visits – and the hundreds of high-spending tourists on board – compared with just one ship two years ago. Already, a few shops accept US dollars.

Fowey's harbourmaster, Captain Mike Sutherland, hopes this will rise to about 50 ships a year by 2006, under a new scheme to attract more cruises to the small ports of Devon and Cornwall.

The initiative – dubbed 'Destination Southwest' – is awaiting confirmation of European subsidies, as Devon and Cornwall are both

eligible for employment-boosting EU funding.

'Cruise passengers are looking for something different – they're starting to say, "Oh, we're bored by the Caribbean". We're offering them a new experience,' Captain Sutherland says.

The new experience is billed as a 'Celtic Trail', involving small ports in Devon and Cornwall, Ireland, Scotland and Brittany.

the needs of tourists and residents. Specialised Destination Management Companies (DMCs) exist that will coordinate the design and implementation of events, activities, tours, transportation – creating and developing a customised programme. This may involve sightseeing tours, water sports, special charters, eating in local restaurants, or providing activities and entertainment for partners.

DMCs ensure that all aspects of a trip or event run to plan. They will assist with special requirements such as customs clearance, immigration and union services, shipments, simultaneous translation, gifts, ground transport, sightseeing services, exhibition and trade show services, excursions and tour planning.

The army moves in to protect Heathrow in 2003.

Image and promotions

Media coverage can have a significant impact of a tourist destination. Media articles that show the tourist destination to be rundown and unpopular will have a very negative effect on the area.

Good media coverage obviously has a positive affect on a destination or attraction. An example of this is the London Eye whose phenomenal success has been due in part to the vast array of positive publicity it has received.

Political factors

The threat of terrorism has become the blight of the modern world for travellers. Many people have been put off travelling by recent world events such as 9/11 in the United States and the subsequent bombings closer to home in Madrid and Turkey. London and the key tourist destinations of the UK are always under terrorist alert.

The Visits to Visitor Attractions Survey 2002, published on behalf of the four national tourist boards, shows the impact of 9/11 and the resulting decline of overseas visitors to Britain. Visits to historic properties, popular with overseas visitors, fell by 7%. The Tower of London, Canterbury Cathedral, Westminster Abbey, Windsor Castle and St Paul's Cathedral all saw their visitor numbers drop significantly.

Despite fewer overseas visitors to the UK in 2001 (down 9% to 23 million), a domestic political move – the introduction of free entry to museums and galleries – meant that at least this sector fared well. As we saw in the last topic, entries to museums in London, in particular, rose dramatically. Government intervention certainly seemed to benefit the tourist in this circumstance – a feeling not shared by the many tourist industries that were affected by the Foot and Mouth Disease in 2000.

When tourist attractions are swamped by visitors – as Westminster Abbey often is – careful management is needed.

The Foot and Mouth Disease outbreak in 2000 had a disastrous impact on some tourist destinations.

The Foot and Mouth Disease outbreak, and the drastic restrictions imposed by the government, had a devastating effect on most UK tourist destinations. The most badly affected destinations were rural areas where cattle were farmed, but farm visits, parks and wildlife attractions – even historic buildings – were affected. It is estimated that the foot and mouth epidemic cost the UK billions in lost revenue.

The closure of countryside locations and footpaths during the height of the epidemic contributed to a 25% fall in visits to farm attractions, a 6% drop in visits to country parks and a 4% decline in visits to wildlife attractions. Overall, 26% of attractions were forced to close for part of their normal opening season in 2001.

The government's plans for 'Destination Britain'

In 2004, the government spelt out how it would work with key partners to drive the tourism industry forward. *Tomorrow's Tourism Today* was published as the' joint tourism prospectus' of the Department for Culture Media and Sport, the industry, the regions and local government.

One of the main aims is to reduce the present 'balance of payments' deficit in tourism. British people spent £15 billion more on tourism abroad (in 2002) than overseas visitors are spending here. The deficit has risen from £2 billion in 1990. One way to reduce the deficit would be to persuade British people to holiday in their own country, but a better (and more practical) way is to promote 'Destination Britain' and encourage more overseas tourists to come here. *Tomorrow's Tourism Today* made several points about this:

- Tourism is vital to our economic success, as well as fostering perceptions of Britain throughout the world.

- According to the World Tourism Organisation, we are seventh in the world table of 'inbound' tourism earners, after USA, Spain, France, Italy, China and Germany – but 3 years ago we were fifth.

- We are competing in an ever more challenging market. New destinations and new markets are rapidly emerging, the latter reflecting the increasing affluence and mobility of people in Eastern Europe and Asia.

- VisitBritain has already expanded into several key emerging markets – China, South Korea, Poland and Russia – promoting new websites, and building media and trade awareness. Further market development is under way in other 'Accession States', and in Malaysia and Thailand.

- We know that this country can provide what today's visitors are seeking:

  – short breaks are a dynamic market, appealing to international tourists;

  – there is great potential for further expansion in business tourism, bringing in significant numbers of high-spending tourists who sustain the upper end of the accommodation sector, and businesses in conferencing and exhibitions;

Language schools in Britain attract large numbers of overseas students, who often return as tourists after their courses have finished.

- English universities and language schools attract high numbers of overseas students.

• We are seeing growth in business tourism, and in visiting friends and relations. There is good evidence that these types of visits very often lead to repeat trips – business visitors often return to the UK for pleasure, and overseas students return to the haunts of their youth.

• Britain remains a leading destination for international tourists, and we can make it even more popular. We can appeal both to our existing markets, and to new ones emerging around the globe. Our traditional assets, including our heritage, culture, and countryside, remain strong. But increasingly they are being supplemented by a new awareness of the attractions of our thriving modern culture, and of our place at the cutting edge of many creative activities. Hobby and pastime packages, sports and activities, and film and television tie-ins, are growth areas, and London's position as both major world city and UK gateway remains strong.

Source. Tomorrow's Tourism Today is available at www.culture.gov.uk/global/publications/archive_2004/ tomorrowstourismtoday.

Tate Modern, a showplace for modern culture, has proved very popular with tourists.

Topic 9 The popularity and appeal of destinations

RESEARCHING ALL THE FACTORS

Research the factors that could affect a destination of your choice, and present your findings to the rest of the group. Include recommendations as to how the destination could improve its appeal in the future. The factors may include the following:

• Accessibility

• Availability of attractions and other tourist facilities

• Cost of visiting

• Changes in customer needs and expectations

• Destination management

• Image and promotion

• Political factors.

How Unit 4 is assessed

Unit 4 is assessed by coursework. The evidence should be in four parts, which we suggest you present as four sections within a portfolio. The following guidance outlines how you can achieve the assessment requirements for each of the four parts.

The evidence could be in many different forms to allow for your learning preferences, styles and strengths to be accommodated. There will be itineraries produced for task **(b)** but other tasks could be evidenced through written reports, newspaper articles, radio or television scripts or witness testimonies of oral presentations, accompanied by supporting evidence.

For task **(a)** your evidence will be drawn from one selected area. For task **(b)** your evidence will be drawn from a range of destinations. Evidence for task **(d)** will be drawn from one destination – which could be one of the destinations featured in evidence for task **(b)**.

Task (a) Key travel and tourism organisations

(a.0) Introduction

Give a brief overview of the area in the British Isles that you have selected to study. (It could be a tourist board region, one or more counties or a themed area, for example.)

(a.1) Description of roles

Describe the roles of the key travel and tourism organisations that support tourism to the selected area. (These would include: Government departments and agencies, regional tourist boards and national tourist offices, local authority tourism departments, regional development agencies, tourist information centres, membership organisations, transport operators, accommodation providers, incoming tour operators.)

(a.2) Explanation of interdependencies and interrelationships

Give an explanation of the interdependence and interrelationships of the key travel and tourism organisations in supporting tourism to the selected area.

Task (b) An itinerary including examples of different types of destinations

You will be given details of incoming tourists by your tutor in the form of a pen portrait, and your itinerary should include destinations that meet the needs that are specified in the information you are given. Destinations should be located on a map, and the features that give each destination in the itinerary appeal should be described. There should be an explanation of how the itinerary meets the needs of the incoming tourists.

(b.0) Introduction

In this section you are to describe the factors involved in planning an itinerary for the incoming tourists, according to the following factors: age, group, business, interests, special needs, language requirements.

(b.1) Planning and presenting the Itinerary

In this section you are to present an itinerary to include different types of British destinations suitable for the incoming tourists, including: who the itinerary is prepared for, dates, timing, what is included, contact details, details of destinations and attractions.

Task (c) The scale of tourism to the British Isles

Research and analysis of the scale of tourism to the British Isles in terms of visitor numbers, visitor spending, type of visitor and bed nights used.

NOTE: To achieve the higher mark bands you need to show that you have researched a range of sources of information independently, and provided a thorough analysis, using accurate statistical data.

Task (d) Popularity and appeal

(d.0) Introduction

A description of the selected destination

(d.1) Evaluation

An evaluation of the factors that have affected the popularity and appeal of the selected destination. (These will include: accessibility, availability of attractions and other tourist facilities, cost of visiting, change in customer needs and expectations, image and promotion, destination management, political factors.)

(d.2) Recommendations

Give recommendations of how the selected destination can develop its future popularity and appeal in order to receive more incoming visitors.

NOTE: To achieve the higher mark bands you should show a detailed and critical evaluation of the factors affecting the popularity and appeal of the destination. Recommendations on how the destination can develop should be relevant, feasible and justified.

Bibliography

List all of the sources of information that you have used to complete the assessment for this unit.

Appendices

Include any relevant supporting information in the appendices, such as examples of marketing materials, policies and procedures, etc.

Improving your grades

Generally, you will get better grades by giving more comprehensive explanations, including better examples and showing a deeper understanding of each topic. Your school or college should be able to advise you in more detail, or you could visit the Edexcel website: edexcel.org.uk for more guidance.

General guidelines on presentation of assignments

See page 289 for advice on how to present your assignments.

Departing, travelling and arriving safely are key considerations when we set off on any sort of journey – and we expect our belongings and possessions to travel safely too. They are also key concerns for the tour operators, travel agencies and the organisations that oversee the travel sector.

Ensuring safe and secure travel needs a range of measures to be in place at various locations – at our departure points, during transit, upon arrival and also while we travel round our destination zone. Governments, industry bodies and operators are all active in this process of protection.

Organisations must also ensure that adequate emergency procedures are in place to cope with minor but regular occurrences and also major unforeseen situations.

You will need to be able to apply the knowledge, skills and understanding of this unit in an externally set test, which is likely to have a number of case studies or scenarios for you to analyse.

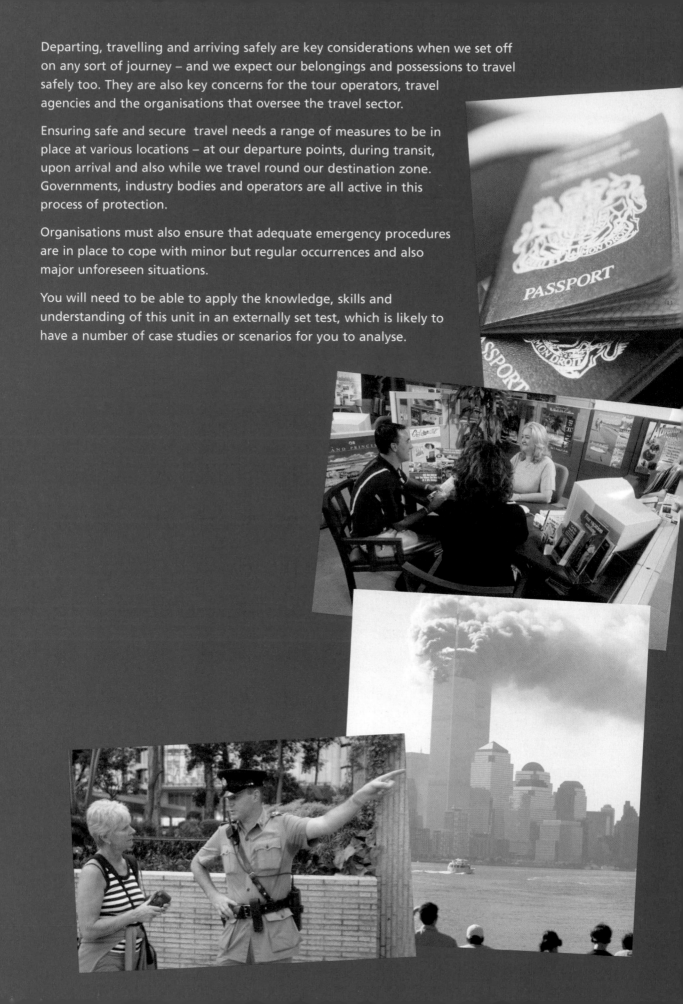

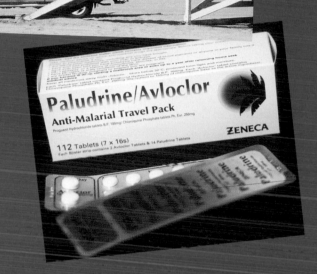

Unit 5

Travelling Safely

5.1 Legal and regulatory requirements

Topic 1	Aviation regulations and ABTA	200
Topic 2	EU and UK legislation	204
Topic 3	Consumer protection	208

5.2 Restrictions on travel

| Topic 4 | Passports and visas | 212 |
| Topic 5 | Health restrictions | 216 |

5.3 Emergency situations

Topic 6	Cancellation, curtailment and insurance	220
Topic 7	Losses and criminal activity	226
Topic 8	Large-scale emergency situations	230

| How Unit 5 is assessed | 236 |

Aviation regulations and ABTA

A number of key organisations regulate the travel sector of the tourism industry – we learned about some of them in Unit 1. In this topic we shall focus on four main organisations – and the regulations they apply to their own members to maintain the highest safety standards. This is known as 'self regulation'.

The safety guidelines and practices are important. They are based on years of experience, including lessons learned from previous incidents and disasters, such as those at UK and foreign airports.

Some of the organisations described below act only in the UK – but other countries have their own equivalent. Others organisations have a pan-European role or a global role. You need to be able to differentiate between these.

The organisations studied are:

- **The Civil Aviation Authority (CAA)**
- **The Association of British Travel Agencies (ABTA)**
- **The International Air Transport Association (IATA)**
- **Joint Aviation Authorities (JAA).**

The first two are UK-specific, and the other two have an international remit. All produce regulations – which must be followed, codes of practice – which *should* be followed, and guidelines – which it is *advisable* to follow, in a range of travel contexts.

The Civil Aviation Authority (CAA)

The CAA is the UK's specialist aviation regulator and has 'under its wing' a range of responsibilities and services. It helps to regulate what goes on in the air – flight paths and frequencies of flights, and what happens on the ground too – airport development and licensing. It offers advice, grants licences to operate, makes safety checks, trains staff and sets standards – as well as informing government policy on all air safety affairs. The CAA also works with 'Eurocontrol' to help protect the whole of Europe – the world's busiest tourist region.

Our main interest here is the CAA's role in safety matters, but some of its other controls and regulations are relevant and will be mentioned to show the scope of its controlling powers. The cornerstone of most aviation legislation is called 'CAP 393' (see opposite). As you can see, there is a very comprehensive set of regulations for aviation, which cover all scheduled, charter, helicopter and taxi-type flights around the UK.

Links to other aviation legislation – including noise regulation – can be found at http://www.legislation.hmso.gov.uk.

The regulatory contents of CAP 393

- The Air Navigation Order 2000
- The Rules of the Air Regulations 1996
- The Air Navigation (General) Regulations 1993
- The Air Navigation (Cosmic Radiation)(Keeping of Records) Regulations 2000
- Permanent Air Navigation (Restriction of Flying) Regulations
- The Civil Aviation Authority Regulations 1991
- The Air Navigation (Dangerous Goods) Regulations 2002

KEEPING THE NOISE DOWN

From your own discussions, observations and some research of the regulations, identify six ways in which airports and aircraft are controlled to reduce noise around urban areas.

The CAA has a 'Safety Regulation Group' composed of a number of departments covering different aspects of UK air traffic services. Their work is vital – although most travellers never see it. Every time a plane pushes back from a terminal building, however, the passengers want to know that these people have done their job to ensure their safety. We will investigate a few departments to give you an overview of their work behind the scenes.

Air Traffic Standards Department

The air traffic standards department works with airports to ensure that their safety systems work smoothly and consistently, especially in the light of increasing air traffic levels (flight frequency). They have, for example, a special programme to help ground crew ensure that there are no 'runway incursions' (see below).

Runway incursions

A runway incursion is any occurrence at an airport involving the unauthorised or unplanned presence of an aircraft, people, or vehicles on the tarmac, which can lead to collisions, crashes, near misses or injuries and accidents.

Worldwide, these are an increasing concern for operators – who now have terrorist threats uppermost in their minds. They usually occur, however, because of poor security systems, lack of communication or just human error amongst pilots, air traffic controllers and ground crew.

REASSURING PRESENCE ON THE GROUND

Discuss what ground staff and emergency vehicles you (as a passenger) would want on standby if you were coming in to land and the pilot said there was a problem with the plane.

Other CAA departments

- The Aerodrome Standards Department issues licences to airports for the purposes of public transport (or flying instruction). They also work to standardise procedures and licensing criteria throughout Europe through their links with international partner organisations, especially the European Aviation Safety Agency (EASA) – see overleaf.

- The Airworthiness Department focuses on the aircraft themselves – their design, condition, etc.

- The Training Department runs regional and international training courses for prospective employees, and advises airport authorities on training needs. They also assess the effectiveness of training amongst staff employed at airports. This can be really important to tourism event organisers – as you can see below.

Air safety and tourism events

The CAA publishes guidelines for tourist events which involve helicopter flights, requiring temporary heliports. This would include events such as the Cheltenham Gold Cup; the Grand National (Aintree); Henley Rowing Regatta; the British Grand Prix (Silverstone); the Open Golf Tournament (various locations); Cowes Sailing Regatta.

You can imagine how chaotic these venues might be in terms of ad hoc arrivals and departures of global visitors/tourists/celebrities and VIPs – and how attractive they would be to terrorist groups. The event organiser and the heliport co-ordinator have to work together to cover all aspects of their 'duties to care' for travellers, spectators and participants, and contingencies and procedures. The CAA would have to ensure that, among other things, the following were adequately covered:

- Competent staff are appointed on the ground
- Rescue and fire-fighting teams are present or on call
- An emergency plan is in place
- Local authorities are fully involved.

- The Publications Department issues a range of leaflets, including: care of passengers, winter flying, bird avoidance, collision avoidance, aerobatics, and ditching – though one would hope that pilots do a little more then read a leaflet on these subjects.

- The General Aviation Department covers all private aerial work and recreational flying, e.g. commercial balloon flights, aerial displays, charity flights, model aircraft events, parachuting.

- The Licensing Department manages the 'Air Travel Organisers Licence' (ATOL) system. Organisers of holidays that include a flight have to hold an ATOL to meet the legal requirement and to ensure that holidaymakers' money is secure, if they go out of business. A leaflet is shown overleaf. If you would like to learn more about ATOLs visit their site at www.atol.org.uk.

WITH AN ATOL PACKAGE
YOUR HOLIDAY STARTS
THE MINUTE YOU BOOK!

MGA 1945

w w w . a t o l . o r g . u k

An ATOL leaflet, produced by the CAA's Licensing Department

Association of British Travel Agents

The Association of British Travel Agencies (ABTA)

ABTA is the main trade association for tour operators and travel agents in the UK. In 2004 its members included 1043 tour operators and 6356 travel agency offices – accounting for 85% of UK-sold holiday packages, and a turnover of £26 billion.

ABTA's primary aim is to give financial protection for customers, through the 'bonding system'. This means that members have to lodge a bond (money) with ABTA to ensure that if, for example, they go out of business, their customers will not be stranded abroad with no way home. The bond would pay any costs. This financial protection for the holidaymaker has been provided for well over 30 years (see right).

ABTA has a commercial role – to promote and develop the general interests of all its members, by influencing

policies, for instance, at government and EU level.

It also has a 'regulatory' role – controlling the actions of its members and covering their liability to customers. When a Cheshire travel group, for example, was unable to meet its liabilities and ceased trading in November 2004, all claims relating to its various companies were handled by the ABTA Claims Department. This comprehensive 'safety net' ensures, not only that the holidaymakers affected are compensated, but also that the whole travel industry maintains its reputation for honesty and reliability. As Ian Reynolds, ABTA Chief Executive said (ABTA website December 2004), 'The travel trade is one of the very few areas of business where reputable companies protect their clients in the event of their failure.'

ABTA's 'bond system'

The source of the bond system is the 'stabiliser' rule introduced by ABTA in 1965, which states that: if an ABTA tour operator wishes to sell their foreign inclusive holidays or other travel arrangements through a third party, they could only do so through ABTA travel agents. Conversely, ABTA travel agents could only sell the foreign inclusive arrangements of ABTA tour operators. This meant that most tour operators and travel agents sought to belong to ABTA and the net of ABTA's safeguards for the travelling public was cast as widely as possible.

- ABTA currently has bonds valued at £201 million for travel agents and £170 million for tour operators.
- To protect consumers' monies and holidays, ABTA paid out £2.2 million in 2001 in respect of travel agents' failures and £90,000 in respect of tour operators' failures.
- In 2003, ABTA dealt with nearly 17,000 complaints. Of these, over 1,200 went to ABTA's independent arbitration scheme – an alternative to a small claims court.

RISKY BUSINESS

Discuss the dangers there might be for customers of a travel agent who has not joined ABTA and its bond system.

The International Air Transport Association (IATA)

IATA prides itself on being an effective, professional trade association for over 270 airlines worldwide – representing 95% of international scheduled flights. Its main aims are to:

1. Ensure that its members' aircraft can fly around the globe safely, securely and efficiently under agreed rules and regulations.
2. Ensure that people, mail and freight can also move round the globe smoothly.
3. Control ticket costs and ensure that tickets are universally usable.
4. Work with governments to set global standards of safety and efficiency.

IATA is involved in a very broad range of activities in the airline industry – aircraft operations (engineering, fuelling, maintenance); airport development (traffic management and infrastructure); cargo (handling, transport of animals); finance (credit cards operations, fraud prevention); passengers (fares, ticketing, in-flight services, baggage); and legal aspects (Customs) – but the one that we are interested in here is safety.

Despite year-on-year losses recorded by many airlines (over $30 billion) IATA members have continued to invest heavily in safety. The IATA website reports:

'Over 1.8 billion people travelled safely in 2004. Tragically, however, 428 people lost their lives in commercial aircraft accidents. To put that into perspective, that is a similar number to 1945 when the industry carried only 9 million passengers. Air transport is the safest form of transport, but every accident is one too many. We are fully committed to further improvements.' What percentage of air travellers in 2004 arrived safely?

Some of the bigger alliances – Star, One World and Sky Team – are now using the new International Operations Safety Audit (IOSA) standard, which is to become a requirement for future membership of IATA, and be at the heart of a global safety drive. This should benefit everyone – passengers, governments and airlines, and create greater public confidence. IATA has a safety advisory committee to help members develop recommended practices and also a Emergency Response Planning Group (ERPG).

WHY SPEND MONEY ON SAFETY?

IATA works to keep the general public safer, while helping its members to run their businesses more profitably, efficiently (and safely). Working in small groups, discuss whether you see any conflict in these aims, and why investment in safety is so important these days. Create a chart or OHP showing your reasons, and then present your ideas.

Joint Aviation Authorities (JAA) and EASA

The JAA, based in the Netherlands, was set up to organise cooperation between aviation authorities in Europe, but its responsibilities are currently being taken over by the new European Aviation Safety Agency (EASA) based in Cologne (Germany). This gives Europe a body (similar to the United States' Federal Aviation Administration) which can draw up the highest safety standards and have them applied across the whole of Europe. These standards cover issues such as

- Certification of aeronautical products
- Approval of maintenance teams and practices
- Approval of operations
- Licensing of aircrew
- Oversight of airports and air traffic services.

Unannounced checks are done on the spot, sometimes randomly and sometimes targeted at suspect aircraft. These investigate as many as 50 aspects, including: the pilots' licences; whether a manual is being carried; compliance with manual procedures; safety equipment carried; and condition of the aircraft.

Since 1996, over 12,000 of these checks have been carried out by inspectors. The inspectors will not normally delay the flight, but do they have powers to request immediate corrective action if the safety of passengers, crew or craft are in doubt. In future, if you are sitting on a plane before take off and the captain announces a short delay due to technical problems, you will probably have an idea that an inspector has been aboard and wants something fixed – so be patient.

ALL THE KEY POINTS

Using your own words, prepare a poster which gives the key points about each of the four organisations featured in this topic.

203

Topic 1 Aviation regulations and ABTA

This topic deals with 'external' regulations – as laid down by governing authorities – in our case the European Union and the British government.

These generally cover *all* organisations – not just the travel sector – but one (the European Package Travel Directive) is industry-specific, and you will need to understand all its applications and implications. Two more general UK Acts are covered in this topic, which have wide-reaching implications for travel organisations. The topic breaks down, therefore into three sections:

- ■ The European Package Travel Directive
- ■ The Disability Discrimination Act
- ■ The Data Protection Act.

It is important to remember that although these Acts and regulations were created a number of years ago they are regularly reviewed, amended and added to.

Staff working in the industry have to stay aware of the current contexts and applications, and this will apply to you too when preparing for your test.

The European Package Travel Directive

From the 1960s to the early 1990s the ABTA 'stabiliser' (which we learned about in the last topic) gave protection for most holidaymakers' money, but a few large collapses and an increasing number of non-ABTA niche-market providers prompted EU chiefs to try to create a better form of protection for consumers. So in 1990 the EC 'Directive on Package Travel' was born. It meant that tours had to be licensed, a fund had to be created to cover contingencies, and travel agents would be held liable for incorrect information in brochures. The Directive also restricted the use of 'additional surcharges' on package holidays. (Flight-only sales are not covered by the legislation.)

Member countries could still retain their own consumer protection, but the regulations harmonise applications to travel throughout Europe. They create civil and criminal liability for tour operators (wholesalers) and travel agencies (retailers) for failures

in the whole of the holiday or component parts such as hoteliers, airlines, airports and transfer companies. The official wording says: 'the organiser shall be liable to the consumer for the proper performance of all obligations under the contract [booking]'. Examples of breaches of the regulations (which trigger compensation payments) might include:

- Food served in the hotel is of poor quality or causes salmonella
- Swimming pool is closed or not maintained hygienically or safely
- A safety rail or balcony gives way and someone is injured at a hotel
- The resort rep fails to do anything about complaints such as mildew in a room.

There are certain situations that the regulations do not cover, including:

- Where an accident happens due to drunkenness or bravado

Sometimes the reality doesn't match the dream.

- Where the failure is due to a third party, outside the package components, e.g. a local motorist
- Where *'force majeure'* occurs – such as war, riots, or natural or climatic disasters
- Excursions bought in the resort.

The package has to be sold as an inclusive deal, containing transport, accommodation and other significant tourism services and be for more than 24 hours. The travel organiser is also liable to provide customers with all additional advice as necessary, such as visa and health requirements, all connections and stopover details, a local rep and contact details, plus insurance and safety advice. In 1998, the Directive was reinforced by a ruling in the European Court (see below).

European Court's landmark decision

The days of stranded holidaymakers are hopefully gone forever. In 1998, James Provan MEP welcomed a landmark decision by the European Court guaranteeing protection for holidaymakers on package tours.

'Every summer some tourists find themselves stranded abroad when their package tour company goes bankrupt. Despite a 1990 EU Package Travel Directive, many people are still forced to pay their own hotel bills and sometimes replacement air fares. The recent European Court decision now guarantees that these payments will be reimbursed.'

The case was brought by an Austrian couple who had been forcibly prevented from leaving their hotel in Crete when their travel company went bankrupt. They had already paid for their hotel in their package, but the hotel manager insisted they pay him again. The European Court, however, judged that the extra hotel payments must be reimbursed by the travel firm's insurance company, under the 1990 Directive.

'Holidaymakers can travel anywhere in the world and know they are protected by European consumer legislation.'

activity

WHO IS GOING TO PAY FOR THIS?

Mr Gloster of Cardiff booked a return flight to Los Angeles, online with 'Direct Deals'. While he was online he was offered accommodation and car hire as additional services at very reasonable prices. He decided to just take the car hire, and he booked, paying (an all-inclusive price) with his credit card. During his trip the car constantly broke down and sometime wouldn't start, and his whole holiday was ruined by the inconvenience.

Is the package covered by the regulations? Can Mr Gloster sue anyone or claim a refund? Would it have made a difference if he had booked the accommodation too?

The Disability Discrimination Act

The Disability Discrimination Act 1994 (DDA) came about through public pressure to persuade operators and businesses to remove barriers facing people with disabilities. The Act has very broad applications in our society which we will mention briefly, but more of the focus will be on the employment, transport and premises applications, as these are more relevant to tourism and travel.

For the purposes of the Act, a person has a disability if he or she has a 'physical or mental impairment, which has a substantial and long-term adverse effect on their ability to carry out normal day-to-day activities'. The Act makes it illegal for any organisation (not just travel and tourism ones) to discriminate against a job applicant or an employee with a disability.

An employer also has a duty to make adjustments to accommodate the employee with a disability in terms of working arrangements and the physical features of premises. In the tourism industry, these adjustments might be:

- altering working hours, i.e. changing shift patterns
- allowing absence during working hours for rehabilitation, assessment or treatment
- acquiring or modifying equipment such as ticket machines or computers
- modifying procedures for testing or assessment, e.g. language training
- altering the premises, e.g. installing lifts or lowering reception-desk heights.

Airports around the world are providing more help for people with disabilities.

In determining what is 'reasonable' for an employer (e.g. a travel agency) to have to do in order to comply with the legislation, the extent of changes, and the financial and other costs must be taken into account. The Act contains some exemptions for small businesses where the costs would be prohibitive.

ACCESS TO PUBLIC PLACES

As a group, brainstorm the problems a person confined to a wheelchair may encounter when using the following:

- Local bus and train services
- A local museum
- A 3- or 4-star hotel in your area
- Bed & breakfast accommodation
- London Underground, or other underground railway service
- Your local coffee shop.

Do any of the above services have to comply with the Disability Discrimination Act 1995? (You might find it useful to look at Part III of the Act on the internet: www.disability.gov.uk/dda.)

Travel services are singled out as key areas. Taxis, for example, must be suitable for wheelchair access and safe transportation. There are clear regulations, too, governing any premises which 'form part of any port, airport, railway station or bus station'. Transport providers are expected to assist with luggage, guide dogs and other aspects of mobility at no additional charge.

Accessibility regulations for 'public service vehicles' (buses), have also been affected. People with disabilities must be able to 'get on to and off regulated public service vehicles in safety and without unreasonable difficulty and, in the case of disabled persons in wheelchairs, to do so while remaining in their wheelchairs'. Regulations also apply to rail and tram accessibility. Adaptations for these include automatic opening doors and wider doors, lower emergency and assistance buttons, lowering of suspension or raising of kerbs.

Tourist attractions and hotels have to comply with these regulations too, and since the 1994 Act was amended and added to in 2000, owners of premises have been busy adding lifts, ramps, and other disabled-friendly furniture and facilities to their premises, such as designated parking and Braille signs.

STOPPING DISCRIMINATION

The DDA has had a major effect on the industry causing employers to think carefully and positively, in a long-term way about how they present opportunities and facilities for employees and tourists with disabilities.

In the event of a complaint of discrimination, any remedies/procedures which must be followed are usually decided by an industrial tribunal. This is an independent body which makes a judgement on whether the organisation has done enough to meet the requirements of the Act (or is exempt). In the case study below (drawn from holidaywhitehead.co.uk) you can see a typical outcome.

The Data Protection Act

This Act was first brought in (in 1984) to regulate organisations holding personal information on people. It was designed to protect customers, staff and members of an organisation from having data on them used unethically or unscrupulously. Under the Act, which was amended in 1998, people have the right to know if information is held on them and what that information actually is. It also details consumers' rights in relation to getting wrong information put right and misuse of information, e.g. selling addresses for marketing mailshots.

In the travel and tourism industry this information might be customers' addresses, personal details, travel plans and travel history, accommodation preferences, and bank details – plus staff records.

There are a quite a number of conditions about holding information in any manual or electronic form (including CCTV footage). Information held on computer databases must be:

- accurate, adequate and relevant
- gathered fairly and legally
- not used for purposes other than the purpose it is kept for
- secure and up to date
- able to be checked by the individual.

Organisations have to apply to the 'Data Protection Registrar' to hold information on clients or staff, giving a reason why and specifying what they will hold, saying also what sources they will use to generate the data. If the information needs to be given to other organisations, then that must be specified at the approval stage too. A fee is payable upon acceptance, and has to be updated every 3 years.

Prohibited data

Under the Act there are categories of 'sensitive personal data' which must not be held:

- racial or ethnic origin
- political opinions
- religious beliefs
- trade union membership
- physical or mental health conditions
- sexual life or orientation
- the commission or alleged commission of any offence.

PROTECTING YOUR DATA

Working in small teams, discuss the following questions, as if you were the database manager for a large city travel agency:

1 Who else would be interested in the type of information held (inside and outside the organisation)?

2 How could you keep it secure (manually and electronically)?

3 How could you keep it up to date and accurate? Design a form for this.

Topic 3 Consumer protection

This topic continues our study of legal protection, focusing more on the traveller as a 'consumer' of a tourism product or service. In the early days of tourism, consumers had very little protection against fraud, or poor quality travel or holiday experiences. Gradually legislation has been brought in to ensure that if standards are low or experiences are not what was expected – or advertised – or if holidays go dramatically wrong, there is a mechanism of recourse. This might lead, for example, to exchanging goods or achieving a refund. We have seen a modern example of this in the EU package travel regulations. Other Acts support tourist goods and services outside the package travel realms, including:

- The Trades Description Act
- The Fair Trading Act
- The Sale of Goods and Services Act.

They apply to all kinds of buying and selling of goods and services, but we shall investigate them from a travel and tourism point of view. It is useful to remember that these types of Act are quite often amended as technology and commercial practices change, so try to access the most up-to-date version for your studies. For your test you will also need to know how travel and tourism organisations meet the requirements of the legislation in their operational practices, which are dealt with at the end of this topic.

The Trades Description Act

The Trades Description Act, introduced in 1968, is designed to protect consumers in general from false description of goods and services. In a travel and tourism context this could mean that if a hotel was described as 'quiet and restful' in a brochure but holidaymakers, once they got there, found it was near a busy motorway, then a false description would have been given. Sometimes, of course, holiday locations have new developments which start after a brochure is printed (often up to a year in advance). Under these circumstances, the operator is obliged to inform the clients of the change in circumstances.

The basic theme is truthful communications so that customers gain a true impression of their location. Nowadays, with 'virtual tours' as a feature of many promotions, these types of misrepresentation are less likely.

Where cases of misrepresentation *are* found, the outcome will be refunds or compensation – maybe even prosecution in serious cases. Apart from the financial penalties and burden of processing claims, operators who mislead their customers are not going to last long in a very competitive marketplace, once word gets round that they are untrustworthy.

ILLEGAL FAKE OR BARGAIN?

Working in small groups, discuss whether you think that the sale in a street market of fake designer-labelled clothing or pirate CDs is a breach of the Trades Description Act or not, and what should be done about it.

The Fair Trading Act

The Fair Trading Act, first introduced in 1973, set up the Office of Fair Trading (OFT). Now, however, most of the OFT's powers come under the Enterprise Act 2002.

When things go wrong, the first step is to make a complaint.

The Enterprise Act (see right) made a number of important reforms, designed to crack down on abuses that harm customers and fair-trading businesses alike, and thus encourage productivity and enterprise. It established the Office of Fair Trading as an independent statutory body, and gave it a greater role in ensuring that markets work well to the benefit of all. The role of the OFT is to investigate and report on business practices in different sectors – including tourism.

Should the OFT wish to investigate the tourism industry, it could:

- Examine practices and regulation to explore whether the needs of consumers are being well served by travel agents and tour operators.

- Make sure that businesses compete on a level footing, and that no price-fixing – for flights, for example – is going on (the Enterprise Act 2002 makes it a criminal offence for individuals to dishonestly take part in the most serious types of price-fixing). Anyone convicted of the offence could receive a maximum of five years imprisonment and/or an unlimited fine.

- Examine whether company directors are operating legally. It is a criminal offence for a disqualified person to be director of a company or be involved in the management of a company, whether directly or indirectly.

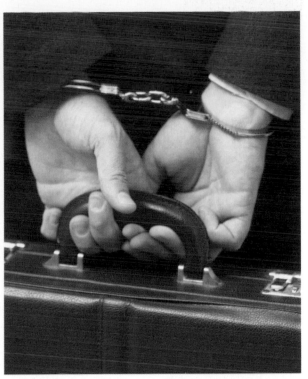

Price-fixing can result in up to five years imprisonment.

- Investigate major cases (called supercomplaints) which can be made to the OFT by a designated consumer body when it thinks that some practice affecting many tourists is harming their interests – over pricing of hotel rooms, for example.

What the Enterprise Act covers

- Enforcement of consumer law – the OFT has stronger powers to seek court orders against businesses who breach certain consumer-protection laws.

- Consumer codes of practice – the OFT has increased powers to help develop effective self-regulation through approving and promoting consumer codes of practice that meet their criteria.

- Merger control – these powers remain much the same as before, working with the Competition Commission.

You can visit the OFT website at www.oft.gov.uk for further information.

activity

TOURISM AND THE OFT

Do you think that the role of the OFT is important to the tourism industry? Give examples to support your views, and use a flip chart to record everyone's ideas.

The Sale of Goods and Services Act

The Sale of Goods and Services Act, introduced in 1979, has been updated by the Supply of Goods and Services Act 1982, the Sale and Supply of Goods Act 1994, and the Supply of Goods to Consumers Act 2002.

The Sale of Goods and Services Act covers everything, including children's toys, though the price would be taken into account.

The main aim of the legislation is to protect consumers from the sale of faulty goods or falsely labelled goods. Whatever kind of goods or services are bought, they must, to coin a famous phrase, 'do what it says on the tin'. That could mean:

- Be as described – in tourism terms, for example, if it says the hotel is '4-star' then it should clearly have all the attributes of a 4-star hotel.

- Fit for purpose – if an attraction, for example, advertises that a ride has 'unsinkable' boats, then they must be unsinkable.

- Of satisfactory quality – that is, not inherently faulty at the time of purchase. Goods should be free from any defects or even blemishes – unless perhaps they are really cheap and tatty seaside souvenirs, which the low price clearly reflects. Safety and durability might come into this category, too. Children's souvenirs, for example, shouldn't break into tiny fragments the first time they are used.

Some factors about the sale of goods are not too well known. For example, if goods do not conform to decent standards it is the *seller* (not the manufacturer) who is responsible. Buyers can request their money back, repairs or replacement as long as the request is 'within a reasonable time' – which, of course, depends on the nature of the goods. The onus, however, is on the consumer to prove that the goods did not work at all, or work properly, or last very long.

This legal area is complex, but it's important for tourism businesses. Some consumer laws give consumers 'civil rights' and others impose 'criminal penalties' on the businessperson. Civil cases involve a dispute between the customer and the supplier of the product. If the customer is right they will normally be compensated in some way. Criminal cases, on the other hand, involve officials prosecuting organisations or suppliers, and may lead to them being punished by a fine and/or imprisonment. Some common examples will help.

Advertising

Adverts must not be misleading and must not be in breach of the Trades Description Act (breaking this Act is a criminal offence). Restrictions on advertising are becoming more complex all the time, especially now that the standards apply to online advertising too. You can find out more from the Advertising Standards Authority at www.asa.org.uk.

Selling tourism goods

All goods must be 'of suitable quality' and be 'fit for the purpose for which they are sold' (e.g. a 'waterproof' watch should not be damaged by you taking a shower). Breaking this law (The Sale and Supply of Goods Act 1979, or its amendments) is a civil matter, and gives the buyer rights to damages or money back or a replacement, depending upon the circumstances.

A customer's right to a refund cannot be taken away by a notice saying 'No refunds' and in certain cases it may be criminal to display such a notice. There may also be safety standards for the goods, and if suppliers ignore them it could make them liable to criminal prosecution – and also face a large claim for damages.

MAINTAINING ADVERTISING STANDARDS

1 Working in small groups, gather some travel brochures or the travel supplements of Sunday newspapers, and look for what you feel might be breaches of the advertising standards. Look for aspects such as:

- advice that might cause someone to break the law
- offensive wording (sexual orientation or religion or race)
- offensive images
- inaccuracy, exaggeration, vagueness.

2 On your own, visit the Advertising Standards Authority website and sum up the key points of their code of conduct for advertising.

Meeting legal requirements

By now you will be aware that the implications of all the legislation that we have discussed are quite far-reaching. Travel and tourism organisations have to make sure that they are up to date with legislation and that they implement effective procedures and practices in their everyday business transactions with the public (see examples, right). Implementation of new practices obviously has a cost in terms of training and awareness, but that has to be weighed up against what it might cost if complaints were made or a law broken.

Travel agencies make great efforts to comply with all the relevant legislation in the various aspects of their work – advising their clients on safety matters, producing their materials, training their staff to cope with emergencies, and operating an appropriate complaints system.

Tour operators employ meticulous planning to ensure that nothing goes wrong on their customers' holidays, as they might be sued and found liable. Clearly they have to invest in a number of areas such as:

- staff training
- equipment
- contingency plans
- insurance.

COMPLYING WITH THE LEGISLATION

In groups, carry out some research to assess what a selected tour operator does to comply with:

1 The Disability Discrimination Act

2 The Data Protection Act

3 The Package Travel Directive.

After you have done your research, consider what the implications would be for travellers if the tour operator did not do a good job under each of these categories.

How organisations keep up with the legislation

- Managers attend conferences and briefings for updates, and then cascade this information to staff in branches or destinations
- Companies with intranet communications send out updates to key staff
- Companies can subscribe to email updates from relevant organisations, such as the DTI or the OFT
- Professional journals and magazines carry articles updating their readers on key topics
- Chambers of trade or tourism associations hold regular meetings where information can be circulated
- The press may carry stories of non-compliance, which staff and organisations can pick up on, to amend their own practices.

Can you add two more ways?

REGULATION MATTERS

Working in small groups, prepare a statement (of no more than 30 words) about why you think all of the consumer-protection regulations are important to travellers and tourists.

211

Topic 3 Consumer protection

Passports and visas

In an ideal world we would all be free to travel where we wanted to, when we wanted to. However, in reality this is not the case. Restrictions imposed by national governments mean that we all have to abide by certain conditions and requirements. The majority of these restrictions are imposed for reasons of the travellers' safety and the security of the countries to which they are travelling. The next two topics investigate some of these restrictions, starting in this topic under the headings:

- **Passports**
- **Visas**
- **The future for passports and visas.**

Each national government needs to control who comes into their country.

Passports

A passport is an official travel document issued by the traveller's country of origin that verifies their identity and nationality. Anyone travelling from the UK to another country (including any within the EU) is required to have a full ten-year, current passport. This includes any journey – even a 4-hour shopping spree in France. The passport needs to be valid for the entire time that the traveller is abroad. In fact some countries require the passport to be valid for at least six months.

In the UK, passports are obtained, renewed or amended through the UK Passport Service. The first stage in obtaining a passport is to complete the passport application form obtainable from Post Offices and other high street partners (such as some travel agencies) or direct from the regional passport office. Alternatively, applications can be made online.

Apart from completing details of the information requested, the application also involves:

- The inclusion of two identical photographs (see rules, right)

- The countersignature (see rules, right) of the application form and one of the photographs if the passport application is for a new or replacement passport or the appearance of the applicant has changed considerably since the old passport – for example in the case of a child

- The inclusion of a birth certificate for applications for new or replacement passports.

Including children on passports

Any UK child under the age of 16 years can be included on one or both of their parents' passports. However, in 2004, in the wake of increased security,

Obtaining a UK Passport

Complete a Passport Application Form
(obtained from Post Office, high street partner or website)

Post to regional
Passport Office
(standard 3 weeks)

Use Post Office
'check & send'
(standard 2 weeks)

Appointment at
Passport Office
(1 week/same day)

Passport photograph rules

In 2004 the regulations as to what constituted an acceptable passport photograph were tightened.

The photographs must be:

- recent (i.e. taken within the last six months)
- 45 mm × 35 mm
- printed on normal photographic paper
- a close-up of your head and shoulders, so that your face covers 70% to 80% of the photograph
- taken against a white, cream or light grey plain background, so that your features are clearly distinguishable against the background
- of you on your own (no toys, dummies or other people visible).

The photographs must:

- be in sharp focus and clear
- have a strong definition between the face and background
- be printed at 1200dpi resolution or better if they are digital or scanned photographs.

The photographs must show:

- no shadows
- your full face, looking straight at the camera
- a neutral expression, with your mouth closed
- your eyes open and clearly visible (with no sunglasses or heavily tinted glasses, and no hair across your eyes)
- no reflection on your spectacles, if you wear them, and the frames should not cover your eyes
- your full head, without any head covering, unless it is worn for religious beliefs
- your face uncovered.

Source: www.ukpa.gov.uk

America ceased to accept children on parents' passports and required anyone entering the country to hold an individual passport. In addition, all passports for entry into America are required to be 'machine-readable' (MRP), which means that they feature two lines of coded data at the bottom of the photograph page that can be 'swiped' at the check-

The first page of the passport application form

Who can be a countersignatory

The countersignatory must be a professional person, or a person of standing in the community. Examples include bank or building society officials, police officers, civil servants, ministers of religion and people with professional qualifications (teachers, accountants, engineers, solicitors, and so on).

activity

PASSPORT PROBLEMS

Imagine that a family of four with two children (aged 2 and 5 years) are on holiday in Spain. Both children are on the mother's passport. Can you think of any situations in which it would have been better to have the two children on separate, individual passports?

in. Other countries may follow America's lead in asking for separate children's passports – and there are obvious advantages in this becoming a standard requirement, despite the fact that it will cost more to the passport applicants.

Length of time for a passport application

The length of time that it takes to obtain a passport depends on the urgency of the application and the amount that the applicant is willing to pay. The standard response to a mailed application is three weeks. However, the Post Office offers a 'check and send' service which, for an additional small fee, means that a member of staff will check that the application form has been completed correctly and the passport will be returned within two weeks. If an applicant needs a passport in a hurry they can visit their regional passport office and receive a passport within 2 weeks or 48 hours – although there are substantial extra charges for this service. The regional passport offices are in Belfast, Durham, London, Glasgow, Liverpool, Peterborough and Newport.

Visas

A visa is a document issued by a government that allows an alien (foreign visitor) to enter the country (entry visa) or for a national resident to exit the country (exit visa). Entry visas can have specific conditions attached to them. For example they may be issued for tourist or business reasons only. Depending on the type of visa, travellers may be allowed just one

visit or multiple visits to the country. Whether or not you need a visa depends on the country that you are visiting and the reason for the visit. Visa requirements vary over time so it may be necessary to contact the Consulate or Embassy of the country to be visited to ascertain whether or not a visa is required. This can be done by using links on the Foreign and Commonwealth Office (FCO) website (www. fco.gov.uk). Foreign visitors to the UK may also need a visa to enter the country. Again, details can be found on the FCO website, as the example below shows.

Do I need a UK visa?

You asked if a national of Bangladesh needs a visa to come to the UK for a business visit.

Yes, you need a visa. Please read *Guidance – Visitors* for more information. Your sponsor, if you have one, may want to read *Guidance – Sponsors*.

To apply for a visa you will need to fill in form *VAF1 – Non-settlement*. In most cases, eligible dependants will also need visas. Any dependants under 16 years old, included on your passport, can be included on the same form, but those older will need to complete separate forms.

If you are applying for a visit visa, or an EEA Family Permit, or are a national of, or are normally and legally living in Bangladesh, please make your application to *Dhaka*.

Visa applications should now be made through our outsourcing partner – VFS. Please visit the High Commission's website for more information.

Source: Foreign and Commonwealth Office website: www.fco.gov.uk

The future for passports and visas

Amid increasing concerns about security and the threat of international terrorism, changes are underway for both passport and visa requirements. These changes are largely made possible by dramatic advances in technology. The two extracts from the *Daily Mail* below show some of the changes that we can expect in the near future.

Traditional passports could have a computer chip added with 'biometric' information about the holder within two years – but at a price, it has emerged.

The UK Passport Service's business plan for the next five years also revealed the cost of a passport is to rise 58% from £33 to £52 by 2006.

Officials are to draw up plans for the new 'smart' passports by next March, and hope to begin implementing the scheme by April 2005.

The chip would carry facial-recognition data about the parameters of the passport holder's face, such as the exact distance between their eyes, and the distance between their nose and chin.

Within a year of the new hi-tech passport books, the agency hopes to introduce a 'passport card' – similar to a credit card – to be used in conjunction with the paper document.

The card would be valid for travel within the EU and 'certain other defined countries' and would feature 'up-to-date security and fraud-prevention features'.

It is likely to feature extra biometric information such as an iris scan or fingerprints, stored electronically on the computer chip.

Source: Daily Mail 27/4/03

A hi-tech visa is to be introduced for travel from Britain to the United States to combat terrorism.

Tens of thousands of Britons planning to travel to the States from the autumn, for business or holiday, will have to be fingerprinted.

An estimated 250,000 will need to apply for the so-called biometric visa. However, there are warnings from the US Embassy that it may not have enough staff to supply them and the tourist industry has warned of cancelled holidays.

The biometric visas are being introduced because the US has ruled that anyone entering the country must have electronic ID, which can be fingerprinting, facial mapping or iris imaging.

All new passports issued after October 26 must contain such data, or the holders must show a biometric visa. The Government has already said that the new passports will not be available before summer next year.

Until then, Britons renewing their passport on or after October 26 will have to visit the US Embassy in London or US Consulate in Belfast, provide an electronic print of the index fingers of each hand, and pay £65 for a visa, which could take months to be issued.

Source: Daily Mail 6/3/04

Health restrictions

In the last topic we looked at the ways in which travel between countries is restricted by passports and visa requirements. With the rapid increase in international travel, the risk of diseases being transmitted between countries also increases and this, in turn, creates further restrictions. In this topic we are going to explore health issues and the restrictions that these put on some travellers and some destinations. In particular we will investigate:

- The main contagious diseases
- The ways in which different countries impose health restrictions on travellers.

The main contagious diseases

A contagious disease is one that can be transmitted from one person to another, though they may also develop after contact with contaminated food or water or from another animal. For example, mosquitoes transmit a range of serious diseases, and rabies is a disease in animals that can be transmitted to humans. The main contagious diseases that are relevant to travellers are:

- Cholera
- Yellow Fever
- Typhoid
- Malaria
- HIV and AIDS
- Hepatitis C.

(Information on all communicable diseases can be found from the National Centre for Infectious diseases – www.cdc.gov)

Cholera

Cholera is an acute infection of the intestinal tract, although rarely fatal if treated promptly and correctly. It is contracted through contaminated food or water and therefore more common in less developed countries. Travellers who abide by food safety recommendations have little risk of contracting cholera. Whilst a semi-effective vaccination is available, it is rarely recommended to travellers.

Typhoid fever

Typhoid fever is an acute, sometimes fatal bacterial fever. As with cholera it is contracted through contaminated food and drink. There are an estimated 16 million cases each year. Vaccination against typhoid is recommended for travel to some areas such as Asia, Africa and the Indian subcontinent. However, the vaccination is not 100% effective. This means that, similarly to other diseases contracted through food and water, travellers need to be careful about what they eat.

HIV and AIDS

HIV and AIDS were first identified in 1981. HIV (human immunodeficiency virus) is the initial infection which results in progressive damage to the body's immune system. In its later stages the disease presents as AIDS (Acquired Immune Deficiency Syndrome) where the body's weakened immune system makes it susceptible to life-threatening infections and diseases such as cancer. Both HIV and AIDS occur throughout the world, with an estimated 40 million sufferers worldwide. It is contracted through body fluids, such as blood, saliva and semen from an infected person. This means that the main risks of infection are through sexual contact, intravenous drug use (where needles are shared) or, less commonly, through blood transfusions in countries where the blood stock is not screened for HIV/AIDS. Whilst no vaccine is currently available, travellers can be advised to minimise the risk by observing safe-sex advice and carrying sterile personal medical kits for use in less developed countries.

Yellow fever

Yellow fever is transmitted to humans by mosquitoes and can vary in seriousness from a flu-like illness to severe hepatitis, with a fatality rate of over 20%. It only occurs in tropical South America and sub-Saharan Africa and is more prevalent during the rainy season when mosquitoes are most active. An effective vaccine is available, but travellers to areas where yellow fever is endemic are also advised to avoid exposure to mosquito bites. Such precautions include wearing clothing that adequately covers all limbs, staying in accommodation that is air-conditioned so that windows can be kept closed, and using an effective mosquito repellent.

Malaria

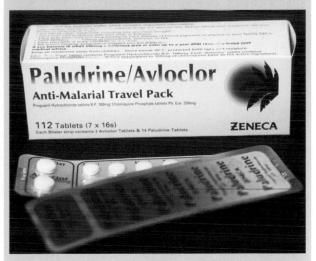

As with yellow fever, malaria is contracted through the bite of an infected mosquito, and can be fatal if not treated. 300–500 million people contract malaria each year, with one million of the cases proving fatal. The disease is particularly common in Africa, Asia, Central and South America and eastern Europe. No vaccine is currently available, but travellers can take a course of drugs before, during and after their visit to a potential area of infection to minimise the risk of contracting the disease.

Hepatitis C

Hepatitis C is an acute, often fatal infection that results in chronic liver disease in 60–70% of those infected. It is transmitted through the exchange of blood. Whilst this may occur during sexual contact, it can also result from blood transfusions, medical or dental work, drug injection or procedures such as tattooing or acupuncture. It is more likely to occur in less developed countries were stringent sterilisation or disinfection procedures are not implemented. It is estimated that 170 million people worldwide are infected with Hepatitis C – with countries in Africa, Asia and Egypt having particularly high rates. There is no vaccine against Hepatitis C, so travellers are advised to be cautious when seeking any medical, dental or invasive cosmetic procedure in high-risk countries.

The ways in which different countries impose health restrictions on travellers

Countries impose health restrictions for two reasons:

• To protect people going to another country from contracting a communicable disease

• To prevent visitors bringing in a contagious disease from another country.

Some countries may require proof that visitors coming in do not have a contagious disease, particularly those coming from a country with a high risk of infection

for a particular disease. Such proof is provided in the form of a completed 'International Certificate of Vaccination'. This certificate is valid 10 days after vaccination and for a subsequent period of 10 years.

The health recommendations and requirements for different countries will obviously vary according to the time that a customer travels and the key diseases that are of both national and international significance at the time. For example, in 2003 the SARS virus placed added restrictions on many international travellers.

Information on health restrictions and advice can be accessed through a number of websites, such as the advice for travellers to Thailand from www.fitfortravel.scot.nhs.uk , shown below.

The difference between 'required' and 'recommended'

It is worth noting, from a travel perspective, the difference between 'required' and 'recommended' health advice. Required means that a customer cannot travel to a country unless they have the stated vaccinations. Recommended means that they can travel without the stated vaccinations – however, in some cases they will find that their travel insurance is invalidated if they were to fall ill and did not have the recommended vaccinations.

Advice to travellers to Thailand

Immunisations: Confirm that those recommended for use in Britain are up to date, especially those for children, and adult boosters of tetanus.

Courses or boosters usually advised: hepatitis A; typhoid; diphtheria.
Vaccines sometimes advised: tuberculosis; poliomyelitis; rabies; Japanese B encephalitis; hepatitis B.

Yellow fever certificate required if over 1 year old and entering from an infected area.

Malaria precautions are essential in Ko Chang and along the borders of Laos, Cambodia and Myanmar, all year round. (There is very little risk in cities and main tourist areas such as Phuket, Pattaya, Bangkok, Changmai, the River Quai Bridge area and offshore islands, except Ko Chang). Avoid mosquito bites by covering up with clothing such as long sleeves and long trousers especially after sunset, using insect repellents on exposed skin and, when necessary, sleeping under a mosquito net.

Check with your doctor or nurse about suitable antimalarial tablets. Prompt investigation of fever is essential. If travelling to remote areas, a course of emergency 'standby' treatment should be carried.

Anyone whose work involves advising customers of the health requirements for foreign travel needs to be fully aware of both recommended and required health advice – as the following customer experience shows.

Vacinations not 'required' but …

'My husband and I were desperate for a bit of relaxation, so decided to book a late break somewhere hot at the end of October. We decided on Tunisia as the weather was still good and there was plenty to occupy our two young children. I specifically asked the travel agency adviser if vaccinations were required and she assured me that they were not, but to consult our GP just to make sure that we were up to date. Anyway when I received a copy of the travel insurance policy it turned out that we all had to have a number of injections or the policy would be invalid. My children were distraught at having to have the injections and the practice nurse asked whether I really felt that it was worth it for just a week's holiday. We had a good holiday, but if I'd known about having to put the children through additional injections for just a week in the sun, I might have gone to the Lake District and put up with a bit of rain!'

activity

GIVING HEALTH ADVICE

You work in a travel agency and the following customers have asked for guidance on health restrictions, recommended/required vaccinations and general health advice. Using the website www.fitfortravel.scot.nhs.uk, write a letter to each customer with your advice.

1 Mr and Mrs Jaines (in their late 60s) going on a two-week safari to Kenya.

2 Mr and Mrs Patel going on an all-inclusive holiday to Mexico.

3 Miss Carmichael and Miss Burns going on a back-packing holiday in Cuba for two weeks.

4 The Wright family visiting friends in Singapore for a month. Their children are aged 2 and 5 years.

Travel insurance and health

Travel insurers normally assume that customers are up to date with their standard 'British immunisations'. These are the standard vaccinations offered to all UK citizens between birth and 16 to protect them against diseases that occur in the UK and can be avoided through the immunisation programme. Currently, these are: diphtheria, tetanus, HIB, meningitis C, polio, measles, mumps, rubella, whooping cough and tuberculosis.

Whilst these immunisations may not be compulsory for travel, a customer may find themselves not covered by their insurance policy if they contract one of the diseases while travelling abroad. Many travellers book a holiday and are totally unaware of whether or not their British immunisations are up to date. You could conduct a quick survey of your peers, your parents – even your tutor – to find out how many know what they are currently protected against.

Topic 6 Cancellation, curtailment and insurance

In the final three topics of this unit we shall investigate a range of 'emergency situations' that affect the traveller. We all hope that nothing will happen to ruin our holiday, but the reality is that every year people's holidays and trips are hit by mini-disasters. Examples might include accidents or injuries occurring in the days or weeks before departure, or perhaps a family bereavement. Illness is also a common factor delaying departures – such as a severe migraine preventing someone from travelling for few days or ear infections preventing people from flying safely.

This topic looks at three emergency situations that are generally regarded as small-scale. Although serious at the time and very stressful, small-scale emergencies are not usually life-threatening. Careful planning and appropriate support from travel and tourism organisations will usually mean that a journey or holiday can be completed or at worst delayed. The industry does of course offer insurance to cover most of these contingencies, which we will also investigate, along with some operators advice on personal health and safety. The topic, therefore is arranged under the following headings:

- Cancellation
- Curtailment
- Medical problems
- Holiday insurance
- Other organisations offering advice and assistance.

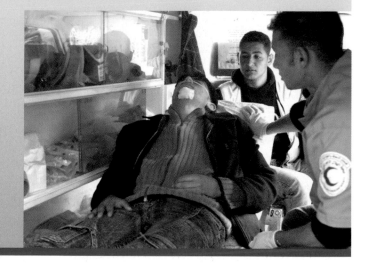

Cancellation

Cancellations can occur for a myriad of unpredictable reasons, such as accidents and injuries involving the traveller. They may also arise, however, because of problems with the operator or at the destination, such as under-capacity or cancellation of a local contract.

When the operator cancels the planned holiday, they must offer the traveller a refund or an equivalent package elsewhere. Some compensation is also usually necessary, calculated on a sliding scale up to the day of departure. The amounts are not usually very high, e.g. 56 days before: £10–£20, 30 days before: £20–£30, 7 days before: £50–£100. See the Thomson Winter Sun brochure extract on the next page for examples.

The operators are careful however to list some exclusions here which are classed as 'out of their

control' such as wars, natural disasters and fire and riots.

Sometimes insurance plans will offer a delayed departure cover if say for example an airport was temporarily closed or temporary bad weather was the cause.

Tour operators will from time to time change a holiday if they can predict that conditions are unsafe (or uneconomic for them). Sometimes this may be minor, e.g. a change of flight or hotel. At other times it may be major, e.g. changing to a different country. Compensation or refunds are usually due in this context.

Tour operators have entered into a contract with their customers so are obliged to meet all the detailed components of that holiday such as flights, level of

Compensation

These scales are based on how many days before your booked departure we tell you of a major change.
See also the 'Important note – events beyond our control'.
Each amount is for each full-fare-paying adult

No. of days	Scale A		Scale B	
	Long Haul & A la Carte	Other holidays	Long Haul & A la Carte	Other holidays
0–7 days	£120	£100	£60	£50
8–14 days	£100	£80	£50	£40
15–28 days	£80	£60	£40	£30
29–56 days	£60	£40	£30	£20
More than 56 days	£30	£20	£15	£10

If the change is not acceptable to you

If any major change indicated above is not acceptable to you, you can cancel your booking. In this case, we will refund all the money you have paid us and will pay you compensation, using the scale below, depending on how many days before your holiday we tell you about the change. The standard payment will not affect your statutory or other legal rights.

No. of days	Amount for each full-fare-paying adult	For each Long Haul or A la Carte adult
14–0 days	£40	£50
56–15 days	£25	£30
more than 56 days	£0	£0

Important note – events beyond our control

Events beyond our control include: war, threat of war, riots, civil disturbances, terrorist activity, industrial disputes, natural disasters, fire, epidemics, health risks, technical problems with transport beyond our control or that of our suppliers, closed or congested airports or ports, hurricanes and other actual or potential severe weather conditions, and any other similar events. See also 'Events Beyond our Control' and 'Weather Watch' in the A–Z Guide, plus the Insurance page for our Delay Protection Plan.

Source: Adapted from the Thomson Winter Sun brochure

hotel, quality of food, excursions, and so on. During each stage of the holiday they are also required to take reasonable care of their customers – so that they travel safely.

Any breaches of the contract or dangers that the holidaymakers are exposed to, such as coaches with bald tyres or unsafe locations for excursions would be their liability. Operators will usually work hard to ensure that local suppliers adhere to safe working practices, but at some extreme destinations the standards we are used to may just not exist, e.g. in Nepal or Africa. Some breaches will also be governed by local or international conventions.

The other side of cancellation is of course the customer cancelling for personal reasons. A sliding scale of increasing charges usually applies here too, based on the number of days ahead of departure (see table below for a typical example).

Number of days before depature	Amount to pay
Over 56 days	Deposit only
30–56 days	50% of holiday
21–29 days	70% of holiday
8–20 days	90% of holiday
7 days or less	The total cost

However if you have taken out a comprehensive insurance policy it will cover you for these types of cancellation costs. Some people leave taking out an insurance policy till very late and expose themselves to the high costs of cancellation – an unsafe travel practice!

activity

I'M CANCELLING BECAUSE …

Working with a partner, compose a letter you could send to an operator with a reason for cancelling a holiday, two weeks before the departure date. Select your reason from the list below. Pass your letter to some colleagues to decide whether a refund would be given.

- Moving house
- Bereavement
- Injury or illness
- Poor weather forecast
- Holiday dates changed at work
- The friends going on the holiday together have fallen out.

When hurricanes strike, resorts must close down temporarily.

Curtailment

'Curtailment' means cutting a holiday short, either by the holidaymaker or by the operator. Common reasons for curtailment are accident, sickness or injury during (or even before) the holiday. Curtailment values are usually in line with cancellations ones. The insurance policy again covers this type of contingency.

Reasons for curtailment should be communicated to the operator as soon as possible – to the rep in the resort, for example. Any paperwork or proof of the reason (such as doctor's notes or diagnosis) should be gathered for use later in the claim process.

In some cases curtailment might be the fault of the holidaymaker – maybe carrying out unsafe or unacceptable behaviour and being asked to leave the hotel, arrested or even deported.

Curtailment can also happen due to what is called 'force majeure' – extreme weather, terrorist activities, or natural disasters, such as the Indian Ocean tsunami (see Topic 8).

Medical problems

Medical problems are all too often the reason for cancellation or curtailment, before and during a holiday. They are also the most compelling reason for taking out holiday insurance. It is not unknown for people to take a chance that nothing will happen, or to just have the E111 form (which offers reciprocal medical care in EU countries) as their insurance.

The need for medical cover can spring from an existing condition suddenly getting worse, or more often, from a holiday incident or a disease picked up while abroad. The Foreign Office (who are responsible for UK citizens abroad) has regular updates for travellers, and this topic will draw some examples of 'horror stories' from their case studies (see below).

Assistance and insurance for travellers with special needs or disabilities usually have to be negotiated separately after advice.

Medical costs are the highest potential charge against travel insurance policies, with the current rate topping the £10 million mark. That would cover you for emergency repatriation, or for a relative to travel out to you, plus any hospital costs for example. There are standard levels set by the industry to cover most global emergencies that could befall tourists, including these, for example:

£600	Two days in a general ward – Mediterranean
£400–£600	Gastro-enteritis – Mediterranean
£10,000	Broken leg – USA
£20,000–£30,000	Heart attack – USA
£15,000	Bronchitis requiring seven days inpatient treatment – Far East
£20,000	Bronchitis requiring seven days inpatient treatment – USA

Holiday insurance

Holiday insurance protection is a must with most travel agencies and tour operators – a condition of booking, in fact. It is a wise decision to make – as shown by the case studies in this topic. Most holiday booking forms will have an insurance section in a fairly standard format, covering aspects such as:

- Data protection – holidaymakers need to be reassured that the personal information they give will only be used for the purposes of the holiday. What companies will want to do is use the information to send out mailshots of information about holidays in the future. Sometimes getting out of this clause is tricky.

- Conditions – there can be many individual conditions attached to the policy. The most common are medical, e.g. breathing, heart or mental health problems, or pregnancy. People who answer 'yes' to one of these conditions will have to undergo a medical screening process before approval/acceptance is given. In some situations travellers may have to pay an additional charge to cover them for a pre-existing medical condition (especially elderly travellers). The policy conditions will usually say that if anything in medical terms changes before travel – after deposits have been paid – the holidaymaker must tell the insurers.

Coverage of possessions can have many small clauses – a maximum limit, or a policy 'excess', such as £50, before they will pay anything. Coverage under all categories is shown in the extract below from Thomas Cook's 2005 Summer Sun brochure.

- Exclusions – these tend to exclude from cover certain sports activities, such as bungee jumping, karting or skiing. A special policy may be needed or an additional premium paid (see below).

- Policy limits. The Thomas Cook's table shows their limits – total amounts for some categories, e.g. personal liability; duration of delays, e.g. up to 10 hrs delay; value limits, e.g. for personal money or luggage. This is based on years of experience of what is 'reasonable' to cover most small-scale emergencies.

---

activity

SKY-HIGH MEDICAL COSTS

Research the costs of repatriation in a hospital plane from an EU capital city to London, and the cost of a helicopter rescue in the Alps.

SUMMARY OF COVER

BENEFIT	CLASSIC TRAVEL INSURANCE	TRAVEL INSURANCE
Cancellation/Curtailment	£10,000	£5,000
Emergency medical expenses	£10,000,000	£2,000,000
Hospital benefit	£30 per day up to £600	£20 per day up to £300
Personal accident	Death £15,000, Permanent disablement £30,000	Death or Permanent disablement £10,000
Luggage and Personal possessions	£1,600, Valuables £400 in all, single article limited £325	£1,000, Valuables £300 in all, single article limited £250
Personal money	£500 (£300 cash limit)	£250 (£150 cash limit)
Personal liability	£2,000,000	£2,000,000
Departure delay	Up to £200 or abandonment after 10 hours £10,000	Up to £120 or abandonment after 12 hours £5,000
Missed departure	£1,000	£500
Mugging benefit	£100 per day up to £1,000	Not applicable
Hijack	£100 per day up to £1,000	Not applicable
Failure of carrier	£1,500	Not applicable
Loss of hotel facilities	£30 per day up to £150	Not applicable
Departure point assistance	£300	Not applicable
Home call service	£150	Not applicable
Kennel/cattery fees	£250	Not applicable
Legal expenses	£50,000	£10,000

Source: Adapted from the Thomas Cook's 2005 Summer Sun brochure

Premiums

The price paid for insurance is called the premium. Premiums vary according to four factors – duration of stay, level of cover, age of the holidaymaker and global location, in the following ways:

- Duration categories are designed to catch our normal holiday patterns, such as 1–3 days (a long weekend), 10–17days (annual holiday), up to 25 or 31 days (long-haul trip). People who have several holidays a year find it easier (and cheaper) to take out annual travel insurance to cover them for a whole year.

- Level of cover – usually at least 2 categories – basic and higher than basic, which pushes up limits and coverage range, or may reduce excesses and conditions.

Expensive jump

A 26-year-old man went on a trip to South Africa. Unfortunately, although he had taken out some insurance, it wasn't adequate to cover him when, on the spur of the moment, he decided to go bungee jumping. After the jump he became nauseous, and whilst swimming later he began to feel extremely dizzy. He was rushed to hospital, where a CAT scan showed that, due to the pressure change caused by the jump, his brain had swollen. Luckily he was able to be treated quickly and given medication. But he had to delay his flight home, and the next available flight was five days later, costing him altogether about £500.

What should he have done to be a safe traveller?

- Age ranges – the usual categories are: up to 3 years, 3–15yrs, adults up to 65, and seniors 65+.

- Location is important because of the level of care available and the cost of services. The destinations are usually grouped into 'European' and 'Worldwide'. Sometimes North America and the Caribbean are given additional premiums.

The insurance company also has to state the 'cooling-off' period – the time during which the holidaymaker can consider the conditions and, if necessary, return the policy. It should also be clear how to contact the insurance company to query anything, how to make a claim should the need arise, or to complain about their service, e.g. via their 24-hour helpline.

Equally, the holidaymaker has a duty to contribute to the policy conditions by taking care of possessions, making medical checks before departure, not exposing themselves to undue risk, such as walking alone after dark. Failure to comply with these or any other conditions can render the policy 'null and void'.

It also makes good sense for the holidaymaker to take a copy of the policy (and proof of payment for it) on holiday with them – it's all part of travelling safely.

Probably the most frustrating part of dealing with such small-scale emergencies is sorting out the paperwork when the holiday is over – reading and understanding the small print that spells out all the conditions of the holiday insurance – then making a claim!

activity

CALCULATING CANCELLATION COSTS

Working with a colleague, collect two different operator brochures and list the main sections of their insurance policies. Then calculate the costs for three different customers – a child under 14, an adult, and someone over 70, who cancel 1 week, 2 weeks, and 30 days before departure. Create a table to illustrate your calculations.

Other organisations offering support and assistance

Other organisations offer valuable assistance in 'small-scale' emergencies:

- Tour operators themselves

- The Foreign and Commonwealth Office (FCO)

- Insurance companies.

Tour operators

Most brochures and travel agents will give pre-holiday advice and guidance, in an effort to help people avoid any small-scale emergencies. They are mostly commonsense points such as:

- Pool and beach safety is important. Few resorts have lifeguards, and children are particularly at risk, e.g. from inflatable toys in pools and the sea, and swimming off unguarded beaches. The local flag system may be unfamiliar.

Some countries have lifeguards on their popular beaches, but many don't.

- Child safety is particularly important. Children are the most vulnerable category of tourist. In addition to the swimming risks there is: road safety (cars coming from the 'wrong' direction), standards and staff of activity clubs they may join, and going on locally organised excursions with leaders.

Resort reps routinely support holidaymakers in the event of small-scale emergencies, by, for example:

- Rearranging flights for someone who was hospitalised
- Completing documentation relating to lost and stolen property
- Arranging for immediate medical assistance
- Coordinating the return of lost luggage
- Liaising between a holidaymaker and their family in the event of their arrest or imprisonment.

activity

PERSONAL BELONGINGS

Working with a partner, devise a set of guidelines that could be issued to travellers concerning security of their: cash, cameras, handbags, passports, jewellery and credit cards.

The Foreign and Commonwealth Office

The work of the Foreign and Commonwealth Office (FCO) is covered in more detail in the next topic. The FCO has a network of British consulates covering most of the globe. They offer consular assistance to British people in difficulty or distress while abroad – due to a lost passport, illness, a death, or a crime, or because they have been arrested or injured. Some of these cases are complicated and can involve human rights issues such as child abduction, forced marriage or the death penalty.

Insurance companies

When something goes wrong on a trip, most insurance companies will assist travellers in the following ways. They will:

- Pay for medical expenses abroad
- Pay for repatriation of a very sick or injured person (or a dead body)
- Pay for some legal expenses
- Compensate the traveller in the event of cancellation or curtailment of the trip
- Compensate for lost or stolen items.

activity

RANKING SMALL-SCALE EMERGENCIES

Discuss which of the following small-scale emergencies you would consider to be the most complicated to solve. Put them in an order, and try to create a flow chart for the first on your list, showing the stages, people and organisations that could be involved.

- Theft of a camera
- A child lost on a busy beach
- A child scalded by a careless waiter
- Loss of contact lenses
- Sickness and diarrhoea
- Being arrested for drunkenness or topless bathing
- Getting mugged.

It is obviously in insurance companies' interest that you are safe and lose nothing while away, as it keeps down their pay outs. So they try to guide travellers on good holiday safety practice, but also on what to do should a problem arise. Any incident should be reported to the local authorities as soon as possible – e.g. police, hotel or carrier – and all documentary evidence collected. It is always reassuring for travellers to know that they can phone someone at the insurers (who speaks their language) at any hour of the day or night.

Losses and criminal activity

This topic explores some further 'small-scale emergency situations' experienced by travellers:

- **Lost passport**
- **Lost money**
- **Lost luggage**
- **Theft and muggings**
- **Arrest and imprisonment.**

Lost passport

Losing a passport whilst abroad can create severe problems for the traveller. At the least it can result in disruption to travel plans. At its most severe it may mean considerable extra expense if the time spent securing new identification means that the pre-arranged transport is missed. All travellers can take a few sensible precautions to minimise the risks and possible problems that may arise from losing their passport. These include:

- Taking a photocopy of the passport so that the details are available in the event of loss.

- Putting the passport in the accommodation's safe or safety deposit boxes when not being used.

- Being vigilant when carrying it around, i.e. making sure that it is secure in a handbag or wallet, and not just casually stowed in a back pocket.

However if the worst happens and a traveller does lose their passport there are some immediate steps that they should take:

1. Report the loss to the resort representative and local police immediately. The local police will provide the traveller with a 'Certificate of Loss' that verifies that the passport has been reported lost.

2. Contact the nearest British Foreign and Commonwealth Consulate, Embassy or High Commission, and provide them with the issued 'Certificate of Loss'. This will ensure that the loss is reported to the UK Passport Office, and will help to provide replacement travel documents.

What are Embassies, Consulates and High Commissions?

There are 'diplomatic missions' and 'consular missions'. Both represent the UK in other countries and protect the interests of UK nationals abroad.

Diplomatic missions are always stationed in the country's capital city, whereas consular missions are elsewhere in the country. In a non-Commonwealth country, the diplomatic mission is known as an 'Embassy'. In a Commonwealth country, it is known as a 'High Commission'.

Depending upon its importance, a consular mission is known as a consulate-general, consulate, vice-consulate or consular agency.

Consular staff can provide British travellers with practical advice, assistance and support, using their local knowledge.

activity

HOW TO NOT LOSE YOUR MONEY

You work in a travel agency and your manager has asked you to produce a short checklist (one side of A4 paper) for customers who are travelling abroad about how to safeguard their money and what to do in the event of loss. You can use pictures and diagrams to make it eye-catching and effective.

not they will be able to claim for the loss on their insurance will depend on the nature of their insurance policy and how careful (or careless!) they have been.

Lost money

The loss of money whilst abroad is always a distressing experience for travellers and can seriously reduce their holiday enjoyment. As with lost passports, travellers can minimise the risk by taking sensible precautions such as not carrying large amounts of currency on them, and making sure that all money, cards and traveller's cheques are kept secure. Travel agents and tour operators also provide sound advice to customers to reduce the risk. Of particular importance is the way in which money is used abroad. Let's look at the three main ways in which travellers carry money and consider the risks involved in each.

1. Foreign currency in cash – probably the most risky, as once it has been stolen or lost it is impossible to trace or cancel.

2. Credit or debit cards – one of the most secure ways of using money abroad, particularly since the introduction of 'chip and pin' which means that anyone stealing a card cannot use it unless they know the PIN code. However, some smaller organisations abroad still accept a card if the person using it just signs for the goods. The sooner a stolen or lost card is reported to the issuer, the less chance the traveller will be liable for any purchases made.

3. Traveller's cheques – if stolen or lost these can be cancelled (if the traveller knows the serial numbers of the stolen cheques) by reporting the loss to the issuer. Once reported, the issuer will provide the traveller with replacement traveller's cheques.

As with passports, any loss of currency, credit/debit cards or traveller's cheques needs to be reported to the local police so that the traveller can obtain a crime reference number for insurance purposes. Whether or

Lost luggage

Travellers may lose their luggage or possessions during transit (on the journey) or at the actual destination. When luggage is lost during transit it should be reported to the airline or tour operator. Both providers will then make efforts to find the missing luggage and may provide some replacement clothing and personal items if there is going to be a delay in retrieving the luggage. If the luggage is stolen or missing at the destination the traveller will need to follow the same procedures as outlined for lost money and report it to the police and obtain a crime reference number. Travel insurance policies cover the loss of luggage, although the amount that can be claimed depends on the

Sometimes, travellers' luggage just doesn't get to the destination.

policy and how much care was taken by the traveller. In addition, some insurance companies require receipts for all items that are being claimed for.

Theft and muggings

Unfortunately an unwanted side effect of tourism development in resorts is often an increase in crime in the area – possibly because the incoming tourists represent 'rich pickings' for a relatively poor local population. Theft, pick-pocketing and muggings are common in many tourist destinations. Travellers are frequently warned about safeguarding their belongings and not venturing into areas that are known to be riskier areas in terms of crime. As with many other emergency situations, travellers who experience theft or muggings need to report the incident to the local police and obtain a crime reference number.

Arrest and imprisonment

So far, this topic has looked at a range of emergency situations that happen to travellers through little or no fault of their own. This final section deals with situations in which the traveller may have placed themselves in a position that results in their arrest or imprisonment. Increasingly we are hearing reports of British nationals arrested for crimes abroad. In many situations the reason for the arrest appears to be a lack of understanding of local laws, as the three examples from the *Daily Mail*, right, show.

Most of the crimes committed by holidaymakers are fuelled by alcohol.

Holiday reps in Faliraki court

Three more holiday club reps have been arrested in the Greek resort of Faliraki, it has emerged. Club 18–30 said three of its staff were being 'detained illegally in breach of their human rights' after they were held by local police.

The arrests bring the total number of British reps known to have been detained in the holiday town on the island of Rhodes over the weekend to five.

The police crackdown follows concerns about violence involving British holidaymakers taking part in organised bar crawls, which were banned last week.

A spokeswoman for First Choice Holidays confirmed that [one of its reps] will be appearing at a Faliraki court charged with organising an illegal excursion that was not organised through a local agent.

Holidaymaker jailed over strip

A British girl who stripped off in a bar during a 'Best Bottom' contest was sentenced to eight months in a Greek prison yesterday. Jemma Gunning, 18, claimed in court that her bikini top fell off accidentally, leaving her in just a G-string.

But her plea fell on deaf ears, and she was jailed within 12 hours of being arrested as the authorities on Rhodes drove home the message that they will no longer tolerate British tourists embarking on booze-fuelled sprees.

British plane spotters face spying trial in Greece

British plane spotters accused of spying in Greece were today meeting members of their legal team. Police arrested the 11 men and one woman in Kalamata last year after they visited a local air base, and accused them of spying – allegations which the group will answer when their trial begins tomorrow.

They all deny espionage, and insist that they are plane spotters and not spies.

They were originally charged with gathering secret information to pass on to an enemy of Greece, which carried a maximum prison sentence of 25 years, but that was reduced to a lesser 'misdemeanour' offence.

Lawyers have had to try to explain the hobby to the authorities, as plane spotting is not a widely recognised pursuit in Greece. Group member Antoni Adamiak, 37, of London, said: 'No one set out with bad intentions. I think it was just a cultural misunderstanding.'

The three examples above are possibly due (as the last quote states) to 'cultural misunderstanding'. However, there are numerous examples of Britons imprisoned abroad for more serious crimes where the possible consequences are more severe, as the following case study highlights.

Prisoners Abroad is the only UK charity providing information, advice and support to Britons detained overseas, their family and friends, and to released prisoners trying to re-establish themselves in society. Caseworkers can often liaise with prison authorities and lawyers overseas, and work closely with the Foreign and Commonwealth Office.

How many Britons are being held overseas?

In total, Prisoners Abroad is supporting 1500 British nationals imprisoned overseas. USA has the largest number – 324 – which can be attributed to the large number of ex-pats. France (193) and Spain (146) follow, the majority of which will be on drug-related charges due to the drug routes across Europe.

The most astonishing increase is in Jamaica, where we currently support 72. More and more women are becoming involved in trafficking drugs out of Jamaica and into England.

What's the worst place to get caught?

South East Asia has the harshest of sentences. The consequences of being caught with drugs can be devastating. Many people sentenced in Thailand may never see outside the prison walls again.

Where are the worst prison conditions?

Prisons in Venezuela are run by gangs of prisoners; violence is rife; prisoners live in an extremely volatile environment. Prisoners also have to pay for everything – from bedding to adequate food. Prisoners Abroad provides all British prisoners in Venezuela with grants to survive this experience.

Due to the climate, prisons in the West Indies are subject to infestations of cockroaches, mosquitoes and rats. Women tend to suffer from gynaecological problems because of the poor sanitation.

Japan's prisons may by physically better, but many Britons return with psychological problems from being kept in solitary confinement for lengthy periods.

How much do penalties differ from country to country?

For trafficking cocaine, a sentence of up to 15 years may be imposed in Venezuela, but if the person were caught in Jamaica they would only receive 2 to 3 years and a substantial fine. In South East Asia, sentences are much harsher as the death penalty can be imposed for drug charges.

What can the British Government do to help people who are arrested? The British Government cannot get a person out of jail, or get them better conditions than are provided for local or other nationals, or give legal advice.

They can, however, give you information on suitably qualified English-speaking local lawyers and the legal system; get a message to family and friends; ensure medical problems are seen to; and take up any complaints of mistreatment.

Source (edited): www.prisonersabroad.org.uk

PRISONERS ABROAD

activity

WHAT SHOULD REPS ADVISE?

In this topic we have looked at five specific emergency situations that can affect the traveller. Imagine that you are responsible for training new reps. Present a 15-minute talk on the advice that they should give to travellers on the following:

- Lost passport
- Lost money
- Lost luggage
- Theft and muggings
- Arrest and imprisonment.

Large-scale emergency situations

In the last two topics we explored some of the small-scale emergency situations that can affect the traveller. In the final topic of the unit we are going to look at more serious, large-scale emergency situations, known as 'force majeure' that can have a profound impact on the traveller. This topic examines some of the major factors that can create emergency situations, under the following headings:

- **Wars**
- **Terrorist attacks**
- **Strikes**
- **Keeping up to date**
- **Natural disasters**
- **Severe weather conditions**
- **Major outbreaks of disease**
- **Other disasters such as transport accidents.**

Dusseldorf Airport, closed by a terror alert.

Wars

Both civil (within a country) and international wars have always had a severe impact on the travel and tourism. Disruptions to travel plans as well as the very real risk of personal injury can deter travellers from going to countries affected. In severe situations it may discourage people from going to adjoining countries or making journeys that involve passing through a war-torn country's airspace. In recent years one of the most devastating wars to affect the travel and tourism industry was the war in Iraq in 2003. Not only did this prevent travellers from venturing to affected regions but also raised concerns about the safety of international travel in general in the light of possible attacks related to the conflict. Americans were particularly affected. Steven Simon, the former senior director of transnational threats in the US National Security Council, warned that popular tourist destinations worldwide could become 'soft targets' and come under attack. Airlines were also perceived as being potential targets, making many travellers reluctant to risk air travel.

Terrorist attacks

The United Nations defines terrorism as: 'Criminal acts intended or calculated to provoke a state of terror in the general public'.

In terms of the effect on the traveller, the impacts of terrorist activity can be similar to those of a war. The 11 September 2001 attacks on the World Trade Centre in New York and the Pentagon in Washington raised global awareness of the devastating impacts that terrorists could bring.

Unfortunately, the number and effectiveness of terrorist groups is growing. The Home Office lists 25 'proscribed' (outlawed in the UK) international terrorist organisations (see page 232). Terrorist attacks are becoming increasingly frequent throughout the world, and all travellers need to be aware of possible risks and minimise them when travelling.. The Foreign and Commonwealth Office offers security tips (see opposite) to British people visiting countries that may be susceptible to terrorist attack.

The events of 9/11 have increased everyone's worries about flying.

activity

WHERE ARE THE TERRORIST ATTACKS?

Below is a Foreign and Commonwealth Office list of some recent terrorist attacks. Using a blank map of the world, identify and mark where each one took place.

- Bomb attacks against hotels in the Sinai Peninsula in Egypt killed 34 in October 2004.
- An attack on a school in North Ossetia in Russia in September 2004 in which hundreds of people, including children, were killed.
- Serious attacks, including assassinations of foreigners in Saudi Arabia in 2003 and 2004 have left a number of Britons dead.
- A car bomb exploded outside the Australian Embassy in Jakarta, Indonesia in September 2004, killing 9.
- Simultaneous blasts which downed two airliners in Russia and a suicide attack outside a Moscow metro station in August 2004 killed nearly 100.
- Simultaneous bombs in August 2004 in two hotels in Istanbul, Turkey.
- Suicide bomb attacks near the US and Israeli Embassies in Tashkent, Uzbekistan in July 2004.

- Simultaneous bomb attacks on commuter trains in Madrid in March 2004 which left 202 dead.
- In February 2004, 116 people died in the Philippines, when the 10,000-ton Superferry 14 caught fire. The disaster was caused by an explosive device.
- A suicide attack on the Moscow metro in February 2004 killed over 40.
- A series of attacks in Istanbul in November 2003 included attacks against HSBC bank and the British Consulate. 3 Britons were killed.
- In August 2003, a car bomb parked outside the US-run Marriott Hotel in Jakarta, Indonesia killed 12.
- Triple bomb attacks in Casablanca, Morocco in May 2002, targeted a Spanish restaurant, a 5-star hotel and a Jewish community centre, killing 45.
- A suicide bombing at the Israeli-owned Paradise Hotel in Mombassa, Kenya in November 2002.
- An attack on a busy nightclub in Bali, Indonesia, killed 202, including 26 Britons, in October 2002.

Examples of international terrorist organisations

- N17 (17 November Revolutionary Organisation) uses violence to highlight 'imperialist and corrupt actions'.
- ANO (Abu Nidal Organisation) whose principal aim is the destruction of the state of Israel. It is also hostile to 'reactionary' Arab regimes supporting Israel.
- GI (Al-Gama'at al-Islamiya) aims to overthrow the Egyptian Government and replace it with an Islamic state. Some members also want the removal of Western influence from the Arab world.
- Al Qaida. Inspired and led by Osama Bin Laden, its aims are the expulsion of Western forces from Saudi Arabia, the destruction of Israel and the end of Western influence in the Muslim world.
- GIA (Groupe Islamique Armée – Armed Islamic Group) aims to create an Islamic state in Algeria.
- ETA (Euskadi ta Askatasuna – Basque Homeland and Liberty) seeks the creation of an independent state comprising the Basque regions of Spain and France.
- EIJ (Egyptian Islamic Jihad) aims to overthrow the Egyptian Government and replace it with an Islamic state. Since 1998, however, it has also allied itself to Osama Bin Laden's 'global Jihad' and has threatened Western interests.
- PKK (Partiya Karkeren Kurdistan – Kurdistan Workers' Party) is primarily a separatist movement seeking an independent Kurdish state in southeast Turkey.
- LTTE (Liberation Tigers of Tamil Eelam) is fighting for a separate Tamil state in the north and east of Sri Lanka.

Source: www.homeoffice.gov.uk

Strikes

Whilst strikes are not as serious as wars and terrorist attacks in terms of possible injury, they can still have a devastating impact on the traveller. Typical strikes that affect travellers include those by transport staff such as airport employees, air traffic control, train and bus services, port and ferry staff and immigration services. Even when the strike is not being held by the staff providing the service, there can still be a knock-on effect. For example, a strike by one airline can disrupt the flying schedules of other airlines.

Travelling is a process made up of a series of distinct parts, and the failure of any one part (however small) can mean that the entire process fails. For example, if coach drivers providing airport-to-accommodation transfers in a destination go on strike, the whole travel process is disrupted.

---

activity

IMPACTS OF STRIKES

Read the article below from the Daily Mail about French transport strikes. As a group, brainstorm a list of all of the potential impacts that the strikes might have.

Tourists hit by French strikes

Travel misery hit British tourists going to and from France today as a French strike affected both air and ferry services. The dispute, part of a long-running row over proposed pension reforms, led to the cancellation of dozens of flights and the scrapping of some cross-Channel sailings.

British Airways cancelled 90 of its 120 planned flights between Britain and France, while bmi was operating only 6 out of its normal 24 flights. Also, low-cost carrier easyJet scrapped 37 flights to and from France.

Dover–Calais ferry operator P&O Ferries was able to operate up to 7a.m. UK time before a walkout by French dockers halted sailings. P&O also had to cancel one of its Portsmouth to Cherbourg sailings, with passengers being moved on to the Portsmouth–Le Havre route. Some passengers unable to sail from Calais switched to the Channel Tunnel shuttle trains run by the Eurotunnel company which were running normally.

Source: Daily Mail, 3/6/03

Keeping up to date

Finally, it should be stressed that the relative safety of travelling to different destinations varies over time according to the political situation within each country. Current information on the safety of specific countries can be obtained from the Foreign and Commonwealth website, as can be seen from the March 2005 advice below:

The FCO advises against all travel to:

Ivory Coast	Somalia	Togo

The FCO advises against all travel to parts of the following countries (see individual Travel Advice Notices for further details):

Afghanistan	Albania	Algeria
Azerbaijan	Burundi	Cameroon
Chad	Colombia	Congo (Democratic Republic)
Ecuador	Eritrea	Ethiopia
Georgia	Guinea-Bissau	India
Indonesia	Iran	Iraq
Israel and the Occupied Territories	Liberia	Mali
Niger	Nigeria	Pakistan
Philippines	Russian Federation	Sierra Leone
Sudan	Uganda	Yemen

Natural disasters

Natural disasters such as volcanic eruptions, earthquakes and flooding can severely disrupt travel plans and, at their most severe, endanger the traveller's life. In addition they can create huge problems for tour operators and transport providers who will need to make emergency provision for customers in affected areas. One of the world's worst natural disasters happened very recently – the Indian Ocean tsunami (see below). Whilst many such disasters predominantly affect long-haul destinations, examples nearer to home are not uncommon. In August 2002, for example, central Europe experienced some of the worst floods in history. Torrential rains resulted in 82 deaths and sparked mass evacuation of major tourist destinations such as Prague and Croatia. Both Salzburg and Vienna in Austria were declared disaster zones. The flooding created further problems including mud and landslides in Switzerland.

activity

VOLCANIC THREAT?

There are a number of volcanoes throughout the world that are currently 'dormant' but could suddenly erupt in the future. Using an internet search engine, identify five such volcanoes that are in popular tourist destinations.

The Indian Ocean tsunami – one of the worst natural disasters ever

The earthquake which triggered the Indian Ocean tsunami had a magnitude of 9.3 on the Richter scale. It struck at 7.58 a.m. (local time) on December 26 2004, just 41 miles off the coast of north-west Sumatra, ripping apart the sea bed 15 miles beneath the surface.

The resulting waves travelled thousands of miles across the Indian Ocean, and when they struck land they claimed the lives of nearly 300,000 people in countries as far apart as Indonesia, the Maldives, Sri Lanka and Somalia.

The first and worst hit was Banda Aceh in northern Sumatra, where 200,000 are now thought to have been killed in just 15 minutes.

The tsunami waves radiated out, sweeping across Thai resorts as some Christmas revellers were rising and others were already on the beaches.

The waves crossed the Indian Ocean, striking the coast of Sri Lanka, the Maldives and south-east India with devastating force.

The final toll in Indonesia was about 126,000 dead and 93,000 missing. The number of homeless was estimated at 800,000. However, the exact number of victims will probably never be known. Despite high early estimates of Britons killed, the final toll is thought to be about 61.

Tourists caught up in the disaster

Vast areas saw entire villages wiped out in minutes. Many of the areas affected were prime tourist destinations and a huge range of organisations and agencies worked together to come to the aid of those involved in the tragedy. Local governments, aid agencies, volunteers and tourism organisations such as tour operators assisted in the grim task of attempting to identify victims or arrange for the transportation home of the bodies of those who had perished. Many more were injured and both they and their families needed support and help. Flights were arranged for those that were able to fly home – but many arrived at UK airports with little more than what they were wearing when the tsunami struck. At Manchester Airport, tour operator and airline staff were on hand to give out clothing and provide transport home. Some were even provided with a locksmith to break into their own homes since many had lost all personal items including their house keys.

The scale of the disaster is hard to comprehend and the impact that it might have on future tourism in this area is uncertain. However, one aspect that has been very clearly highlighted is that natural disasters are frequently one of the greatest threats to the traveller – because they are often totally unpredictable and frequently catastrophic in effect.

What the tsunami did to a hotel in Thailand

Severe weather conditions

Severe weather conditions may be caused by extreme amounts of wind, rain, snow, storms or temperature. Such conditions can cause acute disruption for travellers, as well as proving highly dangerous. Whilst sub-zero temperatures and snow are clearly a necessity for the winter sports market, blizzards frequently halt transport services both in the UK and abroad, leaving passengers stranded at airports and

other transport termini. Temperatures at the other end of the thermometer can be equally perilous. Extremes of heat generate risks of forest fires and heat-related illnesses – and 15,000 people died in France due to the 2003 summer heatwave.

In recent years, the huge increase in long-haul trips, particularly holidays in the Caribbean, has raised the profile of hurricanes – severe tropical storms with destructive wind speeds. They form in the southern Atlantic Ocean, eastern Pacific Ocean, Gulf of Mexico or Caribbean Sea and create torrential rains and gale-force winds that lead to extensive flooding and damage (see below).

Hurricane Ivan

September 2004 saw the devastation that a hurricane can bring when Hurricane Ivan hit Cuba and adjoining islands. The category 5 storm had wind speeds of up to 155 mph – so strong that trees were uprooted, buildings destroyed and waves up to 25 feet high hit the coastline. Over 5,000 UK holidaymakers were evacuated to the Dominican Republic and Cancun (Mexico) whilst others, still to leave the UK, saw their holidays cancelled.

Source: Daily Mail, 3/6/03

activity

REASSURE AND PREPARE

Read the advice below to people caught in a hurricane. Imagine that you are a holiday representative at an all-inclusive resort in Barbados and have been informed that a hurricane is heading your way. Your guests have assembled in the lounge and are anxious about what they should do. Work out what you would say to your guests – remember that you need to reassure them that they are going to be safe but also give them appropriate advice about what they should do if the storm hits.

Major outbreaks of disease

In Topic 6 we looked at some of the main contagious diseases that the international traveller needs to be aware of and take precautions against. Sometimes major emergency situations arise due to the sudden and unexpected outbreak of a particular disease. In

Bird flu

Bird flu (also known as 'avian flu') is a severe strain of the flu virus that can prove fatal in humans. It is unique, in that it is passed from birds to humans, and was first identified in Hong Kong in 1997. Further outbreaks have been reported in other countries such as the Netherlands. The threat of this disease is considered so severe that the World Health Organisation has warned that it could pose a more serious threat to health than SARS.

SARS

SARS (Severe Acute Respiratory Syndrome) was first identified in November 2002 in the Guangdong Province of China – killing more than 800 people and sparking an international health crisis. The travel plans of thousands were disrupted as fears grew. It was recognised that SARS was easily transmitted, and many were concerned about the potential dangers of travelling  on planes with fellow passengers who might be infected. Crossing international borders became time-consuming as officials checked any travellers that they thought might be infected. Reports of SARS infection continue, with further outbreaks reported, such as that in Beijing in April 2004, and the immediate quarantine of those thought to be at risk.

Norwalk virus

The Norwalk virus is a highly contagious gastro-intestinal illness that can be spread through close contact, and food and drink. Whilst short-lived (usually about 48 hours) it can cause severe diarrhoea and vomiting and is particularly dangerous for susceptible people – the elderly, very young or people with weakened immune systems. It has become a problem for many travel and tourism providers, particularly those whose customers come into close contact within confined spaces such as hotels, transport, etc. In the summer of 2003, Norwalk hit the P&O cruise ship Aurora, with 430 passengers contracting the virus. So severe was the outbreak that the Greek government refused to allow the Aurora to dock at the port of Piraeus, resulting in doctors having to ferry medical aid out to the ship.

Eleven of the British holidaymakers involved in an horrific coach crash in Turkey were returning home today [26/9/02] after abandoning their breaks in the sun. They were due back at Manchester airport less than 48 hours after flying out to the popular holiday destination.

Three Britons remain in hospital in Turkey, following the collision between the Airtours coach, another bus and a car during the early hours of yesterday, the British Consul said. His staff were still liaising with those in hospital or recovering at their hotels. He added: 'It is too early to say what happened in the accident and the investigation is in the hands of the Turkish police.'

The accident left five local people dead, including the drivers of the two coaches. A total of 46 Britons were taken to hospital following the accident. It happened during a 90-minute transfer between Dalaman Airport and Marmaris as the tourists prepared to start their holidays after a MyTravel Airways flight.

A spokeswoman for Airtours said: 'The vast majority of the passengers have decided to stay on and continue their holidays but 11 have requested to return home, and we are bringing them back to Manchester today.'

Yesterday's accident was the latest serious crash involving British holidaymakers in the area in the past seven years.

In 1995, two people died and 35 others were injured when a coach carrying First Choice holidaymakers collided with a minibus on its way to Dalaman Airport.

In 1999, 20 British tourists heading for a belly dancing show with operator Oracle Tours escaped serious injury when their coach collided with a car and rolled off the road in Soke.

A year previously, a British woman was one of six people who died when an Airtours coach collided head-on with a taxi near Izmir.

Source: www.dailymail.co.uk

such situations, tour operators, transport providers and other agencies are required to act swiftly in the interests of the traveller. In recent years there have been a number of examples of such outbreaks, as the information below shows.

Other disasters such as transport accidents

Accidents involving transport are a constant concern for travel and tourism providers. Apart from the obvious risk to the personal safety of travellers there are also issues of having to look after both the injured and their relatives whilst abroad and ensuring that they are provided with transport back to the UK. Such accidents can occur with any form of transport whether it is public, such as air, sea, coach (see example, below) or rail, or has been arranged privately by the traveller – e.g. a hire car or moped. In addition to the immediate problems that arise, such accidents can also have the knock-on effect of making future travellers reluctant to use those forms of transport that have been involved in accidents.

HOW CAN ORGANISATIONS HELP?

In the last four topics we have looked at a wide range of emergency situations that can affect travellers within the travel and tourism industry. We have also explored the ways in which various organisations can provide support and advice to travellers involved in an emergency situation. In pairs, outline how each of the following organisations can offer assistance to the traveller and give one example of an emergency situation that each might deal with.

- Tour operators
- Travel agents
- Transport providers
- Insurance companies
- Passport office
- Medical assistance companies
- Foreign and Commonwealth Office
- British Consul, Embassy or High Commission
- Financial services organisations, such as banks and building societies
- Prisoners Abroad.

How Unit 5 is assessed

This unit is externally assessed. The format will be a $1\frac{1}{2}$-hour written exam, using a question-and-answer booklet. The booklet, provided by Edexcel, will consist of short-answer and longer-answer questions relating to scenarios and information. You should aim to be ready to sit the exam in January and/or June.

The Edexcel website – edexcel.org.uk – will have more guidance on external assessment, including specimen papers and example answers, or you can get more information from your school or college.

The grade you are awarded will depend on how well you meet the assessment objectives. The general areas that assessment objectives focus on are:

1. How you **demonstrate** your knowledge and understanding of specified content, related skills and vocationally related contexts.

2. How you **apply** your knowledge and understanding of the content and contexts.

3. How you use **research techniques** to obtain information and analyse issues and problems.

4. How effectively you **evaluate, judge, draw conclusions** and **make recommendations** about issues and problems.

In general, to gain the higher grades your work will have to show that you:

- Have in-depth knowledge and understanding of the subject content of the unit

- Can apply your knowledge and understanding in vocationally related contexts

- Are able to use appropriate research techniques

- Can analyse vocationally related issues and problems

- Are able to evaluate information to make reasoned judgements, draw conclusions and make recommendations.

You written work will also have to convey appropriate meaning and use vocabulary well. You need to be able to interpret statistical data, from which you extract key points, and to show that you understand trends and can support any conclusions which you might draw in your test answers.

To prepare for your assessment you will need to research a range of aspects about working practices and keep a record of your findings – in a 'revision portfolio' perhaps – in such a way that they will be easy to revise as the exam date approaches. The headings below should help you organise your revision portfolio.

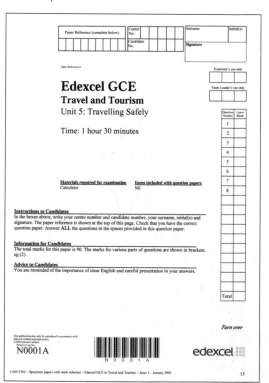

Specimen exam papers are available from the Edexcel website – edexcel.org.uk

1. Legal and regulatory requirements

You need to build up knowledge of key organisations which regulate the industry and be able to differentiate between them and analyse how they affect the industry, by describing the main responsibilities and regulations of each of the following: Civil Aviation Authority, Association of British Travel Agents, International Air Transport Association, Joint Aviation Authorities.

Accurate and up-to-date summaries of the following legislation will also need to be known: EU Package Travel Directive, Disability Discrimination Act, Data Protection Act, Trades Description Act, Fair Trading Act, Sale of Goods and Services Act.

Case studies are likely to be used in the exam to assess your ability to analyse a situation and know which regulation or law applies. A good awareness is also needed of how procedures and practices are put in place by organisations to comply with the legislation.

2. Restrictions on travel

You need to know about restrictions on travel through passport and visa control, and ticketing and boarding, and be able to explain the implications of non-compliance with these measures.

You need to know about restrictions on travel for other reasons, such as disease. You need to have a good awareness of where travellers can obtain advice on precautions and current threats of diseases, such as cholera, typhoid, HIV and Aids, yellow fever, malaria and hepatitis C.

3. Emergency situations

You will need to have good awareness of small-scale emergencies and be able to interpret insurance policies, contracts and agreements to show that you understand their conditions and implications. Emergencies which the questions might pose could be cancellation or curtailment, medical problems, loss of passport, money credit cards or luggage, theft or muggings, arrest and imprisonment.

For all of the above there are key organisations which help travellers, and you may well be asked about their roles and support.

You need to know about large-scale emergencies (force majeure) as well. Questions may assess your knowledge of how the industry deals with these. Your ability to analyse and assess situations (such as the following) and make recommendations will be important in the test: wars and terrorist attacks, strikes, natural disasters, severe weather, accidents and crashes.

Be prepared

You will need to plan your revision to be ready for the exam. Your tutors can also play a role by checking your revision portfolio and setting up a range of visits and speakers so that you have real examples to use. They should also check with the awarding body and brief you on structure, duration and any rules and regulations for taking the papers.

The marking criteria are likely to reward you for:

- Use and understanding of appropriate terminology
- Clear descriptions
- Real examples
- Depth or detail of answer
- Assessment or critical analysis
- Accuracy of interpretation.

Your tutors can also help you by clarify the marking criteria for the assessment, but this will always be based on:

Knowledge and understanding:	25–35%
Application of knowledge skills and understanding:	25–35%
Research and analysis:	20–30%
Evaluation:	10–20%.

The term 'resort operations' refers to the management and implementation of the customer experience within a resort destination. Such operations play a substantial role in the overall activities of tour operating, and are fundamental in ensuring customer satisfaction. When a customer buys a package holiday they are not simply paying for transport, accommodation and food. They will also expect staff to be on hand to coordinate every stage of their experience to ensure that it meets their expectations – dealing with transport, for example, or accommodation problems, providing resort advice, dealing with emergencies and, of course, organising entertainment and excursions.

There are a wide range of staff who provide this function and form the organisational structure of resort operations. Such structures vary according to the tour operator, type of customer and nature of product offered. It is important to have an overall understanding of how a resort office functions and the various staffing roles that may be involved. We will look at a wide range of different jobs and the skills needed for each. Customer-service skills are a crucial requirement for staff working in resort operations, and we will look at how these can be applied to dealing with complaints, hosting a welcome meeting, and providing products and services that meet the needs of different customers.

Much of this unit will relate to the question of how to become a resort representative. 'Repping' has become a very popular career choice in recent years – fuelled largely, no doubt, by TV fly-on-the-wall documentaries! The Open College give the following ten reasons for becoming a rep:

1. Work in the sun
2. See different cultures
3. Meet new people
4. Enjoy unmatched variety
5. Make new friends
6. Make people's holidays one that they will never forget
7. Great experience
8. Feel more independent
9. Feel more responsible
10. Feel a sense of pride and accomplishment when helping holidaymakers on their holiday.

(Source: www.holidayreps.freeserve.co.uk)

Of course, there are also a number of drawbacks to working in resort operations – the long and unsociable hours, not to mention the relatively low pay. But for many it offers a challenging and exciting career – let's see if it's right for you, by exploring the ways in which resort staff operate.

Unit 6

Resort Operations

6.1 The activities of the resort office

Topic 1	Functional areas and departments of the resort office	240
Topic 2	Job roles of different overseas representatives	244
Topic 3	Activities carried out at the resort office	249
Topic 4	Links with the UK office	254

6.2 Duties of a resort representative

Topic 5	The welcome meeting	258
Topic 6	Selling products and services	264
Topic 7	Documentation	268
Topic 8	Dealing with problem situations	272

6.3 The significance of induction, training and product knowledge of staff in delivering high quality customer service

Topic 9	Induction and training	278
Topic 10	Product knowledge	282
	How Unit 6 is assessed	288

Functional areas and departments of the resort office

The range of job roles and departments within the resort office vary considerably according to the tour operator and nature of products and services being offered. In this section we will look at the different overseas staff employed by the tour operator, including:

- Differences in staffing between tour operators
- Administrative staff
- Other overseas representatives
- Team leaders
- Team, area and general managers
- The structure of the specific tour.

Differences in staffing between tour operators

The number of staff employed and the way in which they are structured within a resort will depend largely upon the volume of holidaymakers. At the lesser end of the scale where visitor numbers are small, one member of staff may perform all of the duties within a resort. This is particularly common at the luxury end of the market where small groups enjoy the undivided attention of a designated Tour Guide (often referred to as a Tour Manager). Such a person will oversee all of the arrangements for the group from initially greeting them on arrival, checking them into accommodation and escorting them on excursions (see Cape Town example, opposite).

The level of contact between customer and member of staff on an escorted tour will be considerably higher than on many package holidays. In fact on some, such as trekking holidays in the Himalayas, the tour guide will be with their party for 24 hours a day, sharing meals and accommodation with them. Clearly such a person needs a wide range of highly developed skills as they will be on call to deal with all eventualities.

Single members of staff may also have sole responsibility for less expensive types of holidays. For example, tour operators dealing in a limited range of holidays on the less developed Greek islands may rely on one member of staff to oversee the small number of holidaymakers.

On arrival at Cape Town International Airport you will be met by your South African Tour Guide, who will be providing the local expertise, trade secrets and humour for the next two weeks! You will firstly be taken to the Portswood Hotel on the Waterfront to check in and settle into the Capetonian way of life. In the afternoon carry out a casual city orientation, including various areas of historical and cultural interest in and around the city centre, which provides an insight into the backgrounds of South Africa's diverse communities. The highlight of the afternoon, a trip to the top of Table Mountain by aerial cableway, weather permitting, which provides some of the world's most spectacular views.

For the mass market package holiday resorts, a more structured approach to staffing is usually required – with clearly defined roles and departments. Some of the key departments include:

- Administration staff
- Overseas representatives
- Team leaders
- Team, area or general managers.

Administrative staff

Resort administrators (also known as Commercial Administrators or Administration Supervisors) provide support to the resort staff by liaising with local suppliers such as accommodation suppliers, providing room allocation lists and transfer arrangements. The

Commercial Administrators provide the resort team with support by running the administration function from our resort offices. Working with IT systems and also dealing with customers on the telephone and face to face, you will deal with all aspects of office-based administration including collating information and producing reports and maintaining constant communication throughout the team.

Your main duties include:

- Managing the reservations system and procedures
- Coordinating accommodation requirements to maximise utilisation
- Processing payments to hoteliers and suppliers
- Providing information for suppliers, UK departments and colleagues
- Preparing and analysing reports
- Dealing politely and efficiently with telephone and supplier enquiries
- Maintaining records and systems
- Using IT systems and office equipment
- Dealing with bookings concerning transfers and excursions
- Ensuring all paperwork is completed neatly and accurately with specified deadlines
- Maintaining resort stock rooms and monitoring/ordering supplies
- Producing basic financial spreadsheets on resort income/expenditure.

range of duties varies according to the tour operator but may include any or all of the responsibilities outlined by the MyTravel Group (see previous page):

In larger resorts, there may be additional staff who work in the resort office, such as Flight Sales Administrators – who co-ordinate flight arrangements – and Administration Assistants and secretarial support. Their duties may include providing advice and information to holidaymakers, currency exchange and an excursion booking system.

(see previous page)

Whether British employees or the host country's locals are recruited for the various roles in resort operations varies according to the policy of individual tour operators. As a group, discuss what you think the advantages and disadvantages might be to a tour operator of each policy. For example, how many British employees will be able to speak fluent Greek – and is this an important attribute when working in a highly developed Greek resort?

Many tour operators have a specific finance administration department within a resort. This is largely a 'behind-the-scenes' role and involves safeguarding the cash held in a resort as well as maintaining records of income and expenditure. In most resorts this is a major responsibility because of the large amounts of money that is exchanged. For example, most resort offices provide currency exchange facilities which entail substantial amounts of local currency being available. In addition to this, the majority of holidaymakers book excursions at the resort rather than in advance. With the average excursion costing £35 per person the quantity of money paid to resort reps is frequently high.

Many tour operators now use the services of local agents in the resort to provide much of the administrative support rather than employ their own staff. For example, the Barcello Group in Spain supplies tour operators First Choice with services such as accommodation lists, excursions and airport transfer arrangements.

Overseas representatives

The overseas representative is at the forefront of the customer experience and is largely responsible for ensuring that the holidaymaker enjoys their holiday.

There is a range of different types of rep from transfer and children's to villa and entertainment. We will be looking at the different representative jobs in the next section and their main roles. In preparation for this, have a go at the activity below.

As a group, brainstorm all of the duties that you think might be involved in the role of a resort representative.

Team Leaders

The team leader is the overseas representative who has responsibility for a number of other representatives – typically 6 or 7. Whilst some tour operators call this member of staff a 'Team Leader', others use different titles – 'Head Representative' or 'Supervisor'. The team leader will be on hand to provide advice to reps, help with difficult situations if required and ensure that each rep is carrying out their role correctly.

Team, area and general managers

In large destination resorts all the operations will be co-ordinated through a resort manager. This member of staff will have responsibility for all of the departments explained below. Thomson Holidays refer to this role as 'Team Manager' and outlines the general duties as shown below.

The Team Manager (Resort Manager)

You will manage a team of between 5 and 25 holiday reps/children's reps to provide excellent customer service and achieve the business goals in your resort. This is a hands-on management role where you will be out and about motivating, coaching and developing the skills of your staff. In addition you will have administrative tasks, including accounts, producing reports and managing resort procedures.

Source: www.Thomson.co.uk

Area or General Managers will have responsibility for a large area encompassing a wide range of resorts. Depending on the volume of customers this might be an entire country such as Spain or a number of smaller countries.

WHAT DOES IT ALL MEAN?

Read the Thomson extract, describing the role of a Team/Resort Manager, and discuss the following:

1 What do you think the 'business goals in your resort' might be?

2 What do you understand by the phrase 'a hands-on management role'?

3 What types of 'reports' might the team manager have to produce?

4 Can you think of three examples of 'resort procedures'?

The structure of a specific tour operator's resort operations

As we have already seen there is a huge variation in the way in which tour operators structure their resort operations. The case study, right, outlines the various roles within the Club Med organisation.

Club Med's resort structure is unusual, and heavily influenced by the continental European focus on 'animateuse' – where resort staff are seen as a combination of hosts and entertainers. If you have been on an all-inclusive holiday you may have already experienced this approach to resort staffing.

YOUR DESCRIPTION OF RESORT OPERATIONS

For the assessment you need to produce a description of the different departments and functional areas of a tour operator's resort operations. Investigate one tour operator to identify how they organise the operations in one of their resorts. If you are fortunate enough to be going on a package holiday you might like to carry out your research whilst there by interviewing the staff.

Remember that a tour operator will not necessarily have all of the departments in each resort that we have discussed. However, each of the functions still need to be carried out, so you will need to identify which member of staff has responsibility for each function. For example, the resort representatives may also have responsibility for administration and finance.

Club Med

Club Méditerranée offers its GMs (Gentils Membres) – our guests – unique holidays in outstanding locations, at their own pace and according to their own preferences. Benefit from the expertise of all our GOs (Gentils Organisateurs) and GEs (Gentils Employés) in fields of their own choice. More than 50 activities are provided in our holiday villages, including water sports, beauty care, mini-club.

Structure within Club Med Resorts

Chef de village – and conductor of the orchestra of GO/GEs – his/her aim is to satisfy the GMs, who have come to look for happiness, security, atmosphere, peace of mind and communication. With overall responsibility for village life, the chef de village's experience of organisation and festive activities and his/her personal qualities make this an ideal manager of the GO/ GEs and department heads that he/she supervises.

Chief of service In regular contact with the chef de village, the chief of service's role is to optimise organisation of his/her department by leading a team of GO/GEs in order to help them progress.

Activity leader With extensive experience, the activity leader organises and ensures proper operation of his/her activity while guiding GO/GEs in their approach to their work.

IGO As a GO for integration, he/she welcomes new GOs and helps them to integrate more easily into teams, guiding them in their first steps in the village.

GO/GE As the Club's ambassadors, GOs and GEs do all their best to provide guests with unforgettable experiences. By sharing their joy in life and their professionalism they contribute to maintaining the village's quality of service.

Job roles of different overseas representatives

As we have already said, there are a range of specific jobs available in resort repping. In this section we are going to look at the main categories, which include:

- **Resort representative**
- **Transfer representative**
- **Children's representative**
- **Villa representative**
- **Winter sports representative/Chalet host**
- **Entertainment representative**
- **Young adults' representative.**

Resort representative

The term 'resort representative' is generally used to describe the person who deals with holidaymakers within a resort. However, it should be stressed that whilst First Choice use this job title, other tour operators use alternative titles. At Thomsons, for example, they are referred to as 'holiday reps' whilst MyTravel prefers the title of 'customer-services rep'. Regardless of the title, it is the reps' responsibility to ensure that the holiday meets the needs and expectations of their guests. The number of guests that a rep is allocated to look after will largely depend on the nature of the resort. In a large resort featuring hotels with several hundred bedrooms it is not unusual to have a rep responsible solely for guests at a single hotel – a sole-property rep. In such circumstances the rep will be permanently based at the hotel – possibly with their own desk and available to guests for extended periods of time. Of course, they will only deal with the guests that have booked through their own company, so such hotels will have a number of reps representing the different tour operators who use the hotel. This can often create added pressure for the rep in that they will be keen to show that the service that they offer is equal to or better than that of rival tour operator reps within the hotel – otherwise guests may simply decide to book with a rival company next time! One of the frequent grounds for comparison between companies is the information displayed on the rep's notice board. For example:

Why do we have to depart four hours before our flight when Sunburst holidays only leave two hours before?

How come Sunburst offer exactly the same barbecue at £5 cheaper – can we book with them?

Why aren't you available in the hotel on Sunday and Tuesday like the Sunburst rep?

Why don't you provide a bedroom to get changed in on the departure day, like Sunburst?

Problems indeed for the sole-property rep – but the great advantage of being at just one location is that the rep can be available for longer periods of time, build up effective relationships with the hotel staff, and resolve difficulties promptly. The alternative method of allocation is when a rep has guests in a number of different properties. In this situation, the rep will usually visit all their properties on a rota basis, with guests being notified of the timetable of visits. For example:

> Hi – I'm Nicki, your Sunburst rep.
>
> I'm sure that you will have a fantastic holiday here at the Rexene hotel, but I will be calling in every day to answer your questions and provide any help that I can to make your stay perfect. I will be available in the hotel foyer at the following times:
>
> Saturday: 5.00 p.m.–6.00 p.m.
>
> Sunday: Airport Day
>
> Monday: day off
>
> Tuesday: 5.00 p.m.–6.00 p.m.
>
> Wednesday: 9.00 a.m.–10.00 a.m.
>
> Thursday: 9.00 a.m.–10.00 a.m.
>
> Friday: 5.00 p.m.–6.00 p.m.
>
> If you need to contact me at any other time, please notify reception, who will ensure that your message is passed on.

In situations where small numbers of guests are staying at some properties they may be asked to go to a central hotel to meet with their rep.

Transfer representative

The job of transferring holidaymakers to and from the airport to their accommodation may be done by the resort reps. However, some tour operators designate this role to specific staff. The main responsibilities will include:

- Meeting guests at the airport
- Checking their booking details
- Directing them to the transfer transport (usually a coach, but it may involve a ferry transfer)
- Providing a welcome, and information on the transfer journey

OVERWORKED, BUT COULD DO BETTER

You are employed as a resort rep on the Greek island of Santorini. You are responsible for guests in fifteen hotels in the area. Because they are geographically widespread you hold your daily meeting at one of the hotels that is situated in the town centre – although you also visit guests in their individual hotels on their arrival day and the day before their departure. Attendance at the meetings is low, apart from the Welcome Meeting where the majority of excursions are booked. You are disappointed to receive feedback from your Team Leader that guests have rated your services as a resort rep as 'Poor', with comments such as 'We never saw her'! Your Team Leader has asked you to suggest how the guests' experience could be improved. Bearing in mind that you already feel overworked, what would you suggest?

- Informing guests of their rep's name, and the date, time and location of the Welcome Meeting
- Delivering guests to their accommodation
- Collecting guests for their return journey
- Overseeing the check-in
- Dealing with any problems that may arise such as flight cancellations, medical emergencies and lost luggage.

Children's representative

This job involves looking after and arranging activities for the children who are on holiday with their parents. It is a key role in many holidays, simply because guests with children will often expect to enjoy time on their own, safe in the knowledge that their children are safe and having a good time – so the children's rep is

meeting the needs of both the children and their parents. Many tour operators offer different types of 'children's clubs' depending on the age of the children. This helps the children's reps to ensure that the activities that they provide are suitable for their customers. For example, Thomson offer the three categories of clubs outlined below:

 Tots: 3-5 year olds will enjoy a safe and happy time with a carefully structured programme of play activities.

 Team: 6-8 year olds will experience endless adventures with fun and games to feed their active and enthusiastic minds.

 Tribe: 9-12 year olds will be entertained by sessions filled with challenges to test the most active and creative of thinkers.

KEEPING EVERYONE HAPPY

Read the description of the three Thomson children's clubs above. Can you think of any problems that might occur with a family that had three children, aged 5, 6 and 9? How might the parents' desire for a few relaxing hours on their own not work out?

Villa representative

Many holidaymakers enjoy the freedom of their own villa. Increasingly many holidaymakers opt to take self-catering holidays, and there has been a rapid increase in the popularity of villa holidays. Frequently the reason for choosing this type of holiday is the desire to be semi-independent, which means that guests

may not want the constant intrusion of a resort rep. In fact, many such holidaymakers also book a rental car so that they are free to explore the area themselves, rather than participate in organised excursions. Villa reps look after guests in a number of properties, but the level and frequency of contact tends to be less than with, say, a rep in a hotel. Having said this, when the rep does visit, it tends to be more personalised as it is on a one-to-one basis – as the following extract from a villa rep's diary shows:

Tuesday 15th August

Managed to catch the Blackwells in, this evening – they've been out all the other times I've visited so have just left a message to say that I'd called. Really nice family who seem to be thoroughly enjoying their holiday and exploring the island in their hired car. Was invited to stay for a glass of wine and some olives as they were getting the barbecue fired up. They're not interested in any of my suggested excursions but were interested to hear my recommendations of some good restaurants in the area. Confirmed the details of the return flight and discussed other properties in the area that they might be interested in as they want to return next year.

Winter sports representative/ Chalet host

Winter sports reps carry out many similar duties to a resort rep. However, since the focus of the guests' holiday is usually on skiing or other snow-based activities, there are usually some additional responsibilities as outlined on the right.

In many winter sport resorts, guests stay in chalets. This creates a further job role in the form of the 'Chalet host'. Chalets hosts are basically the 'hired help' for the guests – sorting out general cleaning and housekeeping jobs as well as cooking all of the meals. We are not talking about defrosting a pizza here! Most winter sports operators require their chalet hosts to be gourmet cooks with a proven track record for fine dining.

Entertainment representative

Many tour operators employ representatives whose main role is to provide entertainment for guests. This is particularly popular in large resort hotels and all-inclusive destinations. Such staff may have a background in performing arts, and their daily duties could range from hosting a 'Blind Date' competition, to running a bingo session, to performing in a nightly cabaret.

Ski reps pick guests up and drop them off at the airport, sort them out with skis, passes and lessons. You tell them where all the ski-lifts and classes are, as well as recommending restaurants, shops and runs. You also give them a bit of a history of the resort, maps, as well as general and specific information – which runs are good and get the sun in the afternoon, where the nearest bank machine is, etc. You also have to complete fortnightly health and safety checks, liaise regularly with hotels, suppliers of lift passes and skis, and ski schools in order to maintain relationships. You have to organise après-ski events (mountain meal, dog-sledding, ice-skating, off-piste skiing, snowblade-taster days) and supervise the running of all these. You have to account for expenses and refunds, etc., as well as pay hotel bills and basically balance the books. You also have to solve any customer or supplier problems ('we want a bigger room' or 'your guests stole my skis') and give full reports on all activities. You also do snow reports (depth of snow and forecasts, etc.).

Source: www. careerintravel.co.uk

Young adults' representative

Whilst the duties of a young adults' representative may not differ hugely from those of a general resort rep, there has been a large increase in the number of people wishing to specialise in this particular form of repping. It is therefore worth looking at some of the specific responsibilities that the job may entail.

Well, there are different names for it depending on which tour company you work for, but they basically all do the same thing. The major company is Club 18–30 and you may have seen them on TV recently with their fly-on-the-wall documentary. Other companies use names like Clubfreestyle (Thomsons), Escapades (Airtours) and Twenty's (First Choice).

Your role is to make sure that groups of young men and woman have the time of their life. You will be going on bar crawls, organising beach games (involving alcohol), conducting welcome meetings and doing customer transfers. You will also be handling customer queries and complaints and selling the excursions that are on offer. As well as all this, you will be asked to perform in cabarets and maybe do the odd song or two, or even do a striptease!!

Source: www.careerintravel.co.uk

WHAT'S IT LIKE, BEING A REP?

In Topics 5 to 8 we are going to look at the main duties of reps. In preparation for this, complete the table below.

Type of rep	Advantages of job	Disadvantages of job	Main duties
Resort representative			
Transfer representative			
Children's representative			
Villa representative			
Winter sports representative/ Chalet host			
Entertainment representative			
Young adults' representative			

Nathan Millward, Resort Representative JMC (now Thomas Cook), Zante

What made you decide to be a resort rep, Nathan?

After spending two rewarding years on an HND Travel and Tourism course, I could think of no better way to spend the vacant summer months before a one-year degree top-up at University than to gain some valuable industry experience.

And what was the recruitment process like?

I applied to JMC, a tour operator I was already familiar with through their sponsorship of a Resort Representative's Training course I had been on. I submitted my application to work as a member of their resorts' team during the peak summer months.

After what can only be described as something akin to a *Pop Idol* audition, I successfully made my way through the glitzy interview stages and was finally offered a place.

Tell us a bit about the initial training

Sunny Stockport is the first venue for all JMC's summer reps to be, for it is here that you are prepared for the field of battle.

As our destination for the summer hadn't yet been decided, we quickly realised that for the 120 or so of us in Stockport this was an audition masquerading as a training week.

Those yearning for media stardom in the likes of Ayanapa and Ibiza would have to demonstrate their worth as entertainers and showmen, with the pressures of the week building to a last-minute finale when our destinations would be revealed. After being called into a room one by one and presented with our destination envelopes, I quickly learnt that I and several others from the same group were all off to the Greek island of Zante.

Several more training days followed in Zante, with my only piece of advice being not to fall asleep half-way through a health and safety lecture – it's not a good way to start the summer! Then, after four days on the island, I started my first day's work as a fully-fledged hotel representative. My second piece of advice at this point would be to prepare yourself with a set of dry clothes on your first day, as the 'swimming pool initiation' is not optional.

What did the job mainly involve?

Working alongside two other long-term reps in a recently built apartment-style hotel for about 300 guests, you quickly have to get to grips with juggling a full diary of events and responsibilities – whilst being a constant target of abuse from crazed knee-high children and, on occasion, their parents too.

A typical week would involve a good eight hours a day in your hotel, making sure existing guests are OK, welcoming new ones and celebrating the departure of some of the old ones. Evening entertainment for the guests has to be by far the best part of being a rep. Monday night you're a backing dancer to a soul band. Tuesday night you're eating for free on a Greek meal night. Wednesday night you're a waiter-cum-backing dancer-cum-gay gym instructor in a cabaret. Thursday night you're eventually mastering the '*Music Man*' in front of a packed hotel bar, and Friday night you're having one too many, dressed up as an Hawaiian hula girl for the organised bar crawl.

Sales were also a major part of the job, and more importantly of your pay, with targets set not only for the number of optional excursions sold but also for car rentals and hotel entertainment evenings. Sales training is provided, and targets were often flexible, but from my experience, if you are uneasy with the hard sell then you might want to think again about being a holiday rep.

What advice would you give to someone wanting to be a resort representative?

What anyone looking to become a holiday rep should understand is that at no time are you anything other than a source of information, a person to ask for assistance or a target for abuse. Whether in or out of uniform you will always be the person that people will turn to, whether it's down on the beach on your day off, in the supermarket shopping or in one of the bars relaxing. If you thrive on attention, then this is certainly the job to have.

So what are your lasting memories of being a rep?

The summer cocktail of good and not so good times soon drew to a close and it didn't seem long before we were all faced with the prospect of a reluctant return to normality and a rain-soaked Britain. It's hard to sum up the job and experience of being a holiday representative. You have to be up for a good time whatever your mood, you have to balance this with the composure to handle anything that gets thrown your way, and ultimately, you have to accept that it is often your effort and input that makes or breaks the holiday of so many people. Get this right and you will be hard pushed to find a more rewarding or satisfying experience.

Activities carried out at the resort office

In the last two sections we have looked at the range of staff who work in tour operators, resort offices. In this section we are going to explore some of the specific activities carried out in the resort office, including:

How rooming lists are organised and supplied

How excursions are organised

Liaising with local agencies

Transfers to and from the airport

How the resort office deals with extra rooms to allocation

The procedures for dealing with complaints and emergencies

We will start by having a look at the typical working week of a resort representative.

A typical working week for a rep

	Morning	Afternoon	Evening
Monday	9.00–13.00 Accommodation visits/duties	Need to: Complete Financial paperwork Collect airport rota and all necessary paperwork from the resort office Complete welcome cards for arrivals, and hand in to office Chart the arrivals for all arrival, and check room allocations with hotelier	16.30–19.30 Accommodation visits
Tuesday	9.00–13.00 Accommodation visits/duties	13.30–14.00 One-to-one with Supervisor 16.20–20.20 Airport transfer (Departure and Arrival)	22.10–02.10 Airport transfer (Departure and Arrival)
Wednesday	09.00-13.00 Welcome Meetings	14.00–15.00 Team Meeting 15.00–16.00 Liquidation Hand in excursion tickets Collect guiding list for evening	16.30–19.00 Accommodation visits 19.00–00.30 Medieval Night – including coach pick-ups and drop-offs
Thursday	Morning off	13.45–15.00 Airport meeting in resort office Collect airport rota and all necessary paperwork from the resort office Complete welcome cards for arrivals and hand in to office Chart the arrivals and check room allocations with hotelier	16.30–19.30 Accommodation visits 19.30–21.00 Party Night in hotel. PR with guests and join in with entertainment
Friday	04.00–06.00 Airport transfer (Departure and Arrival)	17.35–21.35 Airport transfer (Departure and Arrival)	22.10–02.10 Airport transfer (Departure and Arrival)
Saturday	09.00–13.00 Welcome Meetings	16.30–19.30 Accommodation visits and welcome meetings	21.00–01.30 Guiding Bar Crawl
Sunday	Day off		

source: www.firstchoice.co.uk

---

a c t i v i t y

HOURS PER WEEK

Using the chart, work out how many hours the rep would work in a typical week.

The chart gives a broad outline of the general duties during a typical week in the life of a resort rep – but what is it like in practice? Read the account overleaf, written by a family rep.

The rep's day can start very early when there are guests to collect from the airport.

Good morning (4.30 a.m.)

Your alarm is going off and it's time to get up to go to the airport and meet the new holidaymakers who are staying for one or two weeks. They are due to arrive at 7.00 a.m. You apply your make-up, put on your uniform and make sure your appearance is immaculate. You need to be at the airport at least 1 hour prior to the aircraft arriving. You leave for the airport, arrive and gather all your paperwork for the new people who are about to arrive.

Passenger arrival (7.00 a.m.)

Fifteen minutes to go until they arrive. This will give you time to check your paperwork and familiarise yourself with the passenger list. You check your appearance and get ready for that friendly smile (even at 7.00 a.m.). The passengers are here – they're tired, restless, children crying, and normally confused. You try to gather up the herd and send them off to the right coaches to be dropped off at their hotels. You check to make sure everybody who should be there, is, and then it's time to leave. (Please bear in mind that this should all run smoothly, but rarely does.)

Transfer to the hotels

You are now on board and travelling to their hotels, so it's time for the running commentary of the sights and general information about the island. (This is the speech you have now given about fifty times.) You normally find that at this time of the morning people don't really take any notice of you, so maybe throw in some extra lines about a completely different island, just to amuse yourself.

Customers to their hotels

You arrive at the first hotel and you call out the names on your list and they hopefully correspond with the people on board. They get out, and you show them to the reception area, and then it's back on the coach to go to the next hotel. This process can take up to 3 hours. Once this has been done, it's back to your base, to gather your thoughts for the Welcome Meeting.

Welcome Meeting

You now go back to the main hotel where you will be holding the meeting. You find the manager, and make sure the complimentary drinks are ready and that you have all your paperwork with you. The meeting should last around 45 minutes and should be informative and interesting. You talk about the island, places to go, their hotels and more importantly the excursions that they can go on. Remember you want to encourage people to book as many as you can, because this is where you earn extra money, known as commission. Once these have been booked, you stay a while and see if anybody has any questions, and answer them accordingly.

Back to base

You now go back to base and sort out your paperwork and the bookings that you received from the Welcome Meeting. Administration is an important part of your role as this has to be kept up to date and accurate at all times. You now have time to grab a drink, eat some food and generally unwind. It's 2.00 p.m. and you now have your hotel visits to carry out.

Hotel visits

You arrive at your first hotel and you first go to the notice board and check that all the information and notices are up to date. Now it's time to mingle with the guests and generally be around if anybody needs you. Times can vary between each hotel, depending on how many people need to see you. Then it's back to base and get ready for the evening.

Evening hotel visits

These visits are set, as customers will expect you there at that particular time. Customer enquiries can vary, and you will deal with complaints as well as general enquiries. The complaints are normally about the room that they are staying in – maybe it's too small, it's not what they booked or it's generally not good enough. This needs to be dealt with and rectified as soon as possible (if you can).

This account has been based on a typical day in the life of a holiday representative. In addition, you will have to guide some excursions (both day and night) and you may have to star in the 'reps' show' at least once a week (that's fun).

Now that your day is finished why not go for a drink with your friends or just go straight back and hit the sack – the choice is yours.

How rooming lists are organised and supplied

The rooming list is the record of guests' details and accommodation reservations. Typically it will include the guests' names and accommodation and room numbers. It will also provide details of any specific requests made by a guest such as 'ground floor preferred' or 'adjoining room for children'. Rooming lists are usually sent by the tour operator's Head Office to the resort office two to three weeks in advance. The actual allocation of guests to specific rooms is done by the resort rep or, sometimes, by the accommodation provider such as a hotel. The rooming list is then used by the transfer rep to enable them to direct arriving guests to their allocated accommodation.

Sometimes, reps have to accompany excursions.

How excursions are organised

Whilst some tour operators organise their own excursions, many of the larger companies now use local agencies to provide all of the excursions offered to guests. The process of booking the guests onto an excursion is completed by the resort rep – usually at the initial welcome meeting or during one of their pre-arranged visits to the accommodation. Details of bookings are then faxed to the excursion provider who sends a return fax with details of pick-up points and times. The staff member responsible for escorting the excursion may vary. Often the resort reps will take turns at accompanying excursions and it will form part of their expected responsibilities. In other situations a specific excursion guide will be provided by the agency. This is often the case when the excursion is of a specialist nature such as a historical or cultural tour.

Liaising with local agencies

Local resort offices liaise with a wide range of different local agencies in order to provide guests with the services and products expected. We have already mentioned large independent organisations who provide services such as excursions, rooming allocations and transfers – Barcelo in Spain is a typical

example. Resort reps will also liaise with local companies such as restaurants and bars for the provision of services such as welcome meetings. Most tour operators offer customers the opportunity to pre-book car hire, and the resort rep will be responsible for liaising with the car hire company to ensure that arrangements are met.

Transfers to and from the airport

Large tour operators will employ a supervisor or Airport Controller at all major destination airports. Their role is to oversee the transfer arrangements to and from the airport and liaise with the transfer representatives. The transfer reps will be responsible for meeting the incoming guests, checking their reservation details and directing them to the appropriate transfer transport. This is usually a coach, but sometimes a car might be used or even a ferry for access to smaller islands. It is standard practice for a rep to accompany guests on the transfer journey and deliver them to their accommodation.

How the resort office deals with 'extra rooms to allocation'

'Extra rooms to allocation' refers to a situation where there are insufficient rooms for the number of guests arriving. This may be due to an overbooking or, more commonly, a problem with some of the accommodation that had been reserved. For example, a hotel having to close due to an outbreak of illness or unexpected problem such as flooding. In such

Handling agents

'Handling agent' is the term that tour operators use when referring to an individual or organisation that undertakes some of the responsibilities in the resort on behalf of the tour operator. Other titles that refer to the same function might be ground arrangements, ground operator, ground handling agent or destination management company. The role of the handling agent will vary, but generally includes providing services such as accommodation transfers, car hire and excursions. They will also deal with some problem situations, such as overbooking and reallocation of accommodation. Most large tour operators use the services of a handling agent in resorts. The advantages are that the handling agent will be local and have a network of connections with local providers. In addition, their services relieve much of the pressure that would otherwise fall on the tour operator's resort staff.

situations, the tour operator needs to find additional accommodation for the incoming guests. Most tour operators will rely on an agent in the resort to source the additional rooms. However, it will be the resort representative's role to explain the situation to guests and deal with any dissatisfaction that might arise.

The procedures for dealing with complaints and emergencies

In Unit 2 we looked at the specific skills required when dealing with a complaint – it will be useful if you are familiar with this before considering the following section on complaint handling within resort operations.

One of the challenges of working in resort operations is the vast range of different customer situations that need to be handled. Whilst many of these situations will be pleasant, such as advising guests on the best restaurants in the area, other situations may be less welcome.

It is a fact of any resort rep's life that guests will often be less than satisfied with an aspect (or several aspects) of their holiday and expect the rep to put it right for them. In recent years there has been a growing realisation that the rep plays a central role in identifying and sorting out complaints at the resort rather than allowing the guest to return to the UK and seek compensation for their disappointment. A recent survey by Direct Line found:

'Two in three British travellers will suffer in silence rather than complain about a bad holiday. People resist moaning because of too much hassle or because complaints fall on deaf ears. The main holiday complaints were for travel delays, poor quality accommodation, service from holiday reps, misleading information and poor food.'

activity

WHAT ARE THEY COMPLAINING ABOUT?

As a group, brainstorm a list of complaints that a resort rep might have to handle for guests who have been:

1 Delayed by six hours on an outbound flight that was due to leave at 17.00 hours on Friday.

2 Delayed by nine hours on a return flight that was due to depart at 21.00 hours on a Sunday.

Clearly the more quickly a rep can identify that a guest is unhappy about an aspect of their holiday and do something about it, the less likely the guest is to have a ruined holiday – and later ask for compensation from the tour operator.

One of the most frequent complaints on package holidays is actually totally beyond the control of the resort staff – that of transport delays. However, it is the resort staff that often bear the brunt of the guests' dissatisfaction. The journeys to and from the holiday resort are an essential part of the package. On the way there, guests are excited and want to see what the resort and their accommodation is like. On the return journey, most people are simply eager to get home as quickly as possible – perhaps in time for work the next day. Any prolonged delays can spoil the initial excitement or create problems in getting home later than anticipated.

Of course, not all reasons for guest dissatisfaction arise because of transport delays. Many complaints are generated through disappointment that the holiday does not meet the guest's expectations. Remember that the majority of customers will have probably spent a considerable length of time going through brochures to choose their holiday and paid hundreds (if not thousands) of pounds for the product. Before they arrive they will have built up an image of what they think the holiday is going to be like – and will be very disappointed if any aspect falls short of their expectations. It is interesting that complaints about late availability deals (where the customer does not know any details of the accommodation) actually result in far less complaints than from customers who book well in advance and know all of the details of their package holiday. This may be explained in part by the fact that customers on late availability have not built up an image of what they expect. However, with all types of package holiday customers, typical complaints in the resort include:

- Poor accommodation/facilities
- Inadequate health and safety provision
- Noise and building work
- Promised facilities and services being unavailable
- Out booking to other accommodation.

Each tour operator will have a specific procedure for handling complaints. Inevitably one aspect of the procedure will require the resort rep to complete documentation. Reps working for the tour operator First Choice complete a Customer Service Report Form (CSR) when a guest has a complaint.

CUSTOMER SERVICE REPORT – CSR

No: RV 0034

REPRESENTATIVES' NAME:

Lead Name: REFERENCE: Adult   Child   Infant   Resort

Accommodation name(s)   Arrival date: Accommodation type: Twin/Apartment/Villa

Room number: Board basis: Bed & Breakfast/Half Board/Full Board/Self-Catering/All Inclusive

DETAILS IF INCIDENT
Date incident was reported: _____

ACTION TAKEN

I believe that the facts stated by me in this report are true.

Representative's name: **Signature:**
(BLOCK CAPITALS)
                Date:

This report is for internal use only. If a claim is to be pursued it must be made in writing to the Customer Relations Department in the UK. Please include your full name, address and holiday booking reference on all correspondence.

Guest's name: **Signature:**
(BLOCK CAPITALS)
                Date:

Source: Based on First Choice Overseas Representatives Handbook.

This form outlines three main areas – what the complaint was about, what action was taken, and the outcome. The guest is given the top copy of the CSR and the bottom copy is retained in the resort office. If the action taken by the rep includes giving the guest some financial compensation (for example a refund for a welcome food pack that was not provided) a further form known as Compensation in Resort form (CIR) also has to be completed.

Another aspect of most resort staff's role is dealing with emergency situations such as illness, accidents, crime or hazardous situations such as severe weather conditions. These situations are covered in detail in Unit 5 Travelling Safely.

activity

TWO PROCEDURES EXPLAINED

Design a page for a resort rep's staff handbook that explains the procedure for two of the following activities:

- How rooming lists are organised and supplied
- How excursions are organised
- Liaising with local agencies
- How transport is arranged for transfers to and from the airport
- How the resort office deals with extra rooms to allocation
- The procedures for dealing with complaints and emergencies.

253

Topic 3 Activities carried out at the resort office

Links with the UK office

The provision of a package holiday is a complex process stretching from the initial enquiry and booking through to the customer experiencing the holiday. Whilst the organisation of resort operations is a key feature of this process it does not constitute the whole process. Staff within the resort are continually reliant on and in contact with the UK Head Office to ensure that the whole process operates efficiently. Before the resort staff even take up their positions, their Head Office will have already completed a large proportion of the organisation necessary in providing the package holiday. This will have included negotiating transport and accommodation, developing excursion packages, marketing and, of course, taking customer bookings.

In this topic we are going to look at some of the ways in which head office deal with their internal customers – in other words the staff within the resorts. In particular we will look at:

- Notification of customer details
- Accounts and reports
- Customer satisfaction
- Dealing with emergencies
- Up-dates such as building works.

Notification of customer details

The process of booking a customer on to a package holiday is co-ordinated through the UK head office. All details of bookings then need to be relayed to the staff in the resort so that they know who they are expecting and what individual requirements are. Details will include:

- Names of all customers in the group (and ages if under 18 years)
- Flight times
- Accommodation details
- Any extras that have been booked (such as taxi transfer from airport, car hire, welcome pack in accommodation, excursions, etc.)
- Any individual requirements or specific needs (such as wheelchair access).

Whilst head office will make every effort to ensure that the correct information is relayed to resort staff, problems sometimes arise due to insufficient or inaccurate information. This complaint letter (opposite) to a UK tour operator shows the sort of problems that can arise when information is inaccurate.

Accounts and reports

There are some obvious concerns in the fact that whilst head office arranges a customer's holiday, it is the resort staff (thousands of miles away) who actually coordinate the guest's holiday experience. In order to streamline this process, tour operators use a variety of reporting procedures to ensure that there is continuous liaison between head office and their resort staff. A wide range of documentation is used to

Dear Sir,

We have just returned from a two-week holiday to Florida with your company and I have to say that we were less than impressed with the organisation at this end. When we booked, we stressed that we had two small children and therefore needed connecting or adjoining rooms in the hotel. We were assured that this was no problem. On arrival we found that, not only were our rooms not together, they were in fact on separate floors of the hotel. We expressed our dissatisfaction to our rep, who was sympathetic, but said that she had us down as 4 adults so did not know that we wanted to be together. As the hotel was fully booked, it was five days before they could move us to adjoining rooms – which meant that my husband and I had to each sleep with one of our children to ensure that they were safe. Since you must deal mainly with families on this type of holiday, I cannot understand how your communication with your representatives can be so poor. It totally spoilt the first part of our holiday and I would hope that you will consider some sort of compensation.

Yours faithfully,

Fay Longley

achieve this, which includes:

- Representative's report forms (summarising weekly activities, concerns and problems)
- Excursions accounts and reports
- Currency-exchange accounts.

We will look at documentation in detail in Topic 7.

Customer satisfaction

Most tour operators ask their guests to complete a customer satisfaction questionnaire at the end of their holiday. Sometimes this will be issued on the flight home, but it is more usual for the resort rep to hand out the questionnaires at the accommodation or on the return transfer to the airport. Questionnaires will be collected by the rep and returned to head office, where the results are collated. Many companies summarise the results of these questionnaires and use them in their next year's brochures to indicate the level of satisfaction of previous guests.

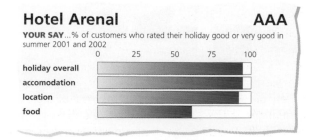

Of course, this use of feedback only focuses on general levels of customer satisfaction. If a tour operator were to receive a number of returned questionnaires that indicated that there was a serious problem within a resort they would act immediately.

Dealing with emergencies

As we discuss throughout this unit, one of the benefits (and possible drawbacks) of working in resort operations is that every guest is different, has specific needs and will expect staff to meet their needs – in essence, no two guests or situations are the same. Frequently, situations will arise that are emergencies – in other words, they need to be dealt with quickly and efficiently. Typical examples include medical emergencies, theft or damage to property, and transport delays. Communication with head office is vital in these situations for a number of reasons, including getting information and advice where needed and ensuring that head office is fully aware of what is going on.

In the most serious situations, such as a guest being taken seriously ill (or perhaps dying whilst on holiday) there are a range of people who need to be involved and informed. In this instance, head office will usually coordinate the communications between all parties whilst working with resort staff and keeping them informed. Actions to be taken may include:

- Liaising with insurance companies to arrange medical treatment and/or transport back to the UK
- Notifying next of kin
- Arranging onward medical treatment in the UK on the guest's return
- Making arrangements for the guest's holiday companions to stay in the resort, if necessary.

In less dramatic situations, such as theft or damaged property, the resort staff may deal with the problem but notify head office of the circumstances and outcome. There will normally be standardised reporting forms that need to be completed and returned to enable guests to make an insurance claim.

Transport disruptions are a constant problem for both head office and resort staff, and result in huge numbers of complaints from customers. At the lesser end of the scale are the delays of several hours that many of us experience when taking a package holiday. Unfortunately, this tends to be part of a standard week's work for most resort staff – and they deal with it by keeping guests informed and perhaps providing vouchers for refreshments if the delay is extended.

REPS NOT WORKING?

'Exclusively Yours' holidays have recently started offering luxury all-inclusive holidays in the Maldives. Communications from their representatives in the resort have not indicated any serious problems. However, the company have just received the first batch of returned customer questionnaires that they mail out to guests once they are home. The following comments appear frequently as responses:

> Organised excursions were appalling – reps had little knowledge of the area.

> Couldn't find our rep when we needed her – she was never in the hotel when she said she would be.

> Lots of problems with the hotel, but the rep just said she couldn't do anything about it – everyone was complaining.

As a group, discuss what action you think head office would take in this situation, and how they would deal with the resort staff.

At the more serious end of the scale are transport delays that can run into several days, due to factors such as strike action by transport workers in the host country.

Up-dates such as building works

Another key area of liaison between a tour operator's head office and the resort office is where there is any potential disruption to the resort or accommodation. One of the main issues is with building work – a particular problem in developing resorts where new accommodation and facilities may be in the process of being built to meet increasing demand from customers. Resort staff will be responsible for notifying their head office of any such work, and the level of disruption that is caused. If there is severe disruption, head office may need to notify customers booked to go to the resort about the situation, and possibly offer alternative accommodation or destinations.

Resort reps with First Choice are required to complete a Building Report Form on a monthly basis, rating the building work on a scale of 1–10 based on factors such as noise, pollution and times of disruption.

Nobody wants to spend their holiday living on a building site.

UNHAPPY AT THE AIRPORT

Imagine that you are working as a resort rep at peak season, with a full plane-load of guests arriving as another group departs. The arriving guests land just as the air-traffic controllers announce a three-day strike. Last week's guests have checked out of their hotel and are now at the airport. The arriving guests are booked into their rooms and every accommodation in the resort is fully booked. And now a number of the departing guests are voicing the following concerns:

- 'I've got an important business meeting tomorrow. I must be back in the UK for it.'

- 'I'm diabetic and only have sufficient insulin for another two days.'

- 'I'll lose three days salary if I'm late back – will you compensate me?'

- 'We've booked a taxi to collect us from the airport and will have to pay for it even if we're not there.'

- 'I suffer from a bad back and need to sleep in a proper bed – I can't stay at the airport.'

- 'My 6-month-old baby only drinks formula Soya milk, but I only have enough for the next 18 hours.'

- 'My father is picking us up from the airport and won't know that we are going to be late.'

As a group, discuss the ways in which you think your UK head office could support you in this situation.

BUILDING WORKS INFORMATION REPORT

This report should be sent to the Building Programme Department in the UK. Please include an Assessment Sheet, Location Map and any relevant photographs. A copy of this report should also be sent to the supplier.

Resort:	Accommodation name:		Accommodation numbers:
Featured in the following brochures:			
Work undertaken by:	Date:		Progress report due:
Authorised by:	Signature:		
See page 2 for a full description of works.			
When did work start?	What departure date should be advised?		
If work has already started, why was advance warning not given?			
Confirmed date of completion of works by supplier:	Completion date in your estimate:		
On which days will work be taking place?	Between what times will work be taking place?		
Where is the work taking place? (Give exact location.)			
Are any areas unavailable due to works taking place?			
Can works be seen from any or all of the guest areas?	What route do contractor's use to access the works?		
Description of site (e.g. dangerous/high risk/ low risk):			
Are the works fenced off?	What equipment is in use on site?		
How noisy are the works?	How dirty are the works?		
Is the proprietor responsible for the works? If not state who is. (see note 1 below)			
What level of compensation is being offered?	Are rooms being allocated away from work?		
Complaints (please list any received):	Names of other UK operators using this resort/location:		
Should guests be informed prior to arrival?	Should guest be reallocated elsewhere?		
Note 1. If hotelier is responsible for works, please advise them they will be liable for any compensation paid or costs incurred due to the work.			

Source: Based on First Choice Overseas Representatives Handbook.

The welcome meeting

In previous topics we have referred to the 'welcome meeting' that many holiday reps conduct for their guests. This meeting takes place soon after guests' arrival at a resort and is an important part of a resort rep's duties. In this topic we are going to look at the welcome meeting in detail with a particular focus on:

- **The purpose of the welcome meeting**
- **Structuring and organising a welcome meeting**
- **The content of the welcome meeting**
- **Producing materials for the welcome meeting.**

The purpose of the welcome meeting

There are a range of reasons for holding a welcome meeting. First, as its name suggests, it provides an opportunity to welcome the guests to the resort as well as allowing them to meet and get to know their designated holiday rep.

Remember that most guests will be excited about their holiday, but perhaps a little apprehensive – what if they don't like the resort, the hotel is poor, or they're nervous about finding their way around? Many guests will have saved hard all year to be able to afford their holiday and they may be anxious that it lives up to their expectations. The welcome meeting

can help to reassure guests that they will have a great holiday. However, sometimes guests will arrive at the meeting having already experienced some disappointment with aspects of their holiday. For example, perhaps they are unhappy with their room allocation, or promised facilities such as a pool are unavailable or the Children's Club is fully booked. The meeting gives the resort rep the opportunity to resolve these problems promptly, so that they do not spoil the rest of the guests' stay.

Two further reasons for holding a welcome meeting include giving information and selling excursions. We will look at each of these, but first have a go at the following activity:

activity

WHAT A WELCOME!

You are a rep in the resort of Puerto Pollensa, Majorca, and are holding the welcome meeting for a group of 25 guests who arrived in the early hours of this morning. The airport transfer rep has told you that the guests' flight from Manchester was delayed by eight hours and many of them were angry about the delay when they arrived, having lost an evening of their holiday. In addition, despite it being July, the island is experiencing some unseasonable weather – heavy rain that is forecast to continue for the next 36 hours. When you arrive at the meeting at 10.30 a.m. you are met by a sea of tired and fed-up guests. What would be your opening lines to your guests?

Structuring and organising a meeting

We have already discussed the importance to the rep of meeting all of their new guests at the welcome meeting – it serves as an introduction, identifies any potential problems and allows information and excursions to be explained. Therefore, the rep needs to ensure that the meeting is well planned to encourage the guests to attend. This involves considering:

- Notification of the meeting
- Date and timing
- Location.

Notification of the meeting

Most holidaymakers are notified of the arrangements for their welcome meeting by the transfer rep on the journey to their accommodation – on the coach from the airport, for example. However, not all guests use the transfer transport. They may have collected a rental car from the airport or taken the option that many tour operators now offer of a private taxi transfer. In this situation it is usual to leave a message for the guests in their accommodation, informing them of the arrangements.

Date and timing

To be effective and useful to the holidaymaker, the welcome meeting needs to be as close to the time of their arrival as possible – there would be little point in telling them about the resort when they had already been there for three days! Ideally the meeting will take place on the day of arrival. However, when guests arrive on a night flight the meeting will be arranged for the following day – although not at 8.00 a.m. if the rep expects them to attend.

Location

The location of the welcome meeting varies according to the number and type of holidaymakers. Where a large number of guests are staying at the same accommodation the meeting will usually take place in one of the public areas of the accommodation such as a bar or reception area. If guests are more widespread in smaller accommodation units they may be asked to meet at a central accommodation. Increasingly, some tour operators are not using their own accommodation but choosing to hold welcome meetings in a local bar or restaurant. This is particularly popular when guests are staying in self-catering accommodation. Regardless of where the meeting is to be held, the rep will need to ensure that everything is confirmed beforehand. This will include confirming that the room is available at the appropriate time, ensuring that staff are aware of the meeting and on-hand to direct guests to the location, and providing any refreshments that are included, such as glasses of wine and soft drinks. In addition, the rep will need to make sure that they have all of the necessary information and handouts with them, including a full list of their guests' details, as well as documentation for booking excursions and handling payments.

activity

WHAT NEEDS TO BE DONE?

Write a checklist for a resort rep of the key stages that they need to go through when arranging a welcome meeting.

In this topic we are exploring the main issues involved in arranging and running a welcome meeting. There is of course a further, very important, consideration – that of customer-service skills. It does not matter how well the welcome meeting is organised, a large part of its success will lie in the effectiveness of the rep's ability to communicate, meet the needs of individual customers, present themselves appropriately, and deal with any complaints or problems. Customer service is examined in detail in Unit 2.

The content of the welcome meeting

The content of welcome meetings tends to follow a similar format with most tour operators. The key sections are:

- Introduction and welcome
- Address of health and safety
- Information provided about the property and destination
- Selling of excursions
- Advice on local amenities.

Introduction and welcome

The introductory section will typically include a welcome and thank you to guests for attending, followed by the rep introducing themselves and their company. Clearly first impressions are important, so it is crucial that the rep gets the introduction right or their guest will simply 'switch off'.

activity

GETTING A GOOD START

Have a go at writing the introduction to a welcome meeting by filling in the blanks in this passage:

'Good morning, and welcome to .... on behalf of .... First let me thank you for taking the time to attend this meeting. I am sure that you will find it .... My name is .... and my role is to...,

Address of health and safety

Providing guests with advice on health and safety issues is an important part of a rep's role, and ensures that their guests have a pleasant and problem-free holiday. Issues that may be covered include:

- Use of pools and swimming in the sea – for example supervising young children and observing flags warning that bathing is unsafe
- Use of accommodation lifts – particularly when supervising young children
- Drinking local tap water – this is rarely dangerous in Europe but sometimes inadvisable because the high mineral content can cause stomach upsets
- Sunbathing – how to avoid sunburn/sunstroke and what to do in the event of either
- Medical emergencies – procedures for dealing with illness or accidents
- Hiring mopeds – many companies advise against this due to poor safety standards and, in fact, travel insurance may not cover accidents on mopeds
- Security of money and belongings – advice on hotel safe deposit boxes and guarding against petty crime such as pickpockets.

The secret to providing good health and safety advice to guests is to provide sufficient information to ensure that they have a healthy and safe holiday – without appearing so negative that they begin to wonder why they came here, if it is so dangerous!

activity

YOU CAN DO BETTER THAN THIS

Read this health and safety advice given by Natalie, a resort rep, and re-write it so that it appears more positive:

'Right then, health and safety – a really important subject, and one that you all need to listen to carefully. The sea on this side of the island has a strong undercurrent that can sweep weak swimmers out to sea. In fact last year three tourists were drowned in the resort. On no account go into the sea if you see a red flag flying. Your hotel is well appointed but unfortunately it has old-style lifts, with sliding-grille doors. Make sure that you accompany your children at all times in the lifts if you want to avoid them losing a couple of fingers. Finally, this area is rife with pickpockets, and many guests have had their holiday ruined when their money has been stolen – so make sure that you watch your belongings at all times.'

Information provided about the property and destination

Most guests will be interested to hear something about the resort and accommodation – but not want a long-winded speech! Reps will often provide handouts of information (such as local maps) to ensure that this section does not become too detailed.

a c t i v i t y

WHAT IS IT LIKE HERE?

Read the extract below from the Thomson Holidays website on the resort of Sorrento, Italy and the Conca Park Hotel. Then write what you would say in your welcome speech to guests about the resort and hotel. Deliver your speech to other members of your group.

Selling of excursions

Advising guests on suitable excursions is a key element of the welcome meeting.

The welcome meeting is the occasion when the rep sells most of their excursions to guests. A large proportion of a rep's earnings come from the commission that they earn on excursions. This means that a rep is clearly going to be eager to encourage guests to book excursions. However, many guests are

Selling excursions increases a rep's earnings.

sceptical about this aspect of the welcome meeting – and, in fact, may view the meeting as an excuse for a sales pitch. Therefore a fine balance has to be achieved by the rep – by explaining excursions in a way that appeals to guests without appearing too eager to persuade them to buy.

The Neapolitan Riviera

Sorrento is a maze of tiny alleys full of piazzas, excellent shops and restaurants, where steep cobbled lanes lead to small pebbled beaches or bathing platforms, and stunning cliff-top views are commonplace.
Heading east, there's historic Amalfi, where the cathedral perches above the piazza, pretty Positano with its maze of near-vertical alleys, and little Maiori with a volcanic sand beach.
The nearby island of Ischia is famous in Italy as 'the green island', because of its luxuriant forests of citrus groves and vineyards. Its hidden beauty lies in its hot springs.

Beaches

The coastline is dotted with tiny pebbled beaches or bathing platforms. The best beach – a dark, pebbly, volcanic sand beach – can be found in Maiori. The area's beaches are crowded in July and August.

Nightlife

Sorrento has many restaurants and bars, and is especially charming in the evenings when you can stroll around the tree-lined streets and do as the Italians do: linger over a meal and a glass of local wine as the sun sets.

Neapolitan food is particularly good, with plenty of fresh seafood, but if you prefer pasta and pizzas, you won't be disappointed – the pizza originated in this region and they are renowned for being the best in the world!

The Conca Park Hotel

Good for families and couples looking for a relaxed holiday in a central location, this busy, recently refurbished hotel is conveniently located, hugging the cliffs near Sorrento's lively centre. The large sun terrace is an attractive place to relax. The atmospheric alleyways and piazzas of Sorrento, with its beautiful views over to the Bay of Naples, are all within easy reach.

Location • 1km to nearest shingle beach (local charge) • 500m to the resort centre • 500m to Piazza Tasso • Due to the hillside location this hotel is not suitable for the less mobile.

For Families • Children's pool • Small garden area • Cots available • Free highchairs.

GETTING THE BALANCE RIGHT

Natalie (the somewhat ineffective rep from the earlier activity) has now turned her attentions to selling excursions. Read her attempt below, and re-write it in a more appropriate style:

'Here at Sunburst Holidays we've got some great excursions for you. Don't be tempted to book your excursions at one of the local agents just because they're cheaper – remember you get what you pay for! One of our best trips is to Barcelona for the day – just £35 per person and half-price for children. Pick-up by air-conditioned coach at 8.00 a.m. and straight to the city where you get a guided tour and then free time to explore. On the way back we stop at a winery that produces Spanish sparkling wine. Of course they'll try to sell you crates of the stuff, but you get a free sample as well. I strongly advise you to book this today as it gets full very quickly and we don't want you to be disappointed. You can pay with cash, traveller's cheques or credit card.'

Advice on local amenities

Apart from receiving information on the accommodation and destination, most holidaymakers will be keen to know about local amenities. Such information might include:

- Public transport
- Local festivals
- Entertainments (theatres, nightclubs, etc.)
- Restaurants and bars
- Visitor attractions
- Public services such as doctors, dentists, etc.

More detailed information on specific amenities is usually given on a one-to-one basis at the end of the welcome meeting.

Producing materials for the welcome meeting

Whilst much of the welcome meeting involves the holiday rep talking to their guests, there will also be a range of materials available for the guests to take with them. These might include:

- Invites to special events
- Information booklets – often the rep will keep an information folder at each accommodation for the guests to read through
- Maps
- Booking forms for excursions.

At the end of the formal part of the welcome meeting a rep will thank guests for attending and explain how they can contact the rep during their holiday. This will usually involve informing them of when and where the rep will be holding their daily meetings and the location of the tour operator's noticeboard.

RUN YOUR OWN MEETING

Part of the assessment for this unit requires you to arrange and run a welcome meeting. Imagine that you are a single-property resort rep at the Hotel Papagayo Arena Resort Hotel in Playa Blanca, Lanzarote. Using the information opposite, plan and carry out a welcome meeting for a group of guests who have just arrived at the hotel. You will need to find out some details about the resort of Playa Blanca, and possible excursions in the area, to include in your meeting. Such information can be found in holiday brochures or on the internet. The meeting should include the following sections:

- Introduction and welcome
- Address of health and safety
- Information provided about the property and destination
- Selling of excursions
- Advice on local amenities.

Your meeting should include some printed materials that are suitable to be handed out to guests.

Hotel Papagayo Arena Resort

●●●●

Playa Blanca

The Papagayo Arena Hotel is located on the beachfront at the Southern end of Playa Blanca. It offers modern accommodation in a great location that enjoys views far out to the sea, Fuerteventura and Los Lobos.

Location On the coarse sand beachfront; 2.5km to Playa Blanca resort centre

Features Three swimming pools; sun terrace and sun loungers; Five restaurants including Pizzeria, Grill; Oriental, International buffet and French à la carte (at a supplement, reservations required) restaurant; Six bars; 24hr reception

Activities See All Inclusive Features for free activities and entertainment: Tennis court; Disco; Saunas; Turkish Bath; Massage; Bicycle Hire; Evening entertainment programme

For Children Two pools; Kids' club (4-12 years); highchairs and cots available

Rooms have up to 4 beds, air conditioning, satellite TV, direct-dial telephone, hairdryer, bathroom and balcony or terrace. Prices are based on 2 adults sharing on **All Inclusive**. A limited number of twin rooms for sole use and junior suites (on request) are available at a supplement.

Child prices: age limit 12

488 rooms.
Official rating: 4 star (applied for)

Offers & Options
- Honeymooners and guests celebrating wedding anniversaries will receive complimentary bottle of wine and flowers on arrival
- Pre-bookable late checkout until 6pm available £28 per room
- Pre-bookable sparkling wine available £8
- Pre-bookable flowers available £19
- Pre-bookable champagne available £30

All inclusive features

Food
Buffet-style breakfast, lunch and dinner. Snacks are available throughout the day until late (excluding meal times).

Drinks
An unlimited amount of soft and alcoholic drinks (excluding international brands) from 10am to midnight

Sports & Leisure
Organised activities, aerobics, aquaerobics, basketball, darts, gym, French bowls, mini golf, table tennis, tennis, whirlpool and volleyball

Entertainment
Daily activities and evening entertainment

NB - All Inclusive features are based upon what the hotel plans to offer once open. All services are therefore provisional and subject to change

Please see 'All You Need To Know' (pgs 506-530) for more details

HOLIDAY HIGHLIGHTS

Partners in Excellence
Highly Commended Award 2003

FREE kids, subject to availability

Hotel run kids club (4-12 years)

4 bedded rooms available

Beach front location

Wide range of activities on site

Daily daytime activities and evening entertainment

Please see 'All You Need To Know' (pgs 506-530) for more details

Source: Thomas Cook brochure

Selling products and services

Selling products and services to guests is an important part of the holiday representative's role. Not only does this aspect of the job help to satisfy customers' needs and expectations but also provides much of the rep's income in terms of the commission that they earn. In this topic we are going to look at:

- The products and services sold
- Selling during accommodation visits
- Effective selling skills.

The products and services sold

The 'welcome meeting' provides one of the main opportunities for a resort rep to sell products and services – and, in fact, 50–70% of excursion bookings are taken at the meeting. This may be for a number of reasons:

- The rep has the opportunity to fully explain the different products sold and answer any questions.

- The holidaymaker has just arrived and is eager to arrange some excursions to ensure that they have something arranged for later in their holiday.

- It is often easier for the holidaymaker to plan and book all of their excursions at one time so that they can budget effectively for them.

- The holidaymaker has not yet had the time to explore the area and, possibly, find cheaper deals with local providers.

The range of excursions offered will depend on the type of holiday and customer. Excursions might be categorised according to duration, theme, or what is included.

Duration

Whilst the majority of excursions tend to be either half-day or one-day in duration, many tour operators are offering longer excursions that include staying overnight for one or more nights. For example, holidaymakers in Tunisia can go on two-day or three-day visits to the Sahara Desert, stopping off at historical attractions on the journey.

Theme

The theme of any excursion will depend largely on the facilities and attractions in a resort as well as the interests of the particular holidaymakers. Themes might include.

- Local familiarisation – such as visits to the local town or surrounding countryside

- Historical or cultural visits – to castles, museums, archaeological sites, etc.

- Social events – such as barbecues or themed evenings based on local culture

Historical and cultural excursions often include a specialist tour guide.

- Sporting activities – such as diving, waterparks, horse riding, etc.
- Shopping trips
- Specialist themes – for example wine tasting, art lectures, etc.

What's included

The cost of excursions will depend largely on what is included in the excursion. At the cheapest end of the range it may simply include transport – for example a familiarisation trip to a local town. More expensive excursions may include overnight accommodation and meals as well as entertainment. Some common inclusions in an excursion are:

- Transport. This may be by coach, ferry or private car. With some excursions the transport may be the main part of the trip, such as with boat trips or jeep safaris.
- Meals/entertainment. Where trips involve a full day or longer, specified meals may be included in the excursion. In addition there may be some form of entertainment. In fact some of the most popular excursions in the mass package holiday market are those that focus on a meal with entertainment, such as a Greek Night with typical Greek food and dancing.
- Entrance charges. Where excursions are to historical or tourist attractions the cost of the trip

Greek Night – with 'typical' Greek dancing

will usually include the entrance fee. Typical examples include trips to theme parks or water parks, museums and art galleries, castles and ruins.

- Tour guide. Historical and cultural excursions will frequently include the services of a specialist tour guide who is able to explain historical information in detail.
- Activities/tuition. Some excursions may focus on particular activities and include the cost of such activities in the charge. Activities such as snorkelling and sailing are particularly popular, and usually include the hire of all equipment, and possibly tuition.

Excursions are not the only product or service to be sold by overseas representatives. Most will also be able to provide car hire and tickets for a range of attractions and events. In addition, the majority of resort offices offer currency exchange facilities.

Selling during accommodation visits

Whilst the majority of products and services are usually sold at the welcome meeting, the rep has further opportunities during accommodation visits.

PLANNING EXCURSIONS

Research the destination of Sorrento in Italy. In pairs, suggest one possible excursion for holidaymakers that fit each of the following criteria:

1 A half-day familiarisation excursion
2 An evening social event
3 A two-day cultural trip
4 A one-day boat trip
5 A one-day historical excursion that visits two main destinations and includes lunch.

The advantage of selling in this situation is that the rep can deal with holidaymakers on a one-to-one basis and accurately identify their needs and therefore make appropriate recommendations. It should, of course, also be remembered that many customers do not actually go to the welcome meeting so may be unaware of what is offered.

Effective selling skills

To sell effectively, the holiday rep must first fully understand the product or service that they are recommending, and be confident that it will meet or exceed the customer's needs and expectations. Clearly this requires the rep to be completely familiar with the products or services that the organisation offers. There are a number of selling skills used by holiday reps, which include:

• Raising customer awareness
• Establishing rapport with the customer
• Investigating customer needs
• Presenting the product or service
• Closing the sale
• Delivering after-sales service.

Raising customer awareness

Frequently customers do not buy particular products and services from a tour operator simply because they are not aware that they exist. Therefore, one of the key selling skills that a resort rep needs to acquire is the ability to raise customers' awareness by highlighting products and services that they think might satisfy the customers' needs and expectations. For example, a package holiday customer may be new to the resort or country and have little idea about the

range of activities and attractions that are available. The initial part of the selling process is, therefore, to tell the customers what is available so that they can make an informed choice as to what will suit them.

Establishing rapport with the customer

'Establishing rapport' with the customer means to encourage a conversation in which you are both communicating at the same level. This requires good judgement for, while no customer likes to be ignored, people do not like to feel that they are being pressured or rushed by over-enthusiastic sales staff. In fact many package holiday customers complain that they felt pressured to buy excursions from the resort rep. Initial rapport is usually established by the resort rep at the welcome meeting and continued during property visits.

Investigating customer needs

Initially, the easiest way of identifying customer needs is to ask 'How can I help you?' The reply will indicate what further questions need to be asked to establish the customer's specific needs. For example, a holidaymaker may say that they are interested in culture, sporting activities, something suitable for the whole family, etc. This allows the rep to ask additional questions about what they have done and enjoyed in the past so that the rep has a good understanding of the types of products that might be suitable for them.

WHAT ARE YOU LOOKING FOR?

In pairs, play the role of a package holiday customer in Tenerife and a resort rep. Before the activity, the customer should write down the type of excursion that they would like to go on. The resort rep should try to identify exactly what type of excursion their customer is looking for by using no more that five questions.

Presenting the product or service

In any selling situation the member of staff and the customer will discuss and hopefully agree what products or services can meet the customer's needs. A resort representative needs to be able to present the product or service to the customer in a way that satisfies the customer's needs. This process usually involves considering the available options and possibly suggesting compromises. For example, a package holiday customer may want to hire an open-top jeep but find that it is outside their budget. The rep may suggest a less expensive type of car – or hiring the jeep for a shorter length of time. The customer will often expect to see examples of the product or service that they are considering buying. For example, holiday reps will usually have photographs of the various excursion destinations.

Closing the sale

'Closing the sale' means actually getting the customer to buy the selected product. Not all sales can be closed straight away. Often the customer may want to go away and think about it or discuss it with someone else. In these circumstances, it is frequently acceptable to suggest that the rep contacts the customer later to find out their decision.

Delivering after-sales service

Good customer service and selling skills does not end when the customer hands over his or her money. The service should continue after the sale has been made to show that the member of staff really cares about the customer.

Sometimes the after-sales service will be immediate, such as asking customers if they have enjoyed their excursion and listening to the comments that they make. In other situations, there may be a need for further service. For example, if a customer has not been satisfied with a particular product, the rep will

SELLING PRACTICE

For this activity you are going to practise selling skills at a welcome meeting. Read the description of the following three excursions offered by Thomas Cook Holidays in Australia. Take turns at describing each excursion to customers at a welcome meeting.

Coffs Harbour – Travel to Crescent Head for picturesque surf beaches followed by a drive to Nambucca Heads where you can paint your own personal postcard on the rocks along V-Wall. Continue into Coffs Harbour for whitewater rafting, scuba diving, 4-wheel drive safaris or bushwalking.

Hunter Valley – Visit some wineries and enjoy the scenery whilst making your way to the coastal town of Port Stephens. Spend the afternoon exploring this small seaside village, go fishing, laze on the beach or take a cruise to see the dolphins.

Katoomba – Travel via Blackheath with its interesting shops and historic buildings before continuing to the world-renowned Jenolan Caves for a guided tour. Continue on to Lithgow then via the scenic Bell's Line of Road through eucalypti forests and apple orchards.

have to resolve the situation and possibly give the customer a refund or offer an alternative product.

You need to understand that selling is an important part of a holiday representative's job because it helps to ensure that customer needs and expectations are met. However, it is equally important to understand that gaining an actual sale is never the only objective in a selling situation. Pressuring a customer to buy a product or service that they do not really want may result in a short-term gain, but the end result is almost certainly a dissatisfied customer – who will probably not return.

In the last topic we looked at the role of selling. The process of selling to package holiday customers also includes the completion of a range of documentation. In this topic we are going to look at some of the more common documentation used, under the following headings:

- Overview of documentation used
- Receipts
- Liquidation reports
- Excursion booking forms
- Car hire booking forms.

Overview of documentation used

We have already discussed a number of the different forms used by the holiday rep but it is useful at this stage to summarise the main documentation used and its purpose. The box oppoisite shows the range of documentation used by First Choice Holidays, with their guidance for their reps. (We will look at examples of some of these forms in the next topic when exploring how the holiday rep deals with some common problem situations.)

1	**Customer service report form (CSR)**	Used to record details of a customer's complaint and what action was taken. One form can be used for an individual customer or relating to a situation affecting a number of customers. Can also be used for situations such as strikes, power cuts, etc. that have not resulted in direct complaints but may do so in the future.
2	**Compensation in resort form (CIR)**	Completed when the rep or a supplier has given a customer a refund or compensation. This can only be used by the rep for small amounts of compensation. For example refunding the charge of a grocery pack in accommodation, where the pack was not provided.
3	**Customer service journal**	This is an internal form used by the rep to record ongoing details of complaints and problem situations.
4	**Accident, illness report form (AIR)**	Used to report any accident or illness suffered by a customer that could be related in any way to the products and services offered by the holiday company or its suppliers.
5	**Emergency medical first call form**	This form is completed if a customer is receiving medical treatment, is hospitalised or has died and wants to call on their Assistance Company (i.e. medical insurance company) to guarantee the payment of costs.
6	**Repatriation request form**	Used when a customer requests to return early to the UK and needs their Assistance Company to cover the cost. Only used in emergencies such as the serious illness of a relative at home.
7	**To whom it may concern form**	Used to record the details when a customer reports the loss or damage of personal belongings.
8	**Accommodation switch form**	This form is used when a customer decides to change or upgrade their accommodation for reasons that are not the fault of the holiday company. The form is used to calculate any additional charges that the switch might have incurred.
9	**Trades Description Act form (TDA)**	Used to record details of any situation where the brochure description of the accommodation or resort does not match the reality.
10	**Building work report form**	Used by the rep to record details of any building work that occurs in or around the guests' accommodation. The form is completed as soon as the rep is notified of any such building work.

Receipts

A receipt is a written record of any financial transaction that takes place between the holiday company and the customer. As a representative of the holiday company, the holiday rep will be required to complete receipts on a regular basis for excursions, car hire, currency exchange and compensation payments. Most receipt procedures are in 'triplicate' –

that is, there are three copies. The guest will receive the top (first) copy as proof of their purchase. They will be required to show the receipt when claiming the product or service that they have purchased, for example when commencing an excursion. The second copy is usually for the supplier (excursion provider or a car hire company, for example) to notify them that the product or service has been purchased. The final copy remains with the holiday rep

activity

WHICH FORM?

Look at the following situations and decide which forms the holiday rep should complete:

1 Guest has an accident in their accommodation and is treated at a local clinic.

2 The guest's luggage is damaged during transfer from the airport.

3 Guest wants to return home due to a major fire in their house.

4 Guest complains that the promised Children's Club is closed at their hotel.

5 Guest complains about the poor standard of food in the hotel restaurant.

6 Guest has a heart attack and is hospitalised.

7 Hotel manager tells the rep that the hotel's water supply will be cut off for 18 hours due to a local plumbing problem.

8 Guest does not like their bedroom and wants to upgrade to a larger room with sea view.

9 A number of guests at one hotel are suffering from sickness and diarrhoea.

activity

TAKING AN EXCURSION BOOKING

Using a mocked-up blank excursion booking form, take turns at role playing a guest and a holiday rep. As the holiday rep, complete an excursion booking form for the following customers for a trip to a local Water Park. The cost is £23.50 for adults and £15.75 for children aged 3–14 years. Under-3-year-olds are free.

1 Miss James and Miss Carmichael, both adults, staying at the Villa Nova apartments.

2 Mr and Mrs Soames and their three children aged 2, 6 and 15 years, staying at the Hotel Continental.

Liquidation reports

Liquidation reports are maintained on a regular basis (usually weekly) by the holiday rep, and are a breakdown of the financial details of all sold excursions. Copies go to the holiday company's head office and the excursion agent.

Excursion booking forms

The excursion booking form (see example opposite) is a record made each time a guest books an excursion. Details would typically include the name of the excursion, the name of the guest who is making the booking, the name of their accommodation, the number of adults and the number of children going on the excursion, the price and the rep's signature. The guest will receive a copy of the excursion booking form.

Car hire booking forms

Many holidaymakers reserve a hire car when making their original holiday booking or simply find a local company when they arrive in the resort. However,

others book a car through their holiday rep on arrival at the resort. The advantage of booking with the rep is that their company will have ensured that they only use reputable car hire companies who conform to minimum safety standards. The rep will liaise with the selected car hire company to check on availability of vehicles and take bookings from guests. Copies of the booking will be issued to the guest and the car hire company.

Reps will only use reputable car hire companies.

MISTAKES CAUSE PROBLEMS

Mr and Mrs Brownlow and their two children aged 13 and 17 have booked for a Greek Night offered at £32 per adult and £21 per child under 14 years. The coach pick-up is at 7.00pm from outside the main gate of their hotel. The holiday rep has made a number of errors when completing the form. Identify the errors and discuss what the possible consequences of each might be.

Excursion Booking Form

Excursion: Greek Night   **Date of excursion:** 06.07.06

Pick-up time: 1700 hours   **Pick-up point:** Hotel foyer

Customer name: Brown   **Accommodation:** San Jose

	Cost (£)
Number of Adults: 2	64
Number of Children: 2	42
Total:	106

Signature: T. Hamilton   Date: 2 July 06

When completing any form of documentation it is vital that all details are recorded accurately and clearly. The reasons are obvious – incorrect details may well result in the guest not receiving the products or services that they requested. In addition, errors can result in financial loss for the company when amounts have been wrongly calculated.

Even in this electronic age, filling in forms is an important part of a rep's job.

Dealing with problem situations

Much of a holiday representative's role will involve dealing with problem situations that arise. In this topic we are going to look at some of the more common problems that may need to be dealt with, and how the rep should handle each. In particular we will look at:

- **An overbooking**
- **A dirty room**
- **Noise due to building work or other customers**
- **Accident**
- **Lost or stolen passport.**

An overbooking

An overbooking occurs when there is insufficient accommodation for the number of arriving guests. This can occur for a range of reasons, although one of the most common is an administrative error at head office when the original bookings were made. Late availability deals are particularly susceptible to this problem when many of the holidays may have been sold as recently as the day beforehand. Other reasons for overbooking can arise where a particular accommodation is suddenly not available such as hotel that has been closed down due to a health scare or unfinished building work. Strikes and transport delays can also result in a shortfall in capacity. For example, when a group of departing guests are unable to leave due to transport problems

but the newly-arriving guests reach the destination, as planned. In extreme circumstances the original guests may have to stay overnight in their accommodation, resulting in there being no available accommodation for the new arrivals. Whatever the reason for the overbooking, it is vital that the holiday rep is fully aware of what is going on and taking prompt action to re-allocate guests to alternative accommodation. Large tour operators use the services of local agents who take on most of the responsibility for accommodation and re-allocation. Part of the holiday rep's role will be to liaise with such an agent and ensure that alternative accommodation is found. Research has found that one of the major complaints from holidaymakers is that they are not provided with sufficient information and updates on what is happening in a situation such as this. The holiday rep

WHAT COULD THE REP DO?

Read the holidaymaker's account below of a situation that involves both an overbooking and a dirty room. In pairs, discuss how effective you think the holiday rep was in dealing with the problem, and suggest how they could have dealt with it better.

I'd booked a week's holiday in Morocco at the end of the summer season for my elderly mother and me. We only booked a couple of weeks before the holiday, but were really looking forward to a bit of sunshine. I'd specified that we wanted a twin room with balcony and sea view (which I'd had to pay a hefty supplement for).

When we arrived at the airport, the rep could not find our name on the rooming list but said it would be OK. Anyway, we arrived at our five-star Hotel

Kasbah and everyone else checked in and went to their rooms. We were left sitting in reception for two hours with our cases – no one came to speak to us. Eventually a porter came and said he would take us to our room. We followed him for what seemed like hours through the darkness in the grounds until we finally came to a beach bungalow which he opened and showed us in.

After he had left we had a chance to look around. The whole place smelled of mildew and as we turned the light on in the bathroom some large cockroaches scuttled away. Light fittings were hanging off the wall and the sheets on the beds were very damp. My mother, who is a bit fierce, said 'we're not staying here' and we made our way back to reception and complained to the rep who was still there. He explained that we were not on his rooming list so the hotel had opened one of its bungalows for us – this accommodation was usually closed this late in the season because the weather wasn't so good. My mother said that she wasn't moving from reception until they found us something better.

We sat there for three and a half hours and missed dinner. Eventually the rep came over to us and said that he had found us a sea-view room in the main hotel but it would mean that two guests arriving the next day would have to have our bungalow. He didn't seem very pleased with us and left us to carry our own cases to the room where we had a meal of the free biscuits that were left in the room.

The following evening, as we came out of dinner, we heard a newly arrived couple saying to the receptionist that they were not willing to stay in the beach bungalow that they had been given.

can ease this situation by ensuring that all of their guests are aware of what arrangements are being made and giving some idea about how long it will take to resolve the situation. Where the delay is extended, the rep may need to make additional provision such as ensuring that guests receive refreshments.

A dirty room

In theory, dirty accommodation is unacceptable and should not happen. However, in reality it is often a problem that a holiday rep needs to deal with. Whilst

blatantly filthy accommodation is a clear reason for a customer complaint that needs to be dealt with seriously, there are degrees of unacceptability that the rep needs to consider carefully. Different cultures and countries have different expectations as to what is an acceptable level of cleanliness. The average UK citizen used to staying in sanitised British hotels may find the presence of lizards wandering into the bathroom in Greece unpleasant. In Greece, because of the lifestyle and open nature of accommodation, this may be seen as fairly usual – and certainly not dirty! In such a situation, the rep needs to use tact to explain to the holidaymaker that certain aspects of accommodation are an accepted part of visiting foreign countries – just as much as having to put toilet paper in a bin rather than flush it away, or having a shower that soaks the entire bathroom and empties through a hole in the middle of the room. However, where accommodation is truly dirty the rep needs to take more severe action. In many cases this may simply involve making arrangements for the accommodation to be cleaned again. If the problem is more difficult it may involve re-allocating the guests to alternative accommodation. In the latter situation, it is clearly important for the rep to ensure that the problem is resolved before any other guests are allocated the dirty room.

Noise due to building work or other customers

One of the continual problems for many holiday reps is building work. The problem is usually that the noise spoils the holidaymakers' enjoyment of the destination or disturbs their sleep. This is a double-edged sword for holiday companies – because new building work means that future capacity in a destination can be increased, or facilities improved. The work, however, often disrupts the enjoyment of current holidaymakers. In an ideal situation, every holidaymaker should be made aware of any building work in the area of their accommodation before they book a holiday. In fact, if you look at some of the main tour operators' summer brochures you will see that building work may sometimes be mentioned as a problem at specific destinations or accommodation.

Particular problems occur when either the holidaymaker claims that they were unaware of any building works or where such work is new and unexpected. In this situation a holiday rep will try to re-allocate the guest to alternative accommodation if possible. Where re-allocation is not possible, the rep needs to be aware that a complaint to the tour company at the end of the guest's holiday may be likely and needs to complete the necessary documentation as well as notifying head office of the situation. As we discussed in the previous topic, it is the holiday rep's responsibility to keep abreast of any new building work and notify head office of the details.

In some situations, noise from other guests can be a major cause of complaints for a holiday rep. This is particularly a problem in the more highly developed resorts that attract a younger target market, but also cater for the family and older markets. For example, San Antonio in Ibiza is seen as one of the 'clubbing

Building new hotels for future tourists is a noisy business, and can ruin the enjoyment of today's holidaymakers.

Clubbers going back to their accommodation can get very noisy in the early hours of the morning – when other holidaymakers might be trying to sleep.

capitals' of Europe for many young adult holiday companies. It also offers package holidays to families and older customers. The many bars, nightclubs and entertainment venues mean that clubbers are frequently still on the streets and noisily returning to their accommodation in the early hours of the morning – not the best holiday environment if you are a family that has just managed to get the baby to sleep! Holiday reps on young adult holidays are trained in how to deal with the noise problem from their customers – in severe situations it can involve asking guests to leave the accommodation. But this type of disturbance from other guests is not confined to the young adult customer. A karaoke session in the hotel bar, a baby crying all night, a couple having an argument in the next bedroom, a group having an impromptu water polo session in the hotel pool at 3.00 a.m. – all of these and many more may prove a headache for the holiday rep the following day.

A further serious problem situation that can arise due to noise is where accommodation is situated near to major transport provision such as an airport or main road. Once again, this should be mentioned in the brochure so that guests are prepared for the disturbance. However, it can be a particular problem with package holidays where accommodation is allocated on arrival – usually the cheaper, late-availability deals.

Accident

When a guest has an accident, the holiday rep has two main considerations. First, and clearly of most importance, is the well-being of the guest and any accompanying guests. All reps will have a list of nominated local doctors, dentists and hospitals or clinics in the destination. Therefore, if the guest has not already made their own arrangements for emergency treatment, the rep will be able to provide the contact phone numbers. Most of the larger tour operators have a nominated 'Clinic Rep', who is one of the standard holiday reps. This role involves the additional responsibilities of notifying the guest's insurance company of the accident, visiting the guest in hospital to ensure that they have everything they require and looking after accompanying guests.

ACCIDENT/ILLNESS REPORT FORM

CUSTOMER'S DETAILS
Customer's full name: Mr/Mrs/Miss
Booking Reference: Date of Birth:
Customer's Accommodation:
Date form completed:
Location of incident:
Date and Time of incident:
Nature of incident:

Weather at time of incident:
Who does the customer consider to be at fault?

Customer's signature: Date:

Dear Guest

We are sorry the above incident has occurred during your holiday.

Our local representative's are available should you require any further assistance in this or any other matter during the remainder of your stay.

Thank you for your help in this matter.

Source: Based on First Choice Overseas Representatives Handbook.

When accidents happen to guests, their rep must do all they can to help.

Where the accident is so severe that the guest and their companions need to extend their stay in the destination, the rep may also need to find accommodation and re-arrange return flights.

The second factor that the holiday rep will need to consider is whether or not the accident has been caused in any way by the products or services provided by their company or its suppliers. This would be a consideration, for example, for an accident in the accommodation, in its facilities such as the swimming pool, or during transport such as that used on an excursion. If this is the case then the rep will be aware that the guest may be able to make a claim against the company for damages. As discussed in the last topic, First Choice require their reps to complete an Accident/Illness Report Form (AIR) when there is any chance that the accident may be the result of products or services supplied by the holiday company.

Lost or stolen passport

In Topic 8 of Unit 5 Travelling Safely, we looked at the steps that a holidaymaker needs to take if they lose their passport whilst abroad. Holiday reps clearly need to be aware of the procedure, and advise their guests accordingly. To recap, the guest will need to:

1. Report the loss to the resort representative and local police immediately. The local police will provide the traveller with a 'Certificate of Loss' that verifies that the passport has been reported lost.

2. Contact the nearest British Foreign and Commonwealth Consulate, Embassy or High Commission and provide them with the issued 'Certificate of Loss'. They will ensure that the loss is reported to the UK Passport Office and help to provide replacement travel documents.

Regardless of the reason for a problem situation or complaint, the resort staff need to do their utmost to resolve the situation and ensure that their guests enjoy the rest of their holiday.

PEOPLE WITH PROBLEMS

For this activity, take turns at playing the roles of the resort representative and the customers in the following scenarios:

Scenario 1. Customer: 'My wife and I booked this hotel because the brochure promised a relaxing break. We've been kept awake every night by the building work next door on the hotel's extension.'

Rep: *Your company was not aware that the hotel was going to be carrying out building work. The hotel is full for the next three days and you cannot move the guest to a different room.*

Scenario 2. Customer: 'My children all have sickness and diarrhoea – as have a lot of other people in the hotel. I'm sure that the flies crawling all over the buffet are the cause – what are you going to do?'

Rep: *You are aware that the local environmental health office has been notified because of concerns about the outbreak of gastro-intestinal illness at this hotel. As yet, no cause has been identified. Your head office has instructed you not to alarm guests until a cause has been established.*

Scenario 3. Customer: 'We were informed at the airport that there had been an overbooking problem and we had been moved to this hotel. We are not happy – there is no evening entertainment or children's club and it's miles from the local town'.

Rep: *You knew that there was going to be a problem when head office notified you of the overbooking problem. The resort is full and there is no chance of moving the family to their original hotel.*

Scenario 4. Customer: 'My wife slipped in the bathroom of our apartment three days ago because the cleaner had not mopped the floor properly. She is now in the local hospital with a broken hip. I've been trying to contact you since the accident but you haven't answered my messages.'

Rep: *You are totally unaware of the accident and have not received the messages. You have visited the apartment in the last three days, but because there was no one there you assumed they were on a trip somewhere.*

Scenario 5. Customer: 'We went out last night and my wife's handbag was stolen. Unfortunately all of the family's passports were in it.'

Rep: *The family of four are due to take their return flight to the UK this afternoon.*

Induction and training

In the final two topics we are going to explore how holiday reps are inducted and trained, and the importance of product knowledge. For many holidaymakers the holiday rep is the only personal contact that they will have with the tour operator. Therefore it is vital that they project a positive and professional image of the company. Holiday companies invest a great deal of time and money in the training of their reps to ensure that they can carry out their role competently. This topic will focus on the various aspects of induction and training, including:

- Recruitment
- In-house training
- Mentoring
- External training
- Work shadowing
- Visits.

Recruitment

Whilst training is crucial to the role of a competent holiday rep, the initial stage for holiday companies is effective recruitment. This means ensuring that candidates are interviewed and selected who already possess suitable interpersonal skills and qualifications. The majority of UK tour operators recruit their overseas resort staff in the UK – although there are exceptions to this where locals in the host country are employed. Recruitment takes place throughout the year, but predominantly from January to April for summer-season staff. The recruitment process is often challenging, and may include one-to-one interviews, group interviews, group tasks and problem solving, presentations, etc.

In-house training

Most tour operators provide some basic training for their newly employed reps before sending them to their resorts. This initial training is referred to as 'induction' and provides an introduction to the company and the roles and responsibilities of a holiday rep. Induction usually lasts one to two weeks, and will often be a residential training course in a hotel. The content will include lectures, presentations, role plays and possible short tests. The in-house induction also gives the trainers the opportunity to assess the new reps' skills and decide which types of resorts they would be most suitable for. In extreme circumstances the trainers may decide during induction that certain candidates are not suitable after all, and they will be asked to leave the course.

It is standard practice for reps with companies such as TUI to only learn of their overseas destination on the final day of the induction training. Prior to starting the induction they will have been asked to come ready prepared for being sent to their destination, with appropriate luggage and passport. The following day they will transfer to their resort in preparation for the next stage of their training – 'resort training' – which typically takes two weeks.

The newly-arrived reps will be trained by experienced reps in each resort. There will be a particular focus on product knowledge about the resort, country and accommodation types as well as continuing training on administration procedures. Health and safety is also a major part of the resort training phase. For example, all First Choice reps have to carry out a monthly health and safety check of the accommodation that they are responsible for. The company provide them with a checklist to complete that has to be signed by the hotel manager to say that they agree with the rep's report. The report is then sent to First Choice Head Office. The checklist requires the rep to carry out checks such as:

- Fire alarms – to ensure that they are working.
- Fire exits and signs – to check that they are clearly marked and free from obstructions.

- Bedrooms – to ensure that they conform to minimum safety and cleanliness standards.
- Swimming pools – the rep will look at aspects such as water clarity, the provision of safety equipment and lifeguards and clearly displayed safety instructions.
- Food temperature – in all-inclusive accommodation, the rep will also be required to check the temperature of the food with a probe.

activity

TRAINING FOR PORTUGAL

Imagine that you have just been recruited as a resort rep in Portugal. Identify five topics that you would expect to be trained in before you travel to the resort and a further five topics that you would expect to learn about once you arrived in Portugal.

Mentoring

Mentoring refers to when an experienced member of staff is assigned to a new rep to provide them with advice and support over a long period. The mentoring role is usually undertaken by a senior rep or supervisor.

Health and safety training – including checking the swimming pool – is an important part of resort training.

External training

Most of the large tour operators carry out all of the reps training in-house. However, some of the more specialist rep jobs may require the rep to have gained external qualifications before they are able to undertake the role. For example, children's reps may be required to have child care and first aid qualifications. Similarly, reps who work on sporting holidays such as winter sports or water sports will need to have qualifications in any sports that they are coaching.

Winter sports reps who act as coaches have to be expert skiers.

Work shadowing

Most holiday companies include 'work shadowing' in the initial stages of rep training. This involves accompanying an experienced rep on their duties to see what the job involves. For example, during the first week of resort training the new reps will normally go on all of the excursions offered to see what they involve. This is clearly crucial since they will shortly be responsible for selling the excursions to new guests at the welcome meetings.

WORK SHADOW QUESTIONS

You have just been sent to the resort of Cala'n Bosch in Minorca where you are going to have responsibility for guests staying in a range of luxury self-catering villas in the resort. For the first week you are going to work shadow Angie who looks after guests in similar apartments. Angie has asked you to write a list of ten questions for her by tomorrow. You suspect that this is a bit of a test to see whether you can come up with a list of relevant questions. What would your questions be?

Visits

As discussed above, new reps will be expected to go on visits such as excursions to build their product knowledge. Other visits during the initial resort training will include touring the area and visiting all accommodation. During accommodation visits they will meet key staff such as hotel managers and private accommodation owners. This is a crucial part of the training since reps need to establish a good working relationship with all providers.

TRAINING A NEW REP

In Topic 7 we discussed some of the documentation used by holiday reps. One such document was the 'Accommodation Switch Form', an example of which is given below. If you cannot remember what all of the abbreviations such as CIR and CSR stand for refer back to the table on page 269. In pairs, take it in turns to role play an experienced rep and a new rep who is work shadowing. The experienced rep should explain the purpose of the Accommodation Switch Form and how to complete it.

ACCOMMODATION SWITCH FORM

Use this form to calculate the cost to the guest when requesting a change of accommodation.

Guest name:
Reference number:
Holiday dates:
Flight details:
Booked accommodation:
Accommodation type:
Date of switch:
New accommodation:
Accommodation type:
Reason for switch:

Costs per week/per night		Number of adults	Number of children
Brochure price of new accommodation per person (A)			
Invoice price of booked accommodation per person (B)			
Difference in Price per person	(C)		
Cost of change (adult/child)	(C x PAX)		
Price for switch of accommodation	D+E=F		
Total cancellation fee (if applicable)	(G)		
Total cost of switch	(F+G)		

Authorised by Rep/Admin		
Authorised by manager	Date	

- Is CSR attached Y/N
- Booked accommodation Rep advised?
- New accommodation Rep advised?
- Original room list amended by Rep?
- New rooming list produced?
- Cancellation fee to be paid to original accommodation?

Guidelines

- If switch is due to guest request the whole form must be completed.
- If switch is due to CIR the top section only is completed.
- Confirm cancellation fee with your Manager.
- This form must be handed in/faxed to local Admin/Ops.

Your Manager must authorise all switches.

Source: Based on First Choice Overseas Representatives Handbook.

Product knowledge

In the last topic we discussed the value of induction and training for new reps and the importance of good product knowledge. In this final topic we are going to explore product knowledge in more detail by looking at:

- The excursions the company operates
- Company information on policies and prices
- Company profile
- Legal and regulatory requirements
- Health and safety
- Resort and destination information
- Property requirements.

The excursions the company operates

We have already discussed how selling excursions is one of the main responsibilities of holiday reps. Clearly it is vital that the rep has an extensive knowledge of all of the excursions on offer, including what's included in each excursion, availability and timings, prices, and suitability for different types of guests. Many reps are expected to actually accompany guests on excursions, which means that they need to have sufficient knowledge to conduct the excursion and answer guests' questions.

activity

GET YOUR ANSWERS READY

You are a newly employed holiday rep on the Greek island of Corfu. You are about to conduct your first excursion with guests to a 'Greek Night'. Your supervisor has warned you that the most frequently asked questions on this particular excursion are as listed below, and asked you to see if you can find out the answer to each.

1 The meal starts with 'mezze' – what is this?

2 How many types of Greek dances are there?

3 The dinner includes Retsina wine – is this different from standard wine?

4 Why do the dancers smash the plates at the end of the meal?

5 What is moussaka?

6 What's the name of the unusual stringed instrument that the band plays?

Company information on policies and prices

In Topic 7 we looked at a range of documentation and procedures that holiday reps will need to follow. All reps will need to have a sound knowledge of these policies and how to implement them.

Company profile

During the initial induction training, holiday reps will be expected to acquire a sound knowledge of the company and the range of products and services that it offers. This is an important element of the selling process, since a satisfied guest may ask for details of other holidays offered by the tour operator and expect the rep to be able to provide the information.

activity

FOUR COMPANY PROFILES

Split into four groups and prepare a company profile of one of the following tour operators: First Choice, TUI, MyTravel, Thomas Cook. Present your profile to the other groups.

Legal and regulatory requirements

Whilst tour operators and resort staff strive to provide the very best possible holiday experience for their customers, much of their work is regulated by legislation and codes of conduct, and holiday reps need to have a good understanding of how this may impact on their role. The three main areas of importance are:

- Codes of conduct
- Employment legislation
- Consumer legislation.

Codes of conduct

'Codes of conduct' are specific regulations that apply to members of professional bodies. The most widely applied code in resort operations is for members of ABTA (the Association of British Travel Agents). Some of the key ABTA regulations are shown below – but you are strongly advised to have a look at the full code that can be found on their website, www.abta.com.

The ABTA code of conduct

This Code of Conduct is binding upon all Members of the Association.

Association of British Travel Agents

Aims of this code of conduct

- To ensure that the public receive the best possible service from Members.
- To maintain and enhance the reputation, standing and good name of the Association and its membership.
- To encourage initiative and enterprise in the belief that properly regulated competitive trading by and between Members will best serve the public interest and the well-being of the travel industry.
- To ensure that Members and their staff are familiar with this Code and the Articles of Association.

1. CONDUCT BETWEEN MEMBERS AND BETWEEN MEMBERS AND CLIENTS

1.1 Standard of service

(i)   Members shall maintain a high standard of service to Clients.

(iv) Members shall make every effort to ensure that the Travel Arrangements sold to their Clients are compatible with their Clients' individual requirements.

(v)   Members shall comply with all relevant statutory and regulatory requirements.

1.2 Minimum standards on brochures

(i)   A Member shall ensure that his brochure complies with the principles, rules and procedures contained in 'ABTA's Standards on Brochures' as published by the Association from time to time.

1.3 Advertising and promotion

(i)   No Advertising or Promotion or any other publication, whether in writing or otherwise, shall contain anything which is likely to mislead the public.

1.4 Booking procedure

(ii) Members shall ensure that any special requests relating to disabilities or medical conditions are noted and, where appropriate, passed on to Principals effectively and in accordance with any agency agreement.

1.5 Booking conditions

(i)   Members shall ensure that their Clients are aware of booking and other published conditions applicable to their Travel Arrangements before any contract is made.

1.6 Passports, visa and health requirements

(i)   Before a contract is made, Members shall inform their Clients of health requirements which are necessary for the journey to be undertaken and shall draw to the attention of Clients travelling abroad the availability of the D.O.H. leaflet Advice on Health for Travellers.

1.7 Insurance facilities

(i)(a) Members shall draw their Client's attention to the availability of insurance cover to suit their Client's requirements.

1.10 Alterations to travel arrangements and Emergency contact

(i) When alterations are made to travel arrangements for which bookings have already been accepted, Members shall inform their Clients immediately they are advised of the situation and Retailers shall act as intermediaries between their Principals and Clients in any subsequent negotiations.

2. CONDUCT OF PRINCIPALS IN RESPECT OF CONFIRMED TRAVEL ARRANGEMENTS

2.1 Cancellation by Principal

(i) A Principal shall not cancel travel arrangements after the balance due date unless it is necessary to do so as a result of force majeure, or unless the Client defaults in payment of such balance.

2.2 Significant alterations to travel arrangements by Principals

(i) Except for reasons of force majeure, a Principal shall not make a significant alteration to previously confirmed travel arrangements unless he does so in time to inform agents and direct Clients not less than 14 days before the departure date of the travel arrangements.

2.4 Overbooking

(i) A Principal shall exercise reasonable care and skill to ensure that travel arrangements are not cancelled or altered as a result of overbooking.

2.5 Building works

Where a Principal becomes aware or ought reasonably to have become aware of building works which may reasonably be considered to seriously impair the enjoyment of travel arrangements he must, without undue delay, notify Clients of the situation, provide them with accurate information about the extent of the building works and offer them the opportunity to transfer to alternative travel arrangements at the price of the original travel arrangements or to cancel without penalty. Furthermore, he must ensure that all prospective Clients are alerted to the situation.

Employment legislation

Generally speaking, the UK employment legislation applies to overseas staff in the same way that it applies to UK staff. However, there are some additional requirements that need to be considered:

- Health agreements and insurance – Any UK citizen is entitled to free (or reduced cost) medical treatment in EU countries if they have an E111 form. Most tour operators will also advise resort staff to have private medical and personal possessions insurance. In addition, the tour operator's own insurance will cover staff for personal and public liability.
- Work permits – In countries outside the UK where work permits may be required, it is usually the responsibility of the tour operator to make the appropriate arrangements for resort staff.

- Passports and visas – All overseas resort staff will require a valid passport, and for some countries outside Europe a visa is also required.
- Contracts of employment – The same legislation applies in terms of contracts of employment to overseas staff as would apply to staff within the UK. The law requires all staff employed for more than 4 weeks to have a written statement of their terms and conditions of employment.

Consumer legislation

We have already discussed consumer legislation in Unit 5 in relation to promotion and sales. Much of the same legislation applies equally to overseas resort operations. Let's look at how some of this legislation might affect resort operations.

BREACHING THE CODE OF CONDUCT?

Read the following report on a customer's experience when booking a package holiday with an ABTA travel agent, and discuss ways in which the travel agent may have breached the ABTA code of conduct.

Peter Steel had decided to book a late-availability deal for himself and his wife in August. They had been to the Greek islands on many occasions and wanted to try a different island. Peter went to the local travel agency for advice. His requirements were straightforward – a week in August, self-catering in a destination that was relatively unspoilt – and no sea crossings because his wife had a phobia about sailing. The travel agency consultant was extremely helpful and, after two hours of searching and discussion, found him an excellent deal to the island of Thassos – a three-and-a-half hour flight straight into the small island. As the holiday was in four weeks time, Peter was required to pay the full price of £698. When they got home from the travel agents, Peter and his wife looked through the guidebooks to find out more about their holiday – but were puzzled that no airport was shown on any of the maps. He returned to the travel agency, where the consultant confirmed that there was, in fact, no airport and access to the island involved a ferry transfer. Peter reminded her of his requirements for no sea travel and asked that his holiday be changed to a different destination. The consultant claimed that he had not specified 'no ferry transfer' and that if he cancelled the holiday now he would forfeit most of the cost.

Package Travel, Package Holidays and Package Tour Regulations (1992)

This EU legislation has a substantial impact on resort operations and staff. The act is extensive, but two elements that directly affect resort staff are:

- Every effort must be made to ensure that the accommodation that the customer has booked should be available and not overbooked.

- No false or misleading statements about the accommodation, facilities or holiday should be made.

Whilst the legislation covers all aspects of the package holiday from the initial booking to the actual experience, there are specific requirements during the holiday, as the extract overlleaf, from the Department of Trade and Industry website, shows.

Trade Descriptions Act (1968)

As with the above legislation, this act states that all aspects of the package sold to the customer must be accurate.

The Supply of Goods and Services Act (1982)

This legislation requires the tour operator and travel agent to carry out the booking correctly and with 'reasonable care and skill'.

The Unfair Terms of Consumer Contracts Regulations (1982)

Tour operators are required to ensure that all contracts are written in clear and understandable language and do not include unfair or unreasonable terms.

What happens if something goes wrong with the holiday?

Where, after departure, a significant proportion of the services contracted for are not provided or the organiser becomes aware he will be unable to procure a significant proportion of the services to be provided, he must make suitable alternative arrangements, at no extra cost to the consumer, and possibly compensate the consumer.

Am I responsible for the hotel in Spain/Tunisia?

Yes. The Regulations make the tour operator liable for the proper performance of the obligations under the contract, irrespective of whether such obligations are performed by the tour operator himself, or by another supplier of services such as the hotel.

Am I responsible if something happens to the consumer when he is on holiday?

The tour operator is liable to the consumer for any damage caused to him by the failure to perform the contract or the improper performance of the contract unless the failure or improper performance is due neither to any fault of the tour operator nor to another supplier of the package services, because, for example, it was the fault of the consumer or a third party unconnected with the provision of the services contracted for, or was due to unusual or unforeseeable circumstances which could not have been avoided even if all due care had been exercised. For example, if the conditions are primitive the tour operator needs to warn prospective customers. Similarly if tourists tend to get harassed, etc.

source: www.dti.gov.uk

---

activity

BREAKING ANY LAWS?

Read the holiday experiences below. In pairs, discuss which laws or code of conduct may have been breached, and what you think the resort staff should do about it.

1 Wayne and Bob are on a young adults' holiday and have booked an evening barbecue excursion. They claim that they were told by their rep that the trip included unlimited free wine and beer, all evening. Now that they are at the barbecue they are complaining that drinks are limited to four per person.

2 Katie Barton and her daughter are spending a week in the Gambia. On their third day they complain to the rep that they are unable to go to the beach because of the constant harassment by traders. Katie states that she should have been warned that the holiday might not suit two women travelling on their own.

3 The Starchen family are staying for two weeks in the Costa del Sol on an all-inclusive holiday. Both of the children have had severe sickness and diarrhoea for four days – as have a large number of fellow guests. Staff have told Mrs Starchen that the problem has been going on for over three weeks and that the manager had informed the tour operator of a possible problem.

4 Dr Bull is staying in Minorca with his family, and booked and paid for a hire car at the travel agent at the time of booking the holiday. When he picked it up he was charged a further £129 for insurance. He complains that he should have been told by the travel agent that this charge would be made.

5 Due to an over-booking error, the Thomas family were notified one week before their departure date that their accommodation had been changed. They were given the option of cancelling the holiday and receiving a full refund, but decided to accept the alternative accommodation. The travel agent assured them that the new accommodation was, in fact, better than what they had originally selected. Now that they are in the resort they are dismayed to discover that the hotel is only three star grade (not four as they had been told) does not have a pool and is two miles from the beach.

6 Mr and Mrs Cullen have booked a full-day's tour of Rome. In the poster on the resort reps' noticeboard the excursion is described as 'An informative and fascinating insight into the rich culture and art of this famous capital city. Join our expert guide on a tour of the art galleries and historical buildings.' On their return they complain to their rep that the excursion rep had little knowledge of the history, art or culture of the city and could not answer any of their questions. They claim that they would have been better off doing the trip independently and therefore saving a lot of money.

Health and safety

Throughout this unit we have already discussed the importance of health and safety – and the responsibilities of the holiday rep. These range from carrying out health and safety checks of accommodation to completing building work reports and accident and illness forms. Apart from carrying out appropriate procedures, the holiday rep is also responsible for advising guests on health and safety issues such as:

- Hotel security arrangements, such as the availability of safety deposit boxes

- Health and safety advice such as the use of the pool, balconies and lifts

- Caution against sunburn, and observing beach safety warnings

- How to obtain assistance if there is an emergency or unforeseen problem such as illness, unsatisfactory accommodation or lost luggage.

Safety Deposit Boxes

For your safety and security we would recommend that all valuables and money are secured in a hotel safety deposit box. These boxes are available for a small charge of 1 € per day. Arrangements can be made at the hotel reception desk.

Resort and destination information

When a customer pays for their holiday there is an expectation that they are also paying for expert and efficient customer service from the moment of booking through to the end of their holiday. At their resort they will expect:

- Information on the resort, local customs and culture, entertainment, food, etc.

- Advice on the best places to go, local transport, customs, etc.

Reps may issue the majority of resort information at the welcome meeting. It is usual, however, to have some basic information on the noticeboard, such as a map of the resort together with information on local attractions, restaurants and bars.

activity

WHAT WILL THEY WANT TO KNOW?

In pairs, discuss what you think the main resort information requirements might be for the following types of package holiday customers whilst on holiday.

1 A group of 18 year olds on a young adults holiday in Corfu

2 A coach party of elderly guests on a four-day visit to Rome

3 A couple on an all-inclusive, adults-only holiday in the Dominican Republic

4 A single female on a week's break at a luxury resort in Morocco.

Property requirements

In luxury hotel accommodation, much of the hotel information will be in a folder in the guests' room. However, additional information that is of interest to everyone may be displayed on the property noticeboard or explained at the welcome meeting by the rep. Such information might include:

- The range of facilities and services available, such as water sports, room service, bedroom facilities, etc.

- Opening hours of hotel facilities such as the restaurant, reception and leisure facilities

- Advice on tipping and settling extras accounts

- Accommodation regulations, such as not using the pool at certain times when it is being cleaned.

activity

SUPER CHECKLIST

Using the information in this topic, design a detailed checklist for a holiday rep outlining all of the knowledge that they would need to acquire to carry out their role effectively.

How Unit 6 is assessed

Unit 6 is assessed by coursework. The evidence should be in four parts, which we suggest you present as four sections within a portfolio. The following guidance outlines how you can achieve the assessment requirements for each of the four parts.

The evidence could be in many different forms to allow for your learning preferences, styles and strengths to be accommodated. There will be witness statements for the welcome meeting, problem-solving and sales activity. Supplementary evidence should include completed documentation and supporting material such as information sheets.

Other tasks could be evidenced through written reports or presentations accompanied by supporting evidence and tutor witness testimonies.

Task (a) Resort operations

(a.1) Description

Describe how tour operators organise resort operations to prepare and deal with customers in resort. (This will include: rooming lists, excursions, liaison with local agencies, transfers, complaints and emergencies, overseas staff, administration staff, overseas representatives, team leaders, team, area and general managers.)

(a.2) Liaising with the UK office

Explain the situations that require the resort office to liaise with their UK office.

NOTE: To achieve the higher mark bands you need to give a more detailed explanation of operations and situations, with specific examples from a range of organisations.

Task (b) Welcome meeting, selling, problem situation

(b.1) The welcome meeting

Organise and present a welcome meeting. (This will include: introduction and welcome, health and safety, excursions, local amenities.)

(b.2) Selling

Provide evidence of how you used effective selling skills to sell an additional service (such as excursions or car hire) including completion of the appropriate documentation.

(b.3) Problem situations

Provide evidence of your effective handling of a problem situation for a customer – whose needs and circumstances will be given to you. (The problem situation might be overbooking, dirty room, noise, accident or lost/stolen passport, etc.)

NOTE: to achieve the higher mark bands your welcome meeting needs to be well-structured, use a wide range of materials and fully engage the audience. Your selling skills should be appropriate and effective. The problem situation should be complex and dealt with fully and effectively.

Task (c) Research undertaken to complete all tasks

This section requires you to provide evidence of the research that you have carried out in completing all the tasks in the unit assessment. (It is arguably better to make this your final task, as it will cover all of the other three tasks.)

NOTE: To achieve the higher mark bands you need to have independently used a wide range of sources for your research and referenced them correctly.

Task (d) Induction, training and product knowledge

An evaluation of the significance of induction, training and product knowledge of overseas representatives in delivering high quality customer service.

(Induction and training will include: in-house training, mentoring, external training, work shadowing, and visits. Product knowledge will include: excursions, company information, company profile, legal and regulatory requirements, health and safety, resort and destination information, property requirements.)

NOTE: To achieve the higher mark bands your evaluation must include the practices of a wide range of tour operators and your conclusions should be mainly substantiated by the examples.

Bibliography

List all of the sources of information that you have used to complete the assessment for this unit. This should include books and journals, websites, direct contact with tour operators, etc.

Appendices

Include any relevant supporting information in the appendices, such as examples of training materials, policies and procedures, etc.

Improving your grades

Generally, you will get better grades by giving more comprehensive explanations, including better examples and showing a deeper understanding of each topic. Your school or college should be able to advise you in more detail, or you could visit the Edexcel website: edexcel.org.uk for more guidance.

General guidelines on presentation of assignments (for Units 2, 3, 4 and 6)

Whilst the way in which you present your assessment evidence will not directly affect your grade, it is important that you strive to present it in a professional and well-structured way. The following are a few tips on achieving good presentation.

1. All assignments should be word processed, using a suitable font, such as Ariel. Try to avoid 'casual' fonts, such as Comic Sans.

2. You can use a different font for titles if you wish, but do not use more than two fonts in your work.

3. Be consistent in your font size. Generally, 14 or 16 is suitable for titles, and 12 for the main text.

4. Only use bold for titles – not the whole report.

5. Use italics and 'quotation marks' to show when you have copied text from another source, and indicate the source in brackets after the quote.

6. If you choose to use more than one colour in your work, limit this to two, e.g. blue for titles and black for the main text.

7. Avoid using 'Wordart' for titles!

8. Use 1.5 line spacing throughout your work.

9. Do not cut and paste cartoon-style clipart into your work.

10. If you use photographs in your work, label each image underneath.

11. Insert page numbers into your finished work.

Answers to WHERE ARE YOU ON THE ATTITUDE SCALE? (page 72)

(1) sometimes, (2) sometimes – consider a customer in a wheelchair, (3) never, (4) never, (5) always, (6) never, (7) never, (8) always, (9) never, (10) always, (11) always, (12) sometimes – but you should always act as if the customer is right!

Index

access to products and services 83

accessibility
    Europe 142
    UK 190
    see also transport links

accident, illness report form (AIR) 269, 275, 276

accident report books 78

accommodation
    accommodation providers 42–3, 44, 160–1
    accommodation switch form 269, 281
    additional information 287
    bed-nights used 189
    building works 256
    dirty accommodation 273–4
    Europe 120
    extra rooms to allocation 251
    noisy accommodation 274–5
    overbooking 272–3
    rooming lists 250–1
    UK 177, 184

accommodation providers 42–3, 44
    camping and caravanning 43, 120, 121, 171, 177
    farmhouse accommodation 43
    guesthouses and B&Bs 19, 43, 120
    holiday centres 43
    hotels 42, 63, 99, 120, 145, 167, 206
    non-commercial 42
    self-catering 43, 120

activity centre holidays 122

adventure trips 16–17

advertising 143
    restrictions 210

advice
    FCO advice 231
    health and safety advice 260, 287
    products and services 85

Aerodrome Standards Department 201

Air France 87

air traffic standards department 201

air travel
    airport expansions 34
    budget airlines 27, 39, 129, 137
    charter flights 39, 128
    data 46
    development 25, 39
    Europe 118, 128–9, 142
    helicopter flights 201
    hub and spoke operations 39
    'late availability without guarantee' 38
    late check-in 67, 84
    overbooking 38
    safety and security 140, 200–3
    scheduled flights 39, 128, 139
    UK 174–5
    wide-body jets 25, 39

Air Travel Organisers Licence (ATOL) 201

airports
    airport hotels 63
    airport transfers 251
    Europe 128
    runway incursions 201
    UK 128, 174, 190

Airtours 101

all-inclusive holiday packages 145, 243

Alps 122, 123

Alton Towers 19, 113, 178

ancient times, travel and tourism in 22

ancillary services 44

animateuse 125–6, 243

Areas of Outstanding Natural Beauty (AONBs) 169

arrest and imprisonment 228–9

art galleries 170, 191, 193

arts festivals 181

Association of British Travel Agents (ABTA) 37, 38, 45, 202
    bonding system 17, 37, 202
    Code of Conduct 96, 283–4
    commercial role 202
    regulatory role 202

Athens 111

attitude 72

attractions see visitor attractions

Australia 267

Austria 116, 122, 233

availability of product 99–100

avian flu 234

aviation regulations 200–3

B&Bs 19, 43

babies and children 61, 83
    children's clubs 246
    children's representatives 245–6, 280
    free services 69
    passports 212–13
    safety 225
    travelling unaccompanied 86–8

backward integration 51

Balearic Islands 107, 144

Barcelona 109, 118, 140

Bath 167

Bathing Water Directive 164

beachenders 147

beaches
    awards schemes 164
    beach resorts 123, 162–3, 192

beach safety 225, 260
    rural beaches 163–4

bed-nights used 189

benchmarking 98

Benidorm 146

bird flu 234

Birmingham 167

Blackpool 178

body language 75, 77
    cultural differences 65
    open and closed 75

bookings
    customer details 254
    global booking systems (GBS) 30, 37
    internet-based systems 76, 145
    telephone bookings 66–7

branded multiples 42

British Airways 50
    Club Europe 63
    SkyFlyer Solo Service 86–7

Brittany Ferries 40

brochures 144

bucket shops 48

Budapest 143

Building Report Form 256, 257, 269

building work disruption 256, 257, 274

built attractions 43
    Europe 123
    UK 178–9, 180

bulk buying 38

business customers 61, 194
    communications networks 118
    conference destinations 166–7
    European destinations 108–9, 118
    needs and expectations 12, 63

business letters 76

business travel 11, 15–16, 30, 139
    itineraries 183
    specialist agents 15, 37

Butlins 19, 25, 43, 171

buying behaviours 30

camping and caravanning 43
    Europe 120, 121
    UK 171, 177

canal/river cruises 130

cancellation 220–1
    compensation 221
    customer cancellation 221
    medical problems 222
    operator cancellation 220–1

CAP 393 200

Cape Town 241

capsule hotels 42

car hire 41, 135
  booking forms 270
  child seats 99
  Europe 126

car pick-up and drop-off 67

Cardiff 167

Carlisle 167

Center Parcs 43, 67, 84, 113
  Europe 112
  UK 171, 177

chalet hosts 246

Channel Tunnel 40, 132, 135

Channel Tunnel Shuttle 41

charter flights 39, 128

children see babies and children

Chinese culture 65

cholera 217

cities/towns
  Europe 107–8
  new towns 164
  UK 47, 164–5

Civil Aviation Authority (CAA) 200–1

climate
  climate change 21
  Europe 114–15
  severe weather conditions 21, 233
  UK 172

clinic representatives 275

Club 18–30 60, 73, 247

Club Europe 63

Club Med 30, 43, 52, 113, 145, 243

coach travel 41
  Europe 135

coastal areas
  Europe 106–7
  UK 162–4

codes of conduct 31, 95, 96, 283–4

Commercial Administrators 241–2

commission rates 35, 37

communication links
  Europe 118
  see also transport links

communication skills 74–9
  documentation 78
  face-to-face communication 74–5
  information communication technology (ICT) 78
  listening skills 75, 77
  non-verbal communication 75
  providing information 78
  responding to customers 77
  telephone skills 75–6
  written communication 76

communist country destinations 27
  see also eastern European destinations

company profile 282

compensation 31, 92–3
  cancellation 220, 221
  travel delays 92

compensation in resort form (CIR) 253, 269

competitive advantage 51

complaints 31, 71, 90–3
  appropriate action 92–3
  complaints statistics 90
  effective handling 90
  face-to-face complaints 91
  package holidays 251–3
  reasons for complaints 91
  supercomplaints 209
  on the telephone and in writing 91–2

conference industry 166–7

consumer protection 31, 208–11, 284–6
  codes of conduct 31, 95, 96, 283–4
  Enterprise Act 209
  EU regulations 286
  Fair Trading Act 208–9
  Package Travel, Package Holidays and Package Tour Regulations 285
  Sale of Goods and Services Act 210–11
  Sale and Supply of Goods Act 210
  Supply of Goods and Services Act 285
  Trades Description Act 208, 285
  Unfair Terms of Consumer Contracts Regulations 285

contagious diseases 217–18

contracts of employment 284

Control of Substances Hazardous to Health (COSHH) 99

Cook, Thomas 24

cost of living 126–7, 148

Costa del Sol 107

Costa Verde 107

country house hotels 42

Countryside Agency 168

countryside areas
  Europe 110
  UK 168–9

Cowes Week 157

credit and debit cards 227

crime 140, 228, 260

crisis-response teams 35

Croatia 148

cruises 26, 40, 130–1

fly–cruise packages 40
    passengers 60, 131
    product information 82

cultural attractions 43
    Europe 111
    UK 170–1, 188

Cultural Capital of Europe 111

cultural differences 61
    body language 65

cultural impacts 33

currency exchange facilities 242

currency fluctuations 20

curtailment 222

customer care 31, 58

customer needs and expectations 12, 13, 30–1, 62–5, 85–6
    balancing 33
    business customers 12, 63
    buying behaviours 30
    changing 192
    conflicting needs 84
    consumer protection 31, 208–11, 284–6
    giving advice 85
    group needs 62
    mixed-age groups 63
    motivations 13, 28–9
    and the organisation's objectives 83
    product ranges 30
    providing assistance 85
    specific needs 53, 61, 64, 85–6, 100

customer promise 94

customer questionnaires 96, 255

customer satisfaction 255

customer service 56–101
    benefits 83
    communication skills 74–9
    complaints procedures 31, 71, 90–3
    customer types 60–1
    evaluation and improvement 101
    external customers 59–61
    free services 66–9
    health, safety and security 87
    internal customers (staff) 58–9
    interpersonal skills 70–3
    measuring 94–7, 255
    meeting customer needs 83–9
    monitoring 89
    product knowledge 80–4, 282–7
    quality criteria 98–101
    role play 88
    staffing levels 83
    taking and relaying messages 86
    training 89
    see also customer needs and expectations

customer service charter 94, 95

customer service journal 269

customer service report form (CSR) 252–3, 269

customers
    age groups 60
    business customers 12, 61, 63, 108–9, 118, 166–7, 194
    cultural differences 61, 65
    external customers 59–61
    groups and individuals 60
    internal customers (staff) 58–9
    language differences 61, 65
    life-stages 13
    'mystery customers' 96, 97
    specific needs 53, 61, 64, 85–6

Czech Republic 148

data 46–8
    data gathering 12
    interpretation 46
    and marketing 30
    sources 48

Data Protection Act 207

deaf people 64

decision-making process 13
    buying behaviours 30

definitions of travel and tourism 10–13
    by activity 11
    by purpose of travel 11
    organisational views 10
    supply and demand views 12
    tourism flows 10–11

demographics 34

Department for Culture, Media and Sport (DCMS) 20, 154–5

Department of Trade and Industry 38

destination associations 159

destination branding 24

Destination Britain 194–5

destination management 146–7, 192–3

Destination Management Companies (DMCs) 193

development issues 34

dietary requirements 61, 64

disabilities, people with
    customer needs, meeting 61, 85–6
    deaf people 64
    discrimination issues 86, 87, 205–6
    free services 69
    language issues 64
    learning difficulties 61
    meeting and assisting 64
    mobility problems 61, 69
    sensory disabilities 61, 69
    speech difficulties, people with 64

visual impairment, people with 64
wheelchair users 64, 69, 85

Disability Discrimination Act (DDA) 61, 85–6, 205–6

disaster management 34–5

Disneyland, Paris 83, 95, 113, 118, 125

distribution chain 48–9

diversification 52

documentation 78, 254–5, 268–71
accident, illness report form (AIR) 269, 275, 276
accommodation switch form 269, 281
Building Report Form 256, 257, 269
car hire booking forms 270
compensation in resort form (CIR) 253, 269
customer service journal 269
customer service report form (CSR) 252–3, 269
emergency medical first call form 269
excursion booking forms 270
liquidation reports 270
receipts 268
repatriation request form 269
to whom it may concern form 269
Trades Description Act form (TDA) 269

domestic tourism 11, 14–15

downsizing 34

drinking water 260

driving
car hire 41, 99, 126, 135, 270
Europe 126, 133–5
scenic drives 135

driving sites 179

drug trafficking 229

eastern European destinations 38, 127, 148–9
communications links 118
stag weekends 143
transport links 117

easyJet 129, 145

eco-tourism 17

economic benefits of tourism 14, 19, 187

economic climate 21

Eden Project 69

Edinburgh 165, 171

embassies and consulates 225, 226

emergency medical first call form 269

emergency situations 71, 220–35
arrest and imprisonment 228–9
assistance 224–5, 255
cancellation 220–1
crisis-response teams 35
disaster management 34–5
disease outbreaks 234
large-scale emergencies 230–5

lost luggage 227–8
lost money 227
lost passport 226, 276
natural disasters 233–4
resort operations 251–3, 255–6, 272–7
small-scale emergencies 220–9
strikes 232
thefts and muggings 228
transport accidents 234–5
transport delays 255–6
wars 230, 232
see also terrorism

employment legislation 284

enablers 29

England Travel Bureau 183

English Heritage 180

Enterprise Act 209

entertainment
Europe 125–6
UK 181, 191

entertainment representatives 246

environmental concerns 19, 21, 26, 33, 43–4

Estonia 148

ethical business practices 31

Eurail 132

euro 148

Eurocamp 43, 121

Euroline bus network 135

Europarc 110

Europe 104–49
accessibility 142
accommodation 120
business and conference destinations 108–9, 118
Center Parcs 112
climate 114–15
coastal areas 106–7
cost of visiting and living 126–7, 147–8
countryside areas 110
destination management 146–7
entertainment 125–6
events 124–5
facilities 121–2, 145
heritage and cultural destinations 111
image and promotion 142–5
landscape 116
local culture 127
location and geography 106
natural and built attractions 123
political factors 148–9
purpose-built resorts 113
top destinations for UK travellers 147
tourist towns and cities 107–8
transport and communication links 117–19, 128–41, 142

European Aviation Safety Agency (EASA) 203
European City of Culture programme 111
European Package Travel Directive 204–5
European Union 104
European Union legislation
    Bathing Water Directive 164
    Package Travel Directive 17, 31, 204–5
    tour operator liability 286
Eurostar 132
events 43
    Europe 124–5
    UK 181
exchange rates 20, 148
excursions 16, 242, 251, 282
    booking forms 270
    duration 264
    inclusions 265
    selling 261, 264–7
    themes 264–5
external qualifications 280
extra rooms to allocation 251

face-to-face communication 74–5
facilities
    Europe 121–2
    UK 178
Fair Trading Act 208–9
farmhouse accommodation 43
fashion trends 31
feedback, informal 96, 97
ferry services 39–40, 130, 131
    cross-channel ferries 40, 130, 175
    Europe 130, 131
    overnight crossings 137
    package deals 38
    roll-on, roll-off ships 40
    security 140
    UK 175
film locations 156
fire safety 279
First Choice 18, 37, 242, 244, 256
flight attendants 70
Flight Sales Administrators 242
flooding 233
focus groups 97
food
    dietary requirements 61, 64
    eating out in Europe 126
    food hygiene 71, 204, 225, 279
Foot and Mouth Disease outbreak 193–4
force majeure 205, 222

Foreign and Commonwealth Office (FCO) 225
    terrorism advice 231
    unsafe destination advice 232
Fowey 192
France 15, 108, 122, 134
    heritage tourism 123
    local culture 127
free services 66–9
    car pick-up and drop-off 67
    for customers with specific needs 68–9
    interpretation materials 67–8
    late check-in 67
    late-night openings 66
    online services 67
    telephone bookings 66–7
    translation service 67

geographical features
    British Isles 173
    Europe 116
Germany 108, 117
    events 124
Getaway Travel 90
Glasgow 167
Gleneagles 42
global booking systems (GBS) 30, 37
global distribution systems (GDS) 30
global issues 32–3
    cultural impacts 33
    development issues 34
    environmental concerns 19, 21, 26, 33, 43–4
    investment costs 32
    operational issues 34–5
    over-development and uncoordinated development 32
Going Places 18
golf complexes 113
government
    departments and agencies 45, 154–5
    Tomorrow's Tourism 20, 35, 45, 194–5
    tourism policies and support 19–20, 35, 45, 154–5, 194–5
    see also legislation
Gozo 144
Grand Tour 23
Greece 124, 130, 134, 142, 148, 228
Greek Islands 117
guesthouses 43
    Europe 120

Hadrian's Wall 180
handbag searches 83
handling agents 252

health issues 216–19
    accidents 275–6
    cancellation/curtailment of holiday 222
    contagious diseases 217–18, 234
    disease outbreaks 234
    food hygiene 71, 204, 225, 279
    health restrictions 218
    insurance 222–3
    medical conditions 61, 64
    'required' and 'recommended' health advice 219
    staff medical treatment abroad 284
    vaccinations 216–17, 218, 219
health and safety see health issues; safety and security
Health and Safety at Work Act 99
heatwaves 115
helicopter flights 201
hepatitis C 218
heritage attractions 43, 123, 170
    Europe 111
    UK 170–1, 188
heritage coasts 169
High Commissions 226
Hilton hotels 52
history of travel and tourism 22–7
    ancient times 22
    Industrial Revolution 23–4
    inter-war period 24–5
    Middle Ages 22–3
    post-Second World War period 25–6
    postmodern era 26
    trends and developments 27
HIV and AIDS 217
holiday camps 25, 43, 171, 177
holiday complex resorts 113
holiday-home buying 27
horizontal integration 41
host environments 21, 33, 43–4
hotels 42
    airport hotels 63
    capsule hotels 42
    car pick-up and drop-off 67
    conference business 167
    country house hotels 42
    disabilities, people with 206
    Europe 120
    facilities 145
    health and safety 99, 225
    hotel chains 42
    overbooking 272–3
    safety deposit boxes 287
Hungary 148
hurricanes 21, 233–4
Hyatt Hotels 52

Ibiza 107, 123, 125, 144, 274
immunisation 216–17
in-house training 278–9
incoming (inbound) tourism 11, 14, 46, 47
independent travel 17
Indian culture 65
Industrial Revolution 23–4
industry growth 28–31
    customer expectations 31
    customer needs 30–1
    development issues 34
    enablers 29
    fashion trends 31
    global issues 32–3
    government strategy 35
    motivators 28–9
    operational issues 34–5
    product development and innovation 30
    socioeconomic factors 29
    technological growth 29–30
industry sectors 18–21
    multiples 18–19
    private sector 18
    public sector 19–20
    resort and service sectors 42–5
    small and medium-sized enterprises (SMEs) 19
    travel sectors 36–41
industry standards 73
information communication technology (ICT) 78
information, provision of 13, 100
    accuracy 80–1, 100
    sources 81
infrastructure 27, 32
initiative 71
inseparability factor 13
insurance
    cancellation cover 221
    conditions and exclusions 223
    emergence assistance 225
    lost luggage 227–8
    medical costs 222, 223
    policy limits 223
    premiums 224
intangibility factor 12, 17
integration 18, 34, 37, 38, 50–3
    backward 51
    horizontal 51
    mergers 51
    partnerships and collaborations 52–3
    problems 52
    vertical 51
inter-relationships and interdependencies 48–9, 157
inter-war years 24–5

internal customers (staff) 58–9

internal tourism see domestic tourism

international agencies 45

International Air Transport Association (IATA) 37, 45, 203

International Civil Aviation Organisation 45

internet 27, 144–5
    online services 67

interpersonal skills 70–3
    industry standards 73
    initiative 71
    personal appearance 70–1, 73
    personality 73
    positive attitude 72
    problem solving 72
    required resources 71

interpretation materials 67–8

InterRail 119

investment costs 32

Iraq 230

Isle of Wight 157

Italy 148, 261
    Italian culture 65

itineraries 182–5
    contact details 184
    dates 182
    destination details 184
    presentation 185
    timing 183
    transport and accommodation 184
    visitor requirements 182

Jamaica 229

Japan 229

Jet2 19

job losses 34

Joint Aviation Authorities (JAA) 203

Jorvik Centre 171

journey times 137

Kyoto Agreement 33

Laerdal Tunnel 135

Lake District National Park 169

landscape
    Europe 116
    UK 173–4

Langdale Quest 179

language differences 61, 65
    communication process 65
    translation service 67

language schools 195

late check-in 67, 84

late-night openings 66

Leeds–Bradford Airport 34, 53

legislation
    CAP 393 200
    compliance with 211
    Data Protection Act 207
    Disability Discrimination Act (DDA) 61, 85–6, 205–6
    employment legislation 284
    Enterprise Act 209
    Fair Trading Act 208–9
    Health and Safety at Work Act 99
    host country legislation 20
    Package Travel Directive 17, 31, 204–5
    Package Travel, Package Holidays and Package Tour Regulations 285
    Sale of Goods and Services Act 210–11
    Sale and Supply of Goods Act 210
    Supply of Goods and Services Act 285
    Trades Description Act 208
    Unfair Terms of Consumer Contracts Regulations 285

leisure travel 11, 16

life-stages 13

lifestyle factors 13

liquidation reports 270

listening skills 75, 77

literacy/numeracy learning difficulties 61

local authorities
    tourism investment 34
    tourist departments 156

local culture
    Europe 127
    UK 181

London 158, 191
    entertainment 125
    itineraries 184
    public transport 138–9, 176
    visitor data 186–7, 188

London Development Agency 159

London Eye 193

London Underground 176

long-haul destinations 15

lost property
    lost passport 226, 276
    luggage 227–8
    money 227

low-cost holidays 147

luggage, lost 227–8

lunar holiday plots 145

Luxembourg 111

McDonaldisation 31, 42

Majorca 32, 107, 147

malaria 218

Manchester 167

market profile 25, 26

marketing
    ancillary services 44
    motivational types 28–9

mass tourism 18, 31, 33, 147

media coverage 142–5, 193

medical conditions 61, 64

mentoring 279

mergers 34, 51

messages
    standard message pads 86
    taking and relaying 86

metros 135

Middle Ages, travel and tourism in the 22–3

Milton Keynes 164

Minorca 144

mobile phone use 84

mobility problems 61, 69

money
    cost of living 126–7, 148
    credit and debit cards 227
    currency exchange facilities 242
    currency fluctuations 20
    euro 148
    exchange rates 20, 148
    lost money 227
    traveller's cheques 227
    see also spending

moped hire 260

motivators 13, 28–9
    cultural 28
    extrinsic 28
    inter-personal 28
    intrinsic 28
    physical and personal 28
    status and prestige 28, 31

motorways
    Europe 134
    tolls 134–5
    UK 175–6

multiple holidays 147

multiples 18–19
    branded multiples 42

multiplier effect 14, 187

museums 191, 193

music festivals 125, 171

mystery customers 96, 97

MyTravel 18, 37, 244

national parks
    Europe 110
    UK 68, 168–9

national tourism organisations (NTOs) 45

national tourist boards 155–6

National Trust 159, 160, 180

natural disasters 21, 34–5, 233–4

natural visitor attractions 43
    Europe 123
    UK 178–9

Neapolitan Riviera 261

Neilson 94

Newcastle 167

newspaper and magazine reports 143

niche-market operations 16–17, 19, 26, 38

nightlife 125

9/11 129, 193, 230

noise 274–5

non-verbal communication 65, 75, 77

Norwalk virus 234

Norway 117, 135, 142

Notting Hill Carnival 181

Office of Fair Trading 209

Oktoberfest 124

Olympic Games 124

online services 67

operational issues 34–5

oral communication 74–5

outgoing (outbound) tourism 11, 15, 46, 47

over-development and uncoordinated development 32, 147

overbooking
    accommodation 272–3
    air travel 38

overseas representatives 242, 244–8
    chalet hosts 246
    children's representatives 245–6, 280
    clinic representatives 275
    entertainment representatives 246
    induction and training 278–87
    resort managers 242
    resort representatives 78, 99, 244–5, 248
    team leaders 242
    transfer representatives 245, 251
    villa representatives 246
    winter sports representatives 246, 247, 280
    young adults' representatives 247

Oxford 167

P&O 40, 82

package holidays 17, 37
    airport transfers 251
    all-inclusive holiday packages 145, 243
    booking 254
    complaints 251–3
    consumer legislation 204–5
    customer satisfaction 255
    customer's own packages 17
    excursions 242, 251, 261, 264–7, 270, 282
    problem situations 255–6, 272–7
    supplements 20, 38
    see also resort operations

Package Travel Directive 17, 31, 204–5

Package Travel, Package Holidays and Package Tour Regulations 285

paid holiday time 147

Pamplona 124

Paris 123, 127

partnerships and collaborations 52–3

passports and visas 212–15
    application for 212, 213, 214
    biometric information 215
    children 212–13
    emergency application 214
    entering America 213
    lost/stolen passport 226, 276
    machine-readable 213
    overseas staff 284
    photographs 213
    regional offices 214
    visas 214, 215, 284

perishability of travel and tourism 12

personal appearance 70–1, 73

personal hygiene 70–1

personality 73

political instability 148

Pontins 171

population profile 29

population shifts 34

ports 130–1, 175

positive attitude 72

post-Second World War period 25–6

postmodern era 26

Prague 125

price-fixing 209

prioritising actions 71

Prisoners Abroad 229

private sector companies 18, 37

private–public partnerships (PPPs) 34

problem solving 72

see also emergency situations

product development and innovation 30

product knowledge 80–4, 282–7
    company policies and prices 282
    company profile 282
    excursions 282
    health and safety issues 287
    impersonal, accurate and objective information 80–1
    information sources 81
    legal and regulatory requirements 283–6
    resort representatives 282–7

product ranges 30

products and services
    access to 83
    availability 99–100
    distribution chain 48–9
    outside suppliers 58
    quality criteria 99–100
    reliability and consistency 100
    resort sales operations 264–7

professional bodies and associations 31, 202–3

profile of the industry 25, 26

promotion 142–5, 193

public sector organisations 19–20, 154–9
    declining investment 34
    finance 159
    government departments and agencies 154–5
    local authority tourist departments 156
    national tourist boards 155–6
    Regional Tourist Boards (RTBs) 155
    tourist information centres 159
    voluntary-sector organisations 159

public transport
    Europe 135
    London 138–9

purpose of travel 11, 47, 188

purpose-built destinations
    Europe 113
    UK 171

quality criteria 98–101
    accuracy of information 100
    benchmarking 98
    health and safety 99
    products and services, reliability and consistency of 100
    speed of service 99

quality levels 13

questionnaires 96, 255

rail services 41
    Channel Tunnel Shuttle 41
    development 23–4
    disabilities, people with 206

Europe 118, 119, 132–3, 139
    InterRail 119
    rail passes 119, 132
    steam-train journeys 41
    UK 176, 177, 190
    ultra-high-speed train routes 132
    urban systems 135, 176

rail station service assistants 81

Ramblers Association 159

receipts 268

recruitment 278
    discrimination 206

Regional Development Agencies (RDAs) 155, 158–9

Regional Tourist Boards (RTBs) 45, 155

repatriation request form 269

resort administrators 241–2

resort managers 242

resort operations 238–89
    documentation 268–71
    links with UK office 254–7
    problem situations 272–7
    resort office activities 249–53
    resort office roles and departments 240–3

resort representatives 78, 99, 244–5, 248
    complaints and emergencies procedures 251–3
    induction and training 278–87
    problem situations 272–7
    selling products and services 261, 264–7
    sole-property reps 244, 245
    training 248
    welcome meetings 258–63
    working day 250
    working week 249

resort and service sectors 42–5
    accommodation providers 42–3
    ancillary services 44
    attractions 43–4
    key organisations 44–5
    support services 44

resorts
    beach resorts 123, 162–3, 192
    facilities 121–2
    purpose-built 113, 177

restrictions on travel
    health issues 216–19
    passports and visas 212–15
    unsafe destinations 232

Richardson Sporting 179

Riga 143

risk 13
    adventure trips 16–17
    assessment 17

road travel 41

Europe 117, 133–5
    UK 175–6

rooming lists 250–1

Roskilde Festival 124

Russia 108

safety deposit boxes 287

safety and security 87, 198–235
    adventure trips 16–17
    air travel 140, 200–3
    aviation regulations 200–3
    beach safety 225, 260
    beaches 225
    children 225
    crime 140, 228, 260
    and customer service 83
    FCO advice 231
    ferry services 140
    fire safety 279
    handbag searches 83
    health and safety advice 260, 287
    health and safety team 58
    hotels 225
    implementing procedures 84
    legislation 204–11
    passports and visas 212–15
    quality criteria 99
    swimming pools 225, 279
    see also emergency situations; health issues

SAGA 73

Sale of Goods and Services Act 210–11

Sale and Supply of Goods Act 210

SARS (Severe Acute Respiratory Syndrome) 234

scale of the travel and tourism industry 46–8

Scarborough 44

scenic drives 135

scheduled flights 39, 128, 139

Scottish Destination Management Association 159

seaside resorts 162–3

seasonality 15, 44

self-catering 43
    Europe 120

selling skills 266–7
    after-sales service 267
    closing the sale 267
    customer awareness, raising 266
    customer needs, identifying 266
    product or service presentation 267
    rapport, establishing 266

Semanta Santa 124–5

sensory disabilities 61, 69

September 11 2001 terrorist attacks 129, 193, 230

severe weather conditions 21, 233

short breaks 15, 27, 38, 147
    beachenders 147
    Europe 118

short-haul destinations 15

singles holidays 60

ski resorts 15, 113, 116, 117, 122, 146
    winter sports representatives 246, 247, 280

Slovenia 148

small and medium-sized enterprises (SMEs) 19, 43

smoking etiquette 84

socioeconomics 29, 47

space tourism 160

Spain 15, 146, 147
    business and conference destinations 108, 109
    coastal resorts 107
    events 124–5
    golf complexes 113
    rail service 139
    transport links 136

spas 23, 60

special-interest tourism 26, 38
    see also niche-market operations

specific needs, customers with 53, 61, 64, 85–6
    free services 68–9
    transport 139
    see also disabilities, people with

speech difficulties, people with 64

speeches and presentations 75, 78

speed of service 99

spending
    balance of payments deficit 194
    buying behaviours 30
    by category 47
    cost of visiting 147–8
    multiplier effect 14, 187
    transport 137–8
    UK visitors 187, 191

sporting events
    Europe 124
    UK 181

sporting holidays 179, 280

sports complexes 113

staff
    contracts of employment 284
    customer service 56–101
    employees with disabilities 205–6
    employment legislation 284
    feedback 96, 97
    internal customer service 58–9
    job losses 34
    medical treatment 284
    motivation 59
    multi-lingual staff 61
    passports and visas 284
    quality criteria 100
    resort operations 240–2
    staffing levels 83
    work permits 284

stag parties 125, 142, 143

steam-train journeys 41

Stonehenge 157, 180

strikes 232

sunbathing 21, 260

Superbreak 89, 92

Supply of Goods and Services Act 285

supply-chains 16, 18, 37

support services 44
    see also accommodation providers; tour operators; travel agents

surveys 96, 97

sustainable tourism 17, 26, 27, 33

Swedish culture 65

swimming pools 99, 204, 225, 260, 279

Switzerland 122, 142, 233

Tallinn 143

tangible factual factors (TFFs) 29

tannoy systems 78

taxation 187

taxis 206

technology
    constraints 30
    impact of 20, 27
    new business systems 29–30
    telephone communication
    automated 76
    bookings 66–7
    complaints, handling 92
    taking and relaying messages 86
    telephone skills 75–6

television and radio programmes 143
    terrorism 21, 27, 83, 140, 193, 230–2
    anti-terrorism measures 140
    FCO advice 231
    organisations 232

Thackray Museum, Leeds 62

Thailand 219, 229

theatres and concerts 125

thefts and muggings 228

theme park resorts 113

theme parks 19, 60, 83, 99, 100, 178

Thomas Cook 18, 24, 37, 267